REAL ESTATE PRACTICE TITLES: REAL ESTATE DEVELOPMENT FROM WILEY LAW PUBLICATIONS

CONSTRUCTION OWNER'S HANDBOOK OF PROPERTY DEVELOPMENT
  Robert F. Cushman and Peter J. King, Editors
DEVELOPING RETIREMENT FACILITIES (SECOND EDITION)
  Paul A. Gordon
DEVELOPMENT, MARKETING, AND OPERATION OF MANUFACTURED HOME COMMUNITIES
  George Allen, David Alley, and Edward Hicks
FOREIGN INVESTMENT IN UNITED STATES REAL ESTATE
  Jeremy D. Smith
HOW TO FIND, BUY, MANAGE, AND SELL A MANUFACTURED HOME COMMUNITY
  George Allen
INSTITUTIONAL AND PENSION FUND REAL ESTATE INVESTMENT
  Stephen P. Jarchow
MANAGING AND LEASING COMMERCIAL PROPERTIES: COMPLEX ISSUES
  Alan A. Alexander and Richard F. Muhlebach
MANAGING AND LEASING COMMERCIAL PROPERTIES: FORMS AND PROCEDURES (SECOND EDITION)
  Alan A. Alexander and Richard F. Muhlebach
MANAGING AND LEASING RESIDENTIAL PROPERTIES: FORMS AND PROCEDURES
  Paul D. Lapides and E. Robert Miller
REAL ESTATE DEVELOPMENT: STRATEGIES FOR CHANGING MARKETS
  Stuart M. Saft

REAL ESTATE FINANCE AND TAXATION: STRUCTURING COMPLEX
TRANSACTIONS
Robert L. Nessen
REAL ESTATE LIMITED PARTNERSHIPS (THIRD EDITION)
Theodore S. Lynn, Harry F. Goldberg, and Michael Hirschfeld
REAL ESTATE PORTFOLIOS: ACQUISITION, MANAGEMENT, AND DISPOSITION
Mark W. Patterson
REAL ESTATE VALUATION: GUIDE TO INVESTMENT STRATEGIES
Terry Vaughn Grissom and Julian Diaz III
REHABILITATING OLDER AND HISTORIC BUILDINGS: LAW, TAXATION,
STRATEGIES (SECOND EDITION)
Stephen L. Kass
RESTRUCTURING TROUBLED REAL ESTATE LOANS
Mark W. Patterson
RETIREMENT HOUSING MARKETS: PROJECT PLANNING AND FEASIBILITY
ANALYSIS
Susan B. Brecht
STRUCTURING REAL ESTATE JOINT VENTURES
Robert Bell

HOW TO FIND, BUY, MANAGE, AND SELL A MANUFACTURED HOME COMMUNITY

HOW TO FIND, BUY, MANAGE, AND SELL A MANUFACTURED HOME COMMUNITY

by
GEORGE ALLEN, CPM®
with
LAURENCE ALLEN, MAI
BARBARA ALLEY
MICHAEL CONLEY
GRADY HUNT
MARTIN NEWBY
DANIEL OAS
DONALD WESTPHAL
CRAIG WHITE, ACM

Wiley Law Publications
JOHN WILEY & SONS, INC.
New York • Chichester • Brisbane • Toronto
• Singapore • Weinheim

Library of Congress Cataloging-in-Publication Data

ISBN 0-471-13587-9

Printed in the United States of America

10 9 8 7 6 5 4 3

This book is respectfully dedicated to four men who have had significant personal influence on my career as an entrepreneur, real estate management consultant, and author.

George F. Allen, Sr. Earliest and continuing positive role model as father, husband, and hard-working non-ferrous foundryman and business owner.

L.A. "Bud" Meyer. Longtime manufactured home community owner, mentor, and close personal friend.

John G. Held. My first real estate instructor, fellow Certified Property Manager, and a valued editor of this text.

Jerry P. Martin. Prayer partner, loyal friend, and exemplary real estate developer, entrepreneur, and business mentor.

To all four, and many other peers, I express sincere gratitude for your support and relationship to Carolyn and me as friends, clients, and advisors.

G.F.A.

FOREWORD

During the first half of this decade, the manufactured housing industry has enjoyed unprecedented growth. The industry has grown by an astounding 81% since 1990, with home shipments exceeding 340,000 in 1995—a 21-year high!

A by-product of the industry's growth has been renewed interest in manufactured home landlease communities. While manufactured home communities have long been recognized as attractive investments due to their high occupancy rate, stable cash flows and long-term asset appreciation, the lack of detailed public information has made it difficult for those outside the industry to compete effectively for available properties. That is—until now.

On behalf of the Manufactured Housing Institute's National Communities Council, I would like to congratulate George Allen on another fine publication. This book draws upon the expertise of many of the industry's most knowledgeable individuals to provide a comprehensive guide to manufactured home community investing. It provides potential and present investors with necessary tools to successfully identify, acquire, manage, and sell manufactured home communities. This book combines practical real estate investment and management advice with the nuances of manufactured housing and manufactured home community marketing operations.

The future remains bright for the manufactured housing industry with healthy home sales predicted through the turn of the century. As the industry continues to flourish, *How to Find, Buy, Manage, and Sell a Manufactured Home Community* will remain a dependable resource for the serious manufactured home community investor for years to come.

JAMES R. AYOTTE, CAE
Vice President
National Communities Council
Manufactured Housing Institute
2101 Wilson Blvd., Ste. 610
Arlington, VA 22201-3062
(703) 558-0400

PREFACE

How to Find, Buy, Manage, and Sell a Manufactured Home Community is the third in a series of books I've written about this real estate–based segment of the manufactured housing industry. *Mobilehome Community Management* debuted in 1988 and was followed by *Development, Marketing and Operation of Manufactured Home Communities* in 1994. The first edition of both books "sold out" within months of their release! Now comes the first text ever penned describing most aspects of the real estate investment nature of landlease manufactured home communities.

While *Mobilehome Community Management* (originally titled *Mobilehome Park Management*) was the work of a single author, *Development, Marketing and Operation of Manufactured Home Communities* required the input of three industry experts, George Allen, David Alley, and Edward Hicks. This new John Wiley & Sons text, *How to Find, Buy, Manage, and Sell a Manufactured Home Community*, could not have been written without the assistance of more than a dozen knowledgeable contributors and researchers. The subject is that broad and the chapter topics and appendixes demand that much varied expertise and hands-on experience.

Who will benefit from reading this book? Would-be real estate investors, present investors and property owners, property managers, and resident or community managers will all learn from "the basics" herein, and likely feel comfortable with this property type when finished reading this text in its entirety. Lenders, real estate and mortgage brokers, as well as Wall Street researchers and analysts will find industry statistics here unavailable anywhere else. And real estate appraisers, manufactured housing producers and retailers, as well as manufactured home owners and homesite renters will find the insights and information they seek relative to valuation principles, names and addresses of key suppliers, trade association listings, and a host of other data.

One of the most exciting features concerning the release of this landmark text is its providential timing. The manufactured housing industry is enjoying a twenty-year "high" in the production, sale, and placement of new factory-built homes. While the site-built housing industry struggles to interest homebuying consumers in building or purchasing new homes with an average sale price well in excess of $100,000, it's heartening to know that the American and Canadian public is rediscovering and buying manufactured housing in record numbers. So it comes as no surprise that this book makes its timely appearance early in a decade, 1995–2005, that is widely acclaimed as the Decade of Manufactured Housing and the Manufactured Home Community! So build or buy your first manufactured home landlease community as an investment and enjoy the prosperity that will likely follow, when built or bought "right," and at the same time, share in providing affordable quality housing for Americans and Canadians from coast to coast.

If after reading this book you'd like to talk to or correspond with the author or contributors, please do so. Their addresses are listed in the author and contributor biographical sections that follow. For a complete list, however, of all other books, forms, and monographs "in print" relative to manufactured home communities, contact PMN Publishing at P.O. Box 47024, Indianapolis, IN 46247 or call (317) 888-7156.

The author would be especially pleased to learn of your specific ideas and constructive suggestions for improving upon, even enlarging, future editions of this text. This is especially true for industry suppliers and major manufactured home community owners not listed herein.

Finally, I'm often asked to recommend a formula or share key insights to personal and business success. I generally recommend but two.

1. The first is a scripture quotation from Proverbs 24: 3 & 4: "Any enterprise is built by wise planning, becomes strong through common sense and profits wonderfully by keeping abreast of the facts." (*Living Bible Translation*)

2. The second appears on the reverse of one of GFA Management's business card variants:

Management Success Formula

Listen & Learn
Plan & Prepare
Motivate & Manage
—with the—
Right Product or Service
Right Location & Timing
Right Skills & Experience
Right Attitude & Motivation
Right Management & Staff
Right Methods & Resources   © 1985

Keep both these in mind while reading the following pages. The shared knowledge will certainly help one plan and prepare for each stage of the real estate investment cycle, and clearly point the way toward a common-sense organization and application of resources and facts necessary to ensure some level of eventual success. So with that thought, embark on a thoroughly educational, and hopefully profitable, reading and learning experience.

Indianapolis, Indiana   GEORGE ALLEN
April 1996

ACKNOWLEDGMENTS

On the personal side, this book would not have reached fruition but for the encouragement and patience of my wife Carolyn. And for a second time in three years, my administrative assistant Nora Freese labored far more hours than anyone else, typing and retyping, copying and recopying this manuscript and appendixes. In this effort she was ably assisted by Ann Berkemeier.

I have so many helpful friends in the real estate and manufactured housing industries, it's difficult to know where to start and end with words of appreciation relative to researching and preparing this historic text. *Allen Letter* subscribers, annual "Allen Report" participants, International Networking Roundtable attendees, and management consulting clients nationwide have provided the financial base that make a comprehensive work like this possible. I am indebted to every one of them for this loyal support! Herb Tieder of *Manufactured Home Merchandiser,* Jim Visser of *The Journal,* and Mariwyn Evans of the *Journal of Property Management* all regularly provide space in their publications for the introduction and expression of many of the real estate investment and management concepts and manufactured housing statistics introduced in this text. Their interest and encouragement is invaluable and appreciated!

Four manufactured housing industry peers deserve special mention. Ed Clayton effectively manages a manufactured home community I own with my partners. He is the classic "mayor of a small town" resident manager and has taught me as much as I have him. Jim Grange of ROC Communities, Inc., continues to be one of my best friends in the business. He motivated me to first pen the *Allen Letter* and prompts me to continually challenge our industry with new ideas. John Rogosich, CPM, of Choice Properties is a peer and confidant with whom I've field-tested some of the new forms and concepts contained in this book. And Randy Rowe. Occasionally we meet and work with someone who makes a positive and lasting impression as a leader. As such, Randy was *the driving force* behind the recent successful movement that brought organization and recognition to manufactured home community owners and fee-managers nationwide. For this unprecedented achievement the entire industry owes him a sincere and lasting debt of gratitude.

Now for the most important acknowledgment—the contributors who have done so much to make this book the comprehensive and useful reference it is, and will likely continue to be, for years to come. Not only is this the very first book written about the manufactured home community as an investment vehicle, but it's the first time in the history of the manufactured housing industry that so many *bona fide* experts have written together under one title.

Michael Conley, Craig White, Grady Hunt, and Daniel Oas have earned noteworthy regional and national personal reputations as manufactured home community real estate brokers and consultants. Together they represent well more than a half-century of hands-on experience with this income-property type.

Laurence Allen, Barbara Alley, Martin Newby, and Don Westphal have likewise developed notable national reputations as the "go to" resources for their respective specialties as valuation, due diligence, resident relations, and property rejuvenation experts. Sure there are other practitioners, but these are among the very best at what they do.

Supporting material for this text, mainly in the form of appendixes, came from Chrissy Jackson, ACM; Patti Greco, freelance writer; and the staff at the Indiana Manufactured Housing Association, a.k.a. IMHA/RVIC.

Jim Gossweiler, Tom Horner, Fred Goodman, and Jane Kelly have supplied proprietary environmental audit, property comparison rating, operating statement format material, and real estate finance source information that is being shared with the manufactured housing industry at large for the first time.

Finally, a special word of acknowledgment concerning Carlton Edwards, retired housing professor and industry historian. Carl prepared the succinct history of the manufactured housing industry and the RV/MH Heritage Foundation in Elkhart, Indiana. We should *all* aspire to be as active and interested in the manufactured housing industry when we are 85 years of age!

This is truly the "dream team" of writers and experts when it comes to describing and extolling the challenges and benefits of manufactured home community investment.

ABOUT THE AUTHOR

George F. Allen, Jr., CPM, is the founder and president of GFA Management, Inc., in Indianapolis, Indiana. GFA Management, Inc. is one of the few real estate management consulting firms in the United States and Canada specializing in the marketing and operation of manufactured home communities. He has managed, fee-managed, and owned manufactured home communities since 1978. He evaluates all types of multifamily rental communities and facilitates training seminars for state and national trade associations, as well as specially tailored, in-house programs for income-property owners. He is past president and Manager of the Year of the Institute of Real Estate Management's Indianapolis chapter and he is a founding member of the Industry Steering Committee, board of governors member with the Indiana Manufactured Housing Association, and charter member of the board of directors for the Manufactured Home Communities Council of the Manufactured Housing Institute. Mr. Allen is the author of *Mobilehome Community Management, Development, Marketing and Operation of Manufactured Home Communities,* and the popular *Allen Letter.* He received a liberal arts degree from Eastern College in St. Davids, Pennsylvania.

ABOUT THE CONTRIBUTORS

Laurence G. Allen, MAI, is president of Allen & Associates Appraisal Group, Inc., in Bloomfield Hills, Michigan. He is an expert in the valuation of manufactured home communities and has been preparing valuations of manufactured home communities for over twenty years. Mr. Allen received a B.A. degree from Linfield College and a masters of business administration from the University of Michigan.

2000 N. Woodward, Suite 310, Bloomfield Hills, MI 48304
(810) 433-9630

Barbara Alley is vice president and managing partner of Alley & Associates, Inc., in Palm Harbor, Florida, where she is a member of the Due Diligence Team. Alley & Associates, Inc., specializes in the planning, engineering, and constructing of manufactured home communities and large tract developments throughout the United States and foreign countries. Ms. Alley attended DePaul University and the University of Minnesota.

P.O. Box 897, Palm Harbor, FL 34682-0897   (813) 787-3388

Michael Conley is a senior investment associate in the office of Marcus & Millichap Real Estate Investment Brokerage Company in Chicago, Illinois. His business is limited to the marketing and sale of manufactured home communities. Mr. Conley has sold over $100 million of investment property and has been one of the Top Ten producers in the company. He has been a featured speaker at the National Manufactured Housing Congress and at the Multi-Housing World Convention.

8750 West Bryn Mawr, Suite 750, Chicago, IL 60631   (312) 693-0700

Grady Hunt is a licensed Realtor with ROC Communities, Inc., in Denver, Colorado. He has owned and fee-managed properties in the manufactured home community industry, and is presently a regional property manager for ROC. He is an approved instructor in MHEI's Accredited Community Manager program.

6430 S. Quebec Street, Englewood, CO 80111   (303) 741-3707

Martin Newby is chairman of the board of National Manufactured Housing Services, Center for Solutions. Martin Newby Management, one of its several divisions, is headquartered in Sarasota, Florida. Martin has been in the manufactured housing business for thirty years. His firms have a solid national reputation for providing quality resident services and education, as well as fee management. Mr. Newby is a founding member of the Industry Steering Committee.

3801 Bee Ridge Road, Suite 12, Sarasota, FL 34233   (941) 923-1456

Daniel R. Oas is a licensed real estate broker, community owner, and property manager in West Los Angeles, California. He works exclusively in the manufactured housing industry. Mr. Oas has been expanding his business by acquiring older, smaller communities and rejuvenating them. He has written an investment guide monograph describing the acquisition and disposition of manufactured home communities.

12400 Wilshire Blvd., #610, Los Angeles, CA 90025
(310) 207-1600

Donald Westphal is a registered landscape architect in Rochester, Michigan, where he concentrates his business on manufactured home community planning, construction, and image building. He has participated in the planning of more than 400 manufactured home communities, published numerous articles, drafted ordinances, and led community planning seminars. Mr. Westphal became interested in community design while living in a manufactured home. This interest progressed from his masters thesis subject to a successful career in landscape architecture and varied leadership roles within the Michigan Manufactured Housing Association and the Manufactured Housing Institute. He received his bachelor of landscape architecture degree from Michigan State University and his master of landscape architecture degree from the University of Illinois.

512 Madison Avenue, Rochester, MI 48307   (810) 651-5518

Craig E. White, ACM, is president of Craig White Associates and a partner in Knoll-White Partners in Denver, Colorado. He is a nationally recognized expert in the development, management, marketing, and brokerage of manufactured home communities. His company focuses on new community development consultation, investment brokerage, and acquisition and development of manufactured home communities. Mr. White is a board member of the Manufactured Housing Institute and Colorado Manufactured Housing Association.

13390 Harrison Street, Denver, CO 80241-1403   (303) 457-1160

ADDITIONAL CONTRIBUTORS

Carlton M. Edwards is owner of Carl Edwards & Associates in Martinez, Georgia, and he is Professor Emeritus on family housing for Michigan State University. He has done research, teaching, and consulting for the recreational vehicle, mobile home, and manufactured housing industries. He has served as an expert witness for the Technical Advisory Service for Attorneys on matters relating to these industries. Mr. Edwards received a B.S. degree from Cornell and an M.S. degree from Syracuse University. He authored *Homes for Travel and Living: The History and Development of the RV and Manufactured Homes Industries* and has prepared monographs and videos on both RVs and manufactured homes. In 1982 he was elected to the RV/MH Hall of Fame. He has built and used an RV since the 1950s and lives in a manufactured home. He has been on the board of directors of a manufactured home manufacturer and is an officer in a retail corporation and a transport corporation for manufactured homes.

4628 Beaver, Martinez, GA 30907   (706) 860-1639

Nora Freese is marketing manager for Scale Model Homes in Indianapolis, Indiana. She is a researcher and responsible for much of the annual *Allen Report* identifying and describing the largest owners and fee-managers of manufactured home communities.

P.O. Box 47024, Indianapolis, IN 46247   (317) 888-7156

Fredric S. Goodman is a vice president of Management Reports, Inc. (MRI), in Cleveland, Ohio. He has over twenty-five years of experience in the property management industry. Mr. Goodman has managed the implementation and conversion of many manufactured home communities in their use of computerized property management accounting systems. He received a B.S. degree in business administration with a major in accounting from Ohio State University.

23945 Mercantile Road, Cleveland, OH 44122   (800) 321-8770

James C. Gossweiler is a senior vice president of Federated Environmental Associates, Inc., a national environmental consulting and engineering firm in Baltimore, Maryland. He is a registered environmental assessor for the State of California and an NEHA registered hazardous substances professional under the auspices of the United States Environmental Protection Agency. Although the company regularly inspects all real estate types, Federated Environmental has performed due diligence environmental audits and structural engineering inspections of over 265 manufactured home communities in seventeen states. The company's manufactured home community interests ensure affordable, attractive, and environmentally sensitive housing alternatives, with an understanding of the CERCLA (Superfund) and the civil liability concerns of property developers and managers.

1314 Bedford Avenue, Baltimore, MD 21208   (410) 653-8434

Patricia Greco is the owner of Greco Writing in Clinton, Massachusetts, where she is a professional writer and marketing design consultant to the manufactured housing industry. Her custom-designed work, including logos, community and company brochures, trade show handouts, and advertisements, promotes a quality image for a growing industry. She is a regular columnist for the *Allen Letter* and the *Journal of Manufactured Housing*. She is co-creator of the "Vendor Resource Packet," a semi-annual direct mail promotion to all major owners of manufactured home communities in the United States and Canada.

902B Ridgefield Circle, Clinton, MA 01510   (508) 368-1022

Tom Horner, Jr., is the owner of Horner & Associates in Edwardsville, Kansas. He has over thirty years experience in all aspects of the manufactured home community business and has owned or managed this property type in eight states. Another of his companies, Horner Construction, specializes in manufactured home community development. He is a founding member of the Industry Steering Committee. Mr. Horner received a B.S. degree in accounting from Kansas University.

10011 Woodend Road, Edwardsville, KS 66111   (913) 441-0194

Chrissy Jackson, ACM, manages three manufactured home communities for ROC Communities, Inc. in Indianapolis, Indiana. She has over fifteen years experience in property management. Ms. Jackson is an author and seminar leader. She has written a twelve-part series of booklets on different property management areas of concern to owners and operators of communities of all sizes.

3003 Honcoye Tr., Lakeland, FL 33809   (941) 859-7793

Jane Irene Kelly has been the lead reporter for Crittenden Publishing's Manufactured Housing Report in Novato, California. She has been a featured presenter at the International Networking Roundtable. Ms. Kelly received a B.S. degree in magazine journalism from Syracuse University's S.I. Newhouse School of Public Communications.

Box #1150, Novato, CA 94948   (800) 421-3483

SUMMARY CONTENTS

Chapter 1	Manufactured Housing and the Manufactured Home Community	1
Chapter 2	Basics of Real Estate Investment	23
Chapter 3	What to Look for in a Manufactured Home Community	45
Chapter 4	How to Find and Buy a Manufactured Home Community	81
Chapter 5	Estimating Value	109
Chapter 6	The Due Diligence Period: Preparing for Closing	131
Chapter 7	Property Management	153
Chapter 8	The Turnaround Challenge and Rejuvenating Older Manufactured Home Communities	233
Chapter 9	Selling the Manufactured Home Community	251
Chapter 10	Coming Full Cycle	275
Appendixes		281
Glossary		465
Bibliography		481
Index		487

DETAILED CONTENTS

Chapter 1   **Manufactured Housing and the Manufactured Home Community**

§ **1.1**   Introduction

§ **1.2**   Affordability

§ **1.3**   The Manufactured Home Community Secret

§ **1.4**   Manufactured Home Communities as Big Business

§ **1.5**   Manufactured Housing

§ **1.6**   Trends in Manufactured Housing

§ **1.7**   Manufactured Home Community

§ **1.8**   Trends among Manufactured Home Communities

§ **1.9**   Investment Cautions

§ **1.10**   Manufactured Housing Industry Terminology

§ **1.11**   Overall Manufactured Housing Trends

§ **1.12**   Summary

Chapter 2   **Basics of Real Estate Investment**

§ **2.1**   Introduction

§ **2.2**   Investment Risk

§ **2.3**   Motivation to Invest in Real Estate

§ **2.4**   The Search for a Real Estate Investment

§ **2.5**   Research for the Right Real Estate Investment

§ **2.6**   Economic and Financial Feasibility

ANOTHER PERSPECTIVE
Dan Oas

§ **2.7**   Cash-on-Cash Return

§ **2.8**   Unique Characteristics of Real Estate Investments

§ **2.9**   Advantages and Disadvantages of Real Estate

§ **2.10**   Summary

Chapter 3   What to Look for in a Manufactured Home Community

§ 3.1   Introduction

§ 3.2   Typical Property Research Sources

§ 3.3   Fieldwork Property Research Sources

§ 3.4   Document and Organize Findings

§ 3.5   Manufactured Home Community Investment Checklist

§ 3.6   Basic Formulas for Financial and Mathematical Operational
          Analysis of a Manufactured Home Community

ANOTHER PERSPECTIVE
Craig White

§ 3.7   Risk and Reward

§ 3.8   Primary Considerations

§ 3.9   Management Impact

§ 3.10   Project Types

§ 3.11   Project Size

§ 3.12   Summary

Chapter 4   How to Find and Buy a Manufactured Home Community

§ 4.1   Introduction

§ 4.2   Goal Setting

§ 4.3   Property Parameters

§ 4.4   Sources of Manufactured Home Communities for Sale and
          Otherwise

§ 4.5   Time to Go Looking

ANOTHER PERSPECTIVE
Grady Hunt

§ 4.6   Identifying a Geographic Market of Interest

§ 4.7   Defining the Type of Community to Purchase

§ 4.8   Cataloging the Surveyed Manufactured Home Communities

§ 4.9   Summary

Chapter 5   Estimating Value

§ 5.1   Introduction

A PERSPECTIVE BY A MEMBER OF THE APPRAISAL INSTITUTE
Laurence Allen

§ 5.2   Manufactured Home Community Valuation

§ 5.3   Valuation Premises

§ 5.4   Factors in the Valuation of Manufactured Home Communities

§ 5.5   Valuation

§ 5.6   —Cost or Replacement Approach

§ 5.7   —Sales Comparison Approach

§ 5.8   —Income Approach

§ 5.9   —Reconciliation

§ 5.10   Future Outlook

§ 5.11   Summary

Chapter 6   The Due Diligence Period: Preparing for Closing

§ 6.1   Introduction

ANOTHER PERSPECTIVE
Barbara Alley

§ 6.2   Purpose of Physical Due Diligence

§ 6.3   Assemble Team

§ 6.4   Request Information from Seller

§ 6.5   Set up Meetings

§ 6.6   Review Manufactured Home Community Records and Inventory

§ 6.7   Investigate Manufactured Home Community, Permits and Licenses, and Cost Projections

§ 6.8   —Physical Examination Agenda

§ 6.9   —Regulatory Agencies and Utility Companies

§ 6.10   —Feasibility Projections

§ 6.11   Arranging Transaction Financing

§ 6.12   Preparing for Closing

§ 6.13   Summary

Chapter 7   Property Management

§ 7.1   Introduction

§ 7.2   Two Categories of Property Management

§ 7.3   Three Levels of Property Management

§ 7.4   Property Management Visits and Inspections

§ 7.5   Management Action Plan (MAP)

§ 7.6   Sources of Property Management Information

§ 7.7   Property Management of a Particular Property

§ **7.8** Property Takeover Checklist

§ **7.9** Property Standard Operating Procedure (SOP)

§ **7.10** Start-up Package of Forms and Related Aids

§ **7.11** Setting up and Running the On-Site Operation

§ **7.12** Establishing Property Files

§ **7.13** Personnel and Human Relations Matters

§ **7.14** Financial Matters

§ **7.15** Rent Collection Matters

§ **7.16** Managing by the Numbers

§ **7.17** Maximizing Income and Minimizing Expenses

§ **7.18** Loss Control Measures

§ **7.19** Marketing Matters

§ **7.20** —Advertising

§ **7.21** —Leasing and Sales

§ **7.22** —Public Relations

§ **7.23** —Resident Relations

§ **7.24** —Resident Services Enhance Resident Relations
Martin Newby

§ **7.25** Maintenance Matters

§ **7.26** Policies and Procedures

§ **7.27** Purchasing Matters

§ **7.28** Computerization

§ **7.29** Federal Laws Affecting Manufactured Home Landlease Communities

§ **7.30** Evaluation

§ **7.31** Summary

Chapter 8 **The Turnaround Challenge and Rejuvenating Older Manufactured Home Communities**

§ **8.1** Introduction

§ **8.2** Turnaround Strategies

ANOTHER PERSPECTIVE
Don Westphal

§ **8.3** Rejuvenating Older Manufactured Home Communities

§ **8.4** Assessing the Present Manufactured Home Community Condition

§ 8.5   Upgrade Alternatives

§ 8.6   Action Plan and Budget

§ 8.7   Annual Review and Reassessment

§ 8.8   Current Methodologies

§ 8.9   Summary

Chapter 9   Selling the Manufactured Home Community

§ 9.1   Introduction

§ 9.2   Deciding the Right Time to Sell

§ 9.3   Preparing the Property to Sell

§ 9.4   Recruiting the Right Assistance in the Marketing Process

§ 9.5   Estimating the Value Range of the Property

§ 9.6   Identifying the Target Markets and Planning Marketing Strategy

§ 9.7   Preparing and Executing the Marketing Plan

ANOTHER PERSPECTIVE
Michael Conley

§ 9.8   Introduction to Marketing Manufactured Home Communities

§ 9.9   Why People Sell

§ 9.10   —Investment Theory

§ 9.11   When to Sell: Timing

§ 9.12   How to Sell Manufactured Home Communities

§ 9.13   —Seller's Objectives

§ 9.14   —Marketing Strategy

§ 9.15   —When and How to Use a Real Estate Broker

§ 9.16   Summary

Chapter 10   Coming Full Cycle

§ 10.1   Introduction

§ 10.2   Review of Major Themes

Appendixes

A   Top HUD-Code Manufactured Home Producers

B   History of the Manufactured Housing RV/MH Foundation

C   Marking the Decade of Manufactured Housing

D   The 1996 Allen Report on the Largest Community Owners

E	Institute of Real Estate Management Certified Property Manager/Members Experienced in the Management of Manufactured Home Communities
F	Manufactured Housing Industry Periodicals
G	History in the Making
H	Directory of National, Regional, State, and Provincial Manufactured Housing Related Associations and Institutes
I	Readying Your Community for Environmental Audits
J	Loan Amortization Charts
K	A Description of the Old Woodall STAR Mobile Home Park Rating System
L	Real Estate Brokers Specializing in the Marketing of Manufactured Home Communities
M	National Source List of Manufactured Home Communities
N	The 21st Century National Manufactured Home Landlease Community Rating System
O	Due Diligence On-Site Inspection Report
P	Typical Manufactured Home Community Operating Statements
Q	Manufactured Home Community Finance Sources
R	Monthly Manufactured Home Community Integrity Inspection Checklist
S	Directory of Products and Services for Manufactured Home Communities
T	Setting a Value on Your MH Community

Glossary

Bibliography

Index

CHAPTER 1

MANUFACTURED HOUSING AND THE MANUFACTURED HOME COMMUNITY

§ 1.1 Introduction

§ 1.2 Affordability

§ 1.3 The Manufactured Home Community Secret

§ 1.4 Manufactured Home Communities as Big Business

§ 1.5 Manufactured Housing

§ 1.6 Trends in Manufactured Housing

§ 1.7 Manufactured Home Community

§ 1.8 Trends among Manufactured Home Communities

§ 1.9 Investment Cautions

§ 1.10 Manufactured Housing Industry Terminology

§ 1.11 Overall Manufactured Housing Trends

§ 1.12 Summary

§ 1.1 Introduction

Welcome to manufactured housing and manufactured home communities—the potent one-two punch of affordable housing production and distribution, and popular real estate investment opportunity. To fully appreciate and optimize the latter, it is necessary to learn and understand the former.

Manufactured housing per se is defined later in the chapter, but for now suffice it to say that it is "America's most affordable housing option."[1] Designed and fabricated under controlled factory conditions at $25 per square foot, it costs less than half the $55 per square foot characteristic of new site-built homes. This means the average manufactured home price, including both single-section and multisection, is $33,500 versus $154,100 for a new site-built home. The cost differences are just that staggering.[2]

Recent production figures underscore the continuing and increasing popularity of this affordable housing option. In 1993 a total of 254,276 new manufactured homes were produced, an increase of 21 percent over the previous year, compared to only a 9 percent construction volume increase for site-built homes during the same period. The next year, 1994, saw manufactured housing jump another 19.5 percent, as 303,932 new homes were shipped. The year 1994 also saw the total national economic impact of manufactured housing rise 36 percent to $23.3 billion. In 1995 production was at 339,601 new manufactured homes produced by 100 companies working out of 300 factories nationwide. For 1996 new manufactured homes production is forecasted close to 375,000 units. See **Appendix A.**

§ 1.2   Affordability

The term "affordability" has been and continues to be closely associated with manufactured housing and manufactured home communities. But just what is affordability? The best attempt at a working definition of this concept appeared in a seminal document that appeared in 1991, titled the *NIMBY Report* and subtitled, "Removing Regulatory Barriers to Affordable Housing." This report, prepared by a special HUD commission stated, "there is not enough 'affordable housing' when a low-to-moderate-income family cannot afford to rent or buy a decent-quality

---

[1] George Allen, David Alley, & Edward Hicks, Development, Marketing and Operation of Manufactured Home Communities 1 (John Wiley & Sons, Inc., 1994) [hereinafter Allen, Alley, & Hicks].

[2] Manufactured Housing Institute, Quick Facts 1995–1996 (Arlington, Va. 1995).

dwelling without spending more than 30 percent of its income on shelter."[3] So affordability is relative to personal income and the forces of supply and demand within different geographic market areas. Affordability is one of several key reasons why manufactured housing continues to grow in popularity with low-to-moderate-income and soon-to-retire homebuying consumers, making it the "fastest growing component of the U.S. housing market."[4]

§ 1.3 The Manufactured Home Community Secret

Manufactured home communities are the best real estate investment among all asset classes. Why? Because they generally enjoy and perpetuate a stable annuity stream of ready cash flow, which is predicated on the following:

1. Restricted supply of manufactured home communities in which to invest or move a home. Said restrictions are usually local regulatory barriers to affordable housing of all types, a reality that is gradually changing from region to region. Restricted supply also relates to the reluctance of present income-property owners (of manufactured home communities) to sell until personally advantageous or absolutely necessary.

2. No "real depreciation" when this property type is managed and operated properly. Because the majority of on-site improvements are below ground (for example, utility infrastructure), unless a clubhouse or swimming pool is in place, asset depreciation opportunity and experience is generally minimal.

3. Less turnover than with just about any other multifamily property type. Statistically, 95 percent of manufactured homes make but

---

[3] Department of Housing & Urban Development, NIMBY Report: Removing Barriers on Affordable Housing 2 (1991).

[4] E. Homel & S. Sakwa, *Manufactured Housing REITs: Strong Long-Term Fundamentals Support an Overweight Position, in* Morgan Stanley's U.S. Investment Research Real Estate Industry Overview (1995) [hereinafter Homel & Sakwa].

one move—from factory to on-site installation. Most other turn-over occurs when homeowner/renters sell their home on-site and relocate. And this only occurs 10 to 15 percent of the time, compared to the 55 percent turnover common among apartment dwellers.

4. Demographic trends that definitely support manufactured home community living as a viable and desirable lifestyle alternative. As the U.S. population ages in greater numbers, especially the baby-boom generation, and migrates to retirement meccas or even elects to stay where they are, the affordability issue again moves to the forefront as retirees seek to stretch their limited fixed incomes. Young families, faced with the ever escalating prices of new site-built housing, continue in increasing numbers to opt for manufactured housing and manufactured home communities as starter homes and initial, if not permanent, domiciles.

§ 1.4   Manufactured Home Communities as Big Business

There is a fairly recent indication that the manufactured home com-munity is now "big business" on the broader American housing scene. Until 1992 there was but one public manufactured home community holding company; now there are five. **Table 1–1** lists the holding companies, ranked in declining order by number of rental homesites owned or managed.[5]

Private owners, syndicators, and sole proprietors, continue to expand their property portfolios of manufactured home communities as well. The five largest nonpublic firms are listed in **Table 1–2.**

While there are certainly manufactured housing and manufactured home communities in other countries, especially Canada, the vast majority of this housing stock and property type exist in the United States. Great Britain and offshore islands have their version of this affordable duo, and efforts are afoot to bring the same combination to the Russian states as well.

---

[5] G.F. Allen, *Allen Report for 1995,* Community Corner, Manufactured Home Mer-chandiser (Jan. 1995) [hereinafter Allen Report for 1995].

Table 1–1

Public Manufactured Home Community Holding Companies

Company	Trade Symbol	# Sites	# MH Communities
Manufactured Home Communities, Inc.	MHC	28,407	78
ROC Communities, Inc.	RCI	26,231	102
Chateau Properties, Inc.	CPJ	15,689	35
SUN Communities, Inc.	SUI	13,500	44
United Mobile Homes, Inc.	UMH	4,623	22

Table 1–2

Nonpublic Manufactured Home Community Holding Companies

Company	# Sites	# MH Communities
Ellenburg Capital	24,112	65
Lautrec, Ltd.	22,652	58
Clayton, Williams & Sherwood	20,156	56
Uniprop	15,046	40
Clayton Homes	13,440	48

§ 1.5 Manufactured Housing

Because 31.2 percent of all new single-family homes sold in the United States in 1993 were manufactured homes (the figure will likely be closer to 35 percent for 1994 and higher in 1995), the popularity of this affordable housing type is doubly underscored. But just what is manufactured housing? Simply put, it is "detached, single-family dwellings that are produced off-site."[6] The Urban Land Institute in a recent research work paper describes the phenomena:

---

[6] Homel & Sakwa at 3.

According to the U.S. Department of Housing and Urban Development's (HUD's) Manufactured Housing Construction and Safety Standards Act of 1974 (24 CFR 3280), a manufactured home is

> a structure, transportable in one or more sections, which . . . is 320 or more square feet, and which is built on a permanent chassis and designed to be used as a dwelling with or without a permanent foundation when connected to the required utilities, and includes plumbing, heating, air conditioning, and electrical systems contained therein.[7]

Manufactured homes differ from modular, panelized, and precut homes in that manufactured homes (1) bear a label certifying compliance with HUD construction standards—the HUD code, and (2) must include a permanent chassis for transporting the home to its site. "Mobile home" is a term used only to describe a factory-built home constructed *before* the enactment of the Manufactured Housing Construction and Safety Standards Act of 1974.[8]

There are solid reasons for the ongoing popularity of manufactured housing:

1. Speed and efficiency of production is easy to understand. Homes manufactured indoors, out of the elements, and built to production standards are going to generally be superior to those built outdoors where laborers are susceptible to weather conditions and often working under awkward, even unsafe circumstances. Speed and efficiency of production obviously translate into lower housing cost.

2. Flexibility of design. Just about any sort of single-story housing design—even multistory, when modular units are considered—can be effected with manufactured housing. Most conventional housing building materials are now routine options for manufactured housing including asphalt shingles, lap siding, heavy-duty entry doors, and thick insulation.

3. Transportability to installation site. It is often a lot easier to move a completed home onto a difficult building site than incur the labor costs of assembling an entire home there piecemeal, and once the

---

[7] Diane Suchman, *Manufactured Housing: An Affordable Alternative* (Urban Land Institute, Research Working Paper #640, 1995).

[8] *Id.*

manufactured home is in place, as was pointed out earlier, it remains.

4. Today's manufactured homes are full-featured. Virtually anything that can be done with a site-built home (for example, hot tubs, cathedral ceilings, upgraded appliances, and special lighting and sound systems) can be easily placed in a manufactured home. Additionally, today's manufactured homes are larger than in years past. The overall average size, among single-section and multi-section homes, is in excess of 1,330 square feet.

5. Affordability. Though discussed earlier, the point cannot be made too often. The average monthly operating costs for a manufactured home—including mortgage, real estate taxes, property insurance, utilities, site rent, and license fees—total $457. Site-built homes, on the other hand, average $736 per month.[9] Yet another study, the 1993 American Housing Survey, pegs median monthly housing costs, using slightly different parameters, at $309 for manufactured homes and $536 for site-built homes, or 73 percent higher.[10]

§ 1.6   Trends in Manufactured Housing

These are certainly exciting times for the manufactured housing industry. The most obvious trend is its increasing popularity with the American homebuying public—as starter homes and conventional and retirement housing. But there are other trends as well:

1. Today's homes are larger: single-section homes as large as 80 feet long and 18 feet wide; multisection homes from 1,600 to 2,500 square feet. Years ago, single-section homes outnumbered multi-section four-to-one. Now the relationship is, nationally, 53 percent single-section and 47 percent multisection.[11]

2. More of today's manufactured homes, particularly when permanently sited on private, scattered sites, warrant conventional real estate mortgages. Personal property or chattel fixed-rate,

---

[9] Bureau of the Census, Statistical Brief on Mobile Homes (May 1994).

[10] U.S. Commerce Department, American Housing Survey for the United States (1995).

[11] Manufactured Housing Institute, Production Report (Arlington, Va. 1995).

level-pay, self-amortizing loans of 7 to 25 years are still common for homes sited in manufactured home landlease communities.

3. The South and Southeast, and parts of the Southwest, have become hotbeds of activity for manufactured housing sales and placement.

4. Manufactured housing now appreciates in value when it is sited in a good location, is the beneficiary of routine maintenance and care, and is supported by a stable housing market. According to Dr. Carol Meeks of the University of Georgia, the life of a new, year-round lived-in manufactured home is close to 55.8 years.

5. Today, 62 percent of manufactured housing production goes onto private, scattered lots and some subdivision locations; 58 percent of new manufactured homes continue to be sited in manufactured home landlease communities.

6. The industry itself has undergone a transformation. For many years, manufactured housing was equally associated with vehicular and housing interests. Now it identifies almost wholly with the shelter or housing industry.

Manufactured housing truly has comes into its own as a popular affordable housing alternative. It is easy to see why the industry has embraced the century-spanning years of 1995 through 2005 as its own decade—the Decade of Manufactured Housing and the Manufactured Home Community. See **Appendixes B** and **C**.

§ 1.7 Manufactured Home Community

The term "manufactured home community" seems to have as many definitions as it once had name variants. Some would call it a "residential subdivision that contains many features."[12] Others simply opt for the professional property management approach; a multifamily rental or subdivision community occupied by homeowners and their families. The rental or landlease variant far outnumbers the subdivision, condominumized or cooperative-owned types of manufactured home

---

[12] Homel & Sakwa at 3.

communities. And the landlease community is the only alternative of the four that represents a true overall investment opportunity for the private and corporate real estate investor.

It is estimated that there are between 50,000 and 55,000 manufactured home communities of all sizes nationwide. In about half the states, where manufactured home communities are regulated at the state level, the total property count often includes single parcels of land with as few as three or four manufactured homes, and these are officially categorized as manufactured home communities. Of the 50 to 55,000 national total, it is estimated that 24,000 are of institutional investment grade size—numbering at least 50 homesites (some would say 100+ sites) apiece. Only when a manufactured home community numbers 50, 100, or even 150 rental homesites does the property realize an economy of scale able to support a centralized property investment and management office.[13] Smaller manufactured home communities, 50 to 100 sites or smaller, are often excellent investment vehicles for the sole proprietor, recent retiree, and fledgling real estate investor buying to accumulate a portfolio. For example, according to the Indiana State Department of Health, in Indiana there are 1,317 manufactured home landlease communities. Of these, 84 percent are 100 homesites and smaller (smallest is 5 sites) in size. See **Table 1–3** for a detailed breakdown.[14]

There are approximately 500 sole proprietor, partnership, and corporate (both public and private) owners of multi–manufactured home community portfolios in the United States and Canada. Each portfolio operator owns or fee-manages a minimum of 500 rental homesites or five manufactured home communities. One hundred and fifty major owners, of the 500 overall number, who respond to the *Allen Report* survey each year, collectively control 4.5 percent of the aforementioned 50,000 property base and 9.3 percent of the 24,000 institutional investment grade pool. And among these 150 surveyed owners, the average property portfolio size is 15 properties apiece and 232 rental homesites per property in size.[15] See **Appendix D.**

---

[13] Allen Report for 1995.

[14] Researched by Indiana State Department of Health Staff, under supervision of Michael A. Hoover, R.E.H.S. (Aug. 7, 1995).

[15] Allen Report for 1995.

Table 1–3

**Indiana Manufactured Home Community Size Breakdown
by Homesite Count**

Number of Manufactured Home Communities	Number of Homesites Range
583 properties are	5–25 homesites in size
327	26–50
200	51–100
86	101–150
36	151–200
32	201–250
20	251–300
9	301–350
10	351–400
4	401–450
2	451–500
4	501–550
1	551–600
1	601–650
1	651–700
1	700+
1,317 total	

Rent rates? Groundlease rental rates vary widely from market to market. Choice sunbelt locations fetch hundreds of dollars per site per month—for groundlease and water, sewer, and refuse removal services (even that is changing with increasing incidences of submetering utility services)—to just barely $100 per site per month in some rural locations. Where manufactured home communities are in very small supply, like Cook County (Chicago), Illinois, monthly site rent is very high indeed. A good example of the bell-shaped curve, where rents are concerned, is the Indianapolis SMSA (standard metropolitan statistical area) where rent rates among 40 Marion County (metropolitan Indianapolis) manufactured home communities have been tracked faithfully for nine years by the Indiana Manufactured Housing Association. In 1995 the lowest site rent was $110 per month, highest was $260 per month, and across-the-board average was $189 per month. Site rents in this particular Midwest urban market have risen as follows over the years.

1987	=	$118.00 avg/mth	
1988	=	$125.00 avg/mth	6% increase
1989	=	$135.00 avg/mth	8% increase
1990	=	$140.25 avg/mth	3.9% increase
1991	=	$151.40 avg/mth	8% increase
1992	=	$159.70 avg/mth	5.5% increase
1993	=	$173.40 avg/mth	8.6% increase
1994	=	$181.00 avg/mth	4.4% increase
1995	=	$188.69 avg/mth	3% increase

Unlike most other property types, there are no present attempts to research and publish market rent rate averages nationally or regionally. This will likely develop as the manufactured housing industry's national information source and lobbying arm, the Manufactured Housing Institute, restructures and addresses the information needs of its real estate segment.

Physical occupancy within manufactured home communities is generally healthy, thanks in part to the relative scarcity of this property type and the continually increasing popularity of manufactured housing. Nationwide, among the major owners reporting these portfolio statistics, physical occupancy hovers around 94 percent. Couple this with the exceptionally low turnover rates cited earlier (10 percent for home-owner/renters and 3 to 5 percent for the actual homes), the stability of this income-property type as an investment becomes quite obvious. A caveat for the novice investor: Although physical occupancy is important and will be examined further in **Chapter 3** of this text, *economic occupancy* is the true test of not only how "full" one's property is, but how efficiently rents are being collected as well.

Operating expense ratios (OERs) for manufactured home communities were a closely held secret until 1988. At that time a national survey of the nation's largest owners of manufactured home communities produced the first publicly stated OER for manufactured home communities at 37.8 percent. A subsequent survey of the same property owners in 1994 suggested a possible adjustment to 38.2 percent. For pro forma planning purposes, a 40.0 percent Allen Model OER has enjoyed increasing use among novice and experienced investors alike. Experienced manufactured home community operators with full properties, charging market-leading rents, and carefully controlling expenses can often drive the property's OER into the 20 percent range. A chart detailing regional and national OER survey percentages, along with IREM's (Institute of Real Estate Management) garden apartment OER average of 51.1 percent, all using the same standard chart of accounts, is shown as **Table 1–4**.[16] The standard chart of accounts breakdown used in the OER document is the following:

1. Management fee: Any nonsalary and nonwage fee paid to a firm or individual functioning as a manage subcontractor.

2. Administrative and wages: All office-related, on-site salaries and wages paid for leasing, bookkeeping, and management, including outside accounting and legal expenses.

3. Administrative costs: Includes travel and entertainment, dues and subscriptions, bad debt expense, office supplies and postage, contributions, and on-site computer supplies.

4. Telephone: Basic telephone charges and long-distance carrier service fees. No yellow page ad fees.

5. Advertising: Newspaper classified and display, telephone yellow page directory, radio, brochures, business cards, and special signage.

6. Operating supplies: Pool chemicals, lawn fertilizers and seed, ice melting chemicals, and so forth.

7. Heating expense: Natural or propane gas and fuel oil for office, clubhouse, and maintenance facility.

8. Electricity: Street lights, pumps, building lights—and heating, if appropriate.

9. Water/sewer: Public or private system-related fees or costs.

10. Maintenance repair: Trash removal, snow removal, grass cutting, street repairs, not including cost depreciable items in this category.

11. Maintenance wage: If not included in administrative and wage, as may be the case with a small community, includes wages for maintenance supervisor and staff, groundsmen, and possibly pool lifeguards.

12. Real estate tax: Real estate taxes only.

---

[16] Allen, Alley, & Hicks at 288.

Table 1–4

Comparing Operating Expense Ratios (OERs)

Expense Category	Texas A&M Guide	Horner Plan	National Survey III	Allen Model	IREMs Analysis	Apt. Model
		Mobilehome Communities			Apartments	
ADMINISTRATIVE EXPENSES						
Management Fee	NA[1]	5.0%	5.0%	5.0%	4.5%	4.5%
Wages	9.0%	4.4%	4.3%	4.5%	8.4%[2]	8.0%
Admin. Costs	1.5%	2.6%	2.4%	2.5%	7.0%	6.5%
Telephone	NA	0.6%	0.5%	0.5%	NA	NA
Advertising	1.0%	0.2%	0.3%	0.5%	NA	NA
TOTAL	11.5%	12.8%	12.5%	13.0%	19.9%	19.0%
OPERATING EXPENSES						
Supplies	0.5%	1.3%	0.4%	0.5%	2.5%[3]	
Heating	9.0% *[5]	0.3%	0.3%	0.5%	0.9%[4]	0.9%
Electric	*[5]	0.8%	0.9%	1.0%	1.7%[6]	1.5%
Water/Sewer	*[5]	14.0%	9.2%	9.0%	3.1%[6]	3.0%
TOTAL	9.5%	16.4%	10.8%	11.0%	8.2%	7.9%
MAINTENANCE EXPENSES						
Repairs	7.0%[8]	3.4%	5.8%	5.0%	8.5%[7]	8.5%
Wages	*[8]	3.4%	3.0%	3.0%	5.8%[2]	
TOTAL	7.0%	6.8%	8.8%	8.0%	14.3%	14.0%
TAXES AND INSURANCE						
Real Estate Taxes	9.0%	5.4%	6.8%	6.5%	7.4%	7.5%
Other Taxes, Licensing	NA	NA	0.3%	0.5%	0.1%	0.1%
Property Insurance	0.5%	2.6%	0.9%	1.0%	1.6%	1.5%
TOTAL	9.5%	8.0%	8.0%	8.0%	9.1%	9.1%
SERVICE EXPENSES						
Subcontracts	NA	1.3%	NA	NA	NA	NA
TOTAL	37.5%	45.3%	40.1%	40.0%	51.5%[9]	50.0%

[1] NA—Not available in this study. —but possibly included in the wage category.

[2] 9.4% (payroll) plus 4.8% (other payroll) totals 14.2%; To ascertain proportions for lines #3 and #17, use data from column #3.

[3] 0.3% (supplies), 1.2% (building services), 0.6% (other operations) and 0.4% (recreation and amenities) equal 2.5%.

[4] 0.5% (heat fuel) and 0.4% (gas) equal 0.9% for common area only.

[5] Texas A&M included electric and water/sewer expenses with heating expenses.

[6] 1.7% plus 3.1% equals common area only.

[7] 0.4% (security), 2.2% (grounds maintenance), 3.2% (maintenance and repair), and 2.3% (painting and decorating) equal 8.5%.

[8] Texas A&M lumped maintenance wages with repair costs.

13. Other taxes, licenses, and fees: Business-related taxes (for example, personal property) and fees/licenses required to operate the property.
14. Property insurance: Liability and business coverage as desired; also group and workers' compensation insurance, if not included under administrative and wage category.
15. Subcontract: Specialty maintenance needs (electrician, plumber), sometimes even refuse removal, and also wastewater treatment plant operator if not on staff.

The obvious question is this: how can a manufactured home community operate a full 13 percentage points "cheaper" (or 13¢ on the dollar) than a garden-style apartment community? There are several key and related reasons:

1. Far less brick and mortar improvements (buildings) to maintain and repair because of weather and wear and tear.
2. No turnover expense relative to carpet cleaning, wall painting, and appliance upgrade. Manufactured homeowner/renters generally care for their homes inside and out.
3. A unique efficiency that manufactured home communities enjoy that apartments do not. The higher the occupancy in a manufactured home community the less the labor and related costs; fewer vacant sites to mow and maintain and very low turnover equals minimal leasing effort and expense. Conversely, low occupancy in a manufactured home community may be more costly than for a like-sized apartment community, as there is a lot more to do to maintain vacant sites. Operating expense ratio is yet another obvious test of performance efficiency.

The Residents

Who lives in manufactured home landlease communities? To begin with, a unique type of lessee. These lessees are true homeowners (unless renting a manufactured home from a third party) in that they are paying a chattel mortgage on their homes or own them outright. The lessees are also just that, renters who pay an agreed upon amount each month for the groundlease rights to small parcels of land or homesites within the manufactured home community. Living in manufactured home communities are younger families, many under 35 years of age, although the across-the-board average is 35 to 46 among all types of homeowners. The residents typically have limited incomes ($19,925 in 1989 versus $29,642 for all U.S. households.[17] Retirees also frequently reside in manufactured home communities. Most are former owners of larger traditional site-built homes who have opted for the convenient lifestyle and amenity packages characteristic of retirement meccas in the Southeast and West. The median number of occupants per manufactured home continues to be 2.2.[18]

While state laws vary considerably as to content and degree of enforcement, federal laws do not. Several categories of federal oversight particularly affect manufactured home communities:

1. The Fair Housing Amendments Act of 1988 as it relates to race, color, religion, sex, national origin, handicap, and familial status
2. Americans with Disabilities Act
3. Fair Housing Advertising.

§ 1.8   Trends among Manufactured Home Communities

These are exciting times for manufactured home community owners and would-be developers and investors. Ever since the release in 1994 of *Development, Marketing and Operation of Manufactured Home Communities,* land development seminars sponsored by the text's co-authors and the Manufactured Housing Institute have been well attended across the United States. This, coupled with the relaxing of local regulatory barriers to affordable housing in some locales—in part credited to awareness of the problem through the aforementioned *NIMBY* ("Not In My Back Yard") *Report,* have presented many opportunities for new and expanded manufactured home community development.

New and expanded manufactured home communities are featuring larger homesites to accommodate larger homes, resulting in lower property densities. Most new development projects are opting for public

---

[17] Bureau of Census, Statistical Brief on Mobile Homes (May 1994).

[18] U.S. Commerce Department, American Housing Survey for the United States (1995).

utilities whenever possible, thanks in part to the tightening of potable water reporting standards and stiffer environmental regulations on wastewater effluent. All new utility services are now generally underground.

Professionalism, education, and positive business press coverage has finally arrived for the manufactured home community niche. Chief among these developments has been the increased incidence of Institute of Real Estate Management's Certified Property Managers at middle and upper echelons of management over multiproperty portfolios. See **Appendix E.** Close behind has been the industry's development of a professional designation program for the on-site or community manager. The Manufactured Housing Educational Institute, an arm of MHI, now regularly trains and approves on-site managers to be designated as Accredited Community Managers. Industry leaders now meet annually at the International Networking Roundtable to network, learn together, and plan the future of their industry as a true multifamily housing player and no longer an also-ran in the shadow of their manufacturer peers.

Several periodicals and specially prepared monographs now describe the industry and educate would-be investors and other interested partners. The *Manufactured Home Merchandiser* has been joined on the national scene by the *Manufactured Housing Journal.* Both monthly publications cover the manufactured housing industry as a whole, while the *Allen Letter* targets manufactured home community owners and managers nationwide. See **Appendix F** for complete list of industry periodicals. The Urban Land Institute's Research Working Paper #640, "Manufactured Housing: An Affordable Alternative" by Diane Suchman, is the best general industry summary to date. *Real Estate Industry Overview: Manufactured Housing REIT's* by E. Homel and S. Sakwa does a credible job on the community side. And Merrill Lynch's and C.S. First Boston's 1995 monographs have also served to further popularize manufactured housing and manufactured home communities as worthwhile investment alternatives. See the **bibliography** for further details.

Finally, progress seems to be continuing, if not increasing, among manufactured home community residents to control their destiny by purchasing the investment property whereon they reside. Known generally as R.O.C.s or resident-owned communities, such homeowner purchased and operated properties are usually cooperatively (co-op) owned, although subdividing and condominiumizing are options as well. Occurring most frequently in Florida, R.O.C.s have also been consummated in New England, Arizona, California, and a few other areas as well. Typical difficulties an R.O.C. faces include maintaining a viable volunteer homeowner association, signing up enough initial investors (homeowner/renters purchase stock in the cooperative) to proceed, and securing adequate, reasonable financing for the transaction. All of this presumes, of course, that the property owner is interested in selling at a price that makes economic sense for the buyer and lender.

§ 1.9   Investment Cautions

By now a few investment cautions should be in the reader's mind, along with all the glowing reasons for considering investing in a manufactured home community. Here are a few additional items to ponder:

1. Rent increase potential, if not already limited by a seller's recent adjustments, may be shackled by one or another form of rent control or landlord-tenant legislation.
2. Rental homesites in older, existing manufactured home communities may be too small to accommodate contemporary, larger manufactured homes. Densities of more than six homes to the acre of developed ground and older properties are two key indicators of this type of possible functional obsolescence.
3. Utility infrastructure condition is a key factor with manufactured home communities. After all, it is generally the only site improvement in evidence—and it is all or mostly below ground.

§ 1.10   Manufactured Housing Industry Terminology

This section lists the cutting-edge of manufactured housing industry terminology. Most of it is common parlance across the United States today. There are regions, a couple of states, and certainly some individuals who continue to resist using terms that cast their industry in the most favorable light, but progress is being made. The following is a standard message sent to journalists misusing terminology:

Oops . . . you slipped!

Trailers haul livestock and beer. People live in manufactured homes. No one lives in a trailer. For that matter, even the term "mobile home" is rarely used by journalists and news commentators anymore.

Hundreds of thousands of homeowners, according to the last national census, live in manufactured homes located in subdivisions, on scattered homesites, and in attractive land/lease communities. Only in California and Florida is mobilehome park still common parlance.

Furthermore, manufactured homes are no longer sold by dealers but by retail sales consultants employed at home sales and information centers. Resident has replaced tenant, and professional property manager has superseded landlord. Rental agreement is also favored over lease, and manufactured homes are affixed to homesites or sites, not lots, spaces, pads or stalls.

The manufactured housing industry has come a long, long way over the past fifty years. Manufactured homes have more than doubled in size, look exactly like many site-built homes, are every bit as energy efficient, but still more economical to purchase. Today's manufactured home offers every comfort and convenience feature and amenity imaginable, from large garden-style bathtubs to vaulted ceilings with fans to thick pile carpeting.

So, as the Decade of Manufactured Housing and the Manufactured Home Community (1995–2005) dawns, let's call a manufactured home a home, and a manufactured home community a nice place to live!

Terminology

Manufactured housing is the factory-produced product discussed so far. Once it is sold at a retail salescenter or sited in a manufactured home community or on a private building site, it becomes someone's home, a *manufactured home.*

Manufactured home community can be landlease, subdivision, cooperatively owned, or condominium ownership. This term alone has seen more variants and evolution than any other in the manufactured housing lexicon. Simply put, a manufactured home community is where several or many manufactured homes are sited, with semipermanent installation and otherwise, and the occupying homeowner pays rent to the property owner or association dues or a management fee to a homeowner's association.

Resident is the term commonly used to describe the homeowner/renter or lessee who resides in a manufactured home community.

Information center or *office* are used interchangeably, the former more often when a new or resale home marketing effort is in effect on-site.

Homesite and *site* are used to describe where a manufactured home is placed within a manufactured home community or on a privately owned scattered building site.

Single-section and *multisection* clearly describe the two size and floorplan variants of manufactured homes.

Retailer and *retail salescenter* are who sells housing and where manufactured housing is sold. It may be a separate location or on-site at a manufactured home community.

Property manager is a middle level manager with responsibility for one very large manufactured home community, but most frequently two or more separate income-producing properties within a given geographic region.

Resident manager or *community manager* generally lives on-site or nearby the manufactured home community. Some refer to this position as property or community administrator.

Sales and/or leasing consultant is a support person to the on-site manager, although with smaller properties this may be one inclusive job description and responsibility.

Transporter is the firm or individual who is licensed and hired to move manufactured homes from one location to another.

Rules and regulations or *guidelines for living* are self-explanatory and usually required by state statute. The latter term is a "gentler and nicer" sounding description of the former. In subdivisions, *covenants and restrictions,* is the correct term.

Rental agreement is preferred by some over using the term "lease."

Skirting is the material, usually vinyl or prefinished metal sheathing, covering the air space between the bottom of a manufactured home and the ground. Also called foundation fascia.

Tiedowns and *earth anchors* are used to affix a manufactured home to the homesite. May be part of a concrete foundation system or simply augered into the earth at prescribed intervals.

Resale homes and *resale center,* the former refers to homes that have been lived-in and are now for sale. It can also refer to homes that have been repossessed by lenders and are now again for sale.

Trash or *refuse removal* is polite verbiage for one of the services usually included in the monthly rent.

Per capita charges is the extra rent amount sometimes charged for additional people living in a manufactured home to offset increased water and sewer system usage.

Wastewater treatment facility is usually a private system (package plant, filtration system) located on-site or nearby, for processing raw sewage from the manufactured home community.

§ 1.11 Overall Manufactured Housing Trends

In addition to the two categories of trends discussed earlier, a few more bear watching:

1. From a regulatory perspective, there is a possibility that the manufactured housing oversight responsibilities presently administered by HUD will be altered in some fashion.
2. The Manufactured Housing Institute, after 40 years, is restructuring and giving its industry segment members (manufacturers, community owners, retailers, suppliers, finance firms, state associations) more voice and authority in the conduct of present and future activities of the institute. See **Appendix G.**
3. Senior housing may well become a major new added market opportunity for the manufactured housing industry in the years ahead. Already actively producing manufactured housing for retirement communities in the South and Southwest, increasing attention is being paid to providing customized manufactured housing in specially designed, even retrofitted manufactured home communities, as an affordable alternative to meet congregate care, assisted living, and continuing care housing needs. Manufactured housing is far less expensive than building new nursing homes and can be in place in a far shorter time. Senior housing does tend to be more management intense as more resident services are required.

§ 1.12   Summary

The manufactured housing industry and manufactured home communities have truly come into their own over the past five years. Those home-hunters who have not stepped into a contemporary manufactured home have no idea what they are missing. This is quality, affordable, desirable housing. And the manufactured home community lifestyle is getting nothing but better as large portfolio owners continue to set new and higher quality standards for their peers to follow. Through it all, the investment opportunity, on either side of the manufactured housing/manufactured home community fence, is unparalleled as we experience the Decade (1995–2005) of Manufactured Housing and the Manufactured Home Community.

CHAPTER 2

BASICS OF REAL ESTATE INVESTMENT

§ 2.1   Introduction

§ 2.2   Investment Risk

§ 2.3   Motivation to Invest in Real Estate

§ 2.4   The Search for a Real Estate Investment

§ 2.5   Research for the Right Real Estate Investment

§ 2.6   Economic and Financial Feasibility

ANOTHER PERSPECTIVE
Dan Oas

§ 2.7   Cash-on-Cash Return

§ 2.8   Unique Characteristics of Real Estate Investments

§ 2.9   Advantages and Disadvantages of Real Estate

§ 2.10   Summary

§ 2.1   Introduction

One way or another, just about everyone winds up investing in real estate. Whether one makes a significant capital investment to acquire the income stream of an investment property, or simply leases an apartment in a certain part of town, both are investments in real estate. The former is made in the expectation of realizing present and future profit, the latter to make a personal statement of one sort or another. Even buying one's home has elements of the two motivations.

This chapter identifies some of the reasons individuals, partnerships, and companies invest in income-producing real estate. Beyond these reasons, the roles of personal and business goal setting are explored, as well as the direct application of a problem-solving process for finding, evaluating, and consummating investment real estate transactions. Of particular value are several sets of investment guidelines and checklists that are applicable to properties of all types. The chapter ends with a brief overview of economic and financial feasibility.

Interestingly, the principles of real estate investment are fairly consistent among the five major property types, especially residential (multifamily) investment properties.[1] It is simply the terminology and trade practices within each that vary. For the purposes of this chapter, a generic middle road is taken, making the discussion generally applicable to the alternative real estate investment types. Narrowing the focus to manufactured home communities occurs in **Chapter 3.**

As suggested in the opening paragraph, just about everyone will invest in real estate. Whether to impress one's peers with personal achievement or to position oneself to receive a new, healthy and ongoing cash flow, the medium is the same: real estate. The focus of the chapter will be on the cash flow and profit phenomena.

§ 2.2 Investment Risk

The old economist's definition of profit, "the reward for taking a risk" is particularly apt when discussing real estate investments. Real estate, like any business venture, involves taking some degree of risk. For some, as in inheriting a portfolio of stable properties with the inheritance tax financed by an insurance policy, the risk is usually very small—unless the local market or national economy changes quickly and drastically. For others, having a market or economy change during land development or being underinsured when disaster strikes can mean ruin. In either event, risk is definitely a factor that can affect profits. Furthermore, high risks do not necessarily translate into high profits, nor do low risks have to mean low profits. The challenge is sorting out investment alternatives using the time-tested guidelines that follow.

Two things in particular are generally said and believed about real estate as an investment alternative. Real estate usually offers the

---

[1] The five major property types are multifamily/residential, office, shopping center, industrial, and raw land.

greatest potential return on one's initial investment—through cash flows, tax benefits, equity buildup and value appreciation—and real estate has the reputation, among many, as being the "most forgiving" of all investments. Unlike the stock market, where one's financial successes and failures are often dependent on reacting in a timely fashion to quick market dips and rises, real estate decisions, particularly those associated with investment property holdings, can be made at a more considered pace, and even wrong decisions can be undone or reversed at times.

The very principle of *investing,* that is to say, adopting a strategy of curtailing present consumption in favor of greater future potential consumption, lends itself especially well to the real estate alternative. For here, in return for an equity down payment, one in effect purchases the present and future cash flow of an income-producing property, along with other ancillary benefits.

There are at least six factors common among all sorts of investments. When preparing to access the real estate investment market, it is good to have a grasp on one's attitude towards each factor and to ascertain how potential investments measure up against them as well.[2]

Degree of risk involved. Everyone's risk tolerance is different, and it often changes with personal or corporate circumstances. The key here is wisdom. If a significant risk is involved and the potential loss of one's equity position is bearable, then a moderate-to-high risk investment with strong potential for significant return might be justified. On the other hand, an investment with moderate risk, offset with exceptionally good personal marketing and management skills, might be even better—even if the returns are not as great. It now becomes a matter of personal investment goals, degree of involvement, and risk tolerance.

Degree of liquidity. Do not invest in real estate with the idea of getting in and getting out of a property quickly. That only happens when one invests in a REIT (real estate investment trust), the stock market, or a real estate–based mutual fund. It generally takes months, even years, to consummate a real estate transaction in the first place. Sale price fluctuations and negotiations, due diligence period inspections,

---

[2] A good resource is Commercial Investment Real Estate Institute, 430 N. Michigan Ave., Chicago, IL 60611.

arranging finance, and closing preparations all take time and effort. Once in the deal, it can be just as time-consuming to get out, unless one sells in a panic for a discount if not outright loss.

Degree of management required or desired. For some, hands-off management is the ideal, as long as there is desired cash flow and continuing residual benefits. But for others, the idea of directing one's destiny, seeing the rewards of one's handiwork, and hopefully, realizing even greater cash flows and related financial rewards make hands-on property management a "must" experience. It is usually a matter of personal choice, unless property circumstances force a less than desirable alternative. Professional real estate management too is a realistic and, for many, a very desirable alternative. Putting one's investment properties into the hands of a capable, experienced, and motivated Certified Property Manager or fee-management firm can yield positive results.[3]

Fluctuations in value (sale price). Get used to it, it happens. Value is dynamic. It is sensitive to all sort of influences, some short term, others long term. The ideal, for some investors, is to develop a parcel of raw land into one or another type of income property, fill it with bona fide lessees (seeing value increase as the cash flow value increases), and eventually sell it for multiples of what the original raw land was worth. For others, the value roller coaster begins with the acquisition of a turnaround challenge. With a name change, astute management, and hopefully an improving economy (if that was the cause of the property's original downfall in value) increased value will likely be realized. But all this can happen just as easily in reverse. The developer may not be able to lease rapidly enough to meet financial commitments and lose the project altogether, including his or her equity. Same with the turnaround challenge: values can and will fluctuate.

Degree of leverage. Simply put, this is a measure of how much of a property's purchase price can be placed in the hands of someone else— generally a lender or seller—if the latter is willing to carry back financing as in a contract for deed transaction. The interest an investor pays on

---

[3] For information regarding the Certified Property Manager designation, contact Institute of Real Estate Management, 430 N. Michigan Ave., Chicago, IL 60611.

the principle portion of the property's leveraged loan is the price for that leverage. For after all, without the ability to finance or leverage real estate transactions, very few deals would ever consummate. The dollar requirement is just too great for most would-be investors to handle without leverage. Then, it becomes a matter of degree. A 75 percent LTV (loan-to-value) requirement by a bank means that 75 percent of the purchase price is financed or leveraged by the bank. If a loan can be arranged wherein the investor makes an equity down payment of only 10 percent of the sale price, then 90 percent of the deal is leveraged with what has been, on occasion, called "other people's money" (OPM)— seller, lending institution, and so forth.[4]

Degree of tax impact. While this is a matter best handled in confidence with one's personal or corporate accounting and tax advisors, a particular point must not be overlooked. Although real estate as a tax shelter is in legislative disfavor just now, there remain several business-related tax benefits: depreciation of assets, tax credits when and where applicable on certain types of property, write-offs of bona fide business expenses, and mortgage interest deductions.

§ 2.3 Motivation to Invest in Real Estate

By now it should be obvious that there are significant differences between investing one's money in fixed investment vehicles, like savings accounts, and putting a portion of such discretionary funds to work in a dynamic fashion as with real estate investments. Which route to go is obviously a matter of personal choice.

Earlier it was mentioned that there were five major investment real estate property types. Actually there are a lot more:

1. Undeveloped land (low cost, high potential gain)
2. Farmland (row crops, livestock, orchards)
3. Shopping centers (neighborhood, community, and regional centers)
4. Industrial (manufacturing, warehouse, research and development facilities)

---

[4] Robert Allen, Getting Started in Real Estate Investing (1984).

5. Apartment buildings (urban highrise; suburban garden-style; subsidized and nonsubsidized)

6. Single-family homes and duplexes

7. Manufactured home communities (landlease and subdivision)

8. Senior housing (congregate care, assisted living, and continuing care)

9. Condominiums, cooperatives, and homeowner association administered (office-type and multifamily residential)

10. Time-sharing (usually resort areas)

11. Hospitality industry (hotels, motels, bed and breakfasts)

12. Parking facilities (surface-type and garages)

13. Downtown and surburban office buildings.[5]

There is certainly a wide variety of investment property types to consider. And besides being land based, there is a common denominator among these property types that consultant/writer Alan Cymrot points out: "Real estate is a business that buys, sells and leases square feet."[6] Think about it. That is certainly the case with offices, shopping centers, industrial properties, and parking lots. With undeveloped land, the talk is about acres; with apartments, manufactured home communities, houses, senior housing, condominiums, and time-sharing properties the terms are number of rental or housing units—all of which can ultimately be described and valued in terms of square feet or income generated per square foot.

Why is real estate a good investment choice for many investors? There are at least four categorized motivations:

1. Real estate investments generate a variety of income streams. The first is cash flow. Cash flow is what is left after paying operating expenses and mortgage payments or servicing debt. Cash flow before paying the property's mortgage is generally referred to as *net operating income* (NOI). Cash flow remaining after paying the mortgage is commonly described as *cash flow before taxes.* And when this latter amount is mathematically divided by the amount of original equity (down payment), the result is often referred to as the *cash-on-cash return* for that property for that period of time.

---

[5] Alvin Arnold, Real Estate Investor's Deskbook 12-4 through 12-81 (1994).

[6] Allen Cymrot, Street Smart Real Estate Investing 11 (1993).

Cash flow is the first and certainly a very significant attribute of investment real estate.

2. **Property management income.** This is the salary or wages taken out of an income-producing property to pay the owner (particularly if a smaller, hands-on type operation) for services rendered, or to pay a fee-management company to supervise the property for a passive investor. So the decision by the investor-owner is whether to work the property oneself and take this extra stream of income for his or her efforts, or concede it to someone else in return for not having to deal with the day-to-day challenges of property management.

3. **Equity buildup.** This is a noncash item, and simply put, equity value of a property increases as the mortgage principle is paid down with periodic debt service payments.

4. **Reversion** of sales proceeds occurs as a cash item when property is divested for a profit.

Real estate investments increase one's net worth in at least three ways:

1. **Value appreciation,** occurring as a result, generally, of inflationary pressure. As inflation, at any rate, pushes the value of consumer goods upward, investment real estate, even one's personal residence, tends to rise by price (that is, value) as well.

2. **Improvements** to the visual and functional attributes and viability of an investment property, particularly with a turnaround challenge, tend to boost value as well.

3. **Equity buildup,** as previously described.

The tax benefits of real estate investments are couched in cost recovery by way of depreciation of assets, tax credits when and where applicable (most common in certain apartment investments), write-offs of business expenses—especially real estate taxes; and mortgage interest deduction. The tax shelter value of investment real estate is negligible at this time but may change again.

The potential use of leverage also protects and enhances one's net worth. Rather than having to invest most or all of one's equity in a single real estate transaction, thanks to leverage (that is, using other people's money), this equity can be distributed to effect several other real estate investment transactions. The end result is control over several income-producing properties, each generating a stream of income, appreciating in value, experiencing equity buildup, and taking advantage of available tax benefits.

Where and how does one start the real estate investment process in general or decide on a particular strategy (or property, property-type) in particular? Analyzing one's present personal and business situation in terms of resources is a place to start. This is a serious "sit down and think about it" exercise:

_____ 1. Finances. Is the present personal or corporate situation stable and with enough cushion to warrant a new departure of any sort, and if so, to what degree? Here is where that question of degree of risk becomes important: Who else will be affected, and how, by these decisions and their possible consequences?

_____ 2. Time. Is time available now or soon to research and learn all about the probable or desired investment? Is time available to be active in the acquisition search or does one need to rely on a real estate broker? What about the important property management question?

_____ 3. Knowledge of investments in general and real estate in particular. Experienced or novice? Where to go for needed information? If simply expanding one's personal or corporate portfolio, what do present trends predict for the future of one's niche?

_____ 4. Motivation. By now this element should be fairly well quantified. Is this something one feels compelled to do or really wants to do for the profit potential, experience, or other motivating reasons? The old equilateral Success Triangle (see **Figure 2–1**) still teaches a valid lesson. Be equally balanced on one triangle side with "ability and skills" in a given area of interest, compared to "experience and knowledge" on the other side of the triangle. Connect both sides with a firm base of "attitude and motivation" to be successful.

SUCCESS TRIANGLE

APPLIED TO

REAL ESTATE INVESTING

ABILITY & SKILLS

KNOWLEDGE & EXPERIENCE

success

ATTITUDE & MOTIVATION

Figure 2–1. Success triangle. Illustration provided by Patti Greco of Greco Writing, 902B Ridgefield Circle, Clinton, MA 01510 (508) 368-1022.

_____ 5. Personal or corporate investment goals. Now is the time to write them down, review and discuss them. Some general examples:

   _____ ROI (return on investment). Is it a must now or can it be delayed for greater return? What level of ROI is desired/required?

   _____ Location preference: nearby or remote; urban or rural?

   _____ Preference for property type—and why?

   _____ Risk level tolerance?

   _____ Stable property or turnaround challenge?

   _____ Small or large-sized property?

This list is not exhaustive, simply illustrative of the introspection and research that must take place before serious investing begins.

§ 2.4   The Search for a Real Estate Investment

Although a fair number of real estate research and investment formulas and rules of thumb have been touted over the years, they all tend to use one common tool: the problem-solving procedure, also known as the scientific process. There are eight steps to this time-proven routine, and they serve the real estate investment search well. These steps are the following:

Select a Problem, A Task
Consider It a Challenge, An Opportunity
Define It; Document It
Ensure the Situation is What is Appears to be
Study It; Question Every Detail
Break Problem Down Into Parts
Research & Organize Data
Get the Facts; Use the Basic M's of Management
Refine and Digest Data
Internalize and Reflect on Alternatives

Produce and Rework Ideas

Weigh and Decide Combining, Eliminating, Rearranging, Simplifying, Testing and Selecting the Best Alternative(s)

Scheduling and Setting Objectives; Standards of Performance

Implement and Monitor

Take Action (by) Adjusting & Modifying as Necessary

Evaluating Performance and Results

Follow up and Recap Results

Review All Actions

Plan for the Future

§ 2.5   Research for the Right Real Estate Investment

One can customize the classic problem-solving procedure (scientific process) to this real estate investment project, whether working on one's own or utilizing the services of a buyer's broker:

1. Select a problem, a task.   In this case, it is the identification and eventual purchase of a real estate investment. Consider it a challenge or an opportunity—to make money. Concentrate on learning all there is to know about one or more desirable property types as investment vehicles before proceeding. Again, the best motivational mindset is to think of the property or property-type search as a challenge and opportunity to make a statement and a profit.

2. Define it; document it.   Again, assuming a property type, even specific property selection, has been made, the "for sale" property prospectus provides initial data about a specific property or portfolio. Ensure the offering is what is appears to be through verification of the listing agreement with the owner, personal inspection, and research. Do the considered "deals" meet one's personal or corporate investment goals and property parameters?

3. Study it; question every detail.   This is simply a continuation and refinement of the previous step. Begin to apply verifiable property data to published industry norms and standards for that property type. Do not rely solely on the property owner's and broker's input. Following are a few of the research formulas and rules of thumb that break this overall challenge into manageable parts.

The Commercial Investment Real Estate Institute[7] recommends five major market factors to consider at this stage:

- **Inventory:** What is available and occupied in the local market in this particular property type? What else is available for sale or lease?
- **Availability:** Conversely, how many square feet or rental units are unoccupied at the present time in the local market?
- **Absorption:** How much vacant square feet or units/homesites were occupied at the end of the observation period? This may be one month, six months, or one year from when the search was initiated.
- **Competition:** Who are the competition and what is their number and character? Is the market controlled by one or open to many investors?
- **Trends:** What supply and demand dynamics are at work in the market area? The SWOT marketing acronym is helpful at this point, where

S	=	identify strength(s) of the property
W	=	identify weakness(es) of the property
O	=	identify the opportunities in the market
T	=	identify the threats inherent in the market

Another time-tested approach used by experienced real estate investors is to "Look for Good Unchangeables and Bad Changeables!" from the buyer's perspective. Specifically, this means to identify, verify, and quantify:

- **Good Unchangeables:** Property location, property design or layout (density), existing infrastructure (underground utilities, public versus private utilities), durability and serviceability of rental space (a harbinger of functional obsolescence).

---

[7] Commercial Investment Real Estate Institute, 430 N. Michigan Ave., Chicago, IL 60611.

- **Bad Changeables:** Obviously poor on-site management (lax rules enforcement, poor curb appeal, morale and resident problems, and so forth), poor rental collection, low occupancy when competition is full, deferred maintenance.

Once the "good unchangeables and bad changeables" evaluation has been made, use experts (engineers, accountants) to verify observations and help lay plans for future improvements. It goes almost without saying that the more Good Unchangeables and Bad Unchangeables, the better the potential transaction for the buyer. Several bad unchangeables should be a definite warning sign. Finally, attempt to ascertain the seller's true motives for selling, possibly to use as a negotiating tool along with the results of the aforementioned research.

A summary thought about this stage of the problem-solving procedure lies in the reminder that prudent loan underwriting generally requires institutional analysis of the following investment property touchstones:

- Location considerations
- Tenancy level and characteristics
- Leases in effect
- Operating performance
- Property management
- Ownership position
- Hazardous materials on-site.

4. Research and organize data.   Continue to collect facts and organize them in some fashion. There is no single best format for this step. However, one method that does organize such data and serves as a forerunner to the eventual on-site manual of operations or standard operations procedures (SOP), is the *Ms of Management* concept. In this case, key property management resource areas are identified with words that begin with M:

- **Manpower:** All data that has to do with staffing (present and anticipated) of a property; an organization chart, possible job descriptions, wage and salary structure per job.
- **Machinery:** The equipment and tools required for continuing operations, for example, vehicles, lawnmowers, amenities (swimming

pool pump and filter data), wastewater treatment, water well and metering considerations. See the personal property inventory for the property.

- **Material:** Inventory of products and sources of requisite services for the property. This may include handtools, pool chemicals, cleaning and other maintenance supplies.
- **Methods:** The policies and procedures, rules and regulations, and all other such codified and written materials that explain and govern the property management operations of the property, from prospect screening to rent collection to hiring guidelines.
- **Money:** Past and pro forma operating statements and budgets, along with petty cash, purchase orders, and wage and hour guidelines.

Some experienced real estate managers go even further and tab other M words, such as Management, Maintenance (manuals, and so forth), and Marketing (samples of ads).

5. Refine and digest data.   Internalize and reflect on alternative actions. This is the initial stage of creative thinking about how one might really take over and manage/improve a given real estate investment. What does data suggest—a good deal or not? Right type of specific property for acquisition now or at a future date? One may even experience some subconscious or gut-level input at this point.

6. Produce and rework ideas.   This step relates to

- Structuring the transaction.
- Changes to the way the property is marketed (maybe a name change) or managed. Rent increase now (to make deal work), or later after planned improvements have been effected?
- A few more possibilities: combine too small rental units or space into larger ones; eliminate or replace obsolete equipment and utilities; rearrange rent due dates to all be effective the same day; simplify lease, rules and regulations, or Guidelines for Living.
- Select and test possible alternatives using different models and spreadsheets.
- Identify, set, and schedule performance objectives for the possible acquisition and performance standards for employees.

7. Implement and monitor. If and when the real estate transaction is consummated, adjust and monitor plans as necessary and continually record and evaluate performance in key result areas.

8. Follow up and recap results. Periodically review actions and results to date and apply them to plans for the future with similar investment properties.

§ 2.6 Economic and Financial Feasibility

No discussion of real estate investment basics is complete without a review of economic and financial feasibility. Texas A & M's Real Estate Center, in one of its technical reports, defines such feasibility: "An income property is economically feasible if the demand for the space is adequate and if it can generate adequate NOI (net operating income) to support sufficient debt to finance the property and provide a satisfactory cash return to its owner."[8]

Concentrating on the latter half of this definition, having to do with financial feasibility, an example will demonstrate how the rental income and operating expenses of a nonspecific multifamily residential property type can fulfill the definition requirements of feasibility.

Given data for subject property:

- 300 rental units
- $250/month rental rate per unit
- $900,000 annualized rental income assuming no vacancy or collection loss
- $360,000 operating expenses, assuming a 40 percent operating expense ration or OER
- $450,000 annual debt service (DS) or total mortgage payments amounts
- $600,000 owner's original equity or down payment (DP) to purchase subject property

---

[8] Wayne E. Etter, Analyzing Distressed Properties 3 (Real Estate Center, Texas A&M University, College Station, Tex.).

Financial feasibility calculations for subject property:

- Rental Income (300 units × $250/mth × 12 months) $900,000
- Operating Expenses ($900,000 × .40 OER)   −360,000
- Net Operating Income (NOI) $540,000
- Annual Debt Service (DS) or Mortgage Payment   −450,000
- Cash Flow before Taxes $90,000
- Divide by $600,000 original equity or down payment (DP) = 15% cash-on-cash return

It is not the intent of this chapter to introduce or explain income-property valuation as it relates to this example. That will be covered in detail in **Chapter 5.** What this example simply and clearly demonstrates is that the rental income more than covers the property's operating expenses and mortgage obligations. Furthermore, the cash flow before taxes represents a solid 15 percent cash-on-cash return to the investor-owner after the first year of ownership. Obviously, this abbreviated example does not factor in the influence of possible vacancy and collection losses, or for that matter, miscellaneous income. Also it does not factor in any tax influences. The example simply demonstrates that this subject property is financially feasible with cash flow sufficient in quantity, quality, and hopefully, durability.

ANOTHER PERSPECTIVE[9]

§ 2.7   Cash-on-Cash Return

Real estate as a form of investment can be one of the most stable time-enduring investments one can make. Whether one calls *real estate* a home, apartment building, manufactured home community, industrial complex, ranch, or farm, they all have essentially the same characteristics

---

[9] Dan Oas writes enthusiastically and authoritatively about real estate as a desirable personal and corporate investment. His perspective, relative to the manufactured home community and its significant ROI potential, unique characteristics, advantages, and disadvantages, makes the following contribution to the text a most informative addition.

that are associated with the ownership of real property. A thorough understanding of these characteristics and how they can be cultivated results in a wise investment that will produce a solid dependable cash flow for the length of the investment.

What never ceases to amaze is the shear simplicity of real estate. Real estate has always, with a few exceptions, increased in value over time. As with everything in life, value is a subjective thing. The real estate market, like everything else, goes up and down. But when one tracks the market over a long period of time, for example, 20 years, one will see that it always increases over time.

Once an investment property is purchased—one that produces a cash flow after all expenses—it provides a return. Revenues, typically from rents, increase on an annual basis. If one's return the first year is 10 percent, then the second year should be slightly higher, provided there are no unusual expenses. After a few years the return can increase to 15 percent or 20 percent. Meanwhile the loan balance is being paid down. As the cash flow of the property increases, so does the overall value. Review **Table 2–1**. The table demonstrates the cash-on-cash return on a $1,000,000 purchase with $250,000 down payment. The gross income in year one is $160,000 with 37.5 percent expenses for each year and a 5 percent annual increase in rents. The loan is a $750,000 loan amortized over 30 years at 9 percent, which has annual payments of $72,416.

Table 2–1

Cash-on-Cash Return

Yr.	Gross Income	Expenses	Net Income	Debt Service	Cash Flow	Return
1	$160,000	60,000	100,000	72,416	27,584	11.03%
2	168,000	63,000	105,000	72,416	32,584	13.93%
3	176,400	66,150	110,250	72,416	37,834	15.13%
4	185,200	69,450	115,750	72,416	43,334	17.33%
5	194,480	72,930	121,550	72,416	49,134	19.65%
6	204,200	76,576	127,624	72,416	55,208	22.08%

The property is sold at the end of year 5 or the beginning of year 6 with a new operating income of $127,624. Based on the same ratio of income to value as when the property was purchased, this would create a value of approximately $1,275,000. This demonstrates a $275,000 profit on the sale plus the $245,678 in cash flow, which totals $520,678 in gross profits. There are closing costs and commissions on the sale, which will total approximately $75,000. This still leaves a healthy profit. The great thing about real estate is the cash flow and appreciation.

This model assumes annual increases of 5 percent and a fixed-rate loan at 9 percent interest amortized over 30 years. This may be optimistic because in many areas 5 percent annual increases are too high; 3 to 4 percent increases may be more realistic. There may also be a recession, which could hinder an owner increasing rents for one or more years.

More importantly, what should be understood from this model are the principles of real estate investing. One purchases an investment for cash flow and appreciation. The principles are still the same, only the numbers change. The numbers may be in amounts of increases or decreases in rents, the time to get the increases, changes in financing rates, poor management, and a variety of other variables that affect real estate.

§ 2.8   Unique Characteristics of Real Estate Investments

There are many characteristics that differentiate real estate from other forms of investments, but notably two are very distinct. The first is its enduring nature: it is immobile and cannot be transported to another location. At any given point of time one can visit a property, walk across it, and touch it. Management is very critical in real estate and one should not understate the importance of it; however, in the absence of management, there is still value. Stocks, bonds, businesses, mutual funds, and most other forms of investments, on the other hand, need management to retain the value. For example, if the owner of a house were to leave it alone for five years without doing anything, the land would still be there and most likely the house would also. If the owners of Microsoft were to close up shop for five years or a farmer were to not care for his crops, where would the value go? Most likely there would be an extreme drop in value.

Businesses are built on goodwill, reputation, and management. When these are diminished for whatever reason, value is lost. How many of the businesses from the 1920s are still in existence today? From the 1940s? We can easily say that every piece of real estate is still here, and worth a lot more today.

This brings us to the second most important characteristic of real estate, its limited supply. This is illustrated in the famous words of Will Rogers, Jr.: "Buy land, cause God ain't making any more of it." The fact that, other than volcanoes and a few other phenomena, all that there is today is all that there is going to be in the future. Products with limited supply and some degree of demand always increase in value over time. They may have cyclic ups and downs, but in the long run they always increase in value. Diamonds and gold, for example, have over the past 100 years increased dramatically in value. Water is another commodity that has a limited amount in some areas, and there the price of water has increased dramatically and will continue to do so into the foreseeable future.

§ 2.9   Advantages and Disadvantages of Real Estate

Endurance and limited supply are what separates real estate from other forms of investment. When these two characteristics are coupled with tax advantages they create several distinct advantages for investing in real estate. The major advantages to investing in real estate are these:

1. Ability to finance (usually long term and relatively cheap)
2. Control of the management and operations
3. Ability to move one's investment into another property tax free (tax-deferred exchange)
4. Relative ease in selling or liquidating
5. Laws protect the owner and owner's rights
6. Relative ease in leasing or renting
7. Ability to change the use of the property.

There are some disadvantages to owning real estate as well, which are related to its two distinct characteristics. Major problems of owning real estate include

1. Inability to change location
2. Directly affected by the local economy and neighborhood

3. Limited expansion ability
4. Subject to local government ordinances.

The ability to finance property at reasonable rates for long periods of time is one key factor in its desirability, accessibility, and value. When something can be financed cheaply, then it is more accessible to buyers. Real estate is a prime example of this. As interest rates drop, real estate activity typically increases, and increased activity typically brings increased prices. When property is difficult to finance or when financing is unavailable, prices decrease.

The majority of properties are owned by individuals, families, and small partnerships and provide the owners with the ability to control management. This allows properties to be managed, sold, and expanded by the owners. If an owner wants to hold it for five years and then sell, or if the property is to be passed on to the heirs, it is entirely up to the owners. With many other forms of investment, an investor does not have the ability to affect the management arrangements and is subject to the management at hand, good and bad.

By using the IRS Form 1031 Tax Deferred Exchange, a property owner is able to move his investment into another property. This provides incentive for the property owner to expand his investment by selling and purchasing another property of equal or larger debt and price within a certain time.

Real estate is relatively liquid in that one can usually sell a property; it seems there is always someone interested in purchasing it at some price. That is not to say one will get the desired price, but there will always be some value, regardless of the property's condition.

Laws protecting the rights of ownership are very clear. Another person cannot steal the property, hold title or deed, or otherwise legally take possession without the owner's consent or due process. The fact that the title is a recorded document that requires a notary public endorsement provides security, as does title insurance, protecting owners against fraud. One can only hope for such protection in most other forms of business.

Disadvantages are related to real estate's immobility and fixed size. First, a piece of property is affected by the neighboring properties, surrounding area, local government, and local economy. If the general area has problems, then the property often has similar problems. Unlike a business, one cannot just pick up and move to another more favorable area.

The fact that the property can only be developed to a certain degree is the degree to which the investment can be expanded. True, one can raise rents and improve the property, but there are limits as to how much one can grow or improve. The only way to continually grow, other than raise rents, is to exchange into larger properties.

With this knowledge of real estate characteristics, advantages, and disadvantages one can use them to maximize an investment. For example, applying this information, the ideal property would have easy access to financing and be located in a relatively good area with a solid economy and in a business-friendly city and state. The surrounding properties would be clean and well maintained. At this point, this scenario does not take into consideration the actual improvements of the property as they are determined by the proposed or existing use.

How does one determine if a location is in fact good? Typically, buying property in the best part of town costs more than buying elsewhere, and very often the sale price is too high for an investor whose goal is to make money. First, determine the desired time of ownership. This affects the way one looks at property. Is the would-be investor seeking a brief holding period or planning to be in the property for the long haul? Then drive through the surrounding area and use common sense to determine if it is a suitable area. Ask, Why would someone want to be here? Would I want to live or work here? Who is going to buy this property if and when I decide to sell?

Presume the area is acceptable. The next step is the financing. Financing is very important and will have a definite effect on the value of property. This is important even if the seller offers to finance the property. As previously discussed, financing affects not only anticipated acquisition, but surrounding properties as well.

What has not been covered are the actual physical improvements. These consist of the actual structures located on a piece of property, such as houses, apartments, parking lots, shopping centers, offices, and amenities. Because a manufactured home community has minimal improvements (usually only streets, underground utility infrastructure, and possibly a clubhouse or pool), this area of investment analysis, while important, is generally of less concern than other attention areas.

§ 2.10 Summary

Real estate investment, whether on a small scale or large, often offers both novice and experienced investors dynamic and very rewarding returns on and of initial equity investments. But it is not an exercise or experience to be entered into lightly. Although more fortunes have been made in real estate investing than any other alternative, it is true that many have suffered damaging consequences as well. The following chapters are designed to introduce the reader to one property type that, while less well known than others, has consistently demonstrated long-term stability and significant return for its proponents.

CHAPTER 3

WHAT TO LOOK FOR IN A MANUFACTURED HOME COMMUNITY

§ 3.1   Introduction

§ 3.2   Typical Property Research Sources

§ 3.3   Fieldwork Property Research Sources

§ 3.4   Document and Organize Findings

§ 3.5   Manufactured Home Community Investment Checklist

§ 3.6   Basic Formulas for Financial and Mathematical Operational
         Analysis of a Manufactured Home Community

ANOTHER PERSPECTIVE
Craig White

§ 3.7   Risk and Reward

§ 3.8   Primary Considerations

§ 3.9   Management Impact

§ 3.10   Project Types

§ 3.11   Project Size

§ 3.12   Summary

§ 3.1   Introduction

The term "income-producing property" is more specific and to the point than simply "real estate investment." The latter can as easily apply to purchasing a home, parcel of raw land, apartment complex, office building, or shopping center. All five property types are indeed investments in real estate. But only the latter three will likely be purchased for their income-producing potential. Yes, the home could be rented out and raw land leased and farmed, but those are generally secondary uses. The point is that the term "income property" is in itself a helpful reminder that when researching and evaluating a manufactured home landlease community, spend equal time examining the property-specific characteristics (for example, location, layout, and infrastructure) as well as its income-producing and return-on-investment potential (for example, rental rates and operating expenses).

Before turning to the specifics of what to look for when purchasing a manufactured home community, it is appropriate to identify the eight steps that comprise the entire acquisition process:

1. Learn and understand the income-property type to be acquired and its marketing and operational characteristics and peculiarities.
2. Set personal or corporate investment goals and establish specific parameters as to property type for the anticipated acquisition.
3. Identify, research, visit, document, and evaluate prospective income-property acquisition possibilities.
4. Prepare a cash flow analysis and estimate current and future values of for sale properties and prepare preliminary pro forma operating statements.
5. Decide whether to proceed. If so, make an offer.
6. Negotiate.
7. Once the offer is accepted, verify the seller's information and claims, compare with previous research, confirm infrastructure integrity, and arrange appropriate financing. This stage is generally referenced as the "due diligence period."
8. Close and register the real estate transaction and take possession of the income property.

Steps 1 and 2 were covered in part in **Chapters 1** and **2**. Steps 4 through 8 will be covered, to varying degrees, in the remaining chapters and the appendixes of this text. This chapter concentrates on step 3 of the acquisition process. Research and evaluation can be an adventure, a mystery to solve, a unique business opportunity. A sense of excitement, challenge, and anticipation is a mindset that can carry a would-be investor through the often tedious work of researching, documenting, and evaluating an income property.

§ 3.2   Typical Property Research Sources

When an investment property owner puts an income-producing property on the market or for sale, whether with a real estate broker or not, an information packet or prospectus is usually prepared. The prospectus is a summary of pertinent information about the property and its historic income-producing capacity. It often contains photographs of the property and varying degrees of detail about income and operating expenses. It almost always contains a disclaimer, particularly if prepared by a real estate broker or accountant, as to the accuracy and completeness of the information contained therein, such as at the bottom of **Form 3–1.**

In states where manufactured home communities are regulated at the state level, the appropriate regulatory agency's inspection report files (referenced different ways in different states) can be a treasure trove of salient information—particularly if the property has a long or even recent history of discrepancies. In fact, the property may be operating without a current license, so check to be sure, if the property is in a regulating state. Properties have been known to change hands with the buyer unaware that the acquisition is unlicensed and, therefore, facing fines and possible legal action.

Read published data and information about manufactured home communities. Learn the appropriate property-type benchmarks (for example, NOI, GRM, OER %, and density are explained later in this chapter) to research and apply to acquisition candidates. Typical sources include books, trade publications, and national and state trade association newsletters. See the **bibliography** and **Appendixes F** and **H** at end of this text for lists of this material.

Study the property owner's operating statement for the subject property (usually in the prospectus), as well as tax returns, which are usually available after the offer is accepted and the earnest money deposit is in escrow. Also request access to the property's resident files.

State manufactured housing association staffers are also reliable sources for some local market information, particularly as it pertains to their membership base. If an association is oriented toward the manufacturer and retailer, it will generally be of limited value to one's property

FORM 3–1
SAMPLE SUMMARY OFFERING PAGE

Operating Information

Property Address:

Summary

Price:	$1,800,000	
Down Payment 25.00%	$450,000	
Number of Spaces:	163	
Cost Per Unit:	$11,043	
Current GRM:	5.7	
Market GRM:	5.2	
Current CAP:	9.65%	
Market CAP:	11.23%	
Approximate Age:	20 Years	
Approximate Lot Size:	28 + Acres	

Proposed Financing

First Loan Amount: $1,350,000   New

Terms: 8.75%, 25 year amortization

Annualized Operating Data

	Current Rents		Market Rents	
Scheduled Gross Income:	$316,980		$346,920	
Less Vacancy Rate Reserve:	15,849	5.00%	17,346	5.00%
Gross Operating Income:	301,131		329,574	
Less Expenses:	127,273	40.15%	127,273	
Net Operating Income:	$173,858		$202,301	
Less Loan Payments:	133,110		133,110	
Pre-Tax Cash Flow:	40,748	9.06% *	69,191	15.38% *
Plus Principal Reduction:	14,985		14,985	
Total Return Before Taxes:	$55,733	12.39% *	$84,176	18.71% *

* As percent of Down Payment

Scheduled Income

	Current Rents		Market Rents	
No. of Spaces	**Monthly Rent/Unit**	**Monthly Income**	**Monthly Rent/Unit**	**Monthly Income**
163	$155	25,265	$170	27,710
Total Scheduled Rent:		25,265		27,710
Rental Units (6):		900		900
Recreation Building:		250		300
Monthly Scheduled Gross Income:		$26,415		$28,910
Annual Scheduled Gross Income:		$316,980		$346,920

Utilities Paid by Tenant: Electric

Annualized Expenses

Taxes 1995	$9,912
Insurance	4,912
On-Site/Payroll	21,579
Main/Repairs	12,225
Trash	17,748
Water/Sewer	34,853
Gas/Electric	4,963
Office	1,580
Administration	2,000
Reserves	2,445
Prof. Management	15,056
Total Expenses:	**$127,273**
Per Space:	**$780.82**

research effort. When membership representation is balanced, however, or there are two such trade associations within a state, the one with the larger number of manufactured home community owners will likely be the best source of local and industry data, local trends, and additional information.

§ 3.3   Fieldwork Property Research Sources

The research sources mentioned in § 3.2 are documentary in nature. It is vital also to get close to the property and generate another whole body of data—some of it new, some of it based on the empirical work just completed or still under way. Visit the property (or properties, if more than one is being considered in a given geographic area) and document property-specific data and local market data.

"Shop" the property by phone ahead of time. In shopping, the caller pretends to be looking for a place to move or buy a manufactured home. This is the first hands-on indication of staff competence. Is the caller handled in a professional and competent fashion? This is important, whether the property is fully occupied or not. Once on-site, evaluate the property and leasing and sales efficiency using a Standard Shopping Report (see **Chapter 7** for sample Standard Shopping Report).

Conduct a Market Survey

This exercise when properly executed allows the evaluator to compare local market area competition with the subject property relative to property size (total number of rental units—in this case, rental home-sites), physical occupancy (simply count the number of occupied home-sites and divide by total number of developed sites), amount of security deposit if any, lease term, and other appropriate information, for example, what is included in basic rent charge (water, sewer, trash removal service). The last four columns on **Form 3–2** are for basic rental rates researched during four different time frames when this form is used over an extended period of time. For the purposes of an acquisition market survey, however, it may be desirable to white out the last three columns and relabel them to include and compare other such variables as on-site amenities and features, subjective opinion of overall curb appeal, and property condition.

FORM 3–2

MARKET SURVEY
- Rental Community -

Market Area Surveyed

Preparer

Type Properties: _____

Year _____

Use this form to conduct market survey once each quarter or four years in succession.

Name & Address of Property	Phone # Manager Name	Total # of Rental Un.	Estimated Occupancy %*	$ Deposit / Lease Term	Other Info	AVERAGE RENT RATE PER UNIT			
						Date ____ $	Date ____ $	Date ____ $	Date ____ $
1.									
2.									
3.									
4.									
5.									
6.									
7.									
8.									
9.									
10.									
11.									
MARKET AVERAGE	N/A	____	____ %*	N/A	N/A	$____	$____	$____	$____

*Formula = # of occupied units ÷ # available, for physical occupancy%.

This form available for purchase in tablet format.
Property Management Form #101
Copyright Jan 1989

G.F.A
MANAGEMENT
P.O. Box 47024
Indianapolis, IN 46247

Interview current residents and local manufactured home retail sales-center staff. In the first instance, it is generally unwise to disclose one's intent to purchase the subject property. Simply dress casually and inquire, in a friendly fashion, what is good about living at this property and what does a new resident need to be cautious or concerned about? This latter question may evoke concerns about security, water condition or reliability, problems with management, and so forth. The same is true with local retailers. Do not start rumors by overtly advertising one's acquisition intent. Simply ask what manufactured home communities are being recommended to new and resale homebuyers these days and why. Look around. Are brochures on hand for the subject property and other manufactured home communities? If not, why not? This might be something to address once the property is purchased.

Drive through the subject manufactured home community. Take photos or a video of scenes that will help determine whether to continue with the purchase and will identify items to address after closing. These photos and video should be made part of the shopping report mentioned earlier, which is likely being completed during the same visit as the interviews are conducted and the photographs and video being made. Visit again at night to evaluate parking, lighting (if any), and noise level.

Visit the state manufactured housing association office if located in the same market area as the subject property. It is likely the staff will know about the manufactured home community and be more comfortable sharing information in person rather than over the phone. Also visit the county courthouse to verify property ownership records. Purchase a copy of the property tax records (have real estate taxes been paid?) and see what else can be learned about the property. Also visit the local chamber of commerce to obtain information about the economy and housing in the market area. For example, what has been the population trend over the past five years: growing and by how much, or declining, or stable/stagnant? How many major employers are in the area, and what is their present and anticipated business health?

§ 3.4 Document and Organize Findings

Chapter 2 recommended formats for organizing one's data pursuant to effecting a real estate investment. All during the research and investigation stages it is wise to keep these outlines in mind and fill in the blanks along the way. Now is the time to organize, distill, and reflect on the assembled data. Yet another helpful evaluation tool is shown in **Form 3–3.**

The first format is a real estate investor's well-known rule of thumb: "Look for Good Unchangables and Bad Changables!" What were the *unchangables* relative to the subject property: location, property configuration, homesite density, infrastructure serviceability, and condition. What else? What about the *changables?* These generally include quality of management, property name/reputation, degree of rules enforcement, curb appeal—or lack thereof, staff morale and resident relations, collections efficiency, physical and economic occupancy levels, and operation expense control. Notice how all these changables relate back to property management, a key consideration with any type income property. Property management strongly influences the level and pace of success or failure. So document the *unchangeables* and *changeables* (good and bad) to get that all important "feel" for the property in question.

Then organize data, in outline fashion, to compare the various resource areas along with the characteristics of the subject property. One useful tool is the Ms of Management. In fact, if there is no on-site SOP (standard operating procedure) or operational manual for this property, now is as good a time as any to begin one, slotting the research and information into M (management resource) categories:

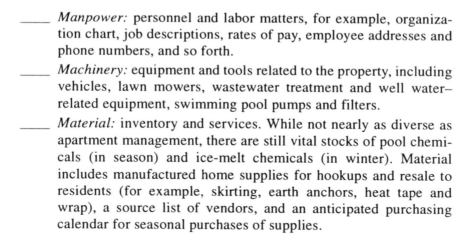

_____ *Manpower:* personnel and labor matters, for example, organization chart, job descriptions, rates of pay, employee addresses and phone numbers, and so forth.

_____ *Machinery:* equipment and tools related to the property, including vehicles, lawn mowers, wastewater treatment and well water–related equipment, swimming pool pumps and filters.

_____ *Material:* inventory and services. While not nearly as diverse as apartment management, there are still vital stocks of pool chemicals (in season) and ice-melt chemicals (in winter). Material includes manufactured home supplies for hookups and resale to residents (for example, skirting, earth anchors, heat tape and wrap), a source list of vendors, and an anticipated purchasing calendar for seasonal purchases of supplies.

FORM 3–3

COMMUNITY CORNER

HOW DOES YOUR COMMUNITY MEASURE UP?

By George Allen, CPM

George Allen is president of GFA Management in Greenwood, Ind. GFA specializes in residential and commercial real estate management. For more information, contact Allen at GFA Management, Box 47024, Indianapolis, Ind. 46247. 317/351-2541.

Some of the most satisfying Community Corner columns have been prepared jointly with community owners and managers who have special knowledge and insight. Such is the case with this month's edition, in which we offer an Evaluation Checklist for Manufactured Home Communities.

J.R. and Shirley Gegenheimer, owners of a number of manufactured home communities in Indiana, have developed a checklist to help home buyers choose the best land-lease communities in which to site their homes.

The points of their checklist were drawn from several sources, including their own long experience as property managers; a similar checklist published by Richard Hoffman in his guidebook, *Mobile Home Parks of Northern California*; input from the *Stephen Pappas Report* published in Arizona; and information from our own files.

While the checklist is designed to be used by prospective home buyers and current land-lease community residents looking for another community, it also serves as a useful self-examination tool for property owners and resident managers who want to see how well their communities stack up.

Would someone want to move into your manufactured home community after completing this worksheet? Decide for yourself by checking the appropriate boxes. Here, with their permission and somewhat modified, is the Gegenheimers' checklist of 60 points in nine categories.

Evaluation Checklist for Manufactured Home Communities

Location

☐ Is the community convenient to employment, shopping, family and transportation?

☐ Is the surrounding neighborhood acceptable and accessible?

☐ Is the response time of police and fire services acceptable? (Ask residents.)

☐ Is the degree of fire protection acceptable? Are there on-site fire hydrants?

☐ Does the area have a good rating for insurance coverage purposes?

☐ Is the degree of security and police protection within the community adequate? Are curfew laws in effect?

☐ Is the community within city or other corporate limits, or do local rules and regulations prevail?

☐ Is the potential for flooding low? Is the community far enough away from a flood plain?

☐ Are personal property tax rates and licensing fees in the area reasonable?

☐ Are public and private schools nearby? (Ask residents about the quality of education.)

☐ What type of amenities are available with in a 5-to-15-mile radius? Are there supermarkets, service stations, shopping malls, beauty salons, laundries and golf courses with in a convenient distance?

☐ Is the number and denomination of churches in the surrounding neighborhood adequate?

☐ Are potential sources of disturbing noise nearby, such as an airport, a busy interstate highway or a railroad line?

☐ Are there any natural barriers that protect the community from outside noise or bad weather?

☐ Is the location of specific home site conducive to energy efficiency and reduced wind impact?

Type of community

☐ Is the community designed for families or senior citizens? Do seniors

receive any special discounts or other considerations?

☐ If it's a family community, are playgrounds and swimming pools safe and monitored?

☐ Is the physical condition of the home sites acceptable? Is the surrounding land wooded or open? Are concrete runners, piers or patios provided?

☐ Are there restrictions on pets? Are there size limits? Must they be kept indoors?

☐ Is the size of the community acceptable? Is it small (50 or fewer sites), medium (51-150 sites) or large (more then 150 sites)?

Type of home permitted

☐ Is a certain type of siding required: wood, vinyl or aluminum, or are there no restrictions?

☐ Are there restrictions on the shape of roof: peaked, rounded or flat?

☐ What type of roofing material is allowed: shingle, galvanized or rubber?

☐ What type of skirting is allowed: vinyl, wood, metal or other materials? Is there a grace period for installation?

☐ Are certain types of decking, carports or screened-in porches permitted or required?

☐ Is the community restricted to single-section or multi-section homes?

☐ Are earth anchors or tie-downs required?

☐ Are there restrictions on the age of the home?

Appearance

☐ Is the entrance to the community clean and attractive? Are there helpful signs?

☐ What is the condition of existing homes in the community, in appearance, size and age?

☐ Is there landscaping—flowers, bushes, and trees—around the home sites?

☐ Are the streets in good condition and of adequate width?

☐ Are street maintenance and snow removal satisfactory? (Ask resi-

FORM 3–3
(continued)

dents.)

☐ Are common areas and facilities well maintained? Is the grass cut? Are the trees trimmed?

☐ Are streets and common areas well lighted?

☐ Is the washing of family vehicles permitted on-site?

Utilities

☐ Are cable TV, telephone, natural gas and electricity metered for each home site?

☐ Are water, sewerage and refuse collection included in the rent or billed separately? What are the rates?

☐ Is the water from public or private wells? Is the supply adequate? How hard is the water?

☐ Is there public or private sewerage treatment? Are there odor problems? (Ask residents.)

☐ Does the community have a state license? Is the license current and posted if required?

☐ Are utility lines above ground or underground?

☐ Are fuel oil or propane heating fuels permitted?

Parking

☐ Is a certain number of parking spaces allotted to each home?

☐ Is parking available for guests within the community?

☐ Are guests permitted to park on the street?

☐ Is storage space available for RVs, boats, campers and travel trailers? Is there a rental fee?

☐ Is there any limit on the size or type of vehicles permitted to park at the home site?

Rents

☐ How much is the basic rent? Is it figured by the month or week or in some other way?

☐ Are there per capita add-on charges for pets, washers and dryers or extra residents?

☐ Is the rental agreement term by the month or year?

☐ Is the leasing agreement set in writing?

☐ What is the history of rent increases over the past two years? (Ask residents.)

☐ Are there a grace periods? Late fees? Service charges?

☐ How large is the security deposit? Is interest earned on this amount?

☐ Is there an entrance or application fee? Is it refundable?

☐ Are the "guidelines for living" (rules and regulations) of the community spelled out in the leasing agreement or separately?

Amenities offered on-site

☐ Is there a clubhouse? Is it free for residents to use, or is there a rental charge?

☐ Are swimming pools free or is an extra membership fee required?

☐ Are there fishing ponds or lakes? Are they stocked with fish?

☐ What other amenities are offered for residents?

General

☐ Are the on-site staff people friendly and helpful?

☐ Is a prospectus available on the community?

☐ All in all, does the community have a good appearance? Is it well maintained and well run?

Certainly, you should find this list helpful in more ways than one. Is it possible we've missed anything? If so, please write and let us know. ☐

A Summary of

'Here's What We're Calling Things Now'

Community Corner column,
Manufactured Home MERCHANDISER - February 1993

- manufactured home community, **not** mobilehome community or park

- resident, **not** tenant

- homesite or site, **not** pad, space, lot

- singlesection and multisection, **not** single-wide or double-wide

- retailer and retail sales center, **not** dealer, street dealer or sales lot

- rules and regulations or guidelines for living

- transporter, **not** toter, hauler or mover

- rental agreement or lease

- skirting or foundation fascia

- leasing consultant, **not** rental agent

- resale center, **not** repo lot

- wastewater treatment plant, **not** sewer plant

- office or information center

_____ *Methods:* policies and procedures. Just the organization of the researched data is a major step in the right direction, but add to it copies of standard leases and addendums, rules and regulations (also known as Guidelines for Living), and existent, if available, policies and procedures relative to rental applicant screening, rent collection, and rules enforcement.

_____ *Money:* income and expenses. Here place the historic and pro forma operating statement and budgets for reference and use. Also include information, if not in the methods section, on petty cash requirements and procedures and a sample purchase order, if used. It may be necessary to create additional tabs to separate pertinent information relative to management, maintenance, marketing, morale (resident relations), and miscellaneous—all Ms of Management.

An additional data format to recall throughout is the one that will likely be used by lenders as they decide whether to underwrite a loan for this transaction. They will closely evaluate these areas, so complete this beforehand:

_____ Location and physical quality of the property and related considerations (for example, infrastructure)

_____ Tenancy (resident) levels (physical and economic occupancy) and typical profile

_____ Leases in effect (verbal, written)

_____ Operating (financial) performance stability in the past and present and anticipated future results

_____ Property management resource(s) on-site and at ownership level

_____ Ownership position of borrower

_____ Hazardous materials on-site or not

§ 3.5   Manufactured Home Community Investment Checklist

In order to generate the information necessary to flesh out the previous three formats, it is helpful to use a detailed checklist tailored to this property type. **Form 3–4** depicts one such checklist specifically designed for the manufactured home community investment.

FORM 3–4

MANUFACTURED HOME COMMUNITY INVESTMENT CHECKLIST

Name of Property:_____Date:_____

Physical Address:_____Zip:_____

Contact Person/Role:_____Phone:_____

1. **Land Characteristics**
   a. Location: (socio-economic image; proximity to schools, public transportation, and shopping; access; etc.)
   b. Adequate size to support viable cash flow and debt service
   c. Overall landscaping and curb appeal
   d. Easement, flood plain, peculiarities of property
   e. Property line characteristics (determined from on-site walk)
   f. Opportunity for expansion in years to come
   g. Zoning restrictions (local)
   h. Environmental concerns...indicators of problems?

2. **Construction and Condition**
   a. All land and improvements inspected and evaluated
   b. Quality of construction, present condition, age, obsolescence
   c. Homesite Density; mix of singlesection and multisection homes
   d. Condition of vacant homesites and utility connections
   e. Anchor installations - complete and in compliance
   f. Street condition, pavement base

3. **Public Areas**
   a. Play area, pool, clubhouse, tennis courts, pond, etc.
   b. Amount of grass to cut; common areas and vacant sites
   c. Adequacy of lighting
   d. Other security/safety equipment

4. **Ancillary Areas**
   a. New and/or resale manufactured home sales on-site
   b. Current licensing (see last inspection report)
   c. Property and/or emergency SOP (Standard Operating Procedures) in effect
   d. Laundry: Size, condition, income and expenses
   e. Garages, shops, sheds, storage areas

5. **Utilities and Equipment**
   a. Water: City or private? See files; condition of lines; quality of water; pressure
   b. Sewage: city or private? Line infiltration; plant size and adequacy; availability of licensed operator
   c. Oil: Condition of system; price of oil
   d. Gas: Natural or propane
   e. Electricity: Power adequate at pedestal, lines buried or above ground; current rates
   f. Cable Television: Contract type; rates; copy of contract; income to property
   g. Plot plans showing all utility locations and shutoffs
   h. All utilities at all homesites

6. **Rental Characteristics**
   a. Entry requirements (qualifications). Resident profile.
   b. Rejected applications kept on file; resident files
   c. Lease: Written or verbal; terms; addendums
   d. Size and number of homesites
   e. Rent structure: Base and adders, due date. Collected on-site or by mail
   f. Rules and Regulations (enforced, posted) - Guidelines for Living
   g. Security Deposit requirement; application fee
   h. Late fees and NSF charges (non sufficient funds)
   i. Delinquent rent status. Collection policy and procedure
   j. Eviction procedure
   k. Rental units: By owner or outside investor(s)
   l. Management and staff job descriptions and evaluations
   m. Review rent roll to confirm rents, vacancies, accounts receivable

FORM 3–4

(continued)

n. Rent inclusions (water, sewer, etc.)
o. Rent control and/or landlord/tenant legislation on effect

7. **General Facilities**
    a. Security measures: Lights, Crime Watch, patrols, sets of keys
    b. Trash Removal: Curbside, dumpster
    c. Off-street parking or curbside
    d. Sidewalks or not
    e. Homes skirted properly
    f. Mail service; Scattered, central, NDCBUs preferred

8. **Additional Considerations**
    a. Physical and economic occupancy compared
    b. Resident relations: Newsletter, socials, resident social group, Home of the Month contest, etc.
    c. Valid state license; Board of Health or regulatory agency
    d. Equipment available with community; Mowers, vehicles, sewer cable, pipe thawer, shop tools, handtools, snowplows, etc.
    e   Referral arrangements with retailers, residents, or others
    f. Complete a Property Information Sheet

9. **Marketing**
    a. Conduct market survey, obtain comparables
    b. Advertising: Newspaper(s), telephone book, etc.
    c. Off-site signage
    d. On-site signage
    e. Flyers and brochures, business cards
    f. Retailer relations
    g. Level of sales training (phone and in-person)
    h. Traffic sheet in effect
    i. Resident profile: Socio-economic, pets, etc.

10. **Neighborhood**
    a. Shopping, schools, churches, medical, fire, police, transportation, employment
    b. Declining or stable neighborhood; urban or rural
    c. Interview resident(s) about community
    d. Chamber of Commerce; map, phone book, etc.

11. **Key Considerations**
    a. Location
    b. Physical quality and curb appeal
    c. Income and Expense history and ROI
    d. Quality of Lessee

12. **Financial Considerations**
    a. Review operating statements; verify all expense and income figures; prepare cash flow analysis
    b. Use formulae:
        1) occupancy percentages, physical and economic
        2) operating expense ratio
        3) break-even occupancy %
        4) NOI and cash flow before taxes
        5) IRV Valuation
    c. Review A/R procedures
    d. Review A/P procedures (including petty cash)

Designed by George Allen, CPM
Form available for purchase in tablet form.
Property Management Form #122

PMN Publishing
P.O. Box #47024
Indianapolis, IN 46247
(317) 888-7156

Potential environmental hazards on-site and lender-required environmental Phase I audits have become so commonplace with real estate transactions that it is instructive to learn what one environmental inspector has ascertained about manufactured home communities:

Environmental Audits and the Manufactured Home Community: What Does the Environmental Audit Company Look For?

Virtually anyone involved in the land acquisition or transfer aspects of the manufactured home community industry has heard the terms 'due diligence' and 'environmental audit'. The latter is tied to the need to perform an environmental inspection of real property prior to purchase in order to reduce or eliminate the chance of losing thousands or hundreds of thousands of dollars on a contaminated property. Environmental management has been simplified through the use of environmental audit companies. But what exactly does an environmental audit company look for when inspecting a property? They review records, maps, and interview people. But is there a special way that properties are inspected?

There is no set physical site inspection protocol *per se*. The audit company uses a checklist of environmental 'red flags' when inspecting a property to ensure that the majority of environmental concerns are investigated. No one list covers all potential concerns. The list Federated uses was developed over a five year period with input from the Resolution Trust Corporation and the American Society of Testing and Materials, and experience obtained through the inspection of over 6,000 properties nationally.

The Federated checklist includes the following specific site inspection 'red flags'; underground storage tanks, above ground storage tanks, bulk chemical storage/drums, railroad spurs/easements, on-lot septic or oil/water separators, on-lot water/cistern/wells, landfill/buried waste, impoundments, pits, ponds, or lagoons, air emissions or stacks, discolored/stained soils, distressed or dead vegetation, herbicide/pesticide use or storage, transformers/PCB equipment, chemical or foul odors, remedial actions/monitoring wells, leachate, drainage or seeps, contaminated adjacent properties, foundations or ruins, farm wastes/manure stockpiles, manufacturing/industrial activities, non-hazardous solid waste/debris, electrical towers/substations, pipelines/transfer stations, equipment/tankers/spray rigs, mining activities, oil/gas wells or production, asbestos-containing materials, lead-based paint, lead in drinking water, radon gas accumulations, non-tidal wetlands/critical areas, archeological/historical concerns, and endangered species concerns.

A compilation of data from 230 environmental assessments of existing manufactured home communities and adjacent expansion tracts provides interesting environmental risk data. The Top Ten environmental concerns observed include accumulations of junk and debris, particularly on immediately adjacent properties (38%); improper disposal of kitchen wastes and related garbage (18%); on-site automobile repairs and related contamination, particularly in resident storage lots (17%); poor/non-existent testing and management of well drinking water (15% of those with wells); improper management of wastewater treatment systems, regulated discharges (11% of those with treatment systems), electric transformer leaks (6%), poor management of pool chemicals (^5 of those with pools); unpermitted destruction of wetlands areas (5%); contamination from historic site or adjacent site uses (2%); and flooding (2%). Of the 230 communities and expansion tracts inspected, 7 were contaminated beyond transferability, 3 had endangered animal species or related confounding problems, and 1 was listed for testing and remediation under the federal Superfund Program. It is interesting to note that 8 of the 10 environmental concerns could have been addressed by responsible on-site community management.

Federated Environmental Associates, Inc. has performed thousands of environmental audits nationwide. Quotations and orders for environmental audits anywhere in the U.S. can be obtained through James C. Gossweiler, REA(CA), RHSP, Senior Vice President of Federated, at (410) 653-8434.[1]

Furthermore, it is never too early to learn all one can about the various types of environmental audits. See **Appendix I.**

§ 3.6 Basic Formulas for Financial and Mathematical Operational Analysis of a Manufactured Home Community

Early on in this chapter the point was made that income-property research and analysis is twofold. Property characteristics, in terms of changeables, unchangeables, mortgage underwriting, and management resources have been identified and reviewed to this point. Now the emphasis switches to the income or financial and mathematical operational

---

[1] Reprinted with permission from The Allen Letter, No. 10 (1994).

research and evaluation of income-property analysis. A lot of difficult work has been done. Much of what was researched to this point is applicable here. It is mainly a matter of applying the data to more than 20 formulas that individually and collectively help one understand the subject manufactured home community much better. These are the financial and operating performance indicators characteristic of investment property analysis for the subject property that will be used in the formulas:

300 rental homesites on 75 acres

280 physically occupied rental homesites

260 physically occupied *and* paid current homesites

$900,000 or $900M potential annual rental income (assuming 100 percent occupancy and collections—300 sites × $250/mth rent × 12 months)

$360,000 or $360M annual operating expenses (assuming 40 percent operating expense ratio—$900,000 × .40 OER)

$450,000 or $450M annual debt service (DS) or mortgage payment amount

12% income capitalization or cap rate, or .12 (based on local, recent comparable sales)

$4,500,000 estimated value (income capitalization approach) of subject property

$600,000 or $600M original equity or down payment (DP) to purchase subject property.

1. Rental Unit Density.   Number of rental homesites per acre of developed ground; degree of spaciousness.

Formula:

$$\frac{\text{\# developed homesites}}{\text{developed acres}} = \text{\# homesites/acre}$$

Example:

$$\frac{300 \text{ sites}}{75 \text{ acres}} = 4 \text{ sites/acre}$$

Note: Industry norm of 4 to 6 homesites/acre is the ideal. Refinements to this calculation can include whether numerator is shown as number of developed *and* rentable sites (implying some developed homesites are, for example, without full array of utility services and *not* included in the calculation); developed acres denominator description generally does *not* including fishing ponds, and so forth. To do so would artificially lower the unit density.

2. Physical Occupancy. Measure of how full an income-property is versus vacancy or the how empty perspective. Vacancy measurement is generally characteristic of commercial real estate, while occupancy parlance is common among owners of multifamily properties.

Formula:

$$\frac{\text{\# occupied homesites and/or rental units}}{\text{total \# homesites and/or rentals available}} = \text{physical occupancy \%}$$

Example:

$$\frac{280}{300} = 93.3 \text{ or } 93\% \text{ physical occupancy}$$

Note: Industry national average is 92.3 percent among the 150 largest owners of manufactured home communities, according to previously cited 1995 *Allen Report*. Again, be careful of the denominator here: 300 available to rent? Or are there some functionally obsolete homesites (too small for contemporary manufactured homes) that should be or have been deleted from the inventory or combined with a neighboring small site to handle a larger manufactured home?

3. Economic Occupancy. The acid test of occupancy measurement. What percentage of available homesites or rental units are physically occupied and paid current, rent current, as well? Also separate out concessioned units or homesites (usually residences for manager or staff) to demonstrate their negative impact on the calculation.

Formula:

$$\frac{\text{\# occupied units } - \text{ \# delinquent/concessioned units}}{\text{total \# available units or homesites}} = \text{economic occupancy \%}$$

Example:

$$280 - 20 = \frac{260}{300} = 86.7 \text{ or } 87\% \text{ economic occupancy \%}$$

Note: A further refinement to this concept is to use actual dollar amounts in the formula instead of unit counts:

$$\frac{\text{\$ amount rent collected}}{\text{gross potential \$ from the property}} = \text{economic occupancy \%}$$

4. Breakeven Occupancy Ratio. Little recognized, but very helpful tool to peg a property's breakeven point during initial infill after development or during the property turnaround process. Use anticipated or actual figures here:

Formula:

$$\frac{\text{operating expenses \$ } + \text{ mortgage or debt service \$}}{\text{rental income \$}} = \text{breakeven occupancy \%}$$

Example:

$$\frac{\$360M + \$450M}{\$900M} = \frac{\$810M}{\$900M} = 90\% \text{ breakeven occupancy \%}$$

Note: As far as the denominator is concerned, use rental income alone, or include additional sources of income (for example, new home sales) *only* if related expenses are part of the numerator as well.

5. Net Operating Income or NOI. Simply how much collected income remains after paying operating expenses and is now available to service debt (mortgage) to produce a residual cash flow before taxes (described later) to the property owner.

Formula:

gross collected income − total operating expenses = NOI

Example:

$900M − $360M = $540M net operating income or NOI

Note: Total operating expenses do *not* include debt service or mortgage payment(s). NOI is one of three key factors in the traditional IRV valuation formula to follow. NOI can be, and should be, measured and evaluated for comparison purposes in three contexts: historical (past NOI performance), present, and future (pro forma NOI performance).

6. Operating Expense Ratio or OER.   Another vital acid test of property management performance; this time expense control efficiency or effectiveness.

Formula:

$$\frac{\$ \text{ operating expenses}}{\$ \text{ total income}} = \text{operating expense ratio OER \%}$$

Example:

$$\frac{\$360M}{\$900M} = .40 \text{ or } 40\% \text{ OER}$$

Note: The manufactured home community norm is generally recognized to be 37.8 percent; the 1995 *Allen Report* pegged it at 38.2 percent. The Allen Model OER%, for pro forma planning purposes, is 40 percent. The OER may be computed using annual figures as shown above, using monthly data, or per line item of operating expense. OER is also known as the "expense ratio" when a particular expense item or category is divided by net sales amount, as in manufactured home sales. Other business types refer to NPM or net profit margin, which is simply the reciprocal of the OER:

$$\text{NPM} = \frac{\$ \text{ operating profits or NOI}}{\text{total sales } \$} = \frac{\$540M}{\$900M} = .60 \text{ or } 60\% \text{ NPM}$$

7. Cash Flow (CF) before taxes. First true measure of profitability. NOI indeed may be such a measure, but it also might be fully consumed by mortgage payments, hence no profit, let alone cash flow.

Formula:

$$\text{annual NOI } - \text{ annual DS } = \text{ CF before taxes}$$

Example:

$$\$540M - \$450M = \$90,000 \text{ CF before taxes}$$

Note: As rewarding as it is to realize a measure of cash flow before taxes, and the more the better, guard against a property's cash flow becoming synonymous with its degree of deferred maintenance— maintenance that should have been effected (for example, street repairs) but was not. The *ideal* is a healthy cash flow before taxes and *no* deferred maintenance.

8. Cash-on-Cash Return (also known as ROI—return on invest-ment and return of investment). The moment-of-truth every investor covets; positive and significant cash-on-cash return.

Formula:

$$\frac{\text{CF before taxes}}{\text{original equity or down payment } \$} = \text{cash-on-cash return}$$

Example:

$$\frac{\$90,000}{\$600,000} = .15 \text{ or } 15\% \text{ cash-on-cash return during first year of operation}$$

Note: Perhaps too obvious to warrant mentioning, but simply put—was investing $600,000 in this real estate investment as down payment a better or worse strategy than placing it somewhere else? Fifteen percent is the performance indicator in this instance, and it does not include measures of equity buildup, appreciation in value, tax benefits, and effects of positive cash flow.

9. Gross Rent Multiplier or GRM. Simply a rule of thumb valuation tool for estimating the value of one property based on the selling price and gross income of a nearby and similar recently sold property. Also known as GIM or Gross Income Multiplier.

Formula:

$$\frac{\text{selling or purchase price of property}}{\text{gross annual rent \$ total at time of sale}} = \text{GRM factor}$$

Example:

$$\frac{\$4,500,000}{\$900,000} = 5 \text{ GRM factor}$$

Note: The GRM is generally calculated using data from two or more local and similar recently sold properties, results averaged or weighted, and then the resulting factor applied to the subject property. The GRM of 5, based on subject property data, could be applied to nearby similar properties coming on the market to estimate their value, for example, another manufactured home community:

$700,000 annual rent × 5 GRM = possible value of $3,500,000

The obvious weakness with GRM is that is has no sensitivity to other types of income that may have been included in the denominator, despite the formula requirement to cite rent dollars only. And as a gross rent calculation, GRM should only be considered as a rule of thumb.

10. Income Capitalization Approach to Value (also known as IRV formula). A handy, helpful triad of formulas when understood and used with good data. IRV abbreviation stands for:

I = annual NOI or net operating income (see earlier formula)

R = income capitalization rate or cap rate

V = value estimate (may be asking price, sale, or purchase price)

Formulas:

I = R × V or .12 × $4,500,000 sale price = $540,000 NOI
R = I ÷ V or $540M ÷ $4,500M = .12 cap rate
V = I ÷ R or $540M ÷ .12 cap rate = $4,500,000 value estimate

Note: A brief word about cap rates. There are more ways than one to calculate a capitalization rate. Observe that the cap rate is being used as a divisor, and not multiplied as is the case with an interest rate, so the larger or higher the cap rate (for example, .10 is of larger numerical value a .12), the higher the calculated value ($540M ÷ .10 = $5,400,000) and the smaller or lower the cap rate (.14 is of smaller numerical value than either .10 or .12), the lesser the calculated value ($540M ÷ .14 = $4,857,143).

11. Per Unit or Homesite Cost Comparison(s).   A helpful way to compare various line items of operating expense, from month-to-month, and among like property types.

Formulas:

(annual) operating expense ÷ 12 months ÷ # units/sites = $/unit/mth
  (month) 1 month of line item expense ÷ # units/sites = $/unit/mth

Example: (citing dollars from two different expense categories)

(annual) $360M ÷ 12 ÷ 300 = $100/unit/mth
(month) $800 ÷ 300 = $2.67/unit/mth

Note: Very useful for tracking performance among especially troubling expense categories.

12. Debt Service Coverage (DSC or DSCR) or Debt Coverage (DC). Appears three ways. Demonstrates to lending institutions that NOI exceeds annual debt service (DS) by a certain amount.

Formula:

$$\frac{\text{annual NOI}}{\text{annual DS}} = \text{DSC or DC}$$

Example:

$$\frac{\$540M}{\$450M} = 1.2 \text{ DSC or DC also written } 1.2/1 \text{ and } 1.20x$$

Note: A 1.2 DSC or DC indicates that annual NOI must exceed annual DS by 20 percent for lending institutions to underwrite a loan. Conservative lending institutions generally require a higher DSC (for example, 1.3/1 versus less conservative sources satisfied with a DSC at 1.05 or 1.1/1).

13. Loan-to-Value (LTV) ratio (also known as Debt-to-Worth Percentage).   How much of an income property's estimated value a lender will underwrite in a loan.

Formula:

$$\frac{\text{loan amount}}{\text{property value}} = \text{LTV}$$

Example:

$$\frac{\$3,600M}{\$4,500M} = .80 \text{ or } 80\% \text{ LTV}$$

Note: Conservative lenders will generally write a lower loan-to-value mortgage, for example, 70 percent LTV, while a highly leveraged deal may be written at as much as 90 percent LTV.

14. Turnover Ratio.   A measure of tenant/resident move-outs over a period of time.

Formula:

$$\frac{\text{\# move-outs per year}}{\text{average \# occupied units}} = \text{turnover } \%$$

Example:

$$\frac{20}{280} = .07 \text{ or } 7\% \text{ turnover}$$

Note: Manufactured home community industry average is in the neighborhood of only 5 percent for actual manufactured home move-outs; a higher percentage results (10 to 15 percent) when including homeowner/renters who sell their manufactured homes in place and relocate. This still compares very favorably with the 55 percent+ national turnover average generally associated with conventional apartment properties.

15. Gross Margin.   Relates to the on-site sale of new and resale homes.

Formula:

$$\frac{\text{net sales \$} - \text{cost of goods sold}}{\text{net sales \$}} = \text{gross margin}$$

Example:

$$\frac{\$600M - \$300M}{\$600M} = .50 \text{ or } 50\% \text{ gross margin}$$

Note: Gross margin can be calculated on an annual basis, as shown above, and certainly on a home-by-home basis as an immediate and ongoing measure of profitability.

16. Conversion Percentages (two related types).   For tracking leasing and sales staff performance.

Formula:

$$\text{\# on-site visits} \div \text{\# phone calls, e.g., } 20 \div 80 = 25\%$$
$$\text{\# approved applications} \div \text{\# on-site visits, e.g., } 5 \div 20 = 25\%$$

Note: Use a daily traffic record (see property management **Chapter 7**) to record telephone calls, on-site visits, and approved applications/sales. Industry norm is 25 percent on both conversion percentage calculations. Weekly totals work best.

17. Calculations of Rent Rate for Commercial Space On-site (for example, beauty shop, convenience or video store, and so forth).

Formulas:

(1) calculate rentable sq. ft. in area to be leased, e.g. 50' × 60' = 3000 sq. ft.

(2) multiply sq. ft. by desired rental rate (e.g., $5.00/sq. ft.)
$5.00 × 3000 sq. ft. = $15,000 rent/yr

(3) divide $15,000 by 12 mths. to calculate monthly rental rate of $1,250/mth

Note: There are four variations of commercial leases to consider:

- Gross lease: lessor has responsibility for paying taxes, insurance, and property maintenance
- Net lease: lessee (renter) pays base rent *and* real estate taxes
- Net net lease: lessee lays base rent plus real estate taxes and building insurance
- Net net net lease or fully net lease: lessee pays past rent plus real estate taxes, building insurance premium, and maintenance charges.[2]

18. Use of Loan Amortization Chart(s). **Figure 3–1** is a miniature example of an amortization chart that often appears on the reverse side of lenders' business cards. A set of comprehensive loan amortization charts is found in **Appendix J.** Using **Figure 3–1,** given a loan term of 10 percent for 30 years, find where the horizontal and vertical lines/column intersect and observe a loan factor of 8.78—that is $8.78 to be paid each month for every thousand dollars borrowed when the loan was effected. For example, a $1,000,000 loan amortized at 10 percent for 30 years and with a loan factor of 8.78 (or $8.78/$1M) would warrant an annual payment of $1,000 × 8.78 = $8780/mth.

---

[2] A. Alexander & R. Muhlenbach, Managing and Leasing Commercial Properties 7–12 (John Wiley & Sons, Inc., 1990).

Why $1,000? That is because 1,000 thousands (1,000 × 1,000) = $1,000,000. A loan payment on $25,000 would calculate as 25 (thousands) × 8.78 = $219.50/mth loan payment.

LOAN AMORTIZATION CARD
MONTHLY PAYMENTS TO REPAY (AMORTIZE)
EACH $1,000 OF A LOAN

YEARS OF LOAN	PERCENT INTEREST							
	6%	7%	8%	9%	10%	11%	12%	15%
1	88.08	86.54	86.99	87.45	87.92	88.39	88.85	90.26
2	44.33	44.73	45.23	45.69	46.15	46.61	47.03	48.49
3	30.43	30.88	31.34	31.80	32.27	32.74	33.22	34.67
4	23.49	23.95	24.41	24.89	25.36	25.85	26.34	27.83
5	19.34	19.80	20.28	20.76	21.25	21.74	22.25	23.79
10	11.10	11.61	12.13	12.67	13.22	13.78	14.35	16.13
15	8.44	8.99	9.56	10.14	10.75	11.37	12.00	14.00
20	7.16	7.75	8.36	9.00	9.65	10.32	11.01	13.17
25	6.44	7.07	7.72	8.39	9.09	9.80	10.53	12.81
30	6.00	6.65	7.34	8.05	8.78	9.52	10.29	12.64

Figure 3–1. Loan amortization card.

19. Cash Flow Analysis is another important step in the operational and financial evaluation of an income property. Several helpful formats have emerged over the years. One that is particularly easy to use is the Income and Expense Operations Analysis (see **Form 3–5**). The format is self-explanatory. Once the heading is complete, insert the property-specific data into the appropriate categories and perform the indicated calculations in Steps A, B, and C.

20. Valuation Calculation Worksheet or VCW. While designed as a nontraditional real estate appraisal tool for the manufactured home community owner (discussed in detail in **Chapter 9**), the VCW is one more helpful tool to reference during the research and evaluation stage of the acquisition process (see **Form 3–6**). Consider the Key Property Characteristics in Step A and Valuation Adjustment Factors in Step B as key indicators to supplement the tools already described. Do not, at this point, use the VCW to estimate a prospective acquisition's value as many of the characteristics and factors are viewed and weighted strictly from the owner/seller's perspective *not* the buyer's.

21. Manufactured Home Community Rating System. There are several such systems in use today. The oldest is the long out-of-print (since 1976 or thereabouts) and defunct Woodall Star System. A copy of it,

FORM 3–5

INCOME AND EXPENSE CASH FLOW ANALYSIS WORKSHEET
for a ground lease-type Manufactured Home Community

Name of Property: _____ Date: _____

Physical Address: _____ Zip: _____

Contact Person/Role: _____ Phone: _____

STEP A. ANNUAL INCOME from homesite rent and other sources.

# Rental Homesites	Type Sites = Sgl., Sec. Multisec, RV, etc.	Avg. Sq. Ft. Per Site	Notes, e.g. Rent Includes =_____	$ Rent Per Homesite Type	Total Monthly Rent $ / Type	
				$	$	/mth
				$	$	/mth
				$	$	/mth
Additional Sources of Income, e.g., parts, service, laundry, cable TV, vending, insurance sales (**exclude** new and resale home $)					$	/mth
				TOTAL Monthly	$	/mth

Mulltiply Total Monthly Income by 12 (months) and put on line #1 of STEP C

STEP B. ANNUAL EXPENSES
(see Chart of Accounts on reverse side of this form)

Administrative Expenses

Management Fee	$_____
Wages	$_____
Administration Costs	$_____
Telephone	$_____
Advertising	$_____

Operating Expenses

Supplies	$_____
Heating	$_____
Electric	$_____
Water / Sewer	$_____

Maintenance Expenses

Repairs	$_____
Wages	$_____

Taxes and Insurance

Real Estate Taxes	$_____
Other Taxes, Licenses	$_____
Property Insurance	$_____

Total Annual Expenses $_____
(insert on line # 4 of Step C)

STEP C. CASH FLOW and INCOME CAPITALIZATION

1. Annual Gross Income (From Step A) $_____
2. Vacancy and Collection Adjust ___% — $_____
3. Annual Effective Gross Income   = $_____
4. Total Annual Expenses (FromStep B) — $_____
5. Annual NET OPERATING INCOME   = $_____
6. Annual Debt Service or Mortgage   — $_____
7. Cash Flow Before Taxes   = $_____
8. Owner's Equity or Down Payment   + $_____
9. CASH-ON-CASH RETURN   = $_____ %
   (first year of ownership)

10. Annual NET OPERATING INCOME $_____
    (see line #5)
11. Local INCOME CAPITALIZATION RATE + @ •____(%)
    (how determined? _____)
12. Capitalized Income VALUE   = $_____
    (compare W - replacement and market valuations)

13. CASH FLOW BEFORE TAXES $_____
    (see line #7)
14. Less Tax Liability (savings)   — $_____
15. Plus Investment Tax Credit   + $_____
16. CASH FLOW AFTER TAXES   = $_____

Designed by George Allen, CPM   8/15/95
Form available for purchase in tablet format
Property Management Form #119
Copyright: August 1995
Revised:

DMN Publishing
P.O. Box #47024
Indianapolis, IN 46247
(317) 888-7156

FORM 3-6

VALUATION CALCULATION WORKSHEET (VCW)
for owners and sellers of ground lease-type
MANUFACTURED HOME COMMUNITIES
operating at 85%+ economic occupancy✦

I.   Name of the Property _____   Date: _____

    Physical Address: _____ Zip: _____

    Contact Person/Role: _____ Phone: (   ) _____

    # Developed Acres: _____   Average monthly site rent: $ _____   Age of property: _____ yrs.

    ✦ # Sites occupied and paid: _____ (+) # sites fully developed: _____ (=) _____ % economic occupancy✦

STEP A.   KEY PROPERTY CHARACTERISTICS . . . viewed from owner/seller perspective of operation
Assign points in 6 Key Characteristics, from low of 1/2 point to maximum of 2 points.

1.   LOCATION. Remote and poor proximity = 1/2 pt.; Good desirability, accessibility and proximity = 1 pt.; excellent neighborhood, desirability, accessibility and proximity to employment, services, transportation = 2 pts. ____ point(s)

2.   NUMBER RENTAL HOMESITES. 5-49 = 1/2 pt.; 50-99 = 1 pt.; 100-199 = 1.5 pts.; 200+ = 2 pts.   ____ point(s)

3.   HOMESITE SIZES. All singlesection (4,999 sq. ft. and smaller) = 1/2 pt; approximately 50/50 mix = 1 pt.; All multisection (5,000 sq. ft. and larger) = 2 pts.   ____ point(s)

4.   UTILITIES. *1. Old, private and poor condition = 1/2 pt.; Private and OK condition = 1 pt.; Private and excellent condition or Public with fair rates and buried = 2 pts.   ____ point(s)

5.   AMENITIES. *1. None = 1/2 pt.; Minimal = 1 pt.; Top quality property with swimming pool and clubhouse - if desirable in local market = 2 pts.   ____ point(s)

6.   OVERALL CURB APPEAL. *1 Marginal to fair = 1/2 pt.; Good = 1 pt.; Excellent and better with landscaping, off-street parking, adequate setbacks, wide curvilinear (vs. grid pattern) streets, lap-sided and shingled homes = 2 pts.   ____ point(s)

7.   ADD POINTS from all 6 categories, deduct from 20, and put result here: _____ point(s)

8.   ACTUAL RENT COLLECTED (no new or resale home sales $, miscellaneous, or rental home income) during last 12 month period.*2. Is there a steady and growing income stream? Y/N___$ _____ income

9.   ACTUAL OPERATING EXPENSES (no debt service or depreciation $; consider including 5% for property management fee and 1% for capital reserves) for same 12 month period. $ _____ expense

10.   OPERATING EXPENSE RATIO (national OER = 37.8%; Model = 40%) Formula: total operating expense + total rent collected; line 9 + line 8 = OER benchmark   _____ %OER

STEP B. VALUATION ADJUSTMENT FACTORS . . . viewed from owner/seller perspective of operation
Decide whether each factor adds to or reduces property's value by maximum of ± $500/homesite

1.   DENSITY OF HOMESITES.*1. 7+/acre = -$500; 6 or less/acre = +$500.   ± $_____
Density formula: # developed homesites + # developed acres.

2.   ECONOMIC OCCUPANCY. Less than 84% = -$500; 85-94% = $-0-; 95% and better = +$500. Formula: see ✦ at beginning of worksheet.   ± $_____

3.   PRESENT RENT LEVEL. *1. low for market = -$500; high for market = $-0-; mid-range for market = +$500.   ± $_____

4.   NUMBER OF RENTAL HOMES ON -SITE. *1. 3% + = -$500; 2% or less = +$500.   ± $_____

FORM 3–6
(continued)

5. ADVERSE OR RESTRICTIVE LANDLORD-TENANT LEGISLATION AND/OR RENT
CONTROL in effect locally? Yes = -$500; no = +$500. ± $_____

6. CONTIGUOUS RAW LAND AVAILABLE AND ZONED for like use?
Yes = +$500; no = -0-. ± $_____

7. OPTIONAL: e.g. licensed to operate, if appropriate. Yes = +$500 or No = -$500. ± $_____ optional

8. OPTIONAL: e.g. significant effect of miscellaneous income stream? *1 and *2. ± $_____ optional

9. OPTIONAL: e.g. resident base and mix; pride in home ownership? Y/N ± $_____ optional

10. OPTIONAL: e.g. effect of area occupancy level and rent structure. ± $_____ optional

11. CUMULATIVE TOTAL OF VALUATION ADJUSTMENT FACTORS at ± $500/site,
with cumulative total not to exceed ± $1.500/homesite on this line: ± $_____

STEP C. VALUATION CALCULATION . . . using data from STEPS A and B above . . .

1. RENT COLLECTED $_____ *3 (-) OPERATING EXPENSES $_____ = $_____ NOI

2. a) NET OPERATING INCOME (from line above) divided by Key Point Total from Step A,
expressed as a decimal (e.g. 9 points + 100 = .09 divisor.
2. b) $_____ NOI (+) _____ point divisor = preliminary value of $_____

3. Preliminary Value $_____ (+) _____ occupied and paid homesites = $_____ per site
adjusted

4. Value per site, $_____ (±)_____ adjustment per homesite from Step B = $_____ site value
value

5. Adjusted Site Value of $_____ (X) _____ # occupied and paid homesites = $_____ subtotal

6. Adjusted Site Value of $_____ (X) _____ # vacant and unpaid homesites   value
                                                    x .50 value discount = $_____ subtotal
7. ADD two subtotals (lines 5 and 6 above) together to obtain the   **Total**
TOTAL ESTIMATED VALUE of the MANUFACTURED HOME COMMUNITY . . . = $_____ **Value**

FOOTNOTES:
*1. These characteristics (Step A) and factors (Step B) will be viewed and valued differently by owners estimating value
and planning to hold vs. owners estimating value and planning to sell and wanting to attract serious prospective
buyers now. The latter perspective will generally be similar to buyers of quality properties.
*2. Cable TV and phone commissions; MH brokerage; rule of parts and service.
*3. A personal judgement call whether to include a 2% vacancy factor here or not.

DISCLAIMER. This VALUATION CALCULATION WORKSHEET FOR MANUFACTURED HOME COMMUNITIES is distrib-
uted as a handy, easy-to-use, self-help guide to estimating the possible value of a manufactured home community. The services
of experienced, certified, licensed real estate value appraisers should always be retained for best results. Accuracy of results
wholly dependent upon data selected and calculated by VCW user.

Designed by George Allen CPM, October 29, 1994

This form available for purchase in tablet format.
Property Management Form #118
Copyright Oct 1994
Revised January 1996

PMN Publishing
P.O. Box #47024
Indianapolis, IN 46247
(317) 888-7156

for historical reference, is included as **Appendix K.** While out-of-date, the "star count" is still common parlance among lenders and some manufactured home community owners and managers. Everyone seems to have loose ideas of "five star" (excellent) properties and "one star" ones—the opposite end of the spectrum. A more detailed discussion of manufactured home community rating systems follows in **Chapter 4.**

ANOTHER PERSPECTIVE[3]

§ 3.7   Risk and Reward

Risk and reward is a fundamental of real estate that is important to understand. If one in looking for a lot of reward, expect to take a lot of risk. Looking for a safe deal? Do not expect a high return. In the manufactured home community business, low returns on investments are those that generate a return on capital in the 8 to 10 percent range, whereas high returns are those in the 17 to 21 percent range.

There are investors who have entered the manufactured home community business because they thought that it would be easy, only to find themselves in the midst of a business more complex than they anticipated. In many cases these investors were expecting a high return without risk or difficulty.

Manufactured home communities are an example of a niche real estate property type that offers a unique investment opportunity and requires standard skills in the areas of acquisition and property management to maximize potential return on investment. Like any other income property type, there are special issues to take into consideration and special things to look for to maximize the potential of the real estate investment.

---

[3] Craig White of Craig White and Associates in Denver, Colorado, has been involved in every aspect of manufactured home community development, acquisition, management, and disposition for more than 20 years. He brings a unique but confirming perspective to the entire theme of "what to look for in a manufactured home community."

§ 3.8 Primary Considerations

Before proceeding any further with the overall issue of what to look for while purchasing a manufactured home community, there are two significant points to emphasize:

1. Do your homework—adequate due diligence is the key to success.
2. Determine why the project is for sale.

Due Diligence

There is an old adage that goes, "the harder you work, the luckier you get." Nothing could be more true of the need for adequate due diligence when a property is purchased. The more knowledge that one has about a property and everything that affects it, the better one's chance for success. Due diligence should include everything there is to be known about the overall site, the local market, and the economics of the investment property. Secure professional help to assess the engineering due diligence and an accountant to assess and review the financial records.

Pay particular interest to the degree to which the project contains physical obsoleteness. Look at the homesite size and determine what is the maximum sized home that can be placed on the homesite. It is not uncommon today to find homesites that are too small to accept the most popular homes being sold. Also make sure the analysis of this critical issue includes a discussion with the planning department of the jurisdiction where the project is located to determine what the setback requirements are for the community.

Make a thorough assessment of physical problems. Physical issues will fall into the categories of cosmetic issues, deferred maintenance, and permanent issues.

Why Is the Property for Sale?

From what the sellers and their agents have disclosed, and one's due diligence, try to ascertain why the property is for sale. To the extent that the reasons involve unresolved problems, such as management problems or marketing problems, an honest assessment must be made as to one's ability to address the issues that have led to the sale of the property.

§ 3.9 Management Impact

As in most businesses, management is the key to the successful marketing and operation of a manufactured home community. Reducing manufactured home community management to its simplest definition includes five activities that must be effected:

1. Fill every homesite
2. Collect every rent dollar
3. Keep operating expenses within budget guidelines
4. Keep every homesite and common areas neat, clean, and tidy
5. Keep every resident happy.

The management of a manufactured home community is just that simple, or just that complex, depending on the present condition of the property. Properties are often differentiated by the degree to which each of these five issues are under control or out of control.

The way to protect oneself in a high-risk project is through superior management. Anyone going into this business should seek experienced assistants or advisors, if only as mentors until familiar with the management of the property. Once everything is running smoothly, the project fully occupied, and the expenses stabilized, the property management function is less critical but still of utmost importance.

In many cases an experienced investor prefers to take a hands-off attitude toward the manufactured home community project. Accordingly, the selection of a fee-management company with proven successful experience in the operation of this property type would be an important decision.

§ 3.10 Project Types

There is a wide range of options available for the investor desiring to acquire a manufactured home community. The choices in project type fall into the following general areas:

1. Full and profitable or turnaround challenge
2. Urban/suburban or rural location
3. Family or adult/retiree resident profile.

Full and Profitable or Turnaround Project

As noted earlier, investment properties such as manufactured home communities typically fall into the categories of being full and profitable or turnaround challenges. The full and profitable property is just what is implied. The fill-up phase of the project is completed, expenses are stabilized, and it is somewhat in "cruise control." This type project has a low risk, but would-be investors should expect to pay a premium price for the property.

The turnaround property is characterized as having high risk and challenge, but represents an opportunity for superior return, provided key issues can be resolved that will facilitate the turnaround situation. Important here are careful due diligence and application of experienced and effective marketing and operating strategies.

Urban/Suburban or Rural Project

The geographical location of the considered project or acquisition is an important decision on the selection of a manufactured home community. The urban/suburban area close to a strong population center is one choice. The rural or small town choice in another alternative.

The closer to the larger urban/suburban areas the higher the competition among investors for available properties. Expect to pay higher prices in urban/suburban locations. The small town and rural locations have unique upside and downside considerations. The upside is relatively lower prices and lack of competition. Selling this property later may be more difficult, and some lenders are reluctant to lend in rural and small town locations, hence the downside.

Family or Adult/Retiree Project

These properties fall into one of two categories: either all-age (family) or adult/retiree. The Fair Housing Act prevails here. The adult/retiree property is referred to as a "55 or older community" under the Fair Housing Act.

In general, the all-age community is more difficult to manage because there are more difficulties with rent collection and covenant (or rules) enforcement. The 55 and older community generally requires a more patient management style because retirees who have "time on their hands" and a desire to be catered to are involved in whatever is taking place around their homes.

§ 3.11   Project Size

What size property should one look for when purchasing a manufactured home community? Manufactured home communities vary in size from five to several thousand homesites. There are several considerations affecting the preference in property size:

Financial.   The amount of capital available for investment, and the ability to borrow from a conventional lender, or seller financing are major considerations regarding the size property that one can afford.

Competition.   The major players in the manufactured housing industry generally restrict their purchases to properties that have 200 or more homesites. Less than 15 percent of the manufactured home communities in existence meet this criteria. The result is that there are many investors seeking this relatively small group of properties, so the sale of larger properties is generally bid upward by the market. By concentrating on properties under 200 homesites in size, the investor can avoid the competition of the largest operators and buy at reasonable prices.

Size and adequacy of management.   As noted earlier, property management is vital for the effective marketing and operation of a manufactured home community. Profitable properties do not just happen. Somebody makes them happen, and that is the role and responsibility of professional property management. Property size is a factor because without a sufficient homesite count, one cannot afford good and full-time management.

In some cases, the property owner lives on-site and performs the property management function. In this instance, almost any size property can be acquired. For properties of up to about 100 homesites, the property management function generally consists of a manager/caretaker who lives on-site and provides limited attention beyond collection of rent. This is one reason for having rents mailed to a central location, to limit the amount of work on-site. The on-site management function should not exceed about 7 percent of the project income; therefore, a project of 50 homesites collecting $150 per month in rent cannot afford more than about $600 per month for the on-site management function.

In a similar fashion, property size has a significant effect on the function of multiproperty supervision, referred to as the property manager. The property manager is that person who provides direction to the on-site manager. Manufactured home communities of less than 200 homesites make it very expensive to justify a property manager, thus the reason why major operators shy away from smaller properties of less than 200 homesites.

One smart strategy regarding the acquisition of smaller properties is to define one's market as where one can drive by automobile in a day and be back to the office or home that night. Within this market parameter, seek out enough small properties to eventually acquire a portfolio of more than 200 homesites. These properties will usually supply extra income to support an adequate property management effort.

Adequate size to attract financing. At some point the need to finance or refinance the property may occur. Many lenders who seek manufactured home communities as debt investments of choice are reluctant to look at properties of less than the 150 to 200 homesite size. This is yet another consideration regarding the size of the community considered for acquisition. Again the strategy of assembling more than one community in a small geographical area is a possible answer. One project of 65 homesites does not usually make a viable business, but a nearby group of five communities, averaging 65 homesites apiece, constitutes a viable business effort.

§ 3.12 Summary

A lot of territory has been covered in this chapter. There is a lot to look for, document, and evaluate when researching a prospective manufactured home community to acquire. It is not a task to be rushed or taken lightly. The best transactions are generally based on informed decisions made after full realization of the nature of the property, its income streams, and operating expenses, along with assessment of available financing and acceptance of the risks involved.

CHAPTER 4

HOW TO FIND AND BUY A MANUFACTURED HOME COMMUNITY

§ 4.1   **Introduction**

§ 4.2   **Goal Setting**

§ 4.3   **Property Parameters**

§ 4.4   **Sources of Manufactured Home Communities for Sale and Otherwise**

§ 4.5   **Time to Go Looking**

ANOTHER PERSPECTIVE
Grady Hunt

§ 4.6   **Identifying a Geographic Market of Interest**

§ 4.7   **Defining the Type of Community to Purchase**

§ 4.8   **Cataloging the Surveyed Manufactured Home Communities**

§ 4.9   **Summary**

§ 4.1   Introduction

It is not difficult to find manufactured home communities. In the United States and Canada, they are a popular housing choice in just about every state and province. The dual challenge, however, is to find the right one and for it to be for sale at a reasonable price at the right time. Furthermore, it is generally a seller's market for this property type because of the positive economic and demographic reasons discussed in **Chapters 1** and **2.** A diligent search and careful selection can produce significant reward for one's labor.

Successful investment in a manufactured home community is like the three-legged stool in **Figure 4–1.** All three legs must be solidly in place to ensure adequate and stable support—or investment. The first requirement is to learn the general characteristics of the manufactured housing industry and particulars of the manufactured home community property type. The second challenge is to be knowledgeable of real estate investment basics in general and the peculiarities of manufactured home community marketing and operations. The final or third leg has to do with the diligent search and considered decision pursuant to acquiring one or more manufactured home communities. This chapter concentrates on effecting that third important step.

There are also three distinct but interrelated stages of this search and decision exercise:

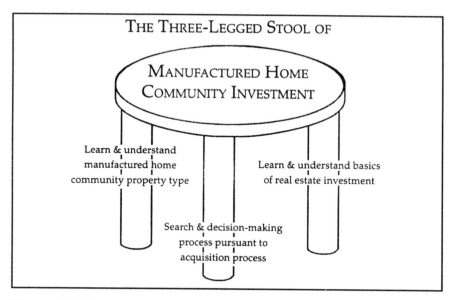

Figure 4–1. Manufactured home community investment. Illustration provided by Patti Greco of Greco Writing, 902B Ridgefield Circle, Clinton, MA 01510 (508) 368-1022.

1.   <u>Set personal or corporate goals</u> as to type and specific property parameters of the manufactured home community to acquire, and when and where appropriate to do so.

2.   <u>Access sources for identifying manufactured home communities</u> nearby, regionally or nationwide, in accordance with one's investment goals. See **Appendixes F, H,** and especially **L** and **M** for a list of such sources, listings, and leads.

3.   <u>Begin the acquisition process.</u> Thinking back to the Problem-Solving Procedure described in **Chapter 2,** this stage of the overall acquisition process requires a would-be buyer to think and operate on parallel tracks. The acquisition effort has reached the point where product (a manufactured home community) is to be actively sought for consideration. With each prospective property, the problem-solving procedure begins anew as the buyer seeks to document, study, and organize data, then decide whether to move ahead or not. The obvious question is whether to look at one potential deal at a time or consider several. The answer to that is usually a function of time and the personnel and financial resources that are available. If a one-person effort, then it does not hurt to rustle the bushes and take a cursory look at several possibilities, then concentrate on one or two offerings that most closely meet one's investment goals and property parameters. If one has staff available to help, then broaden the search and review as many opportunities as practical until several good opportunities or one materializes.

§ 4.2   Goal Setting

Setting investment goals and establishing property parameters is the place to start the search and buy process. Investment goals may be personal, as in the case of an individual investor or basic partnership. They may also be corporate in nature, whether starting off a new business venture with the acquisition of a single property or acquisition of a small portfolio. Goal setting also applies to a business that has been around for awhile and is preparing to grow by investing in manufactured home communities.

In the case of the private investor, setting goals for oneself and perhaps a partner, may be characterized by one or more of these scenarios:

1. Recent or soon-to-be retiree or corporate-downsizing casualty with a financial nest egg to invest. Investor intends to stay active, to varying degrees, and wants to "grow the investment," usually with hands-on management effort.
2. Younger individuals and couples who begin early to amass personal wealth and achieve independence through real property acquisition.
3. The classic partnership, in which one party has financial resources and the other the willingness and ability to "work the investment" to the benefit of both parties.

Depending on the level of personal risk tolerance and available financing, time, and other resources, all three investor scenarios may effect acquisitions ranging in degree from REO (real estate-owned or foreclosed) to full and stable manufactured home communities, from minimal (5 to 10 rental homesites) to much larger size, and with every possible variation in between. The personal investor, however, is rarely able to complete head-to-head with a large portfolio-holding company for the largest manufactured home community listings.

It is difficult to draw a clear distinction between personal and corporate goal setting because many of the companies active in this investment property niche are closely held and run by their founders or CEOs. In these instances personal and corporate goal setting is essentially the same. In instances, however, when CEO decisions are tempered and guided by formal boards of directors, especially in the case of the Real Estate Investment Trusts (REIT), true corporate goal setting usually occurs. In these instances, corporate goals manifest themselves when a company positions itself as a provider of retirement housing and characteristic community lifestyle; or a family-oriented living environment; a Senior Housing specialty firm; one that is known for its manufactured housing sales expertise and performance as well as real estate investment; and on and on. Of course, such pivotal decisions directly affect the type, quantity, and locations of potential acquisitions. A variation to this corporate goal-setting scenario is the syndication of limited partnerships.

Here too, strategic decisions must be made as to objectives and direction. While corporate leaders make these decisions in light of board guidance and potential return to stockholders, would-be general partners and syndicators have to carefully ascertain what they can "sell" to their limited partner investor base. For example, will would-be investors respond well to stable midsize properties with only moderate returns, or is there receptivity to participating in a higher risk venture (for example, moderate turnaround challenge but with good market and economic indicators) with potential for significantly higher returns on investment?

The Real Estate Investment Trust or REIT was mentioned earlier. This too is an investment alternative for the would-be manufactured home community investor. It is the real estate alternative to a mutual fund that allows an investor to invest and observe without the risk of outright property ownership. For example, "A qualified REIT is entitled to conduit tax treatment, i.e., it may distribute income to its shareholders without the imposition of a corporate tax, thus avoiding the 'double tax' burden on regular business corporations."[1]

There are three types of REITs: equity REITs (own real estate directly), mortgage REITs (lenders financing rather than owning real estate), and hybrid REITs. A fourth special type REIT is the umbrella partnership or UPREIT. It allows property owners to transfer holdings into a REIT to create liquidity for partners and raise capital in order to refinance existing debt, acquire or develop new properties, and expand present holdings.[2] The five manufactured home community REITs are

- ROC Communities, Inc., also known as RCI
- Manufactured Home Communities, Inc., also known as MHC
- SUN Communities, Inc., also known as SUI
- Chateau Properties, Inc., also known as CPJ
- United Mobile Homes, Inc., also known as UMH.

Long-time well-known syndicators of limited partnerships specializing in manufactured home communities include

- Lautrec Ltd. of Farmington Hills, Michigan
- Ellenburg Capital of Portland, Oregon

---

[1] Alvin Arnold, Real Estate Investor's Deskbook 6-47 (1994).

[2] *Id.* at 6-49.

- Choice Properties of Troy, Michigan
- Bloch Realty of Birmingham, Michigan
- Windsor Group of Escondido, California (see **Appendix D**).

Whether setting a personal investment goal or strategizing corporate goals, certain orienting questions apply to both scenarios:

1. What is one's (personal or corporate) present financial situation?
2. What are the financial goals, obligations, and commitments that should be or must be resolved over time? Retirement for individuals and retiring debt or meeting projections for businesses are examples of answers to this particular question.
3. How much investment capital is available now and in the near future?
4. What will be the maximum acceptable price and minimum acceptable price and minimum acceptable terms for a real estate investment?

For individual investors the following three questions bring goal setting into even sharper focus:

5. Number of years before planning to live off one's investment income?
6. Income needed at retirement?
7. Number of years retirement income is expected to last?[3]

Some general examples of typical investment goals are these:

1. Earn 20 percent first year return on 10 percent equity investment or down payment
2. Take on a turnaround challenge and work to realize a quick, substantial return *or* treat it as an annuity and steadily improve it over time and sell when the time is right
3. Use property investment as vehicle to write off legitimate business expenses and, if located in or near a retirement mecca, use periodic visits as dual inspection/management and rejuvenation opportunity

---

[3] Milt Tanzer, Real Estate Investments and How to Make Them 16 (1981).

4. As a practical business training ground and source of education funds for one's children while in college or in lieu of a higher education

5. Expand one's business presence in a particular geographic area and add to one's portfolio holdings.

§ 4.3 Property Parameters

There are at least six categories of property or real estate investment parameters to consider and decide upon when acquiring a manufactured home community. The order of the following categories is in declining order of priority, but specific features within each category easily affect its relative level of importance. Do not be unduly restricted to this progression; reorder it to fit the property or properties being considered and personal or corporate investment goals.

Location. Is it good, or not so good, relative to the income-generating ability and nature of the property? Is the property compatible with its surroundings? Any key present or future considerations in this regard? For private investors, the location issue is often one of proximity: Is it close enough to look after? For larger, established portfolio owners the key issues are whether new property locations complement present holdings and orientation, enjoy ease of access by air, or are remote from a central office.

Size, in terms of rental homesite count. The majority of manufactured home communities are less than 100 homesites in size. This is one reason they are so attractive to small private investors. In terms of income potential, it takes roughly three rental homesites to generate the same rental income as one three-bedroom townhouse apartment in the same market area—except for a few retirement areas and specific markets where there are only a few manufactured home communities but very strong demand. Most larger (100+ rental homesites) communities are owned by public and private real estate investment firms, unless still in the hands of the original sole proprietor/developer, or still working through a turnaround or new development lease-up phase.

Acreage is also an important consideration. Has all available acreage been developed or is there expansion property potential? This is especially important if expansion ground has already been zoned and approved for future manufactured home community development.

Density of developed ground is key as well. The number of developed homesites divided by the number of developed acres yields this benchmark. Beware of high density (7+/acre) unless the market clearly supports it, for example, blue-collar rental unit popularity. Low density ensures adequate space for sitting large single-section and multisection homes.

Degree of risk involved.   Certainly a highly personal and corporate-sensitive call, but a decision that must be weighed and made nonetheless. Here are a few possible alternatives:

- Property already full and stable with great curb appeal and no resident or infrastructure-related problems
- Property with low physical or economic occupancy and unstable due to local economy and market, management problems, and perhaps infrastructure failure.
- Property transitioning one way or the other, improving or declining, as a result of the local environs, on-site characteristics, and quality of property management.

Obviously all three risks have their attractions and cautions. The first will be a pride and joy to own and have minimum initial risk, but will likely be priced at a prohibitive premium level. Future negative changes, if the purchase is highly leveraged, could significantly increase the risk level. The second option will certainly have risk involved, but that may be significantly minimized if the transaction is effected at a deep discount or underwritten with very favorable financing terms. The third option is less risky if the improvement trend is spotted early and controlled; the declining trend might not be bad either if the buyer waits until the property hits bottom before acquiring. There is no real magic in any of these decisions. Simply realize during the initial research how vital it is to gain a clear understanding of the property type and its local market, and then make a wise and informed investment decision.

Attitude and fortitude about utilities and infrastructure. Private or public—that is a key question. Most large corporate buyers will not touch the private utility–serviced property offering, particularly if an older community and located some distance from the home office. Until recently, however, private investors in many instances preferred (as some still do) private wells and wastewater treatment systems. Why? If equipment is in good operating condition, it is generally more economical (profitable) to serve a manufactured home community with private utilities than to tap into a city or public system unless the municipality really needs the extra customers and cuts a sweetheart deal with the property owner. This scenario is changing as potable water quality reporting and wastewater effluent standards tighten and violation notices and fines increase. Today, owners of midsize and larger manufactured home communities hook into public utilities when and where possible to reduce regulatory headaches and make their properties more attractive to future investors. Submetering is a corollary consideration in this regard. Is prospective acquisition submetered? If so, this generally reduces overall water consumption by as much as 33 percent; if not, is this something that should be planned and budgeted for soon after closing?

Resident profile and amenity package preferences. Is the potential investor interested in a retirement or all-adult community environment? This resident profile generally makes for a stable tenancy with more attractive homes (residents have more time and money to spend on themselves and homes than when raising children), but it also may represent a greater requirement for features and amenities like clubhouses, swimming pools, and other recreation and social facilities. Family or blue-collar-oriented communities, in some ways, are more management intense because the number of occupants per home is greater and usage of on-site facilities more intense. Some manufactured home community developers and owners frown on having any amenities on-site, figuring they are leasing ground to someone for their home, so let residents go elsewhere for other needs. Assuming such a featureless community can be kept full because of market demand, such a property may well be more profitable than one with a full complement of features and amenities. In the full-featured community it may or may not be possible to charge higher rent to offset all extra operating expenses relative to the on-site amenities. The core issue is to correctly match preferred resident profile, if one has a choice among investment alternatives, with one's attitude about features and amenities requirements in the intended market and what renters may expect and are willing to pay for.

Property management on- and off-site.   Who is to manage? Smaller manufactured home communities are often managed by their owners or a trusted caretaker who is paid a minimal amount or receives a rent-free homesite for usually part-time effort. These are generally referred to as Mom-and-Pop operators. Midsize and larger communities generally have near full-time or full-time staffing depending on the specific needs of the property: low occupancy means more leasing and sales effort and greater curb appeal and site repair requirements; high occupancy should mean a smaller office staff and only moderate expense for grounds maintenance and good curb appeal. Most corporate owners of manufactured home communities employ full-time managers (often couples who share the management responsibilities) to live on-site and manage the asset, functioning like the mayor of a small town. Fee-management services are yet another option. Here the owner of a manufactured home community or portfolio hires a professional property management firm to oversee most or all the day-to-day activities of the investment properties, often including accounting and bookkeeping responsibilities. The management fee, it is important to realize, generally does not include the wages or salary for on-site staff; these are paid by the property per se. For a list of property management firms in the United States and Canada, contact the Institute of Real Estate Management (see **Appendix D**).

There are a potpourri of issues and decision-making points to consider when acquiring a manufactured home community:

Rental manufactured homes or not.   This is not recommended or needed when acquiring a full and stable community. Homeowner/renters generally resent living next to renters who are leasing both home and homesite. Too many times said renters, having no equity or ownership interest in their residence, take less care of them than homeowner/renters. However, if a local market exhibits clear evidence of needing many inexpensive rental homes, acquiring a half-empty manufactured home community and filling it with manufactured homes marketed as rental units can be a very profitable prospect. The key is to keep all rentals full, all rent collected weekly, all homes re-leased quickly, and all well maintained. In time, an exit strategy is to replace worn-out rental homes with homeowner/renters, preferably moving in new homes, until the once half-empty, then highly profitable rental property, becomes a conventional manufactured home community filled with attractive homes and site-rent-paying homeowners.

Presence of rent control or one form or another of landlord-tenant legislation.   Such legislative regulation is a bane to real estate investors and local citizens alike. Not only does its presence in a market discourage new residential multifamily real estate development, but it usually stifles the profitable resale of existing income properties as well. When rental revenues are artificially controlled in this fashion, real estate tax revenues tend to decline, facility maintenance suffers (less dollars available for capital improvements and routine maintenance), and even employment can suffer. Think long and hard before investing in a region where the ability to conduct business is restricted and regulated in any fashion.

Opportunities to develop additional streams of income on-site.   This is usually an area best handled by smaller operator/owners who work on-site or are near enough to see that all revenue producers are nurtured properly. Here are some possibilities:

- New and resale home sales and service.
- Resale home brokerage service (on behalf of residents).
- Homeowner insurance sales.
- Homeowner finance sourcing.
- On-site facilities, for example, convenience store, video rentals, beauty shop, bank machine.
- Sale of parts and related services. Be careful about doing work that has any liability exposure, such as electrical and natural gas hookups.
- Cable TV. Especially good opportunity if a separate business for property owner; otherwise negotiate cash rebate based on monthly sales, unless service is franchised by local municipality.
- Vending machine income (beverage, air, telephone).

- Laundry income (machines, sale of soap).
- Clubhouse rental, especially to outsiders.
- Swimming pool passes, especially to outsiders.

§ 4.4 Sources of Manufactured Home Communities for Sale and Otherwise

There are at least a dozen different sources of leads for names and addresses for manufactured home communities in general and those that are for sale in particular. Some of these sources overlap, but for the most part they should be individually reviewed and pursued each time a new manufactured home community acquisition is sought:

Local newspaper. Metropolitan papers generally have a real estate section that carries classified ads listing investment properties for sale. Individual owners and real estate brokers often place ads for smaller to midsize properties there. Larger manufactured home communities generally will not be listed because these owners already receive a steady flow of solicitation inquires from real estate brokers and large corporate owners who want to list or buy said properties when the time comes.

Also read news stories about manufactured home communities that may be in difficulty with local or state regulatory agencies. This may be an indication that the owner is ready or close to being ready to sell.

Regional real estate–oriented publications. These may be slick magazine or tabloid format. In either event, they too carry occasional listings or ads for manufactured home communities for sale. These publications are usually distributed by local or state realty boards, professional societies (Building Owners & Managers Association (BOMA) and Institute of Real Estate Management (IREM), and so forth), and exchange groups. Get on as many mailing lists as possible. Additionally, some realty companies publish periodic lists of income-producing properties they have for sale.

National newspapers. The *Wall Street Journal* and *USA Today* have weekly real estate sections that occasionally carry ads for manufactured home communities. An ad for a manufactured home community for sale in the *Wall Street Journal* all but guarantees a flood of unqualified inquires, so popular is the property type.

Manufactured housing-related trade publications.

1. *Manufactured Home Merchandiser,* a monthly magazine, in its classified ads section almost always has listings of manufactured home communities for sale. It is not an easy publication to obtain (visit a local manufactured home retail salescenter and ask for a copy) but worth the effort. Call (312) 236-3528.

2. *Manufactured Housing Journal* or simply *The Journal,* a monthly tabloid, also carries occasional ads for manufactured home communities. It is a free publication to those in the business. Call (706) 655-2333.

3. *The Allen Letter,* a paid subscription monthly newsletter, carries regular information about deals that have been consummated and acquisition opportunities available to investors. Call (317) 888-7156.

Manufactured housing trade association newsletters. Not all associations publish newsletters but many do. For names and addresses of state associations in targeted markets, see **Appendix H.**

Manufactured housing regional publications. There are a few newsletters that carry information about recent transactions and properties for sale or available for development (see **Appendix F** for addresses):

1. *The Pappas Report* (Arizona-based)
2. *Manufactured Housing Today* (Oregon-based)
3. *Manufactured Housing Report* (California-based)
4. *WMA Reporter* (California-based).

Local and regional real estate brokers. For those brokers who specialize in marketing manufactured home communities, see **Appendix L.** Only one real estate brokerage, Marcus and Millichap, specializes in manufactured home community marketing on a national level.

Buyer's broker. Recruit a buyer's broker to conduct search for available manufactured home communities.

Direct mail solicitation. Use names and addresses gathered during preceding and following sourcing efforts. The most effective mailings include "bounce back" postcards to encourage prompt reply. Some sources for direct mail contacts include:

1. Manufactured housing association member lists. Some groups are more forthcoming about this than others. Also be aware that most western states have two manufactured-housing-related associations, one made up primarily of manufacturers and retail members, the other comprised of manufactured home community owners and managers. Specify to association executives or staff precisely what is needed. See **Appendix H.**

2. State and county regulatory agency lists of manufactured home communities. These lists are often the best to use because they contain not only the property name, address, size (homesite count), and type of water/sewer utility system, but the name and address of the property owner as well. Plus, many of these agency property files are open to public review, and regulators encourage would-be buyers to visit with them beforehand to avoid potential surprises after closing, for example, lack of operating license, impending legal action, and fines. See **Appendix M.**

3. Commercially marketed lists. There are many variations here. Just be aware that such lists are often compiled from Yellow Page listings in locales across the United States and Canada. Whoever advertises in the Yellow Pages will likely be listed; who does not advertise will not be listed.

Annual Allen Report of Largest Owners. This appears in the January issue of *Manufactured Home Merchandiser* magazine. To obtain a free copy of the current report contact PMN Publishing at (317) 888-7156. See **Appendix D.**

Yellow Page advertisements for manufactured home communities. Use latest edition of this reference to identify some properties in the desired market area.

Networking with other manufactured home community owners is good way to identify leads. Attend state, regional, and national meetings of owners and managers to meet, network, and learn with and from them. Contact the Manufactured Housing Institute for their meeting schedule as well as the state associations mentioned earlier. See **Appendix H.** Many major manufactured home community owners meet annually at the International Networking Roundtable. For information write to INR c/o PO Box 47024, Indianapolis, IN 46247.

Listings on the Internet. A new source for manufactured home communities for sale.

County tax records. Yet another source of leads, especially of those property owners who are delinquent in paying.

Appendix M. This appendix is a comprehensive national list, state by state, of the best primary and secondary sources of manufactured home community lists in the United States.

There are obviously many sources of leads for manufactured home communities to consider for acquisition. It is simply a matter of time, effort, and persistence. One final and generally effective technique involves contacting a targeted state's department of economic development and requesting a list of all manufactured home communities. These departments function to facilitate a prospective buyer's business presence in that state.

§ 4.5 Time to Go Looking

Once the target manufactured home community, or perhaps small group of local properties, has been identified and selected for further scrutiny, take time to visit and document/verify data on hand and determine what still needs to be obtained. Use the Investment Checklist (**Form 3–3**) **Chapter 3.** Here are a few fine-tuning guidelines to consider at this point:

1. Review accumulated property data and formulate a list of questions to ask and things to observe.
2. Visit the properties with a notebook, tape recorder, and camera. Some prefer to use a video camera in lieu of a 35mm picture camera. Also take a large tape measure or measuring wheel.

3. As a matter of courtesy, do not arouse residents or on-site staff during the visit. Drive through, take photos from within car, and if asking anyone questions, use the ruse of "considering moving into the community" and wanting to know what is *good* and *bad* about it.

4. Stay emotionally detached. This will improve the negotiating stance later.

5. Complete the aforementioned Investment Checklist.

Now, with the information gathered

1. Organize all collected data per the guidelines in **Chapter 3.**

2. Decide whether to proceed. Is the investment in accord with goals?

3. Does it fit within the maximum price and minimum term guidelines? If all or most indicators are positive decide whether to proceed.

4. Make an offer.

Prepare a formal written offer or letter of intent to purchase the desired manufactured home community. Never make a verbal offer. The written offer should include all terms and conditions pursuant to acquisition of the property. Some states require an attorney to prepare the offer to purchase, a wise practice in any event. Decide on an earnest money deposit. This is often 10 percent of the purchase price, unless a large transaction, then a $1,000 to $2,000 earnest money deposit check with balance of 10 percent (for example) due shortly after contract is accepted by seller.

Some negotiating points to keep in mind are the following:

1. Again, *never* make a verbal offer.

2. Rarely offer full price except under unusual circumstances, for example, an exceptionally good deal "as is," or if clearly known that seller will not budge. If the latter, attempt to negotiate liberal terms.

3. What to offer? This depends on one's research and desire and the seller's degree and type of motivation for selling.

4. Do not be in a hurry, but set a reasonable time for the seller to accept the offer. There is an old adage that says "if a deal's too hard to make, it probably wasn't meant to be made." This may or may not be true, but it does provide a measure of comfort.

5. Consider some contingency clauses, often called escape clauses, to build into the offer to purchase and contract:

    • Verification of financial statements concerning property income and related operating expenses.
    • Inspection requirements: utility infrastructure, environmental audit, ADA compliance, and so forth.
    • Lease review: ask for completed Estoppel Certificates for every accepted homesite (see **Form 4–1**).
    • Mortgage assumption possibility? Verify loan is assumable and the applicable rate for buyer. Have an attorney verify this.
    • New first mortgage contingency.
    • Personal property inventory.

There are certainly a lot of details to keep in mind while putting a real estate transaction together. For that matter, there is more than one way to go about the process.

ANOTHER PERSPECTIVE[4]

§ 4.6 Identifying a Geographic Market of Interest

In selecting a geographic area in which to invest, the investor should look for ways to make the investment enjoyable, not difficult. Manufactured home communities are not wholly passive investments. They derive their investment value from residents who pay rent, and whenever people are involved, management is required. Therefore, in looking

---

[4] In the next sections, Grady Hunt, an experienced manufactured home community broker from Atlanta, Georgia, shares his thoughts on the subject and concludes with an introduction to rating systems used to grade manufactured home communities.

FORM 4–1

NCR (No Carbon Required)   **ESTOPPEL CERTIFICATE***

Name of Owner _____

Name of Tenant _____

Location of premises _____

Date lease commenced _____   Date lease terminates _____

Lease is subject to the following options to extend: _____
_____.

Tenant certifies that:

1. The lease referred to above is unmodified, is in full force and effect, and constitutes the only agreement between Owner and Tenant with respect to the premises, except: _____
_____.

   ☐ A copy of the lease is attached as Exhibit A.

2. Tenant has no option to purchase or right of first refusal to purchase all or any portion of the leased premises, except: _____.

3. The current monthly rent is $_____ (_____ dollars).

4. Rent has been paid through the period ending _____.
   The sum of $_____ (_____ dollars) has been paid on account of future rent, and the sum of $_____ (_____ dollars) has been paid as a security deposit.

5. So far as is known to Tenant, Owner is not in default under any term or condition of the lease, and no offsets, counterclaims or defenses by Tenant exist, except: _____
_____.

Tenant understands that this Estoppel Certificate may be delivered to a Buyer of the property including the leased premises, or to a Lender who will lend on the security of the property, and that such persons may rely upon the representations made by Tenant.

Tenant agrees to immediately notify the following persons, at the following addresses on the occurrence of any event that would make any of the above representations inaccurate:

Buyer _____   Address _____
                                                    _____

Lender _____   Address _____
                                                    _____

Tenant _____   Date _____

| Rev. by _____ |
| Date _____ |

PROFESSIONAL PUBLISHING

---

* Reprinted by permission of the copyright owner: Professional Publishing, A Division of McKenney's Standard Forms, Inc., 122 Paul Dr., San Rafael, CA 94903; 800-288-2006 • Fax: 415-472-2069.

for an area in which to invest, it is often best to start in one's state, even one's hometown. The key is to pick an area that can be easily visited on a regular basis. If the manufactured home community is inconvenient or difficult to get to, taking care of routine business becomes a hardship and interest in the investment soon wanes.

Starting the search for a manufactured home community in one's locale also improves the odds of selecting markets and properties that are easier to understand, thus avoiding costly location miscues. The United States Bureau of Census tracks population gains and shifts, age changes, income distribution, housing types, and housing cost in all SMSAs (Standard Metropolitan Statistical Area, for example, Atlanta, Chicago) and other cities. This information can also be studied in much smaller geographical areas by looking at census tracts for each targeted city.

Manufactured housing is simply another segment of the overall housing pie. To fully understand how manufactured homes serve the housing market one must also understand the larger picture of the housing business, which includes single-family detached homes, condominiums, and apartments. The local apartment and Realtor® associations often track apartment vacancy and rental rates, median and average home cost, and the gross dollar volume of homes sold in any given area. The local building inspector's office can supply building permit numbers that reflect the volume and value of homes being built in the local market. Officials with the departments of planning and zoning have knowledge of any proposed developments along with the type and cost of housing they will provide.

Quite often SMSAs are comprised of several smaller municipal governments. These smaller government entities understand that for their local communities to prosper they must have expanding job markets and environments in which families wish to live. In order to fully develop their economic potential, nonpartisan economy development agencies are usually established to promote the areas to employers and real estate developers. These agencies can provide a wealth of knowledge as to growth trends and housing needs and opportunities.

As this information is collected, a picture begins to emerge as to the economic health of the local market area. Once the decision has been made to invest in a general market area, more detailed investigation takes place to ascertain what the submarkets are and how they relate to the overall vigor of the general area. As you can imagine, the north, south, east, and west submarkets of any region or city can vary in housing type, demand, and supply. In analyzing the various submarkets, look for such signs as length of time a home is on the market before a sale, median/average home prices, high or low physical occupancy rates for apartments and manufactured home communities, rental rates that vary either way from the overall norm, age of the housing stock, and commercial development in the neighborhood.

Once a full understanding of the entire housing market is known, compare actual costs associated with each housing option. **Table 4–1** is one example of how a housing cost comparison chart might look.

Two stops that are a must during the submarket research are the local zoning department and the school board. The zoning department can assist in determining what zoning regulations impact a particular submarket, such as

1. What zones allow the placement of individual manufactured homes?
2. Can homes be placed anywhere in the county or must they be placed in a manufactured home community?
3. Are there any rent control agencies with jurisdiction over the submarket?
4. Are there any parcels of manufactured home communities zoned raw land in the submarket?

The school board can provide model test scores (for example, SATs) of both middle and senior high students, and in some cases elementary students. These test scores can be compared to other schools in the region as well as national scores to determine the quality of the local school system. This one criteria can determine the long-term vitality of a particular region or submarket.

Before making an investment in any manufactured home community, it is imperative to conduct a complete market survey of all like properties in the SMSA or city. To fully understand the market dynamics, the investor needs to physically see each manufactured home community and speak with the owner or manager. With a minimum amount of research, this survey should look at each of the following areas:

Table 4–1

Housing Cost Comparison Chart

	Conventional Single-Family Home	Rental Apartment Unit	Manufactured Home in a Landlease Community
Cost	$75,000.00		$25,000.00
Down Payment 10%	$7,500.00		$2,500.00
Monthly Payments			
Based upon 30 years @ 9%	$543.12	N/A	
Based upon 15 years @ 11%		N/A	$255.73
Monthly Rent (3 Bdr 2 Bath 1,300 sq. ft.)		$650.00	
Single-section-size Homesite			$200.00
Utilities			
—Water, Sewer	$25.00	$25.00	$25.00
—Trash	$10.00		$10.00
Insurance—Annual (not in total)	($750.00)		($400.00)
—Divided by 12 months	$62.50	$20.83	$29.16
Taxes—Annual (not in total)	($1,000.00)		($250.00)
—Divided by 12 months	$83.33		$20.83
Total Monthly Housing Costs by Housing Type	$723.95	$695.83	$590.72

When an analysis of the income tax benefits is included, the housing cost numbers dramatically improve for the manufactured home and the conventional home, compared to the rental apartment. Manufactured homes in landlease communities generally show a superior cost advantage to other forms of housing in this market, hence manufactured home communities would appear to be a favorable investment.

1. Size—Look at the size of each community by the number of rental homesites and acreage.

2. Rent level—What is the rent quoted to any new resident prospect and what does the rent include, such as water, sewer, trash pickup, lawn care, or cable TV? Are there any incentives being offered to attract new residents?

3. Number of occupied sites—How many sites are occupied as both a raw number and a percentage of the total?

4. Last rent raise and amount—Amount and date of last raise is indicative of the strength of the market. Are there any plans for future raises (in both apartments and communities)?

5. Utilities—Are water and sewer provided by public entity or by private systems for which the community is responsible?

6. Amenities—What does the community have to offer its residents in physical services, and how do these services compare to other communities?

7. Rating—One possibility is a rating of A, B, C, D in reference to both the quality of the community as well as its location.

§ 4.7   Defining the Type of Community to Purchase

There are basically three types of manufactured home communities in which one might invest. The selection of one type over the other is based on the investor comfort with or aversion to risk taking. Each community type carries a different rate of return as well as level of risk. The higher the risk level the higher the potential return, and vice versa.

The three types of manufactured home community investments are as follows:

Stabilized community.   This is a manufactured home community that is currently filled at 93 to 100 percent physical occupancy and has maintained this level for several years. In this situation the investor can earn a return based on his purchase price with little risk of a decrease in the income stream or of losing his money. The return is usually the lowest but the most stable of the three community types.

Turnaround community.   This is a manufactured home community that has been allowed to deteriorate, both economically and physically. The investor purchases low occupancy and deferred maintenance with the intent and plan for curing both and restoring the community to economic health. This return is typically in the mid to high range of the three types of investments.

New development.   In this scenario an investor purchases or options a parcel of land, either zoned or unzoned, and proceeds to develop a new manufactured home community from raw land. With new development, the investor hopes to make the highest return of the three types of investments discussed; however, the possibility for failure is also greatest. If the land is purchased unzoned and must be rezoned, the anticipated return should be even higher.

With these basics in mind, there are a number of physical concerns an investor needs to answer that impact risk as well as profitability:

1.   Is water supplied by public utility or a private system for which the community has responsibility? If water is private, is there a current permit for the well? Does water quality meet federal EPA lead and copper standards as well as local health regulations? Can local officials mandate connecting onto municipal service and, if so, at what cost?

2.   How is wastewater treated—public service, treatment plant, lagoons, septic tank system, or leach field? The public utility alternative offers the least amount of risk to the investor. If the service is private, what responsibility does the community owner have? Will local government officials require connecting onto public service and at what cost? Does the treatment plant have a current Environmental Protection Agency operating permit? Has the plant been operating within or outside of effluent quality levels? Has community age impacted percolation so that septic tanks or leach fields are suffering? What is the true cost of operating each one of these facilities (for example, electricity, outside contractors, chemicals, repairs) and is the facility required to have a licensed EPA-approved operator?

3.   Is the density of the community such that each homesite will accommodate the placement of larger homes that are being purchased by consumers today?

4.   Is the electrical system adequate to accommodate the 150 to 200 amps service required by the modern homes being purchased today?

5.   Based on the age and type of wastewater collection system, is there a groundwater infiltration problem that increases the sewer cost or overtaxes the wastewater treatment system?

6. A lot of older communities were originally built in flood zone areas before such development was prohibited. Is the subject property impacted by flood zone concerns, and if so, how does that impact its ability to lease and re-lease vacant sites or secure financing?

7. Is there, or has there ever been, any type of use on the property that could cause an environmental hazard, for example, gas station, automotive repair facility, underground fuel storage tanks (either home heating fuel or gasoline), old electrical transformers with high levels of PCB, or any buildings with asbestos? Is there a Superfund cleanup site within the same water aquifer that serves the community?

§ 4.8   Cataloging the Surveyed Manufactured Home Communities

In the early years of the manufactured home community industry, when homes were truly mobile, the industry established a rating system so that families moving from one geographic area to another could have some knowledge as to what to expect at their destination. The Woodall rating system qualified communities as One, Two, Three, Four, or Five Star communities with Five Star being the highest possible rating. This system worked very well for decades. Now that manufactured homes and landlease communities have evolved into permanent residences for hundreds of thousands of Americans, and these properties have become institutional-grade investments for many of Wall Street's premier firms, a property rating system should parallel the standard system used with other forms of investment-grade real estate and give the investor a better grasp of the facts at hand.

Most real estate investors grade a property's quality and location because both impact its value. This grading system is A, B, C, and D with A being the highest and D being the worst. Because a property is rated A does not mean it is the best investment possibility, nor does a D mean that a viable investment opportunity does not exist. The rating system is simply a statement as to today's condition. In addition, this rating scale can be very arbitrary, based on the rating user's experience and subjective opinion.

As mentioned earlier, a property's location can have as much impact on value as its physical condition; therefore, both quality and location must be rated. The following is one grading system utilizing quality and location perspective.

A, B, C, D Quality Rating of Manufactured Home Communities

The rating system in reference to a property's quality measures the asset as follows.

1. A RATING—Would indicate the following features are present:
   Curbs and gutters
   Paved off-street parking at each homesite
   Underground storm water collection system
   Amenities to include at least a pool and clubhouse
   All underground utilities
   Standardized installation and setup requirements for each home, e.g., metal or vinyl skirting, sturdy steps
   Security or street lights
   Professional landscaping and signage, especially at entrances
   Uniform, enforced community guidelines (rules and regulations)

2. B RATING—Would indicate features less desirable than those found in an A property:
   Probably no curb or gutter but off-street paved parking
   Minimum amenities of at least a pool and hopefully a clubhouse
   All underground utilities
   Standardized installation requirements but less rigidly enforced than in an A property
   Security or street lights
   Professional landscaping and signage but not as neatly maintained
   Less strict enforcement of community guidelines

3. **C RATING**—Would indicate features less desirable than B properties (probably not an institutional-grade investment asset):

    No curb or gutter but all roads must be paved, with on-street parking

    No storm water collection system

    No amenities or amenities show poor maintenance

    Aboveground utilities

    No standardized installation requirements

    Very few or no security lights

    No landscaped lawns or common areas, with poor or non-existent signage

    No enforcement of community guidelines

4. **D RATING**—Would indicate features less desirable than C properties:

    No curb and gutter, with dirt roads and parking—or maybe pavement but no enforcement of traffic and parking patterns

    Erosion problems with no controls in place

    No amenities, or amenities not maintained or in operational order

    Aboveground utilities

    No standardized installation requirements

    No enforcement of community guidelines

A, B, C, D Location Rating of Manufactured Home Communities

Parameters:

1. PROXIMITY—to jobs, shopping, schools, churches, all of life's necessities.
2. VISIBILITY—how well the community can be seen by general traffic around the area. This includes both primary and secondary roads.
3. ACCESSIBILITY—how easy it is to get into and out of the community.

A LOCATIONS—Near most residents' normal drive pattern to work, school, shopping and known by most local residents because they see it on a regular basis. The community fronts on a primary artery. An example is a community located on a primary artery next to a school, church, shopping district, or other housing development in a fairly well-developed neighborhood.

B LOCATIONS—Further out and on primary or secondary arteries. However, access is easily attained once directions are known. Visibility is usually very good from the roadway. An example is a community fronting on a primary artery with a divided median. This may allow good proximity and visibility but be difficult to get to.

C LOCATIONS—Difficult to find with no visibility. Usually in rural areas but can front on primary or secondary arteries. An example is a community off of an interstate with no immediate access onto the highway, with limited visibility by passing traffic.

D LOCATIONS—Poor proximity, visibility, and accessibility. These communities are tucked away with no directional signage and no roadway frontage in rural areas.

In rating a property, always rate the quality first and the location second. For example, an investor might say, "Cavander's Cove is an A property in a B Location" and indicate this on a market survey as A/B, or say, "Piney Woods is a C property in an A location" and indicate this in the market survey as C/A.

A more comprehensive treatment of such an A, B, C, D rating system will be available in Thomas Horner's soon-to-be-released text: *The Horner 21st Century Rating System for Manufactured Home Landlease Communities*. In the meantime, **Appendix N** contains a summary of the Horner System.

§ 4.9 Summary

A great deal has been covered in this chapter; from setting personal and corporate investment goals to identifying manufactured home community purchase parameters, to sources of prospective acquisitions to the buying process itself. Certainly it is not a simple or quick process. A major lesson to be learned in all of this though is to be patient and diligent, to take one's time and make the effort to effect the right and prudent investment decision.

CHAPTER 5

ESTIMATING VALUE

§ 5.1   Introduction

AN MAI'S PERSPECTIVE
Laurence Allen

§ 5.2   Manufactured Home Community Valuation

§ 5.3   Valuation Premises

§ 5.4   Factors in the Valuation of Manufactured Home Communities

§ 5.5   Valuation

§ 5.6   —Cost or Replacement Approach

§ 5.7   —Sales Comparison Approach

§ 5.8   —Income Approach

§ 5.9   —Reconciliation

§ 5.10   Future Outlook

§ 5.11   Summary

§ 5.1   Introduction

Few exercises better typify man's penchant for simplistic answers to complicated questions than the art of investment real estate valuation. Everyone, it seems, would like to know "right now" how much a subject manufactured home community is worth overall, or some proportionately lesser value per rental homesite. But it just is not that simple if expected to be accurate.

The very best real estate valuations are generally prepared by professional, capable, experienced appraisers who have made this specialty their life's work. It is vital that they have not only a firm grasp on the basics of the valuation discipline, but a working, experiential knowledge of the nuances and peculiarities of various income-property types. This is especially important with manufactured home landlease communities.

To date no one has written a text focusing entirely on the value appraisal of manufactured home communities. The material that follows has been prepared by one of the few MAI appraisers who has specialized in this property type. Laurence Allen has been appraising manufactured home communities for 20 years and is considered to be one of but a handful of experts who know, understand, and apply the industry benchmarks of these income properties to formal valuation reports.

What is an MAI? Simply put, the designation letters stand for Member, Appraisal Institute. The Appraisal Institute is a wholly separate trade association of professional real estate appraisers. The Appraisal Institute provides comprehensive valuation training and eventual certification of real estate appraisers who meet that body's high standards for real estate valuation reporting and professionalism among peers.

Earlier the term "art" was used to describe investment real estate valuation. This was done purposely to distinguish the process from being an empirical science. Appraisers use a problem-solving process (not unlike the one described earlier in **Chapter 2**) to collect pertinent data, apply a variety of formulas, and attempt to understand the property and its operation, as well as prepare charts to compare results generated by various methodology. However, in the final analysis, the appraiser's best estimate of value is a dollar-based snapshot of a given income property in a particular market at a specific point in time. In an instant that picture could change, as new paying or non-paying lessees move in or out, a fire destroys all or part of the facilities, or a major local employer closes its doors or expands and hires more workers.

The real estate valuation process is dynamic. Not only is the final result sensitive to the type changes just described, but interim subvalues, estimated using replacement, market, and income capitalization approaches, are subject to trial and error, accuracy in recording and reporting, and interpretation influences as well. So all this, taken together, demonstrates that the real estate valuation appraisal process is indeed a series of data gathering exercises based on empirical and experiential data, but definitely subject to interpretation and modeling, and sensitive in large part, to the capabilities and background of the appraiser.

AN MAI'S PERSPECTIVE[1]

§ 5.2   Manufactured Home Community Valuation

Real estate valuation is an essential part of the buying and selling process of manufactured home landlease communities. Valuations are preformed by buyers, sellers, and appraisers as part of the acquisition, refinance, and disposition processes. Appraisers are required to be licensed by the state, but buyers and sellers are not when valuing their own properties for acquisition or sale. Buyers and sellers, however, should still understand and use proven valuation techniques in setting their transaction prices. Some of the most common uses for a valuation are to set a listing price, negotiate an acquisition, obtain a mortgage upon acquisition, refinance, and appeal property taxes.

§ 5.3   Valuation Premises

The acquisition and sale of a manufactured home community is one of the most important occasions where accurate property valuations are required. An understanding of valuation techniques is necessary to maximize the effectiveness and accuracy of this process. The following paragraphs introduce and describe the basic valuation considerations as they apply to the value appraisal of manufactured home communities. An understanding of this process will assist one to effectively buy and sell this property type.

Interest Valued

This is the fundamental starting point for any valuation, especially a manufactured home community. There are three interests that can be valued. These are the fee simple, leased fee, and the leasehold. The primary difference among the interests is whether leases are higher or lower than market rent. When the valuation uses market-derived rules of

---

[1] The following material was prepared exclusively for inclusion in this text by Laurence Allen, MAI, of Michigan.

thumb, such as Gross Rent Multipliers and Net Income Multipliers (discussed in § 5.7), the resulting valuation may be inaccurate if the subject property's leases and related rental income are above or below the local market. A leased fee valuation considers the fact that the leases may differ from market, as well as the relationship between current leases and market rents. The buyer may be able to significantly increase the income from the subject property by studying the competitive market and determining that rents are below market and increase them accordingly.

Types of Value

Another important point to clarify before proceeding with the valuation is an understanding of the type value that is needed. Many investors do not understand that there are many different types of value with different definitions. The most commonly utilized value type is market value, but other types include insurable value, assessed value, investment value, and liquidation value. The definition of *market value* is

> The most probable price, as of a specified date, in cash, or in terms equivalent to cash, or in other precisely revealed terms for which the specified property rights should sell after reasonable exposure in a competitive market under all conditions requite to a fair sale, with the buyer and seller each acting prudently, knowledgeable, and for self-interest, and assuming that neither is under undue duress.[2]

The next two types, investment value and liquidation value, are important to understand but rarely used. A property many be worth more to an individual investor than in the market. It could be that the current owner is creating above-market income because he has a positive reputation in the market. He may be able to operate at a lower cost because he buys insurance and supplies in bulk or because he is active in the management himself but does not draw a salary. Additionally he may have a below-market source of capital and is able to buy at a lower than market capitalization rate. All of these characteristics could mean that the manufactured home community has a higher value to a particular owner than to the market. When normal valuation benchmarks

---

[2] Appraisal Institute, The Appraisal of Real Estate 20 (10th ed. 1992).

are applied to this type of operation, a value closer to investment value than market value may be obtained.

Another valuation type is liquidation value. Market value assumes a normal marketing time. If a manufactured home community is old or has to be sold quickly, then the price is often below normal market value. Liquidation value is often 10 to 20 percent less than market value. This is a substantial loss to take when a property must be sold quickly.

Market value is the normal benchmark to use when buying, selling, or refinancing a manufactured home community. The following sections assume that the value being discussed is market value and that the interest being valued is fee simple.

§ 5.4 Factors in the Valuation of Manufactured Home Communities

The real estate appraiser, broker, manufactured home community buyer, and seller generally base value estimates upon the physical characteristics of the subject property, legal status of the property, and economic characteristics of the property and local market. Following is a summary and outline of important factors that should be considered when valuing a manufactured home community.

Physical Characteristics

The inspection of the physical property includes the land, the on-site improvements, and building improvements. The property contains many characteristics that are important to the buyer. Some of the most important include the amount of land, especially the existence of expansion land or excess land that may be able to be developed or sold off to provide additional value. Environmental conditions have now moved to the forefront. A phase I environmental inspection or audit is critical before fully committing to purchase a manufactured home community. In addition to ascertaining soil and water conditions, floodplain maps should be reviewed to determine if flooding is a potential problem. The existence of wetlands is a detriment to development most of the time, but can also be a positive aesthetic amenity. The existence of municipal water and sewer, versus wells and water treatment facilities, should be carefully studied and considered. Location attributes such as accessibility, road access, and visibility are also important.

After land, the improvements are the most important characteristic of a manufactured home community. **Table 5–1** is an appraiser's list of 13 improvement characteristics of a manufactured home community that should be noted during inspection for valuation purposes. The 1 to 5 rating (similar to the One-to-Five Star and A to D ratings in **Chapter 4**) provides an initial indication of the quality of the property's improvement characteristics.

Table 5–1

Appraiser's List of 13 Improvement Characteristics

Characteristics	Rating				
	1 (low)	2	3	4	5 (high)
Attractive entrance					
Wide, paved streets					
Curbs present					
Sidewalk present					
Landscaping					
Underground utilities					
Paved off-street parking					
Street lights					
Patios at least 8' × 30'					
Number of multisectional sites					
Laundry facilities					
Swim pool/recreational amenities					
Community building					
TOTALS					

The rating of improvements provides one of the best indications of the quality of the manufactured home community. The higher the score the higher the quality. Also of concern is the age and condition of improvements and any need for major repairs or replacements in the immediate future.

Legal Status

The legal description must be checked to ensure it describes all the property that is to be purchased. Easements are reviewed to ensure they do not interfere with potential expansion. The zoning ordinance is reviewed to verify that the property conforms and that expansion land is also properly zoned. The presence of rent control or restrictive landlord-tenant legislation should also be considered. Existing assessment and tax rates are researched to determine if the property is over- or underassessed and when an increase in the assessment or tax rates may occur.

Economic Characteristics

A thorough market analysis is an important step in the valuation of a manufactured home community. The first step is to define the local market area. The market area is usually defined in terms of the locations of competitive properties. It is necessary to physically visit and survey competitive manufactured home communities in the market area. This generally will include at least three to five such properties. These can be "shopped" to determine number of rental sites, physical occupancies, present rent levels, and the variety of on-site features and amenities. **Table 5–2** is a summary of rental data that provides an example of the type of information collected. Much of this information should already be available to the appraiser as a result of the buyer's fieldwork.

This data and other characteristics of the market are reviewed and analyzed in order to determine the strength of the existing market and the market position of the subject manufactured home community of terms of its rent level and tenancy. As part of the market survey, it is important to visit the planning departments of the municipalities that comprise the competitive market to determine if any other additions to the supply of manufactured home community sites are proposed or if any other new multifamily properties are planned. It is also helpful to study a zoning map and masterplan to determine if vacant land exists that is zoned or planned for manufactured home communities.

In addition to the competitive supply, it is important to look at the demand factors. What are the current population and demographic

Table 5–2

Market Survey Summary of Property Data

Property #	Existing Sites	Rent	Physical Occupancy	Year Built	Overall Quality/ Condition	Average Homesite Size	Resident Responsibilities
1*	127	$175	98.4%	1970	Average	60×120	Utilities/Trash
2	230	$270	100.0%	1987	Excellent	60×125	Utilities
3	96	$275 SS $330 MS	97.9%	1970	Good	50×100	Utilities
4	108	$225 SS $240 MS $261 MS	98.1%	1972	Good	60×120	Utilities/Trash

* The first property is generally the "subject property," or the property being valued.
1 SS is a site that can only accommodate a single-section home
2 MS is a site that can accommodate a multiple-section home

characteristics of the market area? What has been the historic rate of growth, if any? What is the projected rate of growth? Household growth should also be studied in a similar manner. Other characteristics that are important to research include the income and age distribution within the market area. This information is available from the 1990 U.S. Census, as well as planning agencies that oversee the local market area.

The final step is to put the supply and demand data together to determine the current supply-demand balance and the likelihood of oversupply or shortages of rental homesites in the future. The market position of the subject property can then be estimated, including the rents and physical occupancies that should be possible in the subject manufactured home community.

§ 5.5 Valuation

The previous section describes the basic facts about the property and the market that are important to understand before attempting to place a value on a manufactured home community. These physical, legal, and economic characteristics form the foundation for value. The next step is to consider and apply the three traditional approaches to value: cost, sales comparison, and capitalization of income. The three approaches arrive at value estimates from different points of view.

The *cost or replacement approach* is based upon the principle of substitution, where the premise is that an investor will not pay more for an existing manufactured home community than the cost of acquiring raw land and constructing another such property. The next of the three approaches to value is the *sales comparison approach*. This approach to value involves a comparative analysis of recent sales of similar manufactured home communities in the market area. It is most reliable when there is an abundance of verified transactions to review and when one has access to true and accurate information about the transactions. The third approach to value is the *income capitalization approach*. This approach is the easiest to apply and is generally considered to be the most reliable of the three approaches when valuing a manufactured home community.

§ 5.6 —Cost or Replacement Approach

The basic steps in the cost or replacement approach to value include estimating present raw land value and the replacement cost of the improvements, and subtracting for losses in value, such as physical depreciation of said improvements and functional and external obsolescence.

Land sales that are of comparable size, functional shape, useable topography, have access to public utilities, and the proper zoning for a manufactured home community are often difficult to find. Given that diligent research results in the identification of several comparable land sales that can be verified, the next step is to break the prices down into units of comparison. For manufactured home community land, the most common units of comparison are the sale price per acre and the sale price per rental homesite. For example, a 57 acre parcel of land, zoned for a manufactured home community at six homesites per acre, sold in 1995 for $342,000. The units of comparison would be $6,000/acre ($342,000/57), and $1,000/homesite ($342,000/342 homesites). If the subject property has 300 rental homesites on 50 acres, the indicated land value would be $300,000 or 300 acres × $1,000/site. This process becomes more complicated when comparing land sale, terms of sale, homesite densities, useable land areas, utilities, and location factors.

The next step in the cost approach is the estimation of replacement cost of improvements. This can be done by studying the actual costs of similar, recently built manufactured home communities and by studying standard replacement costs in reference manuals such as the *Marshall Valuation Service*.[3] **Table 5–3** demonstrates the proposed cost breakdown for the expansion of a 100-homesite manufactured home community in the Midwest.

Manufactured home community costs can vary significantly with the layout and design, location, and quality of improvements. The previous cost factors do not include the cost of a community building, any recreational amenities, interest expenses during construction, lease-up costs, and developers' overhead and profit.

---

[3] Marshall & Swift Valuation Service, 911 Wilshire Blvd., 16th Floor, Los Angeles, CA 90017; (213) 683-9000.

Table 5–3

Development Costs

Item	Cost	Cost/site
Earthwork	$14,400	$1,440
Concrete drives	$12,500	$1,250
Asphalt roads	$10,800	$1,080
Sanitary sewers	$7,300	$730
Storm sewers	$7,100	$710
City water service	$5,800	$580
Engineering fees	$4,400	$440
Concrete curb	$3,700	$370
Electrical	$2,400	$240
City sewer tap fees	$1,000	$100
Mailboxes	$500	$50
Miscellaneous	$100	$10
TOTAL	$70,000	$7,000

Another approach for estimating manufactured home community development costs per site, by quality of community, is available through textual resources, such as the aforementioned Marshall & Swift Valuation Service:

Quality	Cost/Site
Average Quality	$ 6,003
Good Quality	$ 8,590
Excellent Quality	$11,183

The *good quality* community is one that caters to larger manufactured homes and represents the median for permanent manufactured home communities. These costs include engineering, grading, street paving, patios and walks, sewer, water, gas, electrical, building, and miscellaneous. The costs do not, however, include the cost of the land, the marketing costs to achieve initial in-fill occupancy, or developers overhead and profit.

The next step in the cost approach to value is to make deductions for all losses in value from the cost when new. This can include losses due to functional inadequacies, such as streets that are unnecessarily wide, too small rental homesites, or a waste treatment facility of inadequate size (functional obsolescence). Another type of value loss is a loss due to adverse land uses in the neighborhood or depressed and overbuilt market conditions (external obsolescence).

The total of the replacement cost of the improvements, depreciation allowance, plus land value results in an estimate of value by the cost approach. Even though this approach may not be the primary indicator of value for a manufactured home community, it does provide some important information about the market. In a seller's market, such a property may sell for more than its replacement cost. In a buyer's market, the price may drop below replacement cost. The cost approach provides a benchmark for equilibrium pricing that can be used to decide if the property is a good buy or a risky buy at the time of consideration.

§ 5.7 —Sales Comparison Approach

The sales comparison approach to value is also based upon the principle of substitution in that a buyer generally will not pay more for a particular manufactured home community than the price that other investors are paying for similar nearby communities. This approach involves research into sale prices compared to the subject property, and the values are adjusted to account for differences in the physical and economic characteristics.

The sources of sales data for manufactured home communities vary but include real estate brokers who specialize in the sale of this property type, appraisers who are active in the local market area, and county assessors who keep track of sales of income properties in the jurisdiction. By way of example, **Table 5–4** summarizes four sales of manufactured home communities with data giving pertinent physical and economic characteristics.

The most important units of comparisons among these sales of manufactured home communities are the sale price per homesite, the Gross Rent Multiplier (GRM), and the Net Income Multiplier (NIM) rate. These units of comparison provide benchmarks for the valuation of a subject manufactured home community.

Table 5-4

Summary of Manufactured Home Communities Sales

Property #	# Sites	Land size (acres)	Year Built	Quality/ Condition	Utilities	GRM	NIM	Price per site
1	426	88.00	1980	Excellent	All	6.30	11.67	$17,878
2	55	29.80	1955	Average	Well/septic	4.69	7.87	$11,818
3	72	20.60	1955	Average	Water/septic	5.27	9.58	$12,639
4	100	73.80	1977	Good	Water/septic	4.75	9.36	$13,100

The next step in the valuation is to adjust the sale price per homesite for various characteristics that differ from the subject property. These elements of comparisons often include differing conditions of sale, market conditions, terms of sale, location, utilities, age and condition, quality, and other physical characteristics. The Gross Rent Multiplier (GRM) and Net Income Multiplier (NIM) rate typically are not adjusted. The rates from the most similar manufactured home communities are selected from the range indicated by the sales. The adjusted price per homesite, Gross Rent Multiplier, and Net Income Multiplier are then applied to the number of homesites to indicate a value. These units of comparisons are used by real estate appraisers and investors. Examples of how these units of comparisons can be utilized are as follows:

Price per site.   This can be approached two ways. First, given a 200-site manufactured home community on the market for $2,400,000, the price per homesite in this case would be $12,000/site. An investor might say that he does not plan to spend more than $10,000 per homesite (indicating a mid-quality manufactured home community in some markets, a lower-quality property in another) and no more than $2,000,000 overall (depending on the degree of leverage available and the buyer's creditworthiness), meaning he is seeking a 200+ site property ($2,000,000 ÷ $10,000/site = 200 homesite size).

Gross Rent Multiplier or GRM.   This is a quick comparison tool. Assuming a known property is worth $2,000,000 (recently sold for that amount) and produced $480,000 in rents last year, the GRM = 4.16 or 4.2 ($2,000,000 ÷ $480,000 rent). Apply this 4.2 factor to another property (subject property) that is generating $400,000/year in rent; the GRM-calculated value is approximately $1,680,000 or ($400,000 × 4.2 factor).

Net Operating Income Multiplier or NOI Multiplier.   This is similar to the GRM but probably a degree more accurate because it allows for the influence of operating expenses. In the GRM calculation, a property with $480,000 annual gross rent was cited. If the NOI is $288,000 (assuming an OER of 40 percent), and the recent sale price is $2,000,000, the NOI Multiplier would be 6.94 ($2,000,000 ÷ $288,000). Applying the 6.94 factor to the second GRM example of $240,000 rent (again assuming 40 percent OER), the NOI Multiplier value would be $1,665,600 or $240,000 × 6.94.

§ 5.8   —Income Approach

The third approach to value is the income approach. A manufactured home community is an income-producing real estate asset. It is typically developed, owned, and operated with the objectives of creating value as well as a return on the required investment by renting homesites to homeowners who will pay rent that is high enough to cover the operating expenses. The most commonly employed technique of valuation is the direct capitalization of net operating income. This technique involves the following steps:

1. By market analysis, estimate the market rent level that the property is capable of achieving.
2. Deduct an appropriate allowance for vacancy and credit losses to arrive at effective gross income.
3. Deduct the estimated operating expenses to arrive at the net operating income (NOI).
4. Capitalize the NOI with an appropriate capitalization rate to yield an estimate of value.

The first step is to obtain a three-year operating history of the property. These statements should be restructured, if necessary, to reflect normal actual operating costs. Often depreciation and interest expenses are included. These need to be taken out because a purchase will involve a new capital structure and the object here is to arrive at net income before interest and depreciation. Another change that often is made is that a management fee is added to the operating expenses. A normal management fee among manufactured home communities is 5 percent of effective gross income. Another adjustment that may be necessary is to remove capital improvement costs that were expensed, such as street repaving, clubhouse roof replacement, or waste treatment plant renovation.

The next step is to compare actual operating history with expense levels of other similar nearby communities. This is done as a check on the expenses of the subject property. For this comparison there are two major units of comparison. One is to compare the costs per site and the other is to compare operating expense ratios or OERs. **Table 5–5** is a listing of operating costs from four manufactured home communities, with the costs per site and operating expense ratios calculated. All

Table 5-5
Summary of Operating Costs from Manufactured Home Communities

Category	MHC #1		MHC #2		MHC #3		MHC #4	
	Cost/site	% of income	Cost/site	% of income	Cost/site	% of income	Cost/site	% of income
Rental income	$2,752	100%	$2,760	100%	$2,791	100%	$2,700	100%
Other income	$0	0%	$0	0%	$0	0%	$0	0%
Effective gross income	$2,752	100%	$2,760	100%	$2,791	100%	$2,700	100%
Utilities	$105	4%	$140	5%	$166	6%	$31	1%
Management fee	$138	5%	$138	5%	$134	5%	$135	5%
Payroll	$36	1%	$104	4%	$133	5%	$68	3%
Administrative	$43	2%	$20	1%	$13	0%	$15	1%
Maintenance/repair	$61	2%	$70	3%	$100	4%	$80	3%
Grounds services	$190	7%	$136	5%	$32	1%	$81	3%
Taxes & insurance	$645	23%	$528	19%	$467	17%	$402	15%
Total expenses	$1,218	44%	$1,136	41%	$1,045	37%	$812	30%
Net operating income	$1,534	56%	$1,624	59%	$1,746	63%	$1,888	70%

numbers are shown in thousands, for example, \$2,752 = \$2,752,000. The expense per site comparison is often more reliable because operating expense ratios can differ significantly among manufactured home communities that have different rent levels but similar operating costs.

A pro forma income statement can now be developed that reflects the information known about the subject manufactured home community. This would include the following:

1. Gross potential rental income: Here consider the current rents at the manufactured home community, and market rents from the market survey, as well as the number of homesites on the property. The result would be a projection for the next 12 months of the rent potential at market rents, if these new rents can be implemented as leases turnover.

2. Vacancy and credit loss: This should reflect the actual experience at the subject manufactured home community, tempered with the normal vacancy levels found in the competitive market area.

3. Effective gross income: This is the gross rental income less an allowance for vacancy and credit loss plus miscellaneous income. This generally does not include new and resale home revenues, which are usually handled as a separate profit center.

4. Operating expenses: This is projected on an item by item basis, based upon a review of the historic costs, and a comparison of these costs with costs at other comparable communities. Property taxes can be projected independently, based upon the current assessment and tax rate.

5. Net operating income: This is the net result of taking the effective gross income less the normal operating expenses but not including debt service.

The next step in the income approach to value is to capitalize the pro forma net operating income into an indication of value through the use of direct capitalization with a capitalization rate. There are several methods of developing capitalization rates. The two most common methods are market extraction and mortgage equity buildup.

Market extraction.   The four sales that were previously summarized (see **Table 5–4**) indicate a range in capitalization rates from 8.57 percent to 12.71 percent. This is the reciprocal of the net income multiplier, that is, 11.67 NIM = 8.57 capitalization rate (1/NIM = 1/11.67 = .0857). The capitalization rate is a property's net operating income divided by its sale price. An 8 to 12 percent range is typically found in the manufactured home landlease communities market, which is often described as a two-tier market. The top tier is the institutional market, which buys high-quality, large, investment-grade manufactured home communities with capitalization rates in the 8 to 10 percent range. The second tier is comprised of individual investors and syndicates, which compete for the lesser quality and smaller-sized manufactured home communities and buy in the 10 to 12 percent range of capitalization rate, often planning to improve their investments so that they can eventually sell in the 8 to 10 percent capitalization rate range.

Mortgage equity. This method typically reflects the local investor who will buy based upon a down payment and a mortgage. The formula for deriving an overall rate is called the *band of investment technique* and is shown as:

$$Ro = (M \times Rm) + ((1 - M)) \times Re)$$

Where:

Ro = the overall rate or capitalization rate

M = the loan-to-value ratio

Rm = the loan constant

Re = the equity dividend rate

An example of this would be a 75 percent loan-to-value ratio (M), an interest rate of 9 percent with a 25-year amortization rate (Rm = 10.90 percent), and a 10 percent equity dividend rate (Re).

$$Ro = (.75 \times .1007) + ((1 - .75) \times .10)$$
$$Ro = .1005 \text{ cap rate}$$

The particular loan-to-value ratio, interest rate, loan amortization term, and equity dividend rate would all depend upon the particular manufactured home community and the time period of the financing.

Another similar method of deriving a capitalization rate is sometimes called the *lender's method* because it entirely reflects underwriting criteria. The formula is as follows:

$$Ro = DCR \times M \times Rm$$

Where:

DCR   =   the debt coverage ratio

M   =   loan-to-value ratio

Rm   =   mortgage constant

The only new factor is the debt coverage rate. The debt coverage ratio is calculated by taking the net operating income and dividing it by the debt service (principle and interest). With a 1.30 debt coverage ratio, the calculation and the resulting capitalization rate is:

$$Ro = 1.30 \times .75 \times .1007$$
$$Ro = .09818$$

In this case both mortgage equity techniques result in an estimated overall rate of approximately 10 percent.

The final step in the income approach is to capitalize the projected net operating income (NOI) by the overall capitalization rate. This is done with the traditional valuation formula $V = I/R$, which indicates that value (V) equals income (I) divided by rate (R). The income is the net operating income and the rate is the overall capitalization rate. For example, if the net operating income is $1350/site and the overall rate is 10 percent, then the indicated value per site would be $13,500/site.

V = $1,350/.10

V = $13,500/site

§ 5.9   —Reconciliation

The last step in the valuation of the manufactured home community is the reconciliation of values from the three traditional approaches to value. Each approach results in a value estimate based upon different considerations.

The cost approach was based upon the replacement cost of the improvements less depreciation plus land value. In general the cost approach produces a value within the general range of the other two approaches. If it is below the indications from the other approaches, it may mean that the market is valuing manufactured home communities based upon current popularity, or it could mean that there is a shortage of zoned properties that is artificially inflating sale prices and rents. Both would be red flags for investors. If the cost approach value is above the other approaches, it could be because values are depressed due to such things as rent controls, the threat of rent controls, or an oversupply in the market. In either case the cost approach can provide valuable insight into the current state of the market.

The sales and income approaches generally result in similar values as long as the value is adequately considering all appropriate factors. In some cases the income approach may be below the comparable sales value because current operators have allowed rents to remain at below-market levels. In other cases the income approach could be low or high because the current management has above- or below-normal operating costs due to their management style or reporting system. In either case if rents and expenses are adjusted to reflect normal levels, then the income approach generally falls in line with the comparable sales value. Sometimes in certain markets there is a lack of sales of manufactured home communities, and to perform this approach sales data is used from other markets. In this case more adjustments are required that may produce a less reliable result.

In the final analysis, the three approaches are viewed as checks and balances. Each can provide valuable information on the state of the market. The final value estimate gives most weight to the approach or approaches that have the most current and reliable information and that best reflect the local market. In general the income approach, when properly done, is the most reliable approach, followed by the sales comparison, and then the cost approach.

§ 5.10 Future Outlook

Manufactured home communities can make an excellent investment. The economics of ownership and operation are superior to many types of real estate investment. The have stable operating costs and generally low capital expenditure requirements. Competition is limited due to the difficulty in finding and zoning land for a manufactured home community. They have stable occupancies and very low turnover rates. The outlook is for continuing periodic rent increases, low physical vacancies, and improved recognition of the product as a quality affordable housing alternative and lifestyle. In the long term, the graying of America will also provide continuing growth in demand. An understanding of the market, the product, solid market research, and application of the three traditional approaches to value provides the foundation necessary for accurate valuations and informed acquisitions and dispositions of manufactured home communities.

§ 5.11 Summary

It should be readily apparent by now that there are a variety of ways to estimate the value of an income-producing property. Each methodology obviously has its merits and shortfalls, but taken together and ensuring a degree of accuracy and veracity, one can estimate the approximate value of an anticipated acquisition or a presently held asset and set an asking or sale price.

CHAPTER 6

THE DUE DILIGENCE PERIOD: PREPARING FOR CLOSING

§ 6.1   Introduction

ANOTHER PERSPECTIVE
Barbara Alley

§ 6.2   Purpose of Physical Due Diligence

§ 6.3   Assemble Team

§ 6.4   Request Information from Seller

§ 6.5   Set up Meetings

§ 6.6   Review Manufactured Home Community Records and Inventory

§ 6.7   Investigate Manufactured Home Community, Permits and Licenses, and Cost Projections

§ 6.8   —Physical Examination Agenda

§ 6.9   —Regulatory Agencies and Utility Companies

§ 6.10   —Feasibility Projections

§ 6.11   Arranging Transaction Financing

§ 6.12   Preparing for Closing

§ 6.13   Summary

§ 6.1   Introduction

A great deal of activity takes place between the time a seller accepts a buyer's offer to purchase—whether by letter of intent or formal contract—and when the transaction is consummated at the closing table.

For the purpose of this chapter, those key activities include, but are certainly not limited to, a series of off-premises surveys and on-site inspections, the securing of necessary transaction financing, preparation for closing, and arranging for property management takeover.

These four activities occur consecutively and often overlap. For example, much of the local market and competition information gleaned during the off-premises and on-site due diligence inspections not only influence the type and amount of financing obtained, but have a bearing on whether the scheduled closing takes place on time, is delayed (as is often the case), or even speeded up—a rare and risky occurrence. Much of the preclosing survey and inspection data is directly tied to a smooth and successful property management takeover by the new owner.

The term "due diligence" has been in common parlance among real estate investment professionals for a long time. Interestingly, it appears in few real estate text glossaries or indexes. It is generally understood, however, to refer to the period of time between the seller's acceptance of an offer to purchase a specific parcel of real estate (for the purposes of this text, an income-producing property) and the commencement of closing the transaction. The due diligence period includes all of those off-premises surveys and on-site inspections that hopefully lead to peace of mind for the buyer and a workable plan for taking control of the property. In fact, the original offer should be made contingent on the successful completion of such fact-finding efforts by the buyer. So the term "due diligence" is used liberally here to describe a buyer's activities during this critical preclosing period of time—although the seller has a responsibility to provide complete and accurate information and data to the buyer during this time as well.

ANOTHER PERSPECTIVE[1]

§ 6.2   Purpose of Physical Due Diligence

The purpose of due diligence is to give the prospective property purchaser the information needed to accurately calculate the feasibility of

---

[1] The due diligence period is so important, so detailed, and so time-consuming that it only makes sense to learn the basics—expressed in five key points—from an expert

the anticipated purchase. It is a thorough investigation of the manufactured home community, both above and below ground, including its physical aspects and status with various regulatory agencies having jurisdiction over it. The feasibility of purchasing a landlease manufactured home community is dependent on a reasonable purchase price, the capital required to rectify existing physical problems with the property, and estimating the operating funds required for existing and ongoing maintenance and operation of the property. Also of importance in the feasibility analysis is the occupancy rate and the rental structure of the property, as well as the anticipated marketing costs and time and effort required to eliminate vacancies.

The following sections outline information required from evaluating the physical condition of the property, as well as from the research and collection of community records and inventory, and from the investigation of all required operating permits and licenses. **Figure 6–1** is a diagram showing the elements that comprise the due diligence process.

§ 6.3   Assemble Team

The due diligence investigation requires expertise in a number of areas, such as engineering, accounting, marketing, financing, and feasibility analysis. This expertise may be provided by one or more persons. The due diligence option period or contingency period in the purchase agreement should be structured with enough time for all team members to assemble their information and enough time for the prospective purchaser to assimilate the findings and project the feasibility of purchasing the property. The absolute minimum due diligence period for a fact-finding team is three days on-site and one day in the office to prepare the final report. The average due diligence period ranges from one to two months.

---

in manufactured home community due diligence, Barbara Alley of Alley & Associates. Suffice it to say that the following information has been developed and field-tested by her and her husband's firm over the past 10 years.

KEY ELEMENTS OF THE DUE DILIGENCE PROCESS

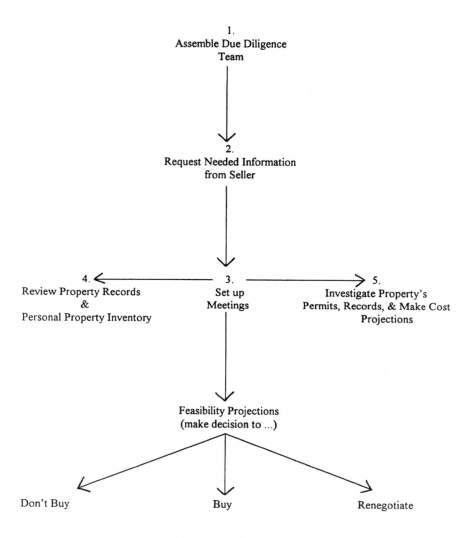

Alley & Associates, Inc.

Figure 6–1. The due diligence process.

§ 6.4   Request Information from Seller

Considerable time, effort, and money will be wasted if the due diligence team arrives at the property without information needed for their review being available to them. The following is a checklist of the information that the seller should have ready for the due diligence team upon their arrival.

Pre–Due Diligence Checklist

____ City or County Permits

____ CO's for all buildings

____ Storm water management permit

____ Consumption use permits

____ Sewage treatment plant

____ Sewage treatment records

____ Water supply permits

____ Water supply records

____ Approvals for sanitary collection system

____ Approvals for domestic water distribution system

____ Boundary survey including all easements and encumbrances

____ Meter records available for both treatment plant and water supply wells

____ As-built drawings of all improvements

____ Have maintenance people available

____ Have treatment plant and water supply operator available

____ Permits for swimming pools, jacuzzi, and so forth.

It is rare for a seller to have all the needed information, but any data and materials that can be provided will speed up the process and simplify the work required of the due diligence team.

§ 6.5   Set up Meetings

It will also be necessary to interview a variety of agencies and resource persons during the course of the due diligence investigation. These persons and agencies should be contacted prior to the due diligence team arriving and specific times set up for meetings and interviews.

The due diligence effort can be characterized as two separate investigations. The first is reviewing manufactured home community records and inventory, and the second, investigating the manufactured home community, permits, and cost projections. The accounting team normally reviews property records and inventory. The engineering or technical personnel investigate the physical aspects of the property and the applicable permits and prepare operating and capital cost estimates.

§ 6.6   Review Manufactured Home Community Records and Inventory

All property records should be reviewed. These include various property files, resident files—including leases, and records of drinking water and wastewater effluent reports from regulatory agencies.

To analyze the financial feasibility of the community, it is necessary to determine its past, present, and anticipated future gross income as well as corresponding operating expenses and resultant net operating income. This is accomplished by reviewing the financial records of the property and interviewing staff personnel.

§ 6.7   Investigate Manufactured Home Community, Permits and Licenses, and Cost Projections

Following is a general list of items to include in the physical inspection and evaluation of the manufactured home community:

Site Investigation Checklist

_____ Zoning classification
_____ Homesite configuration

_____ Street size, congestion, and condition
_____ Drainage type and adequacy
_____ Sewerage handling and adequacy
_____ Domestic water service
_____ Irrigation system
_____ Floodplain presence
_____ Electrical service
_____ Oil, gas, or propane service
_____ Central facilities
_____ Vegetation particulars
_____ Vacant homesites
     _____ Size
     _____ Off-sets
     _____ Impact fees
     _____ Set-up costs, and so forth
_____ Potential to expand existing property
_____ Environmental audit
     _____ For a very comprehensive Due Diligence Checklist see **Appendix O.**
     _____ For a summary description of phase I, II, and III environmental audits, see **Appendix I.**

§ 6.8   —Physical Examination Agenda

Following is a recommended agenda to be used during the physical examination of the on-site manufactured home community:

Meet with manager.   It is essential to meet with the manufactured home community's manager prior to examining the property, to discuss information provided and still needed for the due diligence review. At this time arrange for subsequent meetings with office staff and maintenance personnel.

Review as-built plans and permits.   A review of all existing as-built plans for the property acquaints the buyer with the physical layout of the manufactured home community and the construction standards to which it was built. Once such items as cross-sectional details of pavement construction, utility placement, types of building materials used, and other related physical specifications have been determined, a list of items of concern is developed. This list is investigated in detail in the field and during conversations with maintenance personnel. Also, an engineering expert reviewing the as-builts can often estimate the probability of drainage problems and adequacy of water pressure throughout the property, as well as point out features and criteria that might suggest future potential problems.

After reviewing appropriate permits and licenses made available at the property, a list should be compiled of missing documents and oversight agencies contacted to substantiate their status.

Community drive-through.   At this point, it is helpful to have a small map of the property to use during drive-through inspections. These drive-throughs provide further familiarity with the streets, wastewater treatment plant and lift stations locations, water wells and tanks, RV storage areas, maintenance facilities, recreational areas, drainage swells, and landscaping peculiarities. The drive-throughs also give the inspector an impression of the overall condition of the manufactured home community, as well as the roadways, concrete curbs and gutters, parking pads, turf establishment, the homes proper, and other physical features that can be observed from the street.

Meet with maintenance personnel.   No one knows the physical condition of the community better than those responsible for its upkeep and maintenance. It is extremely important that maintenance personnel are honest and cooperative during their response to inquiries and questions. Following are the types of questions that the maintenance personnel should be able to answer:

1.   Are there any physical or functional problems that should be addressed or repaired on the property?
2.   What is the condition of the sanitary sewer and what maintenance problems have occurred during the last three years?
3.   What is the condition of the water distribution system, is there consistent adequate pressure in the system, how many waterline

breaks have occurred during the past three years, and how were they handled?

4. What kinds of recurring drainage problems occur, and specifically, which areas of the property are most prone to drainage problems?

5. What type electrical distribution system is in place, what kind of pedestals are in use, and what is the physical condition of the pedestals?

It is especially helpful at this point to color-code a street diagram of the property with electric lines marked in red, gas and oil in yellow CATV and communication in orange, water in blue, and sewer in green.

Talk to residents.   Prior to talking to the residents of the community, the community manager must be informed. A wealth of information is available from residents. By talking to residents, certain areas warranting further investigation will likely be determined.

Detailed inspection of community.   Sequentially, it is time for a detailed inspection of the manufactured home community. This generally is an actual walk through the community counting, inspecting, and documenting each homesite and physically inspecting items listed on the Site Investigation Checklist (see § 6.7).

Meet with agencies and utilities.   In § 6.9 is a detailed list of governmental agencies and utilities that should be contacted. In addition to regulatory agencies and utility companies, a meeting of the due diligence team and the seller or seller's representatives should be effected. The due diligence team attempts to establish a neutral rapport with the seller, which eases the exchange of key and sensitive information in a nonthreatening atmosphere. Information obtained in this fashion often includes confirmation of the official zoning of the property, whether there are any outstanding violations with county or state agencies, and a copy of the C.O. or certificate of occupancy, if required. This is also the time to obtain information regarding replacement of existing homes. Additionally, off-sets, impact fees, and set-up costs relative to vacant homesites will be noted.

Further inspection of the community. At this point in the process, problem areas have likely been identified. It is time for a more detailed inspection so that a cost estimate can be made for the correction of existing problems or the anticipated ongoing maintenance expenses associated with these physical problems. This is usually the time when outside consultants or testing companies are hired to locate water leaks, further investigate wastewater treatment facilities, evaluate pavement condition, and offer advice on any number of other problems that have been identified.

Meeting of buyer and team coordinator. Periodic meetings between the prospective purchaser and team coordinator to discuss preliminary findings of the due diligence team is highly recommended. These meetings provide a forum for the exchange of information regarding the community and provides an opportunity to probe for additional unaddressed concerns.

Final report. A report including all of the documentation gathered during the due diligence investigation is prepared by the team. Each subject in this chapter is presented in detail, including estimates to repair or replace as appropriate. An overall evaluation of the property is rendered, including a discussion of the internal and external conditions, visual aesthetics, degree of physical deterioration, and any functional problems that were noted. Factoring in the age of the manufactured home community, income and expense factors, cost to refurbish, and occupancy levels, enough information will be provided to assist the prospective purchaser in making an informed final decision about the property.

§ 6.9 —Regulatory Agencies and Utility Companies

Many manufactured home communities were zoned and built before FEMA, the Federal Emergency Management Act, came into being. If the property is entirely or partially located in the floodplain, this could have serious consequences as to the eventual number of renewable rental homesites available as current residents relocate and the new property owner is not allowed to rerent the homesite because it lies in the floodplain.

The following is a list of government departments that generally have jurisdiction over the manufactured home communities. Included in the list is the type of information generally available from them. Utility companies are listed as sources of ownership, maintenance, and costs.

Local

1. Planning Department: zoning file, floodplain maps, needs for the possibilities of variances, zoning and land use maps and updated data, information about other agencies, and presence of impact fees.
2. Engineering Department: drainage information; utilities concerns, for example, sewer, water, electrical, and gas; local soil maps; proposed area improvements and related assessments; impact fees.
3. Utility Department: sewer and water rates; tap-in fees, impact fees; sewer and water capacity requirements.
4. Building Department: Certificates of Occupancy, permits in force, local codes, known violations and records thereof.
5. Register of Deeds: property ownership, easements and encumbrances, legal description and acreage. A title company can also provide this important information.
6. Power Company: electric, natural gas; types of approved systems; who owns and maintains.
7. Telephone Company: related matters.
8. Cable Television: who owns system, maintains, and invoices users; existence of a formal agreement between property and cable company; whether it can be renegotiated.

State

1. Drainage District.
2. Board of Health: copy of license; property records, pool and jacuzzi reports; violation notices, if any.
3. DER-EPA (Department of Environmental Regulation and Environmental Protection Agency): wastewater treatment plant discharge permit, effluent testing results, flow records, treatment plant violations, domestic water supply permit, domestic water

test results, domestic water violations, domestic water flow records.

4. Utility Commission: rules, regulations; status of utility.

§ 6.10 —Feasibility Projections

At this point, having spent several days at the property consulting with experts, there should be enough information regarding the physical condition of the community and income streams being generated to begin feasibility projections. The buyer meets with the accounting representative/team member to review the operating expenses, rental structure, types of income, other expenses, and capital cost information. In addition, there must be a review of all community records and verification of homesite inventory, physical and economic occupancy rates, and present and anticipated marketing costs. Another meeting with the engineering/technical team members is required to review existing physical problems, costs of repair or reconstruction, and the capital reserve required for existing and ongoing property operations to begin feasibility projections.

Feasibility projections, also called pro forma multiyear operating budgets, incorporate and reflect the anticipated influences of property and market-related factors and variables. Such factors include physical and economic occupancy levels, periodic rent adjustments and ranges, additional income streams, operating expense economies, and the overall impact of improved management and favorable (hopefully) market conditions.

Such projections and budgets are often prepared manually, tracing said influences from year-to-year on both income and expense sides of the ledger, usually showing a gradual if not dramatic improvement in the bottom lines of net operating income and cash flow before taxes. In today's computerized business environment, it is commonplace for this otherwise time-consuming exercise to be performed automatically with one or another brand of spreadsheet software. A caution here is that while manual calculations are indeed time-consuming, the nature of the activity forces an analyst to pay closer attention to the data as it changes from month-to-month and year-to-year. Just be extra careful not to make simple computational errors. See **Appendix P** for a sample operating statement.

The purpose of the feasibility and budget exercise is to see if and how quickly one can turn a profit with a planned acquisition, how quickly or slowly one will achieve desired ROI goals, and whether the sale price and anticipated financing needs must be modified in some way. So do not rush through this step. Carefully plot the subject property's income and expenses for the first several years of ownership. It is invaluable to secure expert advice and guidance during this stage to assist, check, and verify or challenge your assumptions and methodology.

There is a great deal of physical and financial information that a prospective purchaser must obtain and evaluate before closing. Just as a person would not look for a bargain when it comes to hiring a surgeon to perform brain surgery, there are some tasks even in real estate where expert consultation is required. The due diligence inspection process is one. A great deal of expertise is required to be able to investigate the features and review and understand the numbers involved in the operation of a manufactured home community. Here, knowledge is power and protection. Knowing and understanding the shortcomings of a property, if there are any, can provide leverage during the final negotiations and establishment of a final purchase price. At the same time, the expense of hiring such experts pales in comparison to the ultimate cost of a severe mistake or oversight at this point, or a lawsuit at some point in the future. So be prepared with due diligence.

§ 6.11   Arranging Transaction Financing

Early on, the buyer or purchaser of a manufactured home community will have a preference as to manner of payment for the subject property. A good-faith down payment will have already been made (size and form generally dictated by local custom or seller's expectations) at the time a letter of intent or written contract for sale was offered. Now the buyer must decide whether to

1. Effect full payment at closing
2. Effect payment by making a negotiated down payment and assuming an existing mortgage

3.   Effect payment by execution and delivery of a purchase money mortgage where the seller takes back the balance of the sale price in the form of a mortgage[2]

4.   Effect payment through a land contract where the seller retains title until the contract is paid in full.

This is a very important decision and may not rest entirely with the buyer. For example, in the first instance, if the buyer needs a mortgage for less than $1,000,000, she will likely have to obtain it from a local lender, that is, a commercial bank, savings and loan, or credit union. Most large commercial lenders and their respective correspondent or mortgage brokers and bankers will not fund loans of less than $1,000,000 unless other circumstances influence their decision. This means that a buyer would have to at least consider one or more of the other options. Degree of personal or corporate creditworthiness and the condition and quality of the to-be-acquired property also influence whether a lender is interested in underwriting a new loan. Prudent underwriting calls for careful analysis of location, tenancy, leases, operating performance, management, ownership position, and hazardous materials. Anyway, it may well be advantageous for the buyer to effect payment by assuming an existing mortgage, particularly if it is available in the first place and terms are more favorable than what is available with a new loan.

Effecting payment by executing and delivering a contract for deed is probably the most common manner of payment among buyers and sellers of small to midsized manufactured home communities. Such arrangements can be more tax advantageous to contract sellers—as they avoid having to pay the highest tax rate and the property continues to function as an annuity for them throughout the duration of the contract. The major risk, however, is that the buyer (new owner) will not maintain the seller's operational and financial momentum or not improve upon it. All too often contract buyers have been known to perform in a less-than-satisfactory fashion, in effect "milking" the investment (taking most of the cash flow for personal or other uses and not addressing capital repairs and improvements let alone paying normal operating expenses),

---

[2] Alvin Arnold, Real Estate Investor's Deskbook 8-35 (1994).

thus decreasing the value of the asset and eventually lessening or stopping contract payments to the seller altogether. When this occurs the seller is in effect "forced out of retirement" to attempt to resurrect the income property or sell it again.

A typical preliminary commercial loan application is shown as **Form 6–1.** For a list of mortgage brokers, correspondent bankers, and lending sources see **Appendix Q.** A summary comparison of loan characteristics pertinent to conduit-type and life insurance company leaders is shown in **Table 6–1.**

FORM 6–1
PRELIMINARY LOAN APPLICATION

FROM	TO
Name _____	
Company _____	
Address _____	
_____	
Telephone ( ) _____	
Fax ( ) _____	

PRELIMINARY FINANCING INFORMATION

Loan Amount Requested $_____ Estimated Value $_____

Loan is for: (check one) ____ Purchase ____ Refinance ____ Construction

If Refinancing, current lender(s) is/are: _____

Due Date _____ Current Balance $_____

Initial Term Desired _____ years Amortization Term Desired _____ years

Type of Financing Desired:

___ First ___ Second ___ Construction ___ Participation ___ Joint Venture

___ Other _____

PROPERTY & INCOME DATA

Property Address: _____

City/State: _____

Property Type: _____

Acreage: _____ acres & Number Homesites: _____

Sources of Income: _____

Estimated Annual Income: Gross $_____ Net $ _____
(after expenses but before mortgage)

Miscellaneous; Additional Info: _____

_____

_____

Table 6–1

Summary of Loan Characteristics[3]

	Conduit	Life Co.
Quality	C– or better	B+ to A
Loan Size:	$1MM to $15MM	$3MM and up (typically)
Term:	7 to 10 years	5 to 20 years
Amortization:	20 to 30 years	15 to 25 years (30 years on new parks only)
Loan-to-Value:	75% to 80%	65% to 75%
Fixed Rates:	Yes	Yes
Floating Rates:	Yes	Typically no

[3] Material provided by Erik Paulson of Belgravia Capital, Irvine, Cal.

	Conduit	Life Co.
Debt-Coverage Ratio	1.20 to 1.30:1	1.25 to 1.30:1
Appraisal:	Yes—MAI	Yes—MAI
Environmental:	Yes	Yes
Engineering:	Yes	Yes
Survey Requirement:	Yes—Boundary	Yes—ALTA
Assumability:	Yes—1%	Yes—1%
Prepayment:	Variable—5%,4,3,2,1 Fixed—loss of yield	Loss of Yield
Secondary Financing:	No	Generally no
Recourse:	No	No
Ownership Structure:	Single asset entity	N/A

§ 6.12 Preparing for Closing

Preparing for closing is like a dress rehearsal before the opening night of a major performance—but additionally more complicated, potentially litigious, and with proceedings that will influence profitability for years to come. There are roughly four stages involved in preparation for closing an income-property transaction:

1. Prior approval of appropriate legal and procedural documents, such as note or contract; mortgage or deed of trust; assignment of lessor's interest in leases; UCC (Uniform Commercial Code) financing statement; escrow agreement for agreed upon repairs, and so forth.[4]

2. Resolution of title issues and exceptions along with documentation of restrictive covenants, easements, lien waivers, and so forth. An appropriate boundary survey is usually part of this preclosing stage as well.

3. A wide variety of miscellaneous issues may complicate and even delay closing. Some examples include
   - Possibility of hazard insurance requirements
   - Estoppel certificates for existing leases (see **Chapter 4**).

---

[4] Alvin Arnold, Real Estate Investor's Deskbook 4-52 (1994).

4.   As closing nears, be aware that *all* transaction costs need to be prepared not only for payment arranged, but they will be needed in computing financial return during the first year of operation. These costs may well include
   - Real estate commission, if any
   - Legal fees pursuant to transaction
   - Accounting fees relative to financial statement review and pro forma preparation
   - Possible acquisition fee if an advisor's services are utilized
   - Title-related costs, for example insurance
   - Mortgage cost (points and closing fees)
   - Appraisal cost
   - Engineering report(s); survey
   - Environmental study; hopefully only a phase I effort.[5]

Finally, as closing nears, an experienced property manager or possibly the on-site manager for the new acquisition should be given access to appropriate data to complete a Property Management Takeover Checklist (see **Form 6–2**). When properly completed, this document is invaluable to both on-site staff and middle management or the property owner. It pulls together the facts and figures needed for successful day-to-day operations of the property and puts them into a readable and easily referenced data sheet. In some instances, completion of the form may even suggest additional areas of concern to be addressed before closing, so a very worthwhile exercise.

§ 6.13   Summary

During the due diligence period immediately prior to purchasing an investment property, everyone gets involved. The buyer and seller, or their representatives, work long and hard to put the details of the transaction together. The seller, for the most part, provides information and access to records; the buyer's due diligence team immerses itself in research, documentation, and projections. And through it all,

---

[5] Capital Sources for Real Estate, May 1995, at 2.

FORM 6–2

PROPERTY MANAGEMENT TAKEOVER CHECKLIST
for buyers and managers of ground lease-type
MANUFACTURED HOME COMMUNITIES

Name of Property_____Date:_____
Physical Address_____Zip:_____
Contact Person/Role_____Phone:(____)_____
#Developed Acres:_____Avg mthly site rent: $_____Age of property:_____ yrs
Sites Occupied & Paid:_____ (+) # Sites Developed:_____(=)_____%Economic Occupancy

I. GENERAL INFORMATION
- A. Property Description: (e.g. urban/rural; stable/turnaround; family/adult)_____
  _____
  - 1. Travel Direction to the Property:_____
    _____attach map
  - 2. Additional Telephone #:(____)_____Fax #(____)_____Other #(____)_____
- B. Significant Features and Amenities:_____
  _____
- C. Physical Occupancy %:_____% (# sites occupied + # sites available)
- D. Owner - Manager (s) Names & Phone Numbers:_____
  _____
- E. Attach Photographs of Characteristic features: entrance, deferred maintenance items, etc.
- F. Basic Homesite Characteristics:
  - 1. # and type homesite sizes:_____ @ singlesection = _____ sq. ft. each
    _____ @ multisection = _____ sq. ft. each
  - 2. Type site installation and utilities (e.g. piers, slab, runners, utilities)_____
    _____
  - 3. Other characteristics of property (e.g. flat/hilly, density)_____
    _____(# developed sites + # developed acres) = _____density
- G. Current Operating License?_____ Not required_____

II. MANPOWER - PERSONNEL
- A. Staff
  - 1. Names & phone numbers:_____
    _____
  - 2. Pay rates, Seniority, # hours worked each week?_____
    _____
  - 3. Organization Chart (sketch) or attach copy.
  - 4. Job Descriptions Available? Attach copies.
  - 5. Concessions in effect:_____
- B. Other

III. MACHINERY - EQUIPMENT

	description	procedures	history	contents
A. Water System:				
B. Sewer System:				
C. Electric				
D. Gas-natural, propane				
E. Oil				
F. Property Vehicles by type, age				
G. Tools List:				
H. Keys tagged & identified?				
I. Cable TV Contract; % to owners?				
J. Other:				

IV. MATERIAL - SUPPLIES
- A. Supplies: (annual ordering cycle; list of suppliers)
  - 1. maintenance inventory
  - 2. office inventory; equipment & supplies
- B. Forms:
  - 1. Rules & Regulations (Guidelines for Living) attach copy
  - 2. Leases & Addendums. Attach copy
  - 3. Applications. Attach copy
  - 4. Notices. Attach copy
- C. Other:

FORM 6–2
(continued)

V. MONEY
  A. Operating Statements or tax returns. Attach copy of Pro Forma Operating Statement
  B. Budgets - research & evaluate every line item. Attach copy
  C. Accounts Receivable: rent rates, due dates, rent increase history
      1. Complete Rent Roll: Name, address, rent amount, security deposit status (Estoppel Certificates available?)
      2. Rent Records: evaluate delinquent accounts
      3. Delinquent Accounts, Late Fees, NSF Fees, collection procedures
      4. Misc. Income Sources: _____
      5. Deposits, Local bank? Account numbers: _____
  D. Account Payable
      1. Purchase Orders
      2. Open Accounts (credit cards): _____
      3. Petty Cash System in effect?
      4. Approved Vendors: _____
      5. Existing Contracts: _____
  E. Other

VI. METHODS - PROCEDURES
  A. Policies & Procedures Manual (SOP)
  B. Move-in & Move-out Procedures
  C. Existent files for residents, vendors, etc.
  D. Emergency Notebook
  E. Leases: written or verbal
  F. Street Layout. Attach copy

VII. MAINTENANCE
  A. Evaluation; problems, etc.
  B. Deferred maintenance items: _____
  C. Obsolescence; how/why? _____
  D. Street Plans with utilities identified. Attach copy
  E. Other: _____

VIII. MARKETING - SALES
  A. Market Survey, Comparables. Attach copy
  B. Local Newspaper(s) for ads, etc. _____
  C. Local Telephone directory, for ads, etc.
  D. List of Local MH Retailers. Attach copy
  E. Evaluation of Ads, Signage, Brochures
  F. 'Shop' property by phone & in-person
  G. Neighborhood:
      1. Chamber of Commerce Packet
      2. Local Post Office
      3. Schools, stores
      4   Employers
      5. Transportation
  H. Resident Profile: _____
  I. Other, e.g. New Resident Packet; social schedule, etc.

IX. MISCELLANEOUS
  A. Industry Contacts, e.g. MH Association
  B. Night Inspection - Security & lighting
  C. Walk property line, photographs
  D. Interview residents: problem areas?
  E. Brainstorming: Ideas, etc.
  F. Local laws and regulations, Licenses
  G. Biggest Recurring Maintenance Problem

X. OBSERVATIONS - SUMMARY - CONCLUSIONS - RECOMMENDATIONS
  A. List of Deferred Maintenance (especially - rental units & utilities & streets)
  B. Completed Property Information Sheet. Attach copy
  C. New Market Survey completed
  D. Copy of Insurance Policy (workmens comp, liability, bond)
  E. Set of keys, credit cards

Designed by George Allen, CPM
Form available for purchase in tablet form.
Property Management Form # 123
Copyright© October 1995, Revised March 1996

PMN Publishing
P.O. Box #47024
Indianapolis, IN 46247
(317) 888-7156

accountants, attorneys, lenders, title company representation, surveyors, and appraisers all play key and often overlapping roles. No one takes this critical stage lightly. Much money is going to change hands, one way or another, at closing, and it is paramount that buyers fully know and understand what they are purchasing. Then they can walk away from the closing table without misgivings or undue concerns about the future of the property they have acquired.

CHAPTER 7

PROPERTY MANAGEMENT

§ 7.1   Introduction

§ 7.2   Two Categories of Property Management

§ 7.3   Three Levels of Property Management

§ 7.4   Property Management Visits and Inspections

§ 7.5   Management Action Plan (MAP)

§ 7.6   Sources of Property Management Information

§ 7.7   Property Management of a Particular Property

§ 7.8   Property Takeover Checklist

§ 7.9   Property Standard Operating Procedure (SOP)

§ 7.10   Start-up Package of Forms and Related Aids

§ 7.11   Setting up and Running the On-Site Operation

§ 7.12   Establishing Property Files

§ 7.13   Personnel and Human Relations Matters

§ 7.14   Financial Matters

§ 7.15   Rent Collection Matters

§ 7.16   Managing by the Numbers

§ 7.17   Maximizing Income and Minimizing Expenses

§ 7.18   Loss Control Measures

§ 7.19   Marketing Matters

§ 7.20   —Advertising

§ 7.21   —Leasing and Sales

§ 7.22   —Public Relations

§ 7.23   —Resident Relations

§ 7.24   —Resident Services Enhance Resident Relations
Martin Newby

§ 7.25　Maintenance Matters

§ 7.26　Policies and Procedures

§ 7.27　Purchasing Matters

§ 7.28　Computerization

§ 7.29　Federal Laws Affecting Manufactured Home Landlease Communities

§ 7.30　Evaluation

§ 7.31　Summary

§ 7.1　Introduction

Manufactured home community acquisition, property management, and asset disposition are three major stages of investment real estate activity presented in this text. Manufactured home community development is covered elsewhere.[1] Property management is synonymous with real estate management, and while property management is the "administrative and operations" side of manufactured home community ownership, it also has a potentially broad and important marketing use in the sale and resale of manufactured homes, leasing and sale of homesites, and marketing of manufactured housing-related products and services. Manufactured home community property management is a challenging and generally rewarding experience that requires practitioners to be capable and experienced in personnel selection and supervision, resident relations, marketing, sales and leasing, and maintenance matters. The practitioner must be organized, an effective communicator, and a fiscally responsible administrator.

§ 7.2　Two Categories of Property Management

There are two major divisions of professional property management: residential and commercial/industrial. The latter classification generally includes office, retail, manufacturing, and warehouse space. Residential property management is typified by the rental of single-family units and

---

[1] George Allen, David Alley, & Edward Hicks, Development, Marketing & Operation of Manufactured Home Communities (John Wiley & Sons, 1994).

multifamily properties such as apartments, manufactured home communities, condominiums, and cooperatively owned properties.[2] As pointed out earlier, manufactured home communities exist in a variety of forms. The most common type is the landlease or rental community with less than 100 homesites. There are also many larger landlease communities, subdivisions, condominiumized and cooperatively owned manufactured home communities of either family or all-adult (retirement) composition. All require professional property management to some degree. Smaller properties often get by using part-time caretakers; the much larger ones can have staffs numbering a half-dozen or more part-time and full-time employees.

§ 7.3   Three Levels of Property Management

There are three distinct levels of property management. Most basic is the on-site manager, variously referred to as resident manager (when living on-site, as required in some locales), community manager or management team, or even property administrator. The preferred term in the manufactured home community, however, is either resident manager or community manager. This on-site manager obviously oversees the day-to-day activities pursuant to the successful operation of the manufactured home community. On a small property with one part-time or full-time employee, this usually means daily pickup of loose trash, handling telephone inquiries of all sorts—especially from prospective renters, supervising the moving in and out of manufactured homes, dealing with resident concerns, collecting rent, and keeping the property fully occupied, attractive, and well maintained. At larger properties these activities and more are delegated to hourly employees who are supervised by the manager or management team. Many management teams, though not all, are comprised of a husband and wife.

The level above the on-site manager is the property manager. A professional property manager generally is responsible for two or more income-producing properties within a geographic region. The properties may be of the same or differing types, although usually either residential or commercial/industrial and not a cross-mixture. A property manager may well be responsible for several manufactured home

---

[2] Alvin Arnold, Real Estate Investor's Deskbook 1-3 (1994).

communities within a region, or a mix of such properties and apartments. Property managers visit their assigned properties on either a scheduled or unannounced basis, and as frequently as necessary. Typically, a stable, fully occupied property is visited once each month or less; a turnaround challenge may see a property manager on-site more frequently to guide and monitor the on-site manager's activities and progress.

The highest level of property management is generally the executive property manager, who may even be the owner of the property or properties. In any event, the executive-level property manager directs the efforts of one or more property managers and on-site managers in the performance of their assigned duties.

§ 7.4   Property Management Visits and Inspections

The best on-site and property managers are practical, organized, capable, commonsense leaders. They understand when to direct work to be done and when to delegate responsibilities and appropriate authority. Along with that they know that regular, periodic checks help monitor job performance and keep them abreast of what is happening throughout their manufactured home communities or portfolios. The following are examples of the most commonly implemented visits and inspections:

Periodic on-site announced or surprise visits by a property manager. Usually this involves a drive through the property, with or without the on-site manager, then a review of the drive-through observations with the manager. Following this is an updating of the property's management action plan or MAP (see § 7.5) and review of the most recent operating statement, leasing/sales traffic report, petty cash account, resident concerns, and other appropriate matters. It is always a bonus when the property manager gets to chat with a resident or two during the visit.

Periodic nighttime tour of the property.   Regularly effected by the on-site manager and occasionally by the property manager, the purpose is to evaluate lighting needs, parking adequacy, noise level, and so forth.

Semiannual property line walking inspection. This forces the property manager and on-site manager to look at the property from a different perspective; to look for problems with curb appeal, rules enforcement, and deferred maintenance. It is also helpful for spotting previously unidentified water or sewer line leaks and other physical concerns.

Semiannual "four-sided inspection" of every manufactured home on the property. This forces the on-site manager to deal with repair needs and cleanliness issues at individual homesites. The manager should follow up observed and documented problems and rules violations with written notices and subsequent reinspection.

Safety inspection report. One well-known manufactured home community owner, ROC Communities, Inc. of Englewood, Colorado, requires its on-site managers every January to complete an 11-page Safety Inspection Report detailing every possible safety problem area of its property. Major inspection categories include exits, stairs, sidewalks, housekeeping, fire protection, utilities, employees, swimming pools, office, grounds, play areas, and clubhouse. See **Appendix R** for a detailed Integrity Inspection Checklist.

Mystery shopping. This is an inspection, of sorts, that is usually contracted with an outside firm specializing in this type of work. Characteristically, a mystery shopping inspection involves a telephone evaluation and an on-site evaluation. In the first instance, a phone call is placed by the "shopper" to the subject property. During that conversation the shopper observes and evaluates how well or poorly she is interviewed by the on-site leasing/sales consultant or manager (see **Form 7-1** for the typical format). The property is then visited on-site by a shopper or shopper team—often a husband and wife. At that time the property and operations are observed and evaluated relative to curb appeal, rules violations, marketing shortfalls, deferred maintenance, and most importantly, the sales or leasing effort at the information center. Color photographs are taken of as many discrepancies as possible and a narrative report prepared, summarizing the content of the shopping checklist. Mystery shopping is best performed when contracted directly between property owner or executive property manager and mystery shopping firm. This ensures an element of surprise that improves the

FORM 7–1

════════════ **STANDARD SHOPPING REPORT** ════════════

I. GENERAL INFORMATION
A. Property _____
B. Address _____
C. Telephone No. (   ) _____ , Date: Phone _____ Visit _____
D. Person Shopped: Phone _____ , Visit _____ Shopper _____
E. Directions to Property _____
_____

II. TELEPHONE SALES & LEASING EVALUATION (50 possible points)
A. Circle **Yes or No** and assign points appropriately   Possible Points/Points Given
1. Number of rings before being answered? (2=ideal) _____   2/ _____
2. Was answering party SMILING & friendly? _____ Y or N _____ 5/ _____
3. Exact greeting? ' _____ _____ 5/ _____
4. Asked for your name, address & telephone number? _____ Y or N _____ 3/ _____
5. Asked about housing needs? (when, size) _____ Y or N _____ 5/ _____
6. Told pricing information or did you have to ask? _____ _____ 2/ _____
7. ASKED FOR A DEFINITE APPOINTMENT TO VISIT? _____ Y or N _____ 5/ _____
8. Given directions to the community? _____ Y or N _____ 3/ _____
9. Asked how you heard about community? _____ Y or N _____ 5/ _____
10. Given undivided attention during conversation _____ Y or N _____ 2/ _____
11. Thanked for calling? _____ Y or N _____ 5/ _____
12. Length of conversation? _____ minutes _____ _____ 5/ _____
13. How many times was your name used in conversation? ___ _____ 3/ _____
14. Shopper's Comments & Suggestions for Improvement: _____
_____
_____   total = 50/ _____

III. ON-SITE SHOPPING EVALUATION. 50 possible points.
A. Arrival and Curb Appeal (circle **Yes or No** & assign points appropriately)
1. Signage enroute? _____ Y or N _____ 1/ _____
2. Signage in good condition? _____ Y or N _____ 2/ _____
3. Entrance attractive, well-marked? _____ Y or N _____ 2/ _____
4. Route to Information Center clearly identified? _____ Y or N _____ 1/ _____
5. Grounds well-cared-for (e.g. no loose trash)? _____ Y or N _____ 2/ _____
6. Building exteriors well maintained? _____ Y or N _____ 2/ _____
7. Initial overall impression of the property: _____
_____

B. Leasing Consultant or Resident Manager Evaluation.
1. Stood & introduced self? _____ Y or N _____ 2/ _____
2. Greeted confidently & enthusiastically? _____ Y or N _____ 2/ _____
3. Asked for name, address, phone#? _____ Y or N _____ 2/ _____
4. Agent at ease & self confident? _____ Y or N _____ 2/ _____
5. Shopper's name used during conversation? _____ Y or N _____ 2/ _____
6. Information readily offered? _____ Y or N _____ 2/ _____
7. Given undivided attention? _____ Y or N _____ 2/ _____
8. Attire & grooming professional looking? _____ Y or N _____ 2/ _____
9. Any distractions? (smoking, eating, noise,visitors)? _____ Y or N _____ 2/ _____
10. Shopper's Comments & Suggestions for Improvement: _____
_____
_____

C. Rental/Sales Information Center Evaluation
1. Property brochures & business cards available? _____ Y or N _____ 1/ _____
2. Convenient place for completing application? _____ Y or N _____ 1/ _____
3. Office suitable for purpose? _____ Y or N _____ 1/ _____
4. Parking convenient to office? _____ Y or N _____ 1/ _____
5. Shopper's Comments & Suggestions for Improvement: _____
_____

(over)

This form available for purchase in tablet format.
Property Management Form #106
Copyright Jan 1989

DMN Publishing
P.O. Box #47024
Indianapolis, IN 46247

FORM 7–1
(continued)

D. Model & Vacant Apartment/Condominium Evalutation (if applicable)
   1. Initial Impression? _____
   2. Ready to rent? _____
   3. Shopper's Comments & Suggestions for Improvement: _____
   _____

E. Amenities shown and/or explained? _____
   _____
   _____

F. Leasing/Sales Presentation Evaluation:
   1. Asked to complete a Guest Card? _____ Y or N _____   1/ _____
   2. Prospect "qualified" early? (income, family size)_____ Y or N _____   2/ _____
   3. Housing "needs" identified? (size, when. . .) _____ Y or N _____   2/ _____
   4. Good "product knowledge" by consultant? _____ Y or N _____   1/ _____
   5. Good "community knowledge"? (schools, stores. . .) ____ Y or N _____   1/ _____
   6. Practice "benefit selling"?_____ Y or N _____   2/ _____
   7. Quoted prices before you had to ask? _____ Y or N _____   1/ _____
   8. Prospect's objectives answered quickly? _____ Y or N _____   1/ _____
   9. Lease & rules reviewed & explained? _____ Y or N _____   1/ _____
   10. HOW MANY ATTEMPTS TO "CLOSE THE SALE"? _____ Y or N _____   2/ _____
   11. Asked to complete an application? _____ Y or N _____   2/ _____
   12. Asked to leave a deposit, if applicable? _____ Y or N _____   0/ _____
   13. Asked about pets?_____ Y or N _____   1/ _____
   14. Given a sales brochure and/or business card?_____ Y or N _____   1/ _____
   15. Reviewed utility & related costs?_____ Y or N _____   1/ _____
   16. Recommend another community? Name _____ Y or N _____   1/ _____
   17. Shopper's Comments & Suggestions for Improvement _____
   _____

IV. **SHOPPING REPORT SUMMARY**
   A. Spotted as a 'shopper' _____ Y or N _____   0/ _____
   B. Telephone Evaluation.   Total # points = _____
   C. On-Site Evaluation.   Total # points = _____
                                   TOTAL POINTS = _____ out of a possible 100

FOOTNOTES TO STANDARD SHOPPING REPORT:
   •
   •
   •
   •
   •

PHOTOGRAPHS ATTACHED?   YES or NO

SUPPLEMENTAL CHECKLISTS:
   1. Disabled and/or unlicensed vehicles?
   2. Condition of Trash Dumpsters?
   3. Storage Area Condition?
   4. Mailboxes (NDCBU's)?
   5. Condition of Streets?
   6. Resident Relations Indicators?
   7. Parking?
   8. Lighting?

This form available for purchase in tablet format.
Property Management Form #106
Copyright Jan 1989

PMN Publishing
P.O. Box #47024
Indianapolis, IN 46247

accuracy of the shopping report. Many firms follow a training-shopping cycle: train staff in management and leasing/sales techniques; have them professionally shopped; counsel managers and staff as to shopping report results; reshop within two to six months and compare results with original report.

§ 7.5   Management Action Plan (MAP)

There are many useful property management tools and forms introduced in this chapter. One of the most important of all these, however, is a document that unites on-site and property managers in their efforts to plan and implement what is needed at a given manufactured home community. This is called the Management Action Plan or MAP. Popularized by real estate investor Craig Hall in the 1970s, the MAP is simply a written and practical manifestation of George Odiorne's classic "Management by Objectives" concept.[3] Specifically, when the property manager visits with the on-site manager, they identify and agree on a series of actions or tasks that should be effected at that location. This list of activities or actions is written down in short sentences or phrases often beginning with an active verb, and then prioritized. A target completion date and responsible person's initials are attached to each action item, for example:

1.	Repair/replace leaking flushing hydrant	5/31	TD
2.	Change ad in local paper	6/7	PS
3.	Get bids on centralized refuse pickup	6/15	PS
4.	Research semiannual Market Survey	6/18	PS

For a stable property, the list may only have a half-dozen action items; for a turnaround challenge, as many as 20 or 30. Memorandum format is usually adopted for MAPs—TO:, FROM:, SUBJ:, and introductory sentence or short first paragraph. Again, depending on the property, a MAP may go unchanged, other then lining-out completed action items, for a couple of visits or months. An updated version is usually necessary after several items have been lined-out and new tasks handwritten onto the bottom of the memorandum.

---

[3] The New Management by Objectives (1991).

Distribution? The best procedure is that the on-site manager keeps the original copy, the property manager keeps one for reference and updating when on-site, and the executive property manager or property owner is forwarded a copy as a property management progress report. If the manufactured home community is being fee-managed, the MAP should accompany the operating statement mailed to the property owners each month.

§ 7.6   Sources of Property Management Information

- Institute of Real Estate Management
  430 N. Michigan Ave.
  Chicago, IL 60606
  (312) 661-0004 or (800) 837-0706 ext. 4405
  Request catalog of courses and texts; also information regarding Certified Property Manager and Accredited Resident Manager designations.
- Manufactured Housing Institute, Communities Council
  2101 Wilson Blvd., Ste. 610
  Arlington, VA 22201-3062
  (703) 558-0400
  Request "Quick Facts" and information about their Accredited Community Manager program and manufactured home communities council program.
- PMN Publishing
  P.O. Box 47024
  Indianapolis, IN 46247
  (317) 888-7156
  Request publication list. Source of all material in print relative to manufactured home communities.

§ 7.7   Property Management of a Particular Property

Up until now this chapter has reviewed very basic property management characteristics and techniques as they apply to manufactured home communities. At this point the property management expertise focus shifts to a specific property: the recently acquired or presently owned manufactured home community. How is this management accomplished? Professional property managers prepare what the Institute of Real Estate Management (IREM) calls a Long Range Management Plan or LRMP. It is exactly what the title suggests, a long range property management plan that combines regional, neighborhood, and property-specific data with the owner's investment goals and objectives. In fact, much of it may already be part of the investor's present business and marketing plan if this is a newly acquired manufactured home community. Much of the needed information is also likely part of the comprehensive due diligence report prepared earlier. If not existent, however, the LRMP is a worthwhile project to pursue upon takeover of any property or portfolio of properties. Following are the major categories of a Long Range Management Plan.[4]

- Overall Regional Analysis: includes economic and demographic data, trends, usual and unusual characteristics.
- Specific Neighborhood Analysis: describes specific neighborhood and appropriate elements—schools, shopping, transportation, employers, other similar and competing properties.
- Complete Description of Manufactured Home Community: present condition—size, age, homesite density and configuration, utilities, rent structure, amenities, utilities.
- Detailed Analysis of Present Operation: in terms of income streams, operating expenses, employees, equipment, policies and procedures, marketing (sales and leasing).
- Local Market Analysis: recent and comprehensive market survey, analysis of demand, anticipated absorption, typical resident composition and mix.
- A Recommended Marketing and Operating Plan: detailed requisite physical improvements needed for the property; any changes in policies and procedures; personnel and management adjustments; time line for implementation, and related costs of said changes; also appropriate rent schedule. Include an operating budget as well.

---

[4] Institute of Real Estate Management, 501 Course Reference Material (updated periodically).

- Review of Alternative Plans: what alternatives were considered and why not adopted?
- Financial Aspect(s) of Chosen Plan: what will it cost to implement; where will the funds come from; and how will the cash flow be improved—and when?
- Value Appraisal Before and After Planned Changes: present market value of property and how/why this should improve with planned and budgeted changes. Use all three traditional approaches to ascertain value, and describe how/which capitalization rate was calculated and why. Include an "after tax" analysis as part of this step as well.
- Summary and Conclusion of Long Range Management Plan: This is certainly a detailed and often exhausting exercise; probably, for that reason, it is not performed nearly as often as it should be. Once completed, however, the owner and property manager know the manufactured home community well, what it is going to take to maximize one's return on investment, and in what time frame.

§ 7.8 Property Takeover Checklist

At this point, if it has not occurred beforehand, the on-site manager should be given an opportunity to complete a Property Management Takeover Checklist. When completed, this document contains much information from the due diligence reports and Long Range Management Plan (if one was prepared), but in an abbreviated fashion that is helpful to the on-site or community manager. See **Form 6–2** in the previous chapter. The Property Management Takeover Checklist should be supplemented with copies of the latest Market Survey (introduced as **Form 3–2** in **Chapter 3**) and any Mystery Shopping Reports (**Form 7–1**) that were performed prior to acquisition.

§ 7.9 Property Standard Operating
Procedure (SOP)

It is also at this juncture that the on-site or community manager begins compiling the property-specific SOP, if one does not already exist. Once again the Ms of Management, introduced earlier, serve as an adequate and easy-to-use tab system for such an on-site property reference. For example:

> Manpower—personnel-related matters (for example, organization chart and job descriptions)
>
> Machinery—all property-related equipment, tools, and vehicles
>
> Materials—parts inventory and related supplies
>
> Methods—policies and procedures for the property
>
> Money—income, expense, petty cash, purchase order register
>
> Management—reminders and guidelines for the manager
>
> Maintenance—of equipment and vehicles; manuals, property management schedules
>
> Marketing—sales and leasing modus operandi characteristic of this property
>
> Miscellaneous—whatever does not fit other categories.

These tab descriptions are purposely brief as they will be supplemented with more detailed information and property-specific guidance that will also be tabbed and organized according to the on-site manager's preference. The best property SOPs are usually three-ring binders, for ease of effecting changes and updates, and are used as a daily reference to one's assigned property. A key form to put at the front of any SOP is a Property Information Sheet. See **Form 7–2.**

§ 7.10   Start-up Package of Forms and Related Aids

Experienced property managers who take over property acquisitions on a regular basis have a preferred list of forms and aids that they assemble in prepackaged files for quick use. The following is one such possible combination:[5]

- Property or Entity Basic Information Form (**Form 7–2**)
- Marketing and Operations Report (**Forms 7–3** and **7–4** (two formats))

---

[5] G. Allen, Mobilehome Community Management 6–7 (1992).

FORM 7–2

PROPERTY INFORMATION SHEET

PROPERTY_____ PREPARER _____ DATE _____

I. ACCIDENT & CRIME

CATEGORY	IDENTIFCATION	PHONE NUMBER (S)
State Police		
Local Police		
County Sheriff		
Fire Department		
Ambulance Service		
Hospital		

II. UTILITIES

CATEGORY	IDENTIFCATION	PHONE NUMBER (S)
Water Company		
Electric Company		
Fuel (gas, oil)		
Telephone Company		
Cable TV Company		

III. SERVICES

CATEGORY	IDENTIFCATION	PHONE NUMBER (S)
Underground Cable Locator		
Answering Service		
Electrician		
Furnace Repair		
Plumber		
Air Conditioning		
Sewer (clean-out)		
Washer & Dryer Repair		
Glass Repair		
Equipment Rental		
Trash Removal Service		
Insurance Co.		
Attorney		
Pager Call #s		

IV. STAFF

CATEGORY	IDENTIFCATION	PHONE NUMBER (S)
Owner		
Manager On-Site		
Rental Consultant		
Maintenance		
Maintenance		
Property Manager		
Security		

This form available in tablet format.
Property Management Form #111
Copyright Jan. 1993

DMN Publishing, Inc.
P.O. Box #47024
Indianapolis, IN 46247

FORM 7–3

WEEKLY MARKETING AND OPERATIONS REPORT

FOR _____ (property)

For Week of _____ to _____

Date Prepared _____ , Preparer _____

UNIT DATA	# UNITS	*DESCRIPTION OF CONCESSIONS (who?)
Number of Units in Rental Community:	_____	1. _____
Number of Concessions*, models:	(-) _____	2. _____
Number of Units Available:	(=) _____	3. _____

MARKETING & SALES ACTIVITY*[1]

	M	T	W	T	F	S	S	Totals
1. #Ads Run (Size: ____ x ____)								
2. #Phone Inquiries*[2]								
3. #Prospect Visits								
4. #Applications Taken								
5. #Applications Approved								

PRODUCT AVAILABILITY (at time of report)

6. #Units Ready but Not Leased: _____

7. #Units Not Ready (Why? #20): _____

LEASING PROGRESS

8. Present # Occupied Units: _____

9. Present # Vacant Units: _____

10. #Move Out, Futrue (Why?#20) _____

11. #Pre-leased, Future Occupancy _____

12. # Move-ins this week, _____ ,   Unit ID #'s _____

13. #Move-out this week, _____ ,   Unit ID #'s _____

BANK DEPOSITS		PAYROLL	
Date	Amount	Empl.	Hrs.
_____	_____	_____	_____
_____	_____	_____	_____
_____	_____	_____	_____
_____	_____	_____	_____
_____	_____	_____	_____
_____	_____	_____	_____

DEMOGRAPHIC SURVEY: List Move-ins first, then Move-outs . . .

	Last Name	Age	Sex	Family Comp.	Occup.	Month Income	Coming From?	Why Move?	Length Resid.	Other Infor.
14.										
15.										
16.										
17.										
18.										
19.										

20. **NOTABLE INCIDENTS:** SEE #7 and #10 ABOVE, PLUS OTHER OCCURRENCES:

1* Conversion Percentages: Line #3 = #3 ÷ #2; Line #5 = #5 ÷ #3
2* Phone Inquiries: Attach Weekly Prospect Inquiry Report showing calls & visits

This form available for purchase in tablet form.
Property Management Form #102
Copyright Jan 1989

PMN Publishing
P.O. Box #47024
Indianapolis, IN 46247
(317) 888-7156

FORM 7–4

MARKETING AND OPERATIONS SUMMARY
for a ground lease-type Manufactured Home Community

Name of Property _____ during the month of _____ 19 ____

1. Marketing-related performance indicators . . .

		WK #1	WK #2	WK #3	Wk #4	AVG/SUM
	# occupied sites					
÷	# rentable sites					
=	physical occupancy %	___%	___%	___%	___%	___%
	# occupied and paid sites					
÷	# rentable sites					
=	economic occupancy %	___%	___%	___%	___%	___%
	# visits					
÷	# calls					
+	conversion %	___%	___%	___%	___%	___%
	# applications					
÷	# visits					
=	conversion %	___%	___%	___%	___%	___%
	latest shopping score					
	person evaluated					

2. Operations-related performance indicators . . .

	WK #1	WK #2	WK #3	Wk #4	AVG/SUM
rent owed	$				
late charges	$				
court costs	$				
other _____	$				
parts	$				
labor/maintenance	$				
pet fees	$				
cable TV	$				
NSF charges	$				
other _____	$				
total $ owed	$ ____	$ ____	$ ____	$ ____	$ ____
latest OER % (operating expense ration *1)	___%	___%	___%	___%	___%

Remarks & Footnotes: _____

*1 = OER = $ operating expense ÷ $ total income for same period of time = OER %

Designed by George Allen, CPM   2/95
Form available for purchase in tablet format.
Property Management Form # 120
Copyright: September 1995

PMN Publishing
P.O. Box #47024
Indianapolis, IN 46247
(317) 888-7156

- Weekly Prospect Inquiry Report, a traffic report for phone calls and visits (**Form 7–5**)
- Incident/Accident Report (**Form 7–6**)
- Petty cash envelopes and petty cash receipt slips—available from most office supply stores
- Purchase orders, if appropriate
- Summary of Delinquent Accounts, delinquent rent aging form (**Form 7–7**)
- Job Applications (EEOC compliance)
- IRS forms for new employees (W-4s)
- Lease applications
- Model set of Guidelines for Living or rules and regulations (**Form 7–8**)
- Rules Violations Warning Notice(s)
- Written leases and addendums, if used
- Leasing and sales aids, as appropriate
- SOP preparation guidelines—3-ring notebook
- Invoice Distribution Summary (**Form 7–9**)
- Guest Information/Visitor Response cards (**Figure 7–1**).

It is important for a property manager or on-site manager to be fully in control of his or her manufactured home community as soon as possible. The above items help speed that along. Tailor the list to a company's or region's specific needs. For instance, if rent control is in effect, be sure to include a copy of said landlord-tenant law in the takeover package.

§ 7.11 Setting up and Running the On-Site Operation

The remainder of this chapter is a description of much of the hands-on operation of a manufactured home community. The major categories are in a chronological order that may or may not be directly applicable to other such properties. The category titles, while not patterned precisely after the Ms of Management, are close enough in title and content to suggest into which tabs in the property SOP they should be included. This is the order the text will follow:

FORM 7-5

WEEKLY PROSPECT INQUIRY REPORT

FOR (Property)_____

Date	Time	Phone ✓	Visit ✓	Name of prospect	Address, Phone #	Newspaper Which?	Yellow Pages	Radio/ TV	Referral	Passby	Other	Other	Followup: Call, letter, etc.
TOTAL #				N/A	N/A								

CONVERSION %s = 1) # visits ÷ # calls per week = telephone call %. Good = 25%+
2) # applications ÷ # visits per week = visit call %. Good = 25%+

This form available for purchase in tablet format.
Property Management Form #103
Copyright Jan 1989

G.E.A. MANAGEMENT
P.O. Box 47024
Indianapolis, IN 46247

FORM 7–6

| INCIDENT / ACCIDENT REPORT |

(Type or Print All Entries and Attach Photographs)

Date of this report: _____   Vehicular_____ Employee _____
Preparer's Name:_____   Personal Injury _____Fire _____
Rental Community: _____   Property Damage _____Theft_____
_____   Other_____(specify)

1.   Date of incident/accident: _____

2.   Exact location where this incident / accident occurred (address, intersection, etc.). (Attach a diagram if necessary.) _____

3.   Describe in detail what occurred as you know it (use additional pages If necessary): _____
   _____
   _____

4.   What police/fire unit(s) if any, were called to the scene? _____

5.   Was a police investigation made and report prepared?_____ (If you have a copy of the police report, attach a copy to this report.)

6.   Was anyone transported to a hospital or physician's office from the scene of the incident/accident? If so, who? _____

7.   Who/what (hospital, clinic) administered medical treatment? _____

8.   If you know, what type of treatment was given to the patient? _____
   _____

9.   Was anyone formally admitted to a hospital for injuries suffered as a result of this incident/accident? If so, who? _____

10.   If an arrest was made, who was incarcerated and where? _____
    _____

11.   If this was an accident involving a vehicle(s), who was driving? _____
    _____

12.   What damage, if any, was done to the vehicle(s) involved? _____

13.   Witnesses to this incident/accident (name, address, phone number): _____
    _____

14.   Drivers license number(s) of all parties involved (including witnesses): _____
    _____

15.   Name, address and phone number of insurance companies (also agents or representatives): _____
    _____

Footnotes:
This form available in tablet format.
Property Management Form #110
Copyright Jan. 1993

DMN Publishing
P.O. Box #47024
Indianapolis, Indiana 46247

FORM 7–7

SUMMARY OF DELINQUENT ACCOUNTS

For Month of _____ , 19 ___

Property _____   Preparer _____   Manager _____

Unit #, or Address	Resident's Name	Telephone Number(s)	Total Amt. Owed, Incl (NSF & LC)	Late & NSF Charges	Date and Action (1)	Date and Action (2)	Date and Action (3)

This form available for purchase in tablet format.
Property Management Form #104
Copyright Jan 1989.

GFA
MANAGEMENT
P.O. Box 47024
Indianapolis, IN 46247

FORM 7–8

RULES, REGULATIONS AND COMMUNITY POLICIES

Welcome to _____ . To protect your home investment and enhance your enjoyment of living in your new community, certain Rules, Regulations and Policies have been adopted by Management to enhance the desirability of community living. These Rules, Regulations and Policies are established to prevent nuisances and to promote an attractive and desirable manufactured home community, and to insure that each resident has the full benefit and enjoyment of their home and an attractive and desirable environment in which to live.

It is necessary for everyone to adhere to common sense behavior to be happy in the community. As many of the guidelines established by the Management deal with courtesy to your neighbors, they will be second nature to you and no extra effort will be required to follow them.

We are sure you will be content in knowing that our aim is to keep the residents happy and to provide a place where you can live and entertain guests and friends with pride, dignity and comfort. The cooperation of all residents is required to achieve our mutual goals of privacy, safety, comfort and pleasant and enjoyable surroundings.

EMERGENCY PHONE NUMBERS

POLICE . . . .   _____

FIRE . . . .   _____

MEDICAL SERVICE . . . .   _____

OFFICE . . . .   _____

PARK MAINTENANCE . . . .   _____

SCHOOL . . . .   _____

SERVICES (UTILITIES) . . . .   _____

   1. _____   _____

   2. _____   _____

GFA
MANAGEMENT

This Property Professionally Managed by: P.O. Box 47024
Indianapolis, IN 46247

FORM 7–8
(continued)

_____   _____   _____
Leasing Consultant   Move-in Date   Property Manager Approval

RULES AND REGULATIONS

I. **RENTS PAYABLE**

All rents are payable in advance and are due on the _____ of the month. A late charge fee of_____Dollars ($_____) extra will be charged if the rent is not paid by the _____day of the month.

II. **SECURITY DEPOSIT**

A security deposit of _____is due and payable at the time the rental agreement is signed. This money is to be held to satisfy any claim for the damage of the property or any litter left at the time of move-out, or for any damage or loss sustained as a result of a breach or default by the Tenant.

III. **RENT INCREASES**

Management reserves the right to increase lot rents; residents shall, however, receive_____months advanced notice of all proposed rent increases.

IV. **TRANSFER OR SUBLETTING**

Since your home site is rented to you as an individual, it is not transferable to another party. Any assignment, transfer, lease or sublease may be effected only by completing a **new application** which in turn must be approved by management.

V. **PROHIBITED ACTIVITIES**

For the benefit of the other park residents, the following activities are specifically prohibited in the community.
   A. Loud parties or disturbances.
   B. Speeding vehicles.
   C. Automobile, boat, trailer or vehicle repairs.
   D. Loud mufflers.
   E. Burning of any kind.
   F. Nuisances of any kind.
   G. Air rifles, B-B guns, fireworks.
   H. Drunkenness and immoral conduct.
   I. Disabled vehicles.
   J. Peddling, soliciting, canvassing, distributing literature by any religious group or any other form of commercial enter-prise without the permission of the Park Management.
   K. Removal of any plants or shrubs from a lot or manufactured home lot is prohibited.

VI. **YOUR NEW MANUFACTURED HOME**
   A. All manufactured homes will be skirted with an approved material within_____days of moving into the community.
   B. All manufactured homes will be anchored, and all anchoring will be approved by the Management within thirty (30) days of move-in.
   C. Manufactured Home Requirements
      1. Manufactured homes will be no more than_____years old.
      2. Manufactured homes must be a minimum of _____x_____feet.
      3. Manufactured homes must be neat and attractive in appearance.
   D. Each owner is responsible for the maintenance of yards. All yards must be neat and attractively maintained at all times. Management reserves the right to mow yards and impose a charge for mowing against residents and/or owner to be paid at next lot rent payment.

VII. **HOOK-UPS**

Each resident is responsible for water, sewer, oil, gas and electrical installation upon his lot and will be charged for expense of replacing or servicing same where due to neglect or improper use on the part of the resident. The Tenant will make his own application for all utilities, such as telephone, gas, electric and pay all statements rendered by said companies.

VIII. **MANUFACTURED HOME SITES**
   A. Manufactured homes will be placed or removed only by authorized personnel after authorization is given by Management.
   B. All awnings, appurtenances, porches, steps, storage buildings and skirting must be approved in writing prior to installation or may be subject to removal.

FORM 7–8
(continued)

C. No storage under homes will be permitted unless home is skirted with approved skirting.
D. Each resident may arrange his location in a manner where he finds attractive as far as lawns, flowers and shrubs are concerned. Any trees or any temporary or permanent concrete or masonary work must be approved beforehand, and when approved shall not thereafter be removed from premises.
E. All garbage must be placed in proper fly tight, rigid receptacles.
F. Each resident is cautioned against driving rods, stakes, pipes, etc. into the ground or against digging in an area without first checking with the office. Many types of underground installations might be endangered by indiscriminate action. Any damage of this type will be charged to the resident.
G. No sanitary napkins or tampons or other items of this nature are to be flushed into the sewer system.

IX. PETS
A manufactured home community is not the best place to raise a pet. If you wish to have a pet in the community, prior permission must be obtained from the Management. No pets shall be permitted to create a nuisance in the community. Pet owners are responsible for cleaning up waste deposits of pets.

X. TIRES AND AXLES
Residents must retain ownership of their home's tires and axles. Tires and axles must be stored underneath each home or in an appropriate storage building.

XI. REGISTRATION OF GUESTS
All residents must be registered at the office and sign the rental agreement and regulations. Residents shall be responsible and held liable for the conduct of their guests while in the manufactured home community.

XII. VACATING
Your manufactured home community is planned for permanent residence, but if you must leave, it will require _____days notice or your security deposit is forfeited. The Manager must be notified by the resident and the mover at least 48 hours prior to the mobile home toter arriving in the park. It is also up to the owner to get a moving permit from the County Treasurer's office signifying that all property taxes have been paid on the home for the current year and to pay any back rent due before home can be moved.

XIII. RULES VIOLATION
Violation of any park rule or regulation can result in resident eviction. Indiana Code allows owners of manufactured home communities the right to eject persons. "The owner, operator or caretaker of any mobile home park may eject any person from the premises for non-payment of charges or fees for accomodations, for violations of law or disorderly conduct, for violations of any regulation of the State Board relating to mobile home parks or for any violation of any rule of the park which is publicly posted within the park." (Indiana Code 13-1-7-Sec. 34)

XIV. PARK RESPONSIBILITIES
While the Management and owners of your community will exert great effort to assure the safety of residents and the property, they are not responsible for losses due to fire, theft or accident. You the resident are hereby notified that you assume the risk in such matters.

XV. CREDIT CHECK
Home sites shall only be rented to manufactured home owners. Qualifications for site rental will be based on the credit, income, etc. of the manufactured home owner.
I _____do hereby give permission and authorization for the Management of
_____Manufactured Home Community to check my credit and all records
concerning rental of a manufactured home site.

XVI. AMENDMENTS TO RULES AND REGULATIONS
Park Management reserves the right to alter, add to or amend such rules and regulations from time to time, but such changes shall not take effect until written notice thereof is posted within the manufactured home community, or written notice to this effect is delivered to the Tenant.

I have read, understand and agree to abide by these rules set forth by _____
for the benefit of its residence.

(Name)	(Lot)	(Date)

FORM 7-9

INVOICE DISTRIBUTION SUMMARY

Payable to: _____

From: _____

Memo: _____

Date _____

Ck. NO. _____

Approvals ____ / ____

Invoice No.	P.O. No.	Property	Chart of Acct#	Sub #	Memo	Net $

TOTAL $ PAID _____

This form available for purchase in tablet format.
Property Management Form #105
Copyright Jan 1989

DMN Publishing, Inc.
P.O. Box #47024
Indianapolis, IN 46247

The Professional Property Management

Prospective Resident
Information
and
Visitor
Response Cards !

This form available for purchase.
Property Management Form #107
Copyright Jan 1989, Revised Oct 1995

PMN Publishing
P.O. Box 47024
Indianapolis IN 46247
(317) 888-7156

⌘———   ———⌘

VISITOR INFORMATION CARD
To be completed by consultant or visitor <u>during</u> interview.

Today's Date _____   Property _____

Visitor(s) Name(s) _____

Present Address _____

Telephone _____ (Home) _____ (Work)

Type Housing Needed _____

When Needed _____

How Visitor Heard of Community _____

Remarks: _____

_____

Name of Person Completing Visitor Cards _____

⌘———   ———⌘

Figure 7–1. Visitor information and response cards.

⌘——   **VISITOR RESPONSE CARD**   ——⌘

To be completed by visitor after leaving interview.

Dear Visitor ! How did we do ? Please answer following:

1. How did you learn of this property? _____

2. Did you have any difficulty finding the property or office?   ☐ Yes   ☐No

   (details please) _____

3. What was your overall impression of the property and staff?

   Property: Very Good___ Fair___ Poor___ Why? _____

   Staff :   Very Good___ Fair___ Poor___ Why? _____

4. What did you like the most? _____

5. What did you like the least? _____

6. Do you plan to return or lease/buy here?   ☐ Yes ☐ No Why? _____

7. If not, why not? _____

8. Who met with you? _____ Which property? _____

9. Want us to contact you?   ☐ Yes   ☐ No

   If so, name and phone number _____

10. **IMPORTANT:** Consultant to complete address on reverse side before giving to
    visitor!

⌘————   ——⌘

Please mail to:

_____

_____

_____

Figure 7–1. *(continued).*

- Property Files
- Personnel/Human Relations Matters (manpower)
- Financial Matters (money)
- Marketing Matters: Advertising, Leasing, and Sales
- Maintenance Matters
- Policies and Procedures (methods)
- Resident Relations
- Purchasing Matters
- Miscellaneous Matters

§ 7.12   Establishing Property Files

One of the first in-office activities to effect upon takeover of a manufactured home community is to inventory what is on hand and what files, forms, bookkeeping records, and reference manuals may be needed. That is why a start-up package of forms and aids can be so helpful. That way a manager has something familiar to begin working with while inventorying what has been left behind, if anything.

Plan to implement four categories for on-site property files:

- Resident files
- Property files
- Pending files
- Reference files

Resident files.   Generally are of three types: active, closed, and rejected applicant files.

  1. An active resident file is opened and maintained on every lessee on the property, whether renting a homesite, rental unit (apartment), or commercial enterprise (for example, a convenience store). Typical contents include:
      - Original copy of executed rental agreement and addendums, if appropriate
      - Signed and dated original of Guidelines for Living (also known as rules and regulations)

- Copies of late rent notice(s), if any
- Copies of completed maintenance work orders relative to the lessee
- Original or copy of application to rent, along with clearly identified emergency contact(s)
- If possible, a copy of homeowner's title to home or information clearly identifying mortgagor (lender)
- Any other official and unofficial correspondence with lessee.

Keep these files locked up when not in use.

2.   The closed resident files are comprised of individual lessee records of individuals and families who have relocated from the property. These are best kept in a separate location from the active resident files. Also keep secure.

3.   Rejected applicant files must be kept on hand, separate from the active and closed resident files, to demonstrate, if necessary, that application approvals and denials are in strict accords with Fair Housing guidelines and not in any way discriminatory.

Property files.   These vary in number and content according to property location and owner and manager preference. The following is but a sampling of file categories to consider maintaining on-site:

- As-built construction drawings, street layout, utility shutoff locations
- Incident-Accident Reports (completed)
- Correspondence files
- Various blank forms, leases, guidelines
- Past property newsletters
- Swimming pool information and test results
- Wastewater treatment plant information, maintenance records, and effluent test results
- Drinking water reports and test results, if a private system
- Purchasing comparison forms (completed)
- Accounts payable and receivable reports
- Employee performance evaluation reports—should be kept under lock and key.

Each year go through the property files and collect material no longer important to the operation of the property. One alternative is to box such discarded files and put them away in a closet for one more year. Then, if not needed or referenced, dispose of these the following year. Exercise caution though and check to see if certain wage and hour and utility tests (water and wastewater) and related materials must be kept on hand for a longer time.

Pending and reference files.   Used to suit the particular property.

§ 7.13   Personnel and Human Relations Matters

With the typical manufactured home community, personnel and human relations matters can be covered as four distinct but interrelated stages:

- The organization chart
- Job descriptions
- The employment cycle
- Supervision

The larger the property the more complex this resource area becomes. While a full, small-to-midsize (50 to 150 homesites) manufactured home community may need only one part-time or full-time person or couple to effectively manage the day-to-day affairs, properties with several hundred rental sites and a full array of amenities may require six or more full-time staffers. That is where the organization chart comes in handy.

Organization Chart

The organization chart is a graphic way to describe the manning of a property—or any group of jobs within a business. It is also a depiction of the chain of command. **Figure 7–2** shows examples of how small and large manufactured home communities might be staffed.

Typical Small to Midsize Manufactured Home Landlease Community

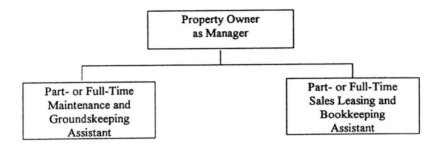

Typical Midsize to Large Manufactured Home Landlease Community

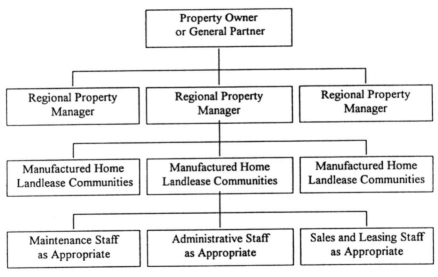

Figure 7–2. Organization chart variations.

Staffing is also influenced by the changing of seasons. Swimming pools may need to be staffed, and depending on the amount of common area and vacant sites with grass to cut, groundskeepers may have to be hired.

Job Descriptions

It seems everyone talks about them, but relatively few owners and property managers regularly use them. Frankly, a simple one-page job description makes employee recruiting and screening a whole lot easier. When one knows ahead of time just what the job responsibilities will be, supervision is a lot easier. A job description need not be much more complicated than a simple description of the job and its purpose set forth in one or two sentences. One should begin with the words, "Responsible for . . ." and continue. In fact, the title, function of the job, and location where the job is performed should be part of the two-sentence description. Additional job descriptions include

1. Duties and responsibilities of the job: listed in several phrases beginning with action words like collect (rent), lease (sites), sell (homes), manage (staff), maintain (equipment).
2. Expected standards of performance: for every clear responsibility there should be a target benchmark so an employee and supervisor can measure progress.
3. Reporting relationships: who the person reports to and the lateral relationships, as well as what jobs report to this one.
4. Job entry requirements: any special education, skill, or work experience requirements clearly tied to the job responsibilities.

The Employment Cycle

Once the organization chart and job descriptions are on hand, the employment cycle of recruiting, screening, selecting, and training begins.

Recruiting often begins with advertising by word-of-mouth among peers and other contacts; in-house advertising in larger companies opens doors to advancement and change of locale. Newspaper and trade publication advertising is common within property management circles.

Be careful that ads do not show direct or indirect bias relative to sex, age, race, marital status, parenthood, national origin, religion, or handicap—unless there is a bona fide requirement. At this time, make sure the job application form is EEOC-correct. For guidance, check with the local chamber of commerce for its helpful booklet, *Employment Law.*

Selection of the right employee for a job opening is very important. Make sure the applicant has the job qualification needed for bona fide job requirements. Do not discriminate. Will maintenance men have to read manuals and schedules to do their jobs? Leasing and sales applicants should be able to convince the interviewer they can communicate clearly and effectively with prospects. If experienced managers are needed, ensure that experience has been appropriate. See **Figure 7–3** for hiring interview tips and preemployment questions.

HIRING INTERVIEW TIPS

Pre-Interview
Review Job Description and Candidate's Application

Private Interview
Appearance and Handshake OK for the Position?
BE FRIENDLY. Put candidate at Ease
Review Job Description Together
Ask Leading Questions and LISTEN

SKILLS & ABILITIES
Identify Level and Confirm Accuracy
Test When Possible

EXPERIENCE
Right Level for Job Requirements
Verify with Reference Checks

MOTIVATION & ATTITUDE
Positive or Negative
Leader or Follower

Figure 7–3. Hiring tips.

MISCELLANEOUS
Ask 'What is personal job performance strength?'
Ask 'What is personal job performance weakness?'
Military? Ask to see DD214 (military resumé)
What questions does candidate have?

Post-Interview
Review and Recap Interview Notes
Make Hiring Decision

Pre-employment Questions

WHAT NOT TO ASK
Place and Date of Birth
Location of Ancestry or Origin
Names, number, ages or addresses of relatives
(unless also employed by the company)
Religion, sex, age, creed, marital status or clubs
and organizations to which candidate belongs
Native Language or Tongue
Who to Notify in Case of Emergency
Disabilities unrelated to the job

WHAT TO ASK
Conviction of Crimes Related to Job Opening
Physical Impairments that Affect Work
Languages Spoken, if Useful
Relatives Working for the Company
Place of Current Residence
U.S. Citizenship
Experience
Education

George Allen
271 Restin Road
Greenwood, Indiana 46142   ©

Figure 7–3. *(continued)*

Training, like the organization chart covered earlier, tends to get too little attention. Any new hire deserves a minimum familiarization with the new job responsibilities. This might easily include

- A welcome letter from the property owner or property manager
- Selections from the company policy manual and property SOP to review
- For leasing consultants, a company-prepared booklet containing a leasing or sales-preferred presentation, or even a few motivating, educational cassettes to listen to and learn from
- For maintenance staffers, some maintenance schedules and equipment lists and SOP guidelines to study and learn.

In any event most training will be on-the-job! Just do whatever is possible to make the transition and learning period easier. Use the job description as a guide.

Supervision

An entire book could easily be written about this aspect of manufactured home community operations. The subject is not all that complicated, but rather the typical on-site manager's job can take on a wide variety of applications: to supervise and effect infrastructure repairs; to sell and lease homes and homesites; to be a human relations specialist, accountant, even social director. In many ways a manufactured home community manager or owner can be likened to the mayor of a small town.

What are some of the basic tools that help make the job manageable? A knowledge of the elements of the management process helps. See **Figure 7–4.** Then there is a variety of helpful aids and reminders that keep one rightly oriented as a supervisor:

"Praise in public, criticize in private!"

"When delegating responsibility, delegate appropriate authority as well."

"Keep it simple!" or the KISS acronym

Practice the ABC Rule of Clear Communication: "Always be *A*ccurate, *B*rief, *C*lear, *C*oncise and *C*omplete!

There is certainly a lot more that could be said, in particular, be an avid reader and benefit from the management wisdom of others. See the **Bibliography** for recommended reading material.

*****   MANAGEMENT WISDOM   *****

Elements Of The Management Process

PLANNING

Proper Prior Planning Prevents Poor Performance

The Problem-Solving Procedure Begins Here

ORGANIZING

Simplicity & Flexibility

Basic Ms of Management

LEADING

Directing & Delegating

Coordinating & Communicating

CONTROLLING

Appraise Performance to Standards

Evaluate & Improve Effectiveness

***

Basic Ms of Management

MANPOWER	Personnel, Labor
MACHINERY	Equipment, Tools
MATERIAL	Inventory, Services
METHODS	Policies, Procedures
MONEY	Income, Expenditures
MANAGEMENT	MARKETING
MAINTENANCE	MORALE
MISCELLANEOUS	MINDS

Figure 7–4. Elements of the management process.

§ 7.14   Financial Matters

Assuming a new property acquisition with few or no existing records, it is paramount to set up one's books right away. Unless an easy-to-use, well-understood computerized system is immediately at hand, one generally uses ledger sheets to set up a method of recording the collection of rent and other monies and other ledger sheets, along with the property checkbook, to record and track expenditures.

The first step is the establishment of a historical tracking and reporting system. The first month's figures are recorded, followed by monthly operating statements, comparing month-to-month and eventually year-to-date experience. **Appendix P** contains a example of such a system.

The next step in the establishment of financial records is the use of a forecasting system. This may well be based on pro forma projections prepared during the due diligence stage of a property acquisition or based on industry standards tailored to a particular property and market. Here, annual budgets come into play along with spreadsheet calculations as to sales, leasing, and so forth.

Before even establishing the above tracking and forecasting system, it is necessary to set up a chart of accounts, with four major segments:

Assets

Liabilities

Income

Expenses

Following is the standardized chart of accounts used by most manufactured home community operators. (Assets and Liabilities are the domain of the operator's accountant and not detailed here.)

Chart of Accounts

INCOME

    Rental Income

    Service Income

Service Labor Income

Additional Source(s) of Income

OPERATING EXPENSES

Management Fee—any nonsalary and nonwage fee paid to a firm or individual functioning as a management subcontractor.

Administrative and Wages—All office-related, on-site salaries and wages paid for leasing, bookkeeping, and management. Includes outside accounting and legal expenses.

Administrative Costs—Includes travel and entertainment, dues and subscriptions, bad debt expense, office supplies and postage, contributions, and on-site computer supplies.

Telephone—Basic telephone charges and long-distance carrier service fees. No yellow pages ad fees.

Advertising—Newspaper classified and display, telephone yellow pages directory, radio, brochures, business cards, special signage.

Operating Supplies—Pool chemicals, lawn fertilizers and seed, ice melting chemicals, and so forth.

Heating Expense—Natural or propane gas, fuel oil for office, clubhouse, maintenance facility.

Electricity—Street lights, pumps, building lights—and heating, if appropriate.

Water/Sewer—Public or private system fees and/or costs.

Maintenance Repair—Trash removal, snow removal, grass cutting, street repairs. Does not include cost depreciable items in this category.

Maintenance Wage—If not included in administrative and wage category, as may be the case with a small community, includes wages for maintenance supervisor and staff, groundskeepers, and possibly pool lifeguards.

Real Estate Tax—Real estate taxes only.

Other Taxes, Licenses, and Fees—Business-related taxes (for example, personal property) and fees/licenses required to operate the property.

Property Insurance—Liability and business coverage as desired; also group and workers' compensation insurance, if not included under administrative and wage category.

Subcontract—Specialty maintenance needs (electrician, plumber), sometimes even refuse removal. Also wastewater treatment plant operator if not on staff.[6]

Accounting System

Although many new manufactured home community operations begin using a manual, cash-basis accounting system, they often wind up opting for one of the following four alternatives:

- Manual, traditional double-entry system, or a single-entry one-write type commercially-marketed system
- Automated or computerized system: several good hardware/software systems on the market today
- Use of a computer service bureau to gather data and provide reports
- Cash-basis: the simplest method and most common among small to midsized properties
- Accrual-basis: income is recorded when received and operating expenses are accrued when obligation is incurred
- Modified-accrual: simplest to administer

In any event, seek the advice of a qualified accountant to help make this important bookkeeping decision.

---

[6] G.F. Allen, *Manufactured Housing Communities Prove a Better Investment than Apartments,* Manufactured Home Merchandiser, Aug. 1992, at 26–27.

§ 7.15   Rent Collection Matters

The following observations about rent may well be subject to legislation and regulation in various locales, so check with the local or state manufactured housing association for guidance. See **Appendix H.**

- Homesite rent is usually paid once each month. Most property owners find it is easier to administer if all rents are due the same day of the month, for example, the 1st, rather than on various days throughout the month.
- When possible, encourage rent to be paid by check or money order, not cash. Having cash around the office only complicates accounting and increases risk of misplacement or worse. Many operations put a NO CASH sign in their office windows. Also consider letting the canceled check serve as the resident's rent receipt.
- Grace period or not? Most operations opt for a period of five working days, some shorter, others longer. At the end of that period, when possible, add either a large enough late charge to make it worthwhile waiting until the end of the month or consider a daily add-on fee of about $2/day.
- Mail-in or collect on-site. There are two schools of thought here. When rent is collected by mail, the USPS cancellation stamp makes a good indicator of whether rent is late or not, and rent collection by mail is generally less labor-intensive. Collecting rent on-site, however, keeps the on-site manager in closer contact with the residents and their concerns. A typical Past Due Rent Notice is shown in **Form 7–10.** A Summary of Delinquent Accounts or late rent collection form was shown earlier as **Form 7–7.**

§ 7.16   Managing by the Numbers

Once employees have been hired, the books set up, and rent starts to come in, it becomes very important to know how to measure various performance indicators. While most of these were covered in earlier chapters, it is now appropriate to apply these formulas to everyday operations.

FORM 7-10

PAST DUE RENT NOTICE

Name _____

Address _____

Site # _____

Date of Notice	Rent Due	Late Charges	Previous Balance	TOTAL AMOUNT DUE
				▲ PAY THIS AMOUNT

THANK YOU . . .For your immediate payment of the Total Amount Due

DMN Publishing, Inc.
P.O. Box #47024 — Indianapolis, IN 46247

Property Management Form #112
Copyright Mar. 1993

Physical Occupancy.   This is the measure of "how full" one's property is. It is probably the most common of all property management indicators. See **Chapter 3** for a formula for calculating physical occupancy. Calculate this at least once each month and record progress on one of the Marketing and Operations Reports, **Form 7–3,** introduced earlier in this chapter.

Economic Occupancy.   Although lesser known, and used less frequently than physical occupancy, it is more of an acid test for the on-site manager. It not only measures degree of physical fullness but accounts for the effect of homesites that are occupied but not contributing rental income to the profitability picture. **Chapter 3** provides the formula for calculating economic occupancy.

Operating Expense Ratios.   OERs can be especially informative. These are measures of efficiency relative to operating expenses, in part and as a whole, compared to income received during the same period. The chart shown earlier in **Chapter 1** as **Table 1–4** is a particularly graphic portrayal of industry OER averages, as well as a pro forma model, per chart of account line item, and totals.

Net Operating Income.   NOI is another often-referenced performance indicator. It is simply the amount of dollars remaining to service debt (that is, make mortgage payments) after all operating expenses have been paid. NOI is also a prime factor in the income capitalization formula for computing the value of a manufactured home community.

Conversion Percentages.   Although not widely known, the conversion percentages of leasing/sales consultants converting calls-to-visits and visits-to-approved applications, when used regularly, help one to keep a keen eye on overall marketing effectiveness. Again see **Chapter 3** for formulas. These percentages should be computed and tracked weekly.

How does the manager use these and other personally preferred formulas to best advantage? Design or use one or another form of weekly marketing and operations report (**Form 7–3** is but one standardized example) and require these benchmarks to be computed and reported regularly. Another format (see **Form 7–4**) places weekly marketing and operations data side by side, to chart progress or otherwise, relative to physical occupancy, economic occupancy, conversion percentages, mystery shopping scores, outstanding accounts receivables, and OER results. Generally, the physical occupancy percentage will not vary much week to week; however, the economic occupancy should rise dramatically between weeks number 1 and 2 and then come close to the physical occupancy percentage by month end. Conversion percentages should be 25 percent or better to match and better industry norms. Accounts receivable amounts should also decrease week by week. OER computation is more instructive compared month to month.

§ 7.17   Maximizing Income and Minimizing Expenses

The following guidelines are fairly comprehensive of the income and expenses in a manufactured home community. They are not the only alternatives available to property owners and managers, but as guidelines they should stimulate thinking about additional income maximization and expense minimization measures. Use **Appendix S** to source vendors.

Maximizing Income

Rent.   Base rent may be supplemented with added changes for additional residents per home, pets, a washer, and so forth. It is increasingly common in many regions to charge separately for water and sewer service, and sometimes for heating fuels, electric service, and refuse removal.

Another rental income possibility, although it should be carefully considered, is the rent (usually paid weekly) for property-owned manufactured homes. One way to maintain discipline and avoid collection problems, as well as reduce wear and tear on the rental homes, is to offer a lease-purchase program to renters.

Is there a clubhouse on-site? Nominal charges for its use and cleaning are not unusual. Similar charges could also apply to property-owned and supplied carports, homesite storage buildings, and secure remote storage areas for boats and RVs.

There are other ways to improve the income flow. Aggressively collect late rents and penalize for bad check writing. Consider investing deposits. When booked and invested separately from weekly and monthly rental monies, security deposits generate interest income that enhances the value of the real estate, especially when state law does not require repayment of all or part of the accumulated interest back to the resident when they relocate. In any event security deposits should be kept—and are often mandated to be kept—in a separate escrow account.

Labor and parts. A second income category includes the sale and installation of foundation skirting, as well as other home rehab and repair services. However, do not commit to projects with high-liability potential (for example, electric and gas-related services) unless properly insured and staffed with qualified, experienced service employees.

Grass cutting and snow shoveling for individual home owners also falls into this revenue group.

Community service revenue. This category encompasses a variety of income-generators, including laundry services, vending machines, videotape rentals, convenience stores, and beauty shops, so long as these services are not included in the homesite base rent. Cable TV franchise fees or rebates and tool rentals to residents may also fit into this category, again if they are not included in the rental agreement.

Some properly licensed property owners and managers sell home insurance to new residents. They may also sell new and used homes on-site, prepare value appraisals, and provide notary services for a fee. Some also offer furniture rentals, housecleaning, and other related services.

Minimizing Expenses

The following list details a variety of line-item suggestions to consider when developing a plan to improve OER performance.

Management fee. This item may not be a factor with your business. Some communities with a single owner provide separate compensation to the owner as a subcontractor, others do not. In the latter instance, the manager's salary will show up in the next category to be discussed: administration and wages.

How can one reduce property management fees? If a third party is managing the property for a fee, tie the fee to measurable improvements in the net operating income (NOI) bottom line, rather than the easier to achieve, off-the-top percentage of rent collected. Whoever is collecting a management fee must be equally concerned with trimming expenses as with collecting rent. Insist on it.

Administrative costs. Simply, run lean. Replace long-term, higher-paid employees with qualified new hires, especially if current subordinates are not shouldering a full workload or have become increasingly complacent about their jobs. Indicators of such problems are long-term unfilled homesites and a growing delinquent rent collection list.

Require office staff, managers, and leasing/sales consultants to clean the clubhouse and their offices each week. Keep accounting functions in-house. In other words, make staff work for their checks.

Encourage residents to mail their rent payments, rather than pay on-site. This reduces office hours (particularly near the first of the month) and the number of deposits made, as well as lowering the risk of employee theft.

Trim ancillary expenses such as travel, entertainment, unnecessary dues, and unread paid-subscription magazines. Avoid funding off-site meals and lodging for industry shows, seminars, and conventions.

It is also advisable not to write off bad debts too quickly. As long as the manufactured home remains on-site, the owner or manager has an opportunity, however small, to collect some or all of the monies owed.

Telephone. All long-distance calls should be faithfully logged. Use a purchasing chart to compare long-distance carriers in your market area. Contract only for the minimum options needed, and keep fax transmissions to a minimum. There is no real need for mobile phones or pagers on-site if employees are properly assigned and the owner or manager is supervising them by regularly getting out of the office to check on job performance.

Advertising. A small, well-designed advertisement can draw telephone inquiries and encourage visits to the property. Choose this rather than wordy promotional copy that loses the reader's interest. Change ads periodically to stimulate new interest.

Do not forget about yellow pages advertising. Determine which directory is most popular and widely distributed in the property's market area and advertise only in that one. Beware of the imitator directories.

If the manufactured home community enjoys a high occupancy rate, save money by buying smaller ads. If occupancy is low, go with larger ads to draw the attention of rental prospects. Ads that run in directories produced by local associations and charities generally have limited effectiveness.

If using business cards, have them printed on both sides. Put a rental coupon, direction sketch map, or "10 Reasons to Move In" on the back of the card. If homes are sold on-site, a loan amortization chart on the card virtually guarantees that it will not be thrown away. The property's color scheme, logo, and preferred print type should be the same on cards, stationery, and signage.

Operating supplies.   One way to save money is to combine needed purchases for several properties. Discounts may also be received if supplies are purchased ahead of season. Use purchase orders to control buying authorizations and freight costs. Diligently avoid open accounts with local hardware, auto parts, and office supply stores and auto repair shops, unless only a few highly trusted individuals have authorized signatures.

The same principle applies to petty cash. Control it closely and record every transaction as it occurs. Petty cash should be handled as a special job responsibility for the manager or a staff member.

Heating expenses.   This wide-open category depends on who supplies and bills for heat. For most properties, this is not a concern beyond ensuring energy efficiency of the office, clubhouse, and owner or manager's residence, plus rental homes if applicable. It can be a vital concern if there are several rental homes to manage.

Electricity.   Are lights turned off when not needed? Street lights should not remain on during the day, and office lights should not burn after hours. Ensure that all electric pumps (sewage lift station, waste-water treatment plant) are cycling properly.

Water and sewer service. The individual metering of water generally reduces home consumption by 33 percent. This point has been demonstrated many times, so seriously consider it. Although most planning guidelines require systems to support 150 to 200 gallons per day usage per manufactured homesite, it has been shown time and again that actual usage is closer to 55 gallons per person per day.

Depending on local environmental conditions and utility guidelines, individual meters can be positioned in pits next to homesites or installed in-line above ground and under the home, with a remote readout device affixed to the exterior of the home. In colder temperatures, meters usually need to be insulated with heat tape and wrapped with installation. Sometimes water meters are installed in-line within the water heater closet, again with a remote digital readout device mounted outside the home. This occurs only in the most frigid of climates.

Repair water leaks as they occur. This can be troublesome, but it is particularly important to fix leaks if they occur under a home or during the winter. Not only does wasted water cost dearly, but erosion and saturated soil can cause problems for home installations.

Maintenance and repair. Compare all maintenance-related products and services on a regular basis. Any vendor used for more than one year can generally be underpriced by a competitor. Annually request bids for large-ticket items.

Work orders should be used not only to schedule and control maintenance service workers, but to document to the use of parts and equipment and completion of work.

Maintenance wages. One indicator of overstaffing is two maintenance workers riding around the property in a pickup truck. The only time two workers are needed on a maintenance task is when job safety dictates and it is clearly a two-person job, as in clearing a clogged sewer line.

Remember this truism about conventional groundlease manufactured housing communities: the higher the physical occupancy, the lower the operating expenses. This is due in part to having fewer sites to maintain (mowing grass, repairing utility risers, and so forth). So capitalize on that and reduce staff as occupancy reaches capacity and stabilizes.

Real estate taxes. This is not an easy line item to categorize, beyond encouraging property owners and managers to consider hiring the services of a property-tax-audit specialist to review present and new assessments. For a fee, these experts can determine if a property can achieve a property tax reduction through the local appeals process.

Other taxes, licenses, and fees. The best advice here is to be vigilant about all tax levies received, checking for accurate calculations and applicability. For example, was any equipment (taxable personal property) sold lately? If so, have this property dropped quickly from the appropriate tax role.

Property insurance. This is another category that should be scrutinized annually. In recent years, insurance premiums have increased markedly, often without obvious justification. This is a good time to review the current policy, increase the deductible, cut premiums, and request estimates from other carriers.

Diligent attention to a wide variety of loss control measures, directed at property facilities and operating characteristics, is a good way to keep insurance premiums under control.

Subcontract. Make sure that independent contractors are job-qualified and properly insured before they start a project on-site. If they are not, the resulting expense could be far more than budgeted due to the cost of reworking the job, as well as liens and unnecessary insurance claims.

Is there a wastewater treatment plant on the property? It may be cost-effective to train and license someone on staff instead of retaining a contractor. This decision can depend on local rates for this technical service and the quality of on-site staff.

§ 7.18 Loss Control Measures

In the list of measures just cited, mention was made of the importance of loss control measures in controlling operating expense. Following is a comprehensive list of such measures tailored specifically for manufactured home communities.

Office building. The kinds of commonsense rules that homeowners follow also apply to office buildings:

1. The facility should be kept clean and equipped with an operable smoke alarm and regularly inspected fire extinguisher within easy reach.

2. Exit doors should be clearly marked with lighted signs. Working fireplaces must be properly screened and maintained.

3. Personal smoking should be kept to a minimum if the facility is used regularly for social gatherings. It is best to avoid the consumption of liquor on the premises as well.

Storage building. Although many of the same risk-reducing measures mentioned above also apply here, there are some standards that manufactured home community owners and managers should review:

1. Consider the proper storage of fuel for lawn mowers or tractors. It is advisable to keep fuels in properly labeled, flammable-liquid storage containers that are approved by a recognized testing laboratory.

2. All welding should be done away from combustible materials. Welding tanks must be chained or bracketed to a wall or cart to prevent them from falling.

3. To reduce the possibility of a flashback, hose fire, or a regulator explosion, reverse flow check valves should be installed next to regulators in gas and oxygen hoses.

4. If woodworking is performed inside the building, wood storage should be kept to a minimum. All sawdust and wood shavings must be removed daily.

Grounds, related measures. Here is a longer list of loss control measures community owners and managers should consider:

1. When electric motors are used for pumping water, sewage, and other functions, lightning arrestors should be installed to prevent property damage.

2. Streets, curbs, and sidewalks should be constantly maintained with no cracks and potholes. Dirt or stone roads should be routinely graded to keep them level, draining properly, and free of potholes.

3. Streets, sidewalks, and rental homesites should be well lit to prevent people from slipping and to discourage theft.

4. Signage should be maintained at all times. Place stop signs at each street exit, speed limit signs at entrances, and other appropriate traffic control signs throughout the property. Make sure signs are replaced when they eventually fade or are defaced.

5. Street corner identification signs are also important as they make it easier for emergency vehicles to locate specific homes, day or night.

6. Speed bumps, if necessary, should be painted in a bright color. Some property owners have found shallow speed dips to be effective as well and not as onerous as speed bumps.

7. All homes should have approved perimeter foundation skirting. Full intact skirting prevents animals and children from climbing underneath homes and minimizes damage during high winds. Property owners should also prohibit the use of combustible materials as perimeter foundation coverings.

8. Rental homes on the property must have sturdy steps and handrails on front and rear entrances, as well as regularly inspected fire extinguishers and working fire alarms.

9. Any body of water on or adjacent to the property must be recognized as a potential problem. Small bodies of water should be fenced off or warning signs posted to alert residents that "No Swimming or Fishing" is allowed. If the community does permit fishing, swimming, or ice skating, highly visible signs must be posted warning residents that they participate in these activities at their own risks. Swimming areas must be clearly indicated and preferably roped-off.

10. Community-owned lagoon systems, sewage lift stations, wastewater treatment plants, and sanitary landfills should be appropriately secured with sturdy fencing and locks. Trash compactors and large dumpsters must be screened and secured as well.

11. Playgrounds also need attention. The equipment should be well-maintained and as safe as possible. Use rubber strap seats instead of wood boards for swing sets. Fresh wood chips should be placed beneath swings and slides to cushion falls. If the play area is fenced, ensure that the entrance is located opposite the side of the playground facing the street.

12.   The swimming pool must be fenced and should be kept locked
      when not in use. Clearly paint depth markings around the pool
      edge and post pool rules in a visible location. If lifeguards are not
      used, have a sign reading SWIM AT YOUR OWN RISK clearly
      displayed poolside. Because diving boards are highly risky, con-
      sider removing them. Ensure that pool chemicals and gases are
      secured and properly used at all times.

13.   Precautions must be taken when propane gas is used on-site.
      Individual homeowner-rented tanks should be secured from falling.
      Tanks should be filled in a fenced, locked area in which fire
      extinguishers are kept close at hand.

14.   Earth anchors or tie-downs should be properly installed and
      secured to homes. Remove earth anchors from vacant homesites
      or at least paint them a bright color to enhance visibility.

15.   Make certain that homes are not installed over an underground
      natural gas line.

16.   When boats on trailers are permitted to be parked next to homes,
      hitches should be safety supported and boat trailer wheels ade-
      quately blocked.

17.   When minor car repairs are permitted within the community,
      require that vehicles not be left unattended when jacks and stands
      are being used.

§ 7.19   Marketing Matters

The "big picture" of manufactured home community marketing can
easily be described in the context of the "Four Traditional Ps of Marketing plus One." These are the following:

Product (or Service).   In this case the product is the vacant rental
homesites in a manufactured home community. How many sites are
available for lease? Are they large enough to accommodate today's
larger single-section and multisection homes? What are the desirable
features and amenities of the property? Are new and resale homes sold
on-site as well?

Place (or Location).   Location is so important for income-producing properties. Is it rural, and easy or hard to find? Is it suburban, and closer to shopping, employment, schools, and community services? Is the location influenced by climate, the regulatory environment, and the local economy?

Price (or Rental Rate).   Study the rent competition in the market. Is the subject property's rent rate leading or lagging? What other income streams are existent or possible? Again, are new and resale homes sold on-site, and in what price range?

Promotion.   The focus of the remainder of this marketing discussion, after the last P of marketing, is on the four traditional marketing measures of advertising, sales and leasing, public (media and press) relations, and customer (resident relations) service.

People.   Usually not thought of as one of the four traditional Ps of marketing, "people" is the "plus One." Product, place, price, and promotion will go nowhere without capable, experienced, and motivated marketers to ensure that the product is right and ready, the place is optimized, the price is right, and the promotion is in place, effective and ongoing. People, as in community staff, must be knowledgeable and enthusiastic about the manufactured housing product and lifestyle, or performance and results will be marginal at best.

The four marketing measures mentioned previously as promotional are not only sequential and progressive but somewhat interrelated. Advertising generally precedes the opportunity to sell and lease. Public relations and customer service—or resident relations—occur continuously, from the time the manufactured home community figuratively "opens its doors," until a resident relocates.

§ 7.20   —Advertising

Off- and on-site signage and print advertising are the two most common vehicles for conveying a manufactured home community's message to the homebuying public. Both must command the attention of passersby and readers and prompt them to action to be effective.

Signage

A highway billboard and directional signs are usually the first property-related messages a prospective homebuyer or homesite rental prospect see. The entrance sign, along with the manicured and attractive landscaping around it, forms the visitor's initial impression of the property and its ownership and management. A tastefully designed, crisp-looking (freshly painted) entrance sign at all entries, announcing the name of the property plus possibly the words "manufactured home community," is the best way to start. Seasonal flowers and pruned shrubs, along with watered, fertilized, and manicured grass, help set a positive tone. Just inside every entrance, a small 2' × 1' sign announcing WELCOME HOME (DRIVE CAREFULLY or HURRY BACK displayed on the reverse side) welcomes and pleases visitors and residents alike (see **Figure 7–5**). Small legible signs clearly pointing the way to the Information Center, if not readily visible from the entrance, are an especially nice and necessary touch when the office is in the center or at the back of the property. Avoid having any "no this and no that" signs at the

Figure 7–5. Signage for visitor's initial impression.

entrance. If there are vacant homesites, a few signs, 2' wide × 3' tall, with THIS CHOICE HOMESITE AVAILABLE, Call (office #), are especially effective when placed on scattered, raked homesites (see **Figure 7–6**). The sign tells visitors the homesite is choice and available and how to get rental information. Once a homesite is leased or sold, as in a subdivision, place a 2' × 2' SORRY, I'VE BEEN TAKEN or RESERVED sign on it. Finally, ensure that all street identification and traffic control signs are in place and in good condition, not faded, leaning, or defaced. Every home should be clearly identified with a number on a front corner. Through all this emphasis on signage, remember the adage: You don't get a second chance to make a good first impression.

Figure 7–6. Signage to advertise homesites.

Print Advertising

Most manufactured home community owners and managers wind up spending most of their advertising dollars on yellow pages directory and newspaper classified ads. Other possibilities include property-specific brochures or flyers, business cards, other locally produced directories (for example, by charitable organizations), premium gifts (for example, property logo and phone number on pens, key fobs, coffee mugs) for local retail salescenter personnel and prospects visiting the property, and sometimes radio and cable TV advertising. The easiest and best approach to deciding what is best for one's market is to try a variety of advertising media over time and keep careful record of how prospects say they first learn of the property. Use a traffic sheet to keep a record of responses (see **Form 7–5**). Then, over time, spend the bulk of advertising dollars on those media alternatives that generate the most traffic and response, whether additional or better-positioned signage, resident referrals, newspaper or directory advertising, or whatever. Two particularly effective and inexpensive classified newspaper ads are as follows (one column wide):

L(.)(.)K
Free booklet
"How to Buy a
Manufactured
Home!" Call
(office #)

That's it! It is not even necessary to identify the property. When placed among "manufactured homes for sale" or "homesite rental" ads, it always pulls in responses from homebuyers and would-be renters. The booklet, *How to Buy a Manufactured Home,* is available from PMN Publishing or the U.S. Government Printing office in Pueblo, Colorado.

A word or two about property flyers or brochures. They are not really needed for full manufactured home communities, other than to perpetuate a local positive image, but they are a very important "must have" tool for properties actively selling new and resale homes and leasing rental homesites. Here, retaining professional help is usually a plus. In addition to having a message that is clear and effective, the brochure's impact will be heightened when a simple and recognizable logo is added, all signage and stationery is tastefully color and print-style coordinated, and the material is professionally produced. Once in hand, keep a good supply of the brochures and business cards at the on-site Information Center and distribute some to local retail salescenters, hotels and motels, the local chamber of commerce office, and wherever else prospects might pick up this type of promotional material. Speaking of business cards—again, use the reverse side! If property is hard to find, put a sketch map on the card. If vigorously trying to fill vacant sites, put a "free rent" coupon there, along with an expiration date. If selling homes on-site, put a loan amortization chart on the back of the card. Perhaps even a mission statement, current year calendar, or list of "5 Reasons to move to . . . ."

§ 7.21   —Leasing and Sales

By way of review, there are six commonly recognized levels of a sale or lease. These are:

ANNOUNCEMENT

Stimulate Attention, Interest, Decision, and Action With Ads

TELEPHONE CONTACT

Qualify Prospect and "Get An Appointment"

PERSONAL CONTACT

Identify Needs and Wants; "Ask"Questions

DEMONSTRATION

Show and "Listen"

AGREEMENT

Answer Objections; "Close"

RENEWAL & REFERRALS

Service and Customer Relations[7]

---

[7] GFA Management, *Personal Sales,* Management Wisdom Card Series (1985).

And directly related to these key levels of a sale are five strategic steps to effecting a personal sale or lease decision:

KNOW BEFOREHAND WHAT YOU'RE GOING TO SAY

Memorize Openings and Closings

Rehearse On Your Own and Practice With Someone

INTRODUCE YOURSELF; EXCHANGE NAMES

Be Cheerful and Positive; Avoid Artificiality

Use Prospect's Name During Presentation

QUALIFY THE PROSPECT

Can You Supply What Is Needed or Wanted and When?

Serious or Looker? Prospect Capable of Purchase?

DEMONSTRATE THE PRODUCT, SERVICE

Review and Stress Features

Answer Objections With Positive Counters

CLOSE THE SALE

"Ask For The Order!"

Perform Follow-up, Paperwork, Service[8]

Once these two generic guidelines are mastered, it is simple to apply this to the manufactured home community leasing and sales effort.

Telephone Presentation for Incoming Calls

1. Answer on the *second* ring with a SMILE on your face and in your voice! First ring should be a reminder to SMILE.
2. Properly greet caller with a friendly "Hello," then mention the name of the property and your first name. This makes it easier to ask the caller's name later.

---

[8] *Id.*

3. Ask how to assist the caller.

4. Assuming interest in the property, describe a couple of features to gauge the caller's interest level. Describe features as benefits!

5. Qualify the caller. Can their housing needs be met at this location? If so, proceed; if not, recommend another location.

6. Is the caller still interested? Invite the prospect to visit the property soon. Get an appointment! Request the caller's full name, phone number, and address, for sending a follow-up note.

7. Before ending the conversation, offer clear travel directions to the property, ask how the caller heard of the property, and say thank you for calling!

8. At the end of the conversation, record appropriate data on the traffic sheet and send a follow-up packet (letter, property brochure, and business card) to the prospect if not visiting on-site for a few days.

Figure 7–7 demonstrates how the front and back sides of a sales and leasing card was designed as an on-site training aid and reminder. These are available on request from PMN Publishing.

On-Site Presentation

The presentation on-site is not a lot different the telephone procedure just described.

1. When rental or sales prospects arrive, stand and warmly greet them as they enter the Information Center. Exchange names and make them comfortable. Offer refreshment, for example, coffee, pop, and juice.

2. Either ask them to complete a Guest or Visitor Card, or fill it in as they provide the appropriate information. See **Figures 7–1** and **7–2** for a dual-card format, where one card is used for this purpose and the other is a takeaway card for the prospect to complete and mail in after the on-site visit.

3. Identify the visitors' housing needs and wants. Can they be fulfilled at this location? If so, proceed; if not, recommend alternatives.

Fold card this way when . . .

• RENTAL PROSPECT PHONES •

Answer on **2nd** ring

SMILE!

Introduce Self

QUALIFY THEM!

Describe Features as Benefits

GET AN APPOINTMENT!

Fold card this way when . . .

• RENTAL PROSPECT ARRIVES •

Stand & Greet

USE GUEST CARD!

Identify Needs and Wants

QUALIFY THEM!

Describe Features as Benefits

GET AN APPLICATION!

Figure 7–7. Sales and leasing card as a training aid.

4. Qualify the prospect. Do they meet the property's entry criteria relative to income, employment, credit history, and favorable past tenancies (answers to the latter two questions will be ascertained later)? Use a qualification survey of some sort or a guide. See **Form 7–11** for one such format.

5. Describe on-site features and amenities as benefits to living at this location.

6. Show them around, whether through model homes or simply a drive through the property to select a homesite on which to locate their home. In warmer climates golf carts are often used for this purpose.

7. Get an application—either for a rental homesite or a new or resale home transaction.

8. Again, put appropriate prospect information onto the traffic sheet—to ascertain what marketing means is working best for the property, to schedule follow-up actions as appropriate, and to eventually calculate conversion percentages, introduced earlier and shown at the bottom of **Form 7–5.**

Application, Lease, and Guidelines (Rules)

These procedures will vary from property to property and should be clearly spelled-out in the properties SOP in the policies and procedures section. Sample homesite lease and guidelines for living are shown as **Form 7–8.**

Related Marketing Opportunities

To this point, leasing and sales advice has been oriented primarily towards the manufactured home community homesite rental effort, and only passing mention of new and resale homes sales. A few additional considerations follow:

New home sales. These represent an opportunity for a handsome secondary source of income, given a supportive market, fair number of vacant rental homesites, and available housing product. Generally, it is necessary to initiate a working relationship with a manufacturer and

FORM 7–11

Rental Prospect Qualification Summary for Multi-family Income-Producing Properties

Applicant's Name(s) _____   Unit #: _____

Person Completing Form: _____   Date: _____

Every Applicant begins with a total of -0- points!
Maximum 25 pts for each of the 4 major categories = maximum score of 100 pts.

A. EMPLOYMENT HISTORY INFORMATION
   1. Number years on present job? _____ years
      Number years on last job? _____ years
         Apply present job tenure to following equivalency data for a point total
         a. 2.5 years or more on same job   = 25 points
            1.5 to 2.5 years on same job   = 20 points
            7 months to 2.5 years on same job   = 15 points
            6 months or less on job   = 10 points
         b. for example: 2 years on present job   = 20 points
         c. **POINTS, TOTAL** (max of 25 points)   = _____ points

   2. Additional considerations:
      Monthly retirement $ _____
      Social Security $ _____
      Liquid assets $ _____
      Recent College Graduates may merit extra consideration.
      If short tenure on present job, use 1/2 of point value.

B. INCOME INFORMATION
   1. Divide total monthly income for individual or couple by quoted monthly
      rental rate. Apply resulting factor to following equivalency data:
         a. 3.5 factor or higher   = 25 points
            3.0 - 3.4 factor range   = 20 points
            2.9 factor or less   = 10 points
         b. for example: $400/wk x 4.2 wks = $1720
            $1720 mth inc: 500/mth rent = 3.4 factor or 20 points
         c. **POINTS, TOTAL** (max of 25 points)   = _____ points
   2. Employer: _____
         Contact: _____
         Telephone #: _____

C. CREDIT INFORMATION
   1. Obtain one or more credit ratings for individual or couple, and calculate a point total (or 'average
   point total' if more than one credit rating obtained) using following equivalency data:
         a. R1 - R2 = 25 points
            R3 - R5 = 20 points
            R6 - R7 = 15 points
            R8 - R9 = 10 points
         b. for example: (R3 rating = 20 points)
         c. **POINTS, TOTAL** (max of 25 points)   = _____ points
   2. Source(s) of rating(s):_____

FORM 7–11
(continued)

D. PAST RESIDENCY INFORMATION

    1. From previous lessor ascertain Payment History

        Rent paid on time?   YES / NO

        Lease fulfillment?   YES / NO

        Tenant Reference (Lease again?)   YES / NO

        Apply these three responses to the following equivalency information and calculate an appropriate point total

        a. Rent paid on time   = 25 points

             Rent usually not paid on time

             (more than 5 days late)

             No information   = 15 points

             Eviction   = 0 points

             Lease not fulfilled   = 0 points

             Would lease to them again? No   = 0 points

        b. for example: 'no info' = 15 points

        c. **POINTS, TOTAL** (max of 25 points)   = _____ points

    2. Landlord contacted: _____

        Telephone # _____

        Date: _____

E. TOTAL POINTS (max of 100 points)   = _____ **POINTS**

F. COMPANY MINIMUM REQUIRED SCORE   _____ **POINTS**

Remarks:

Completed by: _____   Date: _____

Approved by: _____   Date: _____

Rejected by: _____   Date: _____

Attachments:

Credit Report: _____   Drivers License: _____ (copy) _____

    Pay stub: _____   Emergency contact: _____

Designed by George Allen, CPM
Form available for purchase in tablet form.
Property Management Form #121
Copyright: September 1995

DMN Publishing
P.O. Box #47024
Indianapolis, IN 46247
(317) 888-7156

identify sources of wholesale (floorplan) and retail (chattel mortgage) financing to support housing sales. Here, too, train and supervise motivated sales staff to ensure success. Having on-site new home sales generally alienates local manufactured housing retailers because they fear that by sending customers to the subject property to select homesites, they will lose them to the on-site sales effort. So carefully decide whether to utilize local manufactured housing retailers, if they are in place, to fill vacant sites or to go on your own with the on-site sales effort. Also, be aware that proper installation of new homes and aftersale servicing are critical activities to the success of an on-site sales effort.

Resale home sales.   Buying older or resale homes on- and off-site to fill vacant homesites is another potentially profitable activity. The cycle is usually (1) buy as new and in as good a condition as possible but for a discounted price, (2) move home on-site, (3) fix it up, and (4) sell on contract, for cash, or with a lease-purchase agreement. The procedure fills vacancies quickly and profitably when vigorously pursued and monitored closely.

Brokerage.   This is the appraisal and selling of homes on-site on behalf of present lessees. Why pass this opportunity on to an outside real estate or manufactured home broker when the on-site Information Center is regularly in touch with would-be resale home buyers? Just establish a separate set of accounting and forms books and treat the brokerage operation as a separate profit entity.

Rentals on-site.   Usually, this is a last resort for filling vacant homesites for several reasons: lack of equity interest in the home on part of the renter; and homeowner/renters generally resent living near rental units; maintenance of rental homes is ongoing and expensive. On the other hand, when rentals are kept full and collections current, they represent a very favorable source of secondary income for a property. Rentals also make a property very difficult to sell in the future, unless they are sold off beforehand or converted to contract sales.

Products and services to residents.   Another array of products can be marketed to residents and manufactured home owners living nearby. This includes the sale of foundation skirting, entry steps, awnings and car ports, heat tape and wrapping. Services to residents could include set-up and tear-down services, transporter depot service, sale of home-owner's insurance, value appraisals, and notary services.

Sales and leasing in the manufactured home community is a broad and varied, but strategic, subject. Pick and choose the measures and methods that work best for the property and its market. Helpful tips at this point are the two ABC rules of sales: "Always Be Closing!" and "Always be Courteous!"

§ 7.22   —Public Relations

Public relations is an often overlooked but potentially valuable market-ing measure for the manufactured home community. It is also one of the least expensive forms of advertising available to the property owner and manager.

Every time there is a positive noteworthy event or planned hap-pening at a manufactured home community, a press release should be prepared and sent to the local newspaper. A press release is not difficult to write. Use a piece of property letterhead, or just type one up, type the day's date in an upper corner, and then, centered: FOR IMMEDIATE RELEASE. Describe in a few short sentences what has happened or is scheduled to happen (announce awards, yard sales, and so forth) in terms of what, when, and where. If how, why, or how much is appropriate, answer those questions as well. Then, near the bottom of the page, centered, type again: FOR IMMEDIATE RELEASE. Underneath that and off to one side or the other, put the name of a contact person (usually the on-site manager) and phone number. Once prepared, mail copies to the editors of targeted local newspapers.

Another way to garner positive press is to invite a local newspaper editor or town official (mayor) to judge a Home of the Month contest each month. This way, an important third party is used for the sensitive task, and it is a good opportunity to show off the property.

So seek out ways to generate "good press" as an effective and cost-efficient marketing measure.

§ 7.23   —Resident Relations

Resident relations, also known as customer service, is an important enough topic in its own right to be dealt with separately. It is also initially tied in with the ongoing marketing effort of a manufactured home community. For that reason, it is introduced here as the fourth marketing measure. There are seven key steps to effective resident relations in a manufactured home community.

Step 1.   Residents must be the No. 1 priority. Learn what attracts rental prospects to your property in the first place and what keeps them living there happily. To find out what attracts prospects, make certain your leasing consultants always ask callers and visitors how they heard of the community. This should be a regular part of their preleasing presentations. Your consultants will find it easy to remember to do this if they complete a guest card for each prospect they talk to on the telephone or interview in person, or if they keep a weekly prospect inquiry record on a clipboard next to the telephone.

Be especially sensitive to any mention of referrals, whether they come from residents, local retailers, the chamber of commerce, or even other communities.

You also need to know what keeps residents satisfied. One way is to ask them to answer a periodic questionnaire. A better way is the technique suggested by business writer Tom Peters that he calls "Management By Walking Around" (MBWA):[9] You should regularly walk or drive through your communities and chat with the residents. Once you understand what attracts prospects to your property and what keeps the residents happy, you will know what areas of management need to be further strengthened.

Step 2.   Think of those who live in your community as residents, not just tenants; think of inquirers as prospective renters, not just consumers.

You should get to know rental prospects by name as soon as possible, even during the initial telephone inquiries. Using the prospects' names during the first conversations helps convey the friendliness of your community, and taking note of their names provides a practical way to

---

[9] Thomas J. Peters & Robert H. Waterman, Jr., In Search of Excellence (1982).

follow up later. Just as important, you should know and use the names of your current residents in your conversations with them.

Find out what your prospects' housing needs are. Here again the guest cards are helpful memory aids.

If your community has an occupancy problem, check your office hours. More often than not, community offices are open from 9 A.M. to 5 P.M. on weekdays and are closed at lunchtime. Yet many of your prospective renters also have 9-to-5 weekday jobs and cannot come in when your office is open. Perhaps you should consider shifting office hours to 11 A.M. to 7 P.M. so that you can accommodate people who want to visit after work. Also, have a trained leasing consultant on duty during the lunch hour when many working prospects can find the time to call.

Just as it is important to think in terms of residents rather than tenants, it is also important to use up-to-date, positive terminology in your conversations and correspondence. Here are some suggestions on which terms to use and which to avoid:

- Manufactured home, not a trailer or a mobile home
- Sales center, not dealership
- Leasing consultant, not rental agent
- Information Center, not rental office
- Single- or multisection homes, not single-wides or double-wides
- Homes, not units
- Guidelines for living, not rules and regulations
- Rental agreement, not lease
- Resident manager or administrator, not landlord
- Foundation fascia or siding, not skirting
- Wastewater treatment facility, not sewage plant.

These are only a few of the phrases that have become standard terms in the industry. It would be another step in the right direction if we stopped referring to resale homes by size (for example, 70 × 14), the year of manufacture, and even the manufacturer's name in classified advertising.

Step 3.   Make it a high priority to keep your residents satisfied. Community owners need to identify and, if necessary, change or eliminate any policies or procedures that cause dissatisfaction among residents.

Take a tip from the satisfaction guarantee promised by Hampton Inns, a well-known hotel chain: "We guarantee high quality accommodations, friendly and efficient service, clean, comfortable surroundings. If you're not completely satisfied, we don't expect you to pay." How many manufactured home community owners or managers can or would offer such a guarantee?

However, one owner who attended a recent International Networking Roundtable in Florida has a policy that goes a long way toward that goal. Martin Newby of Sarasota, Florida, who owns more than a dozen rental properties, promises to respond in a positive way within one hour to any resident's complaint, question, or request for assistance. Not every issue can be resolved within an hour, but Mr. Newby instructs his on-site managers to give residents a verbal commitment, anytime day or night, as to specifically how and when the matter will be resolved.

Step 4. Ensure that all employees have the opportunity to experience the community from the resident's perspective. Managers and other employees who live on-site experience firsthand both the good and the bad right along with the other residents. They enjoy the same quiet country living and suffer with the same water and sewer problems. In fact, some states require that an identified caretaker reside on the rental property.

Your employees' experiences are enhanced if they are required to pay rent like other residents, rather than have it waived as part of their compensation. The experience of being rent-paying residents should alone raise their consciousness of the need to correct problems as they occur.

Many property owners have stopped giving their employees rent and utility waivers because these indirect forms of compensation are rarely appreciated at their full value after the first month of employment. Moreover, offering free water, electricity, and phone service to employees tends to encourage wastefulness.

It is important that employees who deal directly with residents have good skills in dealing with people. According to writer Bobbie Gee, writing in *SAM's Buy-Line,* likeable people

- Smile easily and often
- Have a good sense of humor
- Are themselves, without pretense

- Are fun
- Compliment easily and often
- Know how to use commonsense etiquette
- Show self-confidence
- Engage others in conversation about themselves
- Are able to laugh at themselves
- Are approachable and touchable
- Are good listeners.

Employees who are deficient in these areas may need counseling or retraining.

Step 5. Organize the working environment so that on-site managers have the authority to perform their assigned jobs as efficiently as possible. Assigning managers duties to perform without giving them the accompanying authority is like trying to drive a 6-inch steel spike with a 1-inch plastic hammer—it simply cannot be done. Job responsibilities have to be matched with an appropriate measure of authority. When this balance is achieved, the results are less failure and frustration and more personal success and job satisfaction.

Step 6. Let residents know that the management appreciates their tenancy. There are lots of ways to demonstrate this appreciation, but they can be summed up in two short phases: "tell 'em" and "show 'em."

Tell 'em. Periodic letters from management should start with a Welcome Aboard letter inserted in the packet of community information residents receive when they move in. Another letter of appreciation should be sent when residents renew their rental agreements—a milestone decision that should not be taken for granted. Also, when it is apparent that residents are going to extra expense and effort to beautify their homes and the grounds around them, make a point not only to send them a letter of appreciation, but also to talk with them personally.

Show 'em. As the budget allows, you should be open to sponsoring a variety of projects to improve resident morale. Among these are publishing a community newsletter (which can pay for itself through advertising); holding seasonal parties (geared toward children in family-oriented communities and toward seniors in all-adult communities); supporting resident participation in local softball teams or bowling leagues; and offering transportation to nearby shopping malls and medical centers.

Step 7.   Recognize top-performing managers and staff with enthusiasm and worthwhile recognition on a regular basis. Increasingly, multiple-property firms are realizing the importance of giving credit where credit is due. ROC Properties in Denver, Colorado, has set the pace for the past several years with its manager recognition program. Manager performance is gauged and evaluated monthly against previously set goals, and interim awards are presented as appropriate. Then, at the annual conference, the top performers who have met their personal goals for the year and are singled out for membership in the President's Club.

Summing it up, implementing these seven steps can help you build an effective resident relations program. But this is only a drop in the bucket of what can be done.[10] The following section describes what one firm, headed by Martin Newby, has done to address resident relations in the highest priority fashion.

§ 7.24   —Resident Services Enhance Resident Relations
Martin Newby

The Martin Newby Management Company has been in business for more than 20 years and owns and fee-manages 10 Florida manufactured home communities. The firm has earned a positive national reputation as program innovator and role model in the area of resident relations. Its success in this challenging aspect of property management is tied to a management style characterized by sensitivity to residents' needs, careful planning, and appropriate activities. A commitment to biblical principles relating to interpersonal relations is practiced at all levels of management.

This firm's success in resident relations can be traced to three distinct steps:

---

[10] G.F. Allen, *Seven Steps to Effective Resident Relations,* Manufactured Home Merchandiser, Sept. 1992.

1. The overt adoption of a customer service mind-set relative to resident relations, and the formation of a Resident Services Division to promote this attitude throughout the entire company

2. The implementation of information-gathering methods by which the Resident Services Department learns what residents expect and want from management

3. The formation of an integrated network of resident relations specialists (on-site manages and volunteer support staff) to design and implement policies and programs for residents, with an emphasis on one-on-one attention to personal and familial needs.

Many property owners and managers would not think a change of emphasis from business-as-usual to outright concentration on customer service and resident relations as a major shift, but for Martin Newby Management that is just what it was. Management and staff committed to move away from "that's how it's always been done" to the proactive position: *What can our company do to make life better for its valued residents?* So began a new corporate vision that today serves as an example for the manufactured home community industry coast-to-coast.

This major shift in orientation was precipitated by (1) a season of unprecedented severe storms, and (2) a change of residency laws in Canada that reduced the desirability of residency in Florida for many people. These influences were seen as harbingers of difficult times for landlease manufactured home communities. Coincidentally, the firm's top management had been self-educating relative to the successful business experience of other entrepreneurs, writer-experts, even other industries, to identify a business success pattern that might work at MNM. Enter the Resident Services Department, a separate functional entity at the corporate level tasked with leading managers and staff in the quest for excellence in everyday resident relations. Few, if any other, property management firms in business today can say they have done the same—let alone match this firm's commitment to learn what residents need and want, and then conscientiously attempt to fulfill those desires.

How does this Resident Services process work? The first step is to ascertain the needs and wants of residents. This is accomplished four ways:

1. Meeting with New Residents. Here the Resident Services repre-
    sentatives' visit provides an opportunity to introduce the corporate
    purpose and function, to convey a warm sense of welcome, and to
    interview the new resident about hobbies, talents, interests, and
    special needs.

2. The Use of Focus Groups. In this instance, a focus group headed
    by a resident services facilitator, meets with a selected group of
    residents under controlled conditions to discuss items of com-
    munity concern. The results are cataloged, and meaningful sum-
    mary reports are generated.

3. The 58-Question Resident Survey. Every quarter, this survey is
    sent to a 20 percent sampling of residents. These surveys enable
    MNM to look back and evaluate performance. Recording results
    of this data on a computer spreadsheet allows easy comparison
    from quarter to quarter and year to year. This effort provides the
    opportunity to focus attention on line-item problems.

4. The Team Member Survey. This is a 48-question survey and
    is structured similarly to the 58-question resident survey. The
    process of information gathering and recording is exactly the same
    as that of the resident survey.

Input from these sources is received and summarized by the Resident
Services Department, which then generates easy-to-read computer
printouts. These measured results are powerful tools for management
use. Ideas are generated in roundtable discussions and plans laid to
implement various prescriptions addressing said needs and wants. Some
actions are effected right away; others require further planning and often
budgetary considerations.

Following are some of the specific and generally unique Resident
Service Department agendas that have earned MNM an industry-wide
reputation for resident relations *par excellence.*

• There is a 24-hour response to residents' requests, complaints, and so
  forth (at least the initial process for cure is addressed and a timetable
  is given for resolution all within 24 hours).

• Rent collection day on-site is a pleasant community-wide affair,
  complete with fresh coffee and doughnuts, free blood pressure

checks, and timely community-interest announcements. All this is usually held in the community activity center.

- Internal promotions show residents how much they are appreciated, for example, drawings for dinners, delivery of flowers on appropriate occasions, cards sent for birthdays and anniversaries, personal visits to the infirm, and so forth.

- Strawberry festivals, chicken BBQs, and other special occasion events directed and served by management say "We appreciate you" as residents.

All this but scratches the surface of what can be done when enlightened property owners and their management teams decide to make good resident relations a top priority in their business enterprise. Any one or more of these services are available for those who appreciate this resident services paradigm. For more information about this firm's unique program, contact Kathy Peters, Director of Resident Services, Martin Newby Management, 3801 Bee Ridge Road, Suite 12, Sarasota, FL 34233.

§ 7.25   Maintenance Matters

Maintenance within a manufactured home community occurs at two levels: property-related and homeowner-related. Property maintenance is concerned with curb appeal and infrastructure upkeep, vehicle and equipment serviceability, energy conservation, and safety. Homeowner maintenance is simply whatever is required to maintain properly one's home inside and out.

Property Maintenance Matters

Curb appeal   (that is, how property looks to the casual passersby). It is immediate and ongoing depending on the season. Common area maintenance (grass cutting, flower planting, and shrub/tree trimming) along with loose trash pickup is a daily occurrence. The earlier cited marketing reminder, "You don't get a second chance to make a good first impression," drives this maintenance activity. Property maintenance includes keeping all signage looking freshly painted and all streets and buildings in good repair and sharp in appearance.

Infrastructure maintenance. This critical maintenance generally includes the upkeep and repair of above- and belowground utilities, particularly water lines and risers. Sewer lines and risers, natural gas connections, and cable TV lines are included when owned by the property. Detailed maintenance procedures are beyond the scope of this text. Local and state codes and guidelines are the starting point for most preventive maintenance programs. What is *preventive maintenance?* It is the property management measures instituted to keep all infrastructure, curb appeal, equipment, and vehicle concerns and assets in topnotch shape and operating condition. This involves, in part, scheduling checks and periodic servicing of the aforementioned attention areas on a regular basis hopefully to prevent unexpected failures. The following are some random maintenance tips:

1. Street surfaces will last longer when refuse is collected at one or two property perimeter pickup points, keeping heavy trash trucks off most roads throughout the property.

2. Sandblasted cedar signs not only look better than flat, painted entrance signs, but tend to stay looking better longer as well.

3. Carefully weatherproofing and adequately protecting exposed water and sewer risers will prevent costly repairs. Factory-insulated water risers usually need only a fresh coat of bright paint to keep them visible and safe from lawn mower hits; unprotected water risers in tile crocks usually need fiberglass packed around them and a sturdy cover on top. Sewer risers should extend about four inches aboveground and be tightly plugged, or capped and cemented shut.

4. One of the easiest ways to protect the integrity and fitness of homesite utilities is to require that every move-in and every move-out be closely observed and supervised by a knowledgeable staff member.

5. Color-code a street map of the property to show specific locations of underground pipes and cables: electric (red), gas/oil (yellow), water (blue), sewer (green), and communications (orange).

Equipment maintenance. The scope of these activities obviously varies from property to property. The most equipment-intense manufactured home community features one or more private water wells and pressure tanks, an EPA-approved wastewater treatment plant or facility of some sort, and one or more swimming pools. The largest equipment, other than automobiles, in a manufactured home community is usually the lawn mowers, a backhoe with snowblade, and a one- or two-man sewer router machine.

- **Wastewater treatment** is a fascinating subject in itself. Most property owners contract out for a state-approved or licensed contractor to monitor the facility's operations and effluent quality. However, if management or maintenance turnover is not a concern, taking requisite courses in the subject and obtaining a class I license is a worthwhile experience and cost-saving exercise. At the very least, obtain sets of manuals, usually from appropriate manufacturers, that describe all on-site equipment and its intended operation. Also, learn how to read and understand the facility's wastewater treatment permit.

- **Water wells** are still in evidence at many manufactured home communities. They usually have one or more pumps and pressure tanks, plus water conditioning equipment if warranted. The tightening of water quality standards is leading to more and more use of public or municipal systems. One of the best resources for water and wastewater equipment parts and supplies is the *USA Bluebook.* Call (800) 548-1234 for a free catalog.

- **Swimming pools** too are an education in their own right. Not only are pumps and filter operations ongoing concerns, but the pool structure itself must be monitored and maintained carefully. Pool chemistry, when the swimming pool is in daily use, is a series of sensitive tests and treatments performed by knowledgeable staff. Here are a few key pool-related formulas using pool data to determine pool capacity:
  - Rectangular pools: length × width × average depth (in feet) × 7.5 equals gallons capacity
  - Round and oval pools: average diameter × average diameter × average depth (in feet) × 5.9 equals gallons capacity

- One gallon of water = 8.3 lbs.; One cubic foot of water = 62.4 lbs.; One cubic foot of water = 7.5 gallons
- One part per million (pm) of any chemical, means 8.2 lbs. of that chemical per million gallons of water.

Vehicles. The number and type of vehicles vary with property size and type operation. For example, northern climate properties almost always have a pickup truck or heavier vehicle on hand capable of plowing snow. Southern properties, however, often have one or more golf carts on hand to drive prospects from home to home and site to site year round. In either event, the property vehicles should be kept not only in good repair but clean and good-looking as well, particularly if the manufactured home community's name and phone number are painted somewhere on them.

Safety. On-the-job safety is an important part of property management. Three key guidelines are especially applicable in manufactured home communities:

1. Know how to properly and safely do the job or repair that needs to be done. Seek assistance if not known.
2. Never work alone on a job or repair that has the remotest possibility of bringing you in contact with electricity or natural gas or a main water line.
3. Mark all underground lines before starting to work. Protect the job site from start to finish with bright-colored flags, tapes, or barriers.

Energy saving ideas. ROC Communities, Inc. sets a good example for other manufactured home community operations with its 15 energy savings ideas. See **Form 7–12.**

Tools. When hiring a maintenance staffer, ask to see his or her personal working tools. Make it clear that the property does not buy or supply hand tools—employees must supply their own. This simple policy saves a property hundreds of dollars every year. What does the property's management supply? Test equipment, if needed, specialty tools, anchoring and sewer augur machines.

FORM 7–12
ENERGY SAVING IDEAS*

1. Assign watering days to residents. (Odd numbered homes water on odd numbered days—even numbered homes on even days.)

2. Install water saving shower heads and toilets in rental homes as fixtures are replaced. Your local water company may offer a rebate for each installed water saving device. Check for leaks.

3. Read water meters on the 5th, 10th, and 25th to ensure accuracy of billing and to check for possible water breaks. If water usage is up and a leak is suspected, read the water meters between 2:00 A.M. and 4:00 A.M.—four times in one month.

4. If a water break occurs, talk to the sewer company as they may give you a rebate if you can estimate the number of gallons lost.

5. Implement a resident water saving program. Offer a free drawing to everyone if usage is reduced by six percent or more.

6. Offer a free toilet fix kit to any resident with a leaking toilet (approximately $ 6–$7).

7. Create a network of vendors who would work at a reduced rate for residents and then publicize the list.

8. Insulate hot water heaters in laundry rooms.

9. Conduct a clubhouse and office 'energy audit' each quarter. Check insulation, heating equipment efficiency, window and door seals, etc.

10. Have power disconnected to empty homesites in order to avoid a fee.

11. Require that new residents show proof that electric service has been switched before the resident occupies a home.

12. Make use of timers for thermostats and lights. Reset outdoor light timers often throughout the year to take advantage of longer daylight hours.

13. Switch outdoor lights in remote areas to motion lights. Monitor them carefully to ensure that the sensor remains in working order.

14. Consider changing outdoor street lights to fluorescent bulbs. There is a connect cost of approximately $10–$15 (for the plug connection) and the bulbs are slightly more expensive than regular light bulbs. However, fluorescents last three times longer than regular bulbs and would save approximately 89 percent in electricity costs.

---

* Used by permission of ROC Communities, Inc.

Homeowner Maintenance

Maintenance for the homeowner begins with the initial installation of the home on-site, continues with routine maintenance inside and out throughout the tenancy, and ends with the infrequent moving-out of a manufactured home.

Installation. Every manufacturer of manufactured homes provides an installation manual with every new home. It details the home-tailored installation instructions designed to provide a stable and safe siting of the manufactured home. The hiring of a competent, experienced, and in some locales, licensed set-up crew at this point also enhances the quality of installation. Another timely resource in the NCSBCS/ANSI A225.1— 1994. This *Manufactured Home Installation* manual is available from NCSBCS at 505 Huntmar Dr., Suite #210, Herndon, VA 22070. Also check with the state manufactured housing association to ascertain what state and local regulations may be in effect regarding manufactured home installations.

Routine manufactured home maintenance. This comprises all the usual household care and maintenance tasks relative to in-home cleaning, appliance maintenance, energy efficiency and savings, home safety, and attractiveness of one's residence. When properly sited, hooked-up to utility services, and fully skirted, the home should be energy efficient and easy-to-maintain. Mowing grass around one's home and keeping the homesite clean and uncluttered is all that is usually needed outdoors.

Preparation to move a manufactured home. This is generally covered in literature available from firms that specialize in transporting manufactured homes.

§ 7.26 Policies and Procedures

By now, the policies and procedures of manufactured home community management should be pretty well in place. The material gathered and organized prior to acquisition now usually only needs to be reorganized with additional subject-specific tabs. Of particular concern at this point is Policies and Procedures. Property owners and their managers should sit down and identify these specific operational areas that require general and property-specific policies. As these are identified and spelled-out, procedures should be discussed and codified as well. A few examples include

1.   Rental policy: Who to rent to—being careful not to violate Fair Housing guidelines. Is there an age or size limit on homes? Is there an income level required of new move-ins? Procedures would then spell out what forms to use and who has approval authority.

2.   Rent collection policy: When is rent due? How strict or lenient is the collection policy? Then spell out a procedure, using dates to control the waiving and action sequence to support the stated policy.

§ 7.27   Purchasing Matters

Skilled purchasing can save a property a lot of money. There are a half-dozen or so pointers that fit most manufactured home community operations.

1.   Plan ahead. Use an annual planning calendar to anticipate and plan for future purchasing needs. Especially pertinent with changing seasons, for example, plan advance purchase of swimming pool chemicals and furniture and snow and ice melting chemicals.

2.   Cooperative purchasing. Either within a company with several like properties, or among peers, combine product and service needs and approach vendors with a group purchase. It takes a leader or organizer to effect the process, but it is ultimately worthwhile. Cooperative purchasing sometimes occurs via the state manufactured housing association for insurance, printing, long-distance telephone service, and so forth.

3.   Use a Purchasing Comparison Chart to research data and compare responses among potential vendor. See **Form 7–13** for format. Save these completed forms for reference and updating from year to year.

4.   Speaking of year to year—always rebid and renegotiate larger ticket purchases every year because costs tend to creep up from

FORM 7–13

| PURCHASING COMPARISON CHART |

- for Products & Services -

_____   _____
Product/Service Being Researched   Potential Purchaser/User of Data

_____   _____
Date(s) of Data   Chart Preparer

Use this form to summarize data and as reference from year to year. Print or type all entries.

	Name/Address of Potential Vendor, Supplier	Telephone # and Contact Person	Pricing Data	Terms	Lead Time Warranty	Additional: References, Point of Origin
1.						
2.						
3.						
4.						
5.						
6.						
7.						
8.						
9.						
10.						
	Averages, Summary					

Footnotes:

This form available in tablet format.
Property Management Form #108
Copyright Jan. 1993

DMN Publishing, Inc.
P.O. Box #47024
Indianapolis, IN 46247

year to year. Rebidding keeps vendors on their toes and competition for the property's business. Use **Appendix S** as a sourcing document.

5. Importance of controls. Use purchase orders whenever possible. Avoid open accounts with anyone, or at least restrict who has signature or approval authority. Require a completed Invoice Distribution Summary (see **Form 7–9**) on every invoice submitted for payment. This form makes it clear what is being billed and why. Monitor petty cash closely, and if credit cards are used, especially for gasoline, require vehicle license plate numbers on every slip submitted for payment.

6. Question every expenditure. What expenses are not really necessary to the efficient operation of the property? For example, require maintenance staff to provide their own hand tools.

§ 7.28   Computerization

Are you thinking of evolving the on-site operation from manual to mechanized or computer mode? Hardware and software suppliers generally recommend the following:

1. Identify needs, for example, in terms of
   - Leasing and sales
   - Resident relations and communication support
   - Property and equipment maintenance and capital improvements
   - Performance monitoring and measurement by management
2. Involve everyone who will have any contact with the acquired system
3. Talk to peers—and yes, competitors, for their input.
4. Research carefully, then decide
5. Plan ahead for installation and training
6. Effect the conversion.

The best comparison of property management software packages is available in publication format from the Institute of Real Estate Management at (312) 661-1930.

§ 7.29 Federal Laws Affecting Manufactured Home Landlease Communities

Two bodies of federal legislation have an effect on how manufactured home communities are configured and managed:

1. The Fair Housing Amendments Act of 1988. This Act expanded the "protected clause" of the 1968 Civil Rights Act to include race, color, religion, sex, national origin, handicapped persons, and families with children.

2. Americans with Disabilities Act. This Act effectively prohibits discrimination on the distribution of goods and services offered by "public accommodations" and "commercial facilities" such as manufactured home community offices and community buildings.

§ 7.30 Evaluation

There is an easy way to ascertain how well or poorly management is progressing. Send out a Property Management Report Card (see **Form 7–14**) with a stamped and self-addressed envelope along with every returned security deposit check to former residents. Surveys of this nature are a good idea during a resident's tenancy as well.

§ 7.31 Summary

Manufactured home community management embodies a lot of conventional property and real estate management wisdom and practices with a healthy dose of common sense and interpersonal relations. Only with this property type does an investor and property owner relate to renters who, for the most part, own their own homes—somewhat like a businessman who rents commercial office or storefront space. Renters have equity interest, in this case in their homes, and tend to be stable renters. Manufactured home community owners and managers should at all times be fair and diplomatic in their dealings with residents and conscientious in caring for the property or properties entrusted in their care.

FORM 7–14

PROPERTY MANAGEMENT REPORT CARD

- for Multi-Family Rental Communities -

_____   _____
Community Being Graded   Return Report Card to

_____   _____
Date Report Graded   Grader (optional)

Please take a few minutes to grade this rental community. Your input is important and will help management do a better job. Simply check appropriate blocks and answer questions. Thanks!

PROPERTY-FACILITY   Poor   Avg.   Good
Overall Cleanliness
Overall Appearance
Condition of Streets
Condition of Buildings
Condition of Laundry
Remarks: _____

STAFF & MANAGEMENT   Poor   Avg.   Good
Courteous
Helpful
Responsiveness
Dependable
Personal Appearance
Remarks: _____

AMENITIES   Poor   Avg.   Good
Swimming Pool
Playground
Other:
Remarks: _____

RESIDENT RELATIONS   Poor   Avg.   Good
Activity for Residents
Services for Residents
Communication Efforts
Remarks: _____

- Do or Would You Recommend this Rental Community to Friends and/or Relatives?
  _____ YES _____ NO   Why /Why Not: _____
- Should there be more Planned Social Activities for Residents:
  _____ YES _____ NO   Why/Why Not: _____
- What Daily Newspaper(s) do You Read?_____
- What Weekly Newspaper(s) do You Read?_____
- Anything Else You'd Like to Bring to Our Attention?_____

Footnotes:
This form available in tablet format.
Property Management Form #109
Copyright Jan. 1993

PMN Publishing
P.O. Box #47024
Indianapolis, IN 46247

CHAPTER 8

THE TURNAROUND CHALLENGE AND REJUVENATING OLDER MANUFACTURED HOME COMMUNITIES

§ 8.1   Introduction

§ 8.2   Turnaround Strategies

ANOTHER PERSPECTIVE
Don Westphal

§ 8.3   Rejuvenating Older Manufactured Home Communities

§ 8.4   Assessing the Present Manufactured Home Community Condition

§ 8.5   Upgrade Alternatives

§ 8.6   Action Plan and Budget

§ 8.7   Annual Review and Reassessment

§ 8.8   Current Methodologies

§ 8.9   Summary

§ 8.1   Introduction

As popular and viable an investment as manufactured home communities are, there is an occasional need, whether anticipated or the result of circumstances, to either implement a marketing and operations turnaround strategy, or rejuvenate an older property. In both instances, it is usually necessary to fill vacant homesites quickly, convert rental units into sold homes, or dispose of them and fill vacant sites. These scenarios often interrelate when an investor acquires an older manufactured home community with vacant rental homesites, some rental homes, a lot of deferred maintenance, deteriorated or outdated signage, and poor curb appeal.

§ 8.2 Turnaround Strategies

As long as 20 years ago, various manufactured home community turnaround strategies were proposed and popularized in the pages of manufactured housing industry trade magazines. One such early procedure involved three stages:

1. Analysis and Recommendation
2. Management Control
3. Marketing Plan—Sales and Leasing Program.

This approach was originated by the Colorado firm ARISTEK, a manufactured home community management firm many years ago. Each stage of its procedure involved specific substeps. The following is a modified version of this approach.

MANUFACTURED HOME COMMUNITY
A TURNAROUND STRATEGY

PROPERTY ANALYSIS AND INITIAL RECOMMENDATIONS

1. Learn and understand property owner's objectives.

2. Perform financial analysis to identify ways to trim operational expenses.

3. Effect on-site familiarization inspections to develop a "feel" for the property.

4. Conduct a local Market Survey relative to rent levels, amenities, and so forth.

5. Develop a preliminary operating plan for taking over—or turning around the property.

6. Prepare a pro forma operating plan to project financial implications of same.

7. Implement Property Management Control.

MANAGEMENT CONTROL IS EFFECTED IN A VARIETY OF WAYS:

1. Emplacement of on-site management team tailored to the property's needs.

2. Comprehensive on-site property inspections: day and night, boundary, infrastructure.

3. Physical inventory of equipment, vehicles, supplies, and files/forms.

4. Evaluations of present staff, if any.

5. Preparation of operating budget for first year.

6. Consideration of a possible incentive program for on-site staff.

7. Begin to formulate a long range plan for the property.

8. Implement policies and procedures pursuant to the property's needs.

9. Decide upon and use a standard accounting system, probably manual at first, computerized later—if justified.

10. Ensure timely and effective maintenance of infrastructure, buildings, equipment, and vehicles. Assemble needed manuals and develop time schedules for preventive maintenance.

11. Take care of repairs and needed improvements ASAP. See that routine maintenance is performed.

THE TWO-PHASE MARKETING PLAN—SALES AND LEASING PROGRAMS

The two phases germane here are planning and implementation. In the first instance, property owner/manager must:

- Identify and understand property's resident or profile.
- Peg the local competition in both sales and leasing.

- Understand new and resale homes market and local rental structure.
- Decide on a USP—unique selling proposition, e.g., property feature or benefit.
- Prepare a workable marketing strategy along with a schedule and budget.

In the second instance, implementation of the plan involves traffic generation through promotion and advertising; leasing and sales performance on the telephone and in-person; and concerted effort at resident relations, referral, and retention.

It should be obvious that this turnaround strategy varies little from the property takeover procedures described earlier in this text. The main difference is the degree of turmoil and challenge one faces when assuming responsibility for the manufactured home community. During the normal acquisition process, the change in ownership and management is generally smooth and friendly—as it should be. With a turnaround challenge, however, the mood can easily go either direction: the new management team is seen (a) as savior, of sorts, by the residents or property owner—if a fee-management firm is hired or if this is a real estate owned or REO property, or (b) a serious threat to the status quo, where some individuals presently in control are concerned. It is with this latter scenario in mind that a shorter, direct takeover and turnaround procedure is recommended:

1. Take control and listen! Get a handle on rent collection and other income streams; pay only the most justified bills, for example, payroll and payroll taxes and utilities. Talk to the present staff: "What's good and bad about the property and operations?" Take detailed notes.

2. Stop the problems! What is the main money drain or problem? Address it first, if at all possible. Be willing to make difficult decisions and follow through.

3. Make a plan and implement it! Using the Ms of Management (described earlier), organize your thinking and efforts and move ahead in a forthright fashion. The sooner a new owner or management team moves from a reactive to proactive stance the better.

4. Establish credibility with the staff, residents, and suppliers. Raise new cash if necessary! A high-energy level, leadership skills, and sensitivity are a must at this point.

5. Look for the positives. Motivate and begin to build the manage-
    ment team! By now momentum should become an ally; use it to
    encourage positive attitude and performance, and a team spirit.
6. Show a profit ASAP! This is the benchmark that will breathe new
    life into an underperforming property, keep staff going, and buy
    time from suppliers, lenders, and residents.

Even these two formulas do not cover fully the variety of challenges
a manufactured home community owner and manager may face with a
new acquisition or even a present investment. There are many variables
that can affect ultimate profitability. Two perspectives, however, identify and quantify the factors that most—and least—affect the property in
question:

1. The "Good Unchangeables and Bad Changeables Rule of Thumb"
    for identifying good acquisition possibilities. Recall that un-
    changeables are quasi-permanent property characteristics such
    as location, utility infrastructure, and homesite density and lay-
    out. Changeables are factors generally relative to management
    quality and diligence, for example, curb appeal, rules enforce-
    ment, rent level and collections efficiency, and degree of deferred
    maintenance. Many would-be investors look for real estate oppor-
    tunities with upside (profit) potential and opportunities with
    good basic (location and infrastructure) characteristics, yet having
    items warranting the investors' improvement efforts. The turn-
    around challenge then, as was pointed out earlier, is generally
    a matter of degree in these areas, the worst case scenario being bad
    unchangeables and bad changeables to be addressed simultaneously.
2. The second approach is to concentrate solely on the property's
    ability to quickly generate maximum income and minimize oper-
    ating expenses. Look at all the key property characteristics then in
    this light:
    •   Location—Is it so poor as not to ever be overcome or is there a
        related feature that will offset and draw prospects? An example
        is a rural popular recreation area with fishing and a quiet
        lifestyle.
    •   Number of homesites—Are there enough to generate the needed
        level of income to cover operating expenses and debt service

and generate a respectable ROI? Is expansion property adjacent or not?

- Size of homesites—Are the sizes adequate for today's larger homes or will it be necessary to sacrifice two small sites to make one larger one? What is the effect of this latter strategy on the number of homesites and rent-generating capability?

- Utilities—Are utilities adequate for present and future property needs? Can all utilities be submetered and residents billed? This would encourage efficiency and add another income stream. At the same time, however, is the infrastructure outdated and costly to operate (wells and wastewater treatment facility), and are water lines subject to frequent leaking and sanitary sewers subject to infiltration?

- Amenities—Can income be generated from clubhouse rental, swimming pool pass fees, and so forth? What operating costs are associated with amenities, and can they be reduced?

- Income—How many income streams are possible at this location? Consider homesite rent, upcharges for additional residents and pets, sale of new homes, value appraisal and sale of resale homes, resale home brokerage, sale of parts and service, homeowner insurance, interest income on security deposits where allowed, late rent penalties and NSF fees, and rental unit income possibilities.

- Operating expenses—Closely review every line item of expense to ascertain whether it might be reduced and how. See **Chapter 7** for practical suggestions.

So there are a variety of approaches for taking over and turning around an underperforming manufactured home community. During the last few years, another specialty has emerged on the property management scene. This is the rejuvenation of older or mismanaged manufactured home communities. While the procedure described in §§ **8.3** through **8.8** is generally applied to profitable properties in an ongoing manner and in a directed effort to ready them eventually for sale and maximum profitability, the following process also applies to the turnaround challenge. One of the industry's pioneer practitioners in this area shares his thoughts and experiences on the subject in the following sections.

ANOTHER PERSPECTIVE
Don Westphal

§ 8.3   Rejuvenating Older Manufactured Home Communities

Many older landlease manufactured home communities suffer from the lack of an ongoing program that will keep them attractive and competitive with other communities vying for residents at similar market level rents. All older communities, whether being readied for sale or newly acquired, can greatly benefit from a process that will result in a fresh new appearance.

§ 8.4   Assessing the Present Manufactured Home Community Condition

The first step in the rejuvenation process consists of a thorough and objective assessment of its present condition. Such an assessment can be performed by the owner's management team or a qualified outside consultant. In most cases, a more objective assessment can be obtained through the use of someone not involved in the day-to-day operations of the community.

The assessment process should include (1) elements under management and resident control, and (2) the layout and organization of the property. It is suggested that a video or still camera and tape recorder be utilized to document existing conditions. These will be useful throughout as a baseline with which to measure progress. The process should begin with a drive-by of the community to assess its appearance from outside and to gauge the visual effect of the entrance or entrances. Note at this time the condition of landscaping, fencing, screening, entrance signs, and adjacent homes and homesites.

Continuing into the community, observe and note the condition of the streets, curbs, and walks as well as the overall appearance of the homes and homesites. Are all driving and walking surfaces clean and in good repair? Are grass and weeds growing in cracks and over the edges of the paved surfaces? Are landscape elements alive and vigorous and in well-maintained and mulched beds? Traffic and informational signage is also important to the overall appearance of the community. Is signage uniform in appearance and does it match the decor of the community in style and color? Does it convey the message in a positive way and use contemporary industry terminology? Is a corporate logo in evidence?

Moving on to the community facilities, assess the overall appearance of the community center building and related facilities. Are all buildings in good repair and modern in appearance, or do they show their age by state of disrepair and the style of decor and color scheme? Is there uniformity in color and architectural style in the structures, or do they add to the overall visual confusion? Is recreation and play equipment in good condition and does it complement other facilities in color and style? Is it safe to use or a potential liability because of age, design, and disrepair? Are the landscape materials in scale with the structures or overgrown? Are all lawn areas well kept, green, and mowed? The community maintenance area and resident storage compound often present a negative image. Are they properly screened, and is the screening in good repair? Are equipment and materials stored there needed or should they be removed from the site?

Most of the review thus far has dealt with elements of the community under management control. This is important because individual residences and homesites reflect the level of maintenance of these management-controlled elements. Management must lead by example and cannot expect residents to live up to a standard higher than it sets for itself.

In reviewing individual homes and homesites, consider not only the exterior appearance of the home, but also the condition of added site elements such as porches, storage units, carports, and foundation enclosures. Is the landscaping appropriate in scale and well maintained? Are lawn areas well kept and green? Once the drive-by and drive-through have been completed, it is important to spend additional time walking the property, camera in hand, to get a complete record and overview of the community.

Once a visual inspection is completed, it is appropriate to review the site layout and organization of the community. A set of construction plans for the total project will assist in assessing the appropriate nature of the layout, the adequacy of roads and parking, and the possibility of homesite size adjustment. Opportunities for adding future homesites in previously unused areas and for expansions to new lands should be considered at this time.

§ 8.5 Upgrade Alternatives

The assessment process has resulted in a list of opportunity areas that should be addressed. Many remedies for the various discrepancies are available and should be considered. Perimeter areas can be visually enhanced by removing unsightly or negative visual elements. These elements, if not easily removed, can be effectively screened with fencing or landscaping. Additional maintenance in the form of pruning, mowing, and mulching might be in order here. Residents with homes in perimeter areas should be encouraged to remove debris and improve the appearance of these high-visibility areas by painting storage buildings, repairing fences, and upgrading plantings.

Entrance signage can be upgraded by simply changing colors and making needed repairs. A more aggressive approach may be undertaken if a new image is needed to update a decades-old style (see **Figure 8–1**). Some property owners go as far as to change the community name (see **Figure 8–2**) in instances where the original name is indicative of old style trailer parks or mobile home estates.

The number of signs in the entrance area also creates a visual effect. Signage concerning speed limit, no trespassing, and office location should be consolidated into one attractive sign conveying the required information in a positive tone. Compare the effects of **Figures 8–3** and **8–4.**

Landscaping at the entrance can be upgraded as well, both by the removal or transplanting of larger, older materials and the addition of new foliage. Professional help in the selection of plantings results in a landscape that remains viable over a long time. Consider an irrigation system in the high-visibility areas. Such systems often pay for themselves in the resulting vigorous plant and lawn growth and the ability to provide a show of seasonal color with annual flowers. Ease of maintenance is another benefit of the upgrade. The grouping of plants in mulched beds for ease of mowing is one such maintenance reducer.

Figure 8–1. Updated image for entrance signage.

Figure 8–2. Updated name for entrance signage.

Figure 8–3. Entrance signage that is not consolidated.

Figure 8–4. Entrance signage that is consolidated.

Paved surfaces can be improved in a number of ways. Immediate cosmetic improvement can be effected with simple sweeping, weed removal, and a sealant coating. Ongoing problem areas in roads and parking lots may require more involved and costly work, such as the removal of poor subbase, additional base improvement, and repaving. Equipment is available that allows the existing asphalt surface to be removed, ground up, and reapplied as base material.

Many older manufactured home communities have wide roads with on-street parking and short homesites that cannot accommodate longer contemporary homes. Explore the possibility of moving the parking off-street and reducing the street width. The narrower street can allow for extra homesite length for replacement homes and reduce clutter from on-street parking.

Many older community buildings project a negative appearance as a result of outdated exterior architectural style, drab color, and materials and an older interior decor and furnishings. Alternatives for upgrade can be as simple as an exterior color change and interior redecorating, or as complete as an architectural change in the outward appearance of the building and reorganization of the interior space for optimum use. Some features once popular in older communities, such as laundry rooms and drying yards, are less desirable today and can provide needed space for exercise rooms and child care centers, even a new homesite or two.

Recreation and play equipment once thought appropriate, such as swings and monkey bars, have become unsightly and an insurance liability. Newer climbing and play structures add a fresh appearance to play lots and provide an attractive visual upgrade. Other facilities on-site should be upgraded with new equipment and surface treatments or removed to make way for more desirable uses. Half-court basketball and sand volleyball are popular new alternatives. Site furnishings, such as benches, trash receptacles, and mail boxes, can be upgraded by painting in theme colors compatible with the other community facilities or replaced with more modern style equipment. Replace individual mailboxes with NDCBUs (Neighborhood Delivery and Collection Box Units) meeting U.S. Postal Service specifications.

The upgrading of management-controlled and resident-controlled elements go hand in hand toward increasing the value of the property. Attractive manufactured home communities stimulate higher home resale values, and attractive homes stimulate homesite rentals and competitive market level rents. It is important then for management to promulgate community guidelines or rules that set a high standard for maintenance of homes and then to enforce the rules uniformly and consistently. Unsightly conditions must be remedied immediately, and unsafe or unhealthy situations removed or corrected.

Individual homesite landscape improvements can be encouraged by community-wide annual spring flower days. Management can lead the way during the week and encourage homeowner participation on a weekend. Shrubs and flowers can be made available at large-quantity cost or reduced prices to stimulate homeowner participation. Awards and recognition of superior efforts can stimulate a healthy competition among residents for the most attractive homesite. An ongoing Home-of-the-Month contest is yet another way to stimulate community-wide beautification of the manufactured home community.

§ 8.6   Action Plan and Budget

Having completed the first two steps in the upgrade process, assessing the problem and considering solutions, the next step is to decide on an action plan to implement the desired changes. It is important to weigh the cost-benefit relationship for each item on the list and begin with a program that will yield maximum visual results at a reasonable cost. Visual results will assist in getting the program started with the residents. To accomplish this, all items on the assessment list should be reviewed, and priorities established. Cost estimates for the various improvements must be obtained and factored into the action plan discussion.

In reviewing the action plan, determine which items should be added to the list of regular maintenance chores and which should be treated as special needs to be accomplished on a phased basis. Some operations may be handled adequately by the maintenance staff and others may require outside contractors. Assess each decision based on the overall effect on the community. Regular maintenance operations should not be sacrificed to accomplish major projects. It may be more cost-effective to contract some tasks to qualified outside companies. The quality of the end result should be of equal importance to price.

If the upgrade work to be done is designed by an outside consultant, competitive bids can be sought utilizing the construction drawings as bid documents. Smaller, less complicated upgrades can be accomplished by negotiating prices with reputable contractors. If a consultant is used, the finished work should be inspected and approved prior to complete payment. In all cases, written proposals for the work to be performed must be prepared and accepted prior to the beginning of work.

§ 8.7 Annual Review and Reassessment

An important ongoing step in the upgrade process is an annual review of the action plan and community inspection by the owner and the management team. The same tour route utilized in the initial assessment process should be retaken and the progress photos compared with the initial base photos. New areas of concern should be identified and noted, and the action plan should be updated to assure that the community presents an image representative of the value of the investment. If these procedures are carried out continuously, the community will not only achieve a higher value, but it will also fulfill the promise of providing a quality, affordable living environment for the residents.

§ 8.8 Current Methodologies

No discussion of takeover, turnaround, and rejuvenation of manufactured home communities would be complete without describing unique methodologies currently used to address routine and special needs with this property type. In the first instance, Hanover Capital Mortgage Group of Indianapolis, Indiana, has developed a new home sales, financing, and customer service package that effectively and quickly fills vacant homesites in manufactured home communities:

SELLING AND FINANCING PRIVATE LABEL MANUFACTURED HOMES ON-SITE

Hanover Group has been active in the manufactured housing industry since 1973. Hanover Group currently owns and manages seven communities (1,164 homesites) in central and southern Indiana, and has marketing agreements with other non-owned communities totaling over 5,000 sites. Ten years ago the Hanover Group identified a need for an on-site new homes sales, finance and service package, that led to the formation of Capital Acceptance Corporation in 1994.

The Need

Many manufactured home communities built in the 1960s and 1970s were designed to accommodate homes no longer than 60' long, and in some cases 70' long. Meanwhile, manufacturers built larger and larger homes, fueled by buyers with private land on which to site their home. Over time, two problems occurred:

1. Vacancies created from normal turnover could not be filled with the new larger manufactured home.

2. Residents could not "trade up" to larger new manufactured homes.

These problems led to reduced income streams and less upgrade potential for many manufactured home communities.

The Hanover Group Response

Many community owners turned to home rental as a way to fill vacancies, and initially Hanover Group tried this approach as well. Rentals, however, do nothing to upgrade the homes in the community. In fact, they do the opposite. So Hanover Group began selling used homes on contract. As the availability of quality used homes became scarce, they turned to new homes. The new homes are manufactured to Hanover Group's specifications to fit on the smaller homesites characteristic of older communities.

Capital Acceptance Corporation (CAC) was formed by Hanover to finance and insure these private label homes. CAC has the flexibility and the experienced underwriters to approve homebuyers with bruised credit histories. The keys to this successful program include:

1. Expert structuring to approve applicants with "bad credit/good stories."

2. Community manager approval in addition to credit approval.

3. Maintain control over specific location of home. CAC only loans on homes sited in a community managed by Hanover Group or in selected communities with whom we have marketing agreements.

4. Closely monitor loan portfolio. Act quickly to repossess home when payments are late.

5. Resell repossessed homes within thirty days.

6. Financial strength to accept higher risk of lending to substandard credit applicants.

Hanover Group and CAC are actively looking for communities with whom to share this successful program. Contact Ronald E. Farren (317) 782-1396 for more information.

Homes Direct, Inc. of Jacksonville, Florida, has developed a nationwide program that effectively "sells-off" the existing rental homes in a manufactured home community through either a lease purchase program or an installment sales program:

HOMES DIRECT PROGRAM FOR CONVERTING RENTAL MANUFACTURED HOMES TO CONTRACT SALES

Homes Direct, Inc. of Jacksonville, Florida, has developed a nationwide program that effectively "sells-off" the existing rental homes in a manufactured home community through either a lease purchase or an installment sales program.

Most community operators agree that resident-owned homes provide distinct benefits over community-owned rental homes, including reductions in management and maintenance time and expense, repair costs, property taxes and insurance, and turnover rates. The homeowner's pride of ownership generally translates into a more stable living and management environment and a much more desirable landlease community.

These programs are designed to provide the community owner with an increase in the overall asset value while reducing the operational aspects of ownership. This too provides an efficient hands-off exit strategy and makes the community much more attractive to potential lenders and investors.

Homes Direct, Inc. handles all aspects of the program, from the initial inventory evaluation and marketing, through to account servicing and collections. Contact Homes Direct, Inc. at (904) 246-6688.

§ 8.9 Summary

The turnaround challenge of manufactured home community management can at the same time be a most difficult and a potentially rewarding experience for an investor/owner/manager. The risks are often great, but so are the ongoing and ultimate rewards. Rejuvenating manufactured home communities also has its challenges and, like the turnaround scenario, can result in personal satisfaction as the living environment is substantially improved and the property value increased. Just be very careful to assess the up-front risks involved, to budget and plan accordingly, and to implement in a forthright, consistent manner. The results will speak for themselves.

CHAPTER 9

SELLING THE MANUFACTURED HOME COMMUNITY

§ 9.1   Introduction

§ 9.2   Deciding the Right Time to Sell

§ 9.3   Preparing the Property to Sell

§ 9.4   Recruiting the Right Assistance in the Marketing Process

§ 9.5   Estimating the Value Range of the Property

§ 9.6   Identifying the Target Markets and Planning Marketing Strategy

§ 9.7   Preparing and Executing the Marketing Plan

ANOTHER PERSPECTIVE
Michael Conley

§ 9.8   Introduction to Marketing Manufactured Home Communities

§ 9.9   Why People Sell

§ 9.10   —Investment Theory

§ 9.11   When to Sell: Timing

§ 9.12   How to Sell Manufactured Home Communities

§ 9.13   —Seller's Objectives

§ 9.14   —Marketing Strategy

§ 9.15   —When and How to Use a Real Estate Broker

§ 9.16   Summary

§ 9.1   Introduction

The "marketing" of a manufactured home community is a better description of the real estate divestiture process for this investment vehicle than simply "selling" the property. The marketing process takes into consideration the timing, the property preparation and valuation, and an appropriate planning process.

This marketing process is characterized by six key steps:

1. Deciding the right time to sell
2. Preparing the property to sell
3. Recruiting the right assistance, if any, to enhance the marketing process
4. Estimating the value of the property
5. Identifying the target markets and planning marketing strategy
6. Preparing and executing a Marketing Plan with the goal of selling the property at the highest price.

So now the manufactured home community investment has come full cycle. Whether developed upon raw land or acquired as an investment, the income property, hopefully, has served its desired purposes and yielded rewarding results.

§ 9.2   Deciding the Right Time to Sell

Divestiture timing is a product of the association of personal or corporate decision making and local market conditions. Hopefully the two conditions are in sync at the appropriate time. This would typically be when an individual (corporation or partnership) has a positive reason for selling when the local market and rent levels support high occupancy at the subject property. Then the seller stands a good chance of maximizing ROI (return on and of investment). Positive reasons for selling might include retirement (on the personal or sole proprietor level) or a desire to liquidate and access another type investment (on the corporate or partnership level). Negative reasons for selling might include failing health, unexpected or overwhelming personal financial reversals, or mounting debt. Market conditions at the time may be soft (low occupancy), stable (high occupancy), or somewhere in between. Ideally, from a seller perspective, right timing and market conditions will coincide. However, short of that, the seller should guard against his personal pressures being known and used as a negotiating lever to his ultimate disadvantage. There is not much to do about market conditions in the short term, unless a new employer comes to town or rent controls are lifted during the due diligence period. Anything less than these scenarios tends to work against the seller. Sometimes, however, seller financing works as an equalizer when local commercial bank financing is not available to underwrite the needed mortgage. So timing is a basic consideration with a variety of scenarios that must be carefully considered before and during the manufactured home community marketing process.

§ 9.3 Preparing the Property to Sell

Much of this topic was covered in **Chapter 8.** For that matter, the entire holding period for an investment like this should be looked upon as a continuing effort to prepare the property to sell, ensuring that the value has every opportunity to appreciate. But beyond all that, there are three distinct categories of effort that enhance this important preparatory step: tighten up, clean up, and get help!

Tighten up.   There are but two ways to improve the NOI of an income-producing property. The first is to maximize income in every possible way; the second is to minimize operating expenses just as aggressively.

To maximize income, the astute owner and property manager must maximize existent primary income streams (that is, raise rents to the highest justifiable levels without destroying all upside potential for the eventual buyer) and secondary streams, such as new and resale home sales, brokerage profits and commissions and sale of products and services to residents. They must also seek to identify and implement new income streams, such as homeowner insurance, cable TV rebates, and vending machine income.

Minimizing operating expenses, like maximizing income, should be an ongoing exercise for conscientious property owners and managers. The easiest way to effect this is to examine regularly every line item of monthly expense and ask, How can this figure be reduced for next month? It works. It also takes time and diligence month on end, year after year.

Clean up. Here is yet another ongoing set of activities that take on greater importance just before and during the time an income property is for sale. As they say in the Navy, "If it doesn't move, paint it! Or stain it." Either way, signs, trimwork, curbs, basketball and tennis court striping, fencing, and building exteriors and interiors should all look freshly painted. Streets should look recently slurried. For maximum curb appeal (that is, how a property looks to the casual passerby or drive-through prospect), fresh and manicured landscaping treatments, grass, completely clean streets and homesites, fully and properly skirted homes, and freshly seal-coated home roofs all help to this end. The property must be infinitely appealing to prospective renters and home-buyers, present residents, employees, and prospective buyers of the manufactured home community.

Get help. This step is not mandatory but is often helpful, even critical, in many marketing situations. Help might be found from three directions:

1. Consultant. A consultant is someone who knows manufactured home communities as well and probably better than the seller. The consultant advises the seller as to how to maximize the value of the investment property before putting it in the market, and the consultant may or may not become involved in one or both of the following assistance areas (see §§ **9.4** through **9.7**). A consultant often "mystery shops" a property for the owner to identify curb appeal, marketing, rules enforcement, deferred maintenance, and resident relations shortfalls that need to be addressed.

2. Appraiser. Real estate appraisers capable and experienced in the area of manufactured home communities are generally difficult to find. Ask to see samples of an appraiser's work with other like properties. How do the appraiser's manufactured home community benchmarks (occupancy, OER, and so forth) compare with industry standards?

3. Broker. Real estate brokers who specialize in marketing manufactured home communities are likewise a rarity. Ask to see samples of previous successfully marketed manufactured home community packages plus references. For a list of manufactured home community specialist brokers, see **Appendix L.**

§ 9.4 Recruiting the Right Assistance in the Marketing Process

Not every manufactured home community owner needs a consultant, appraiser, or broker to help prepare, value, market, and sell the property. In fact, the guidance in this text covers most of the requisite property management bases, even mystery shopping one's own holding. Additionally, the aforementioned Valuation Calculation Worksheet (VCW) (see **Form 3–5** in **Chapter 3**) is a simple and handy way to supplement the three traditional appraisal methods described in **Chapter 5.** But as far as real estate brokers are concerned, they do have the ability to expose property to a much broader market than is usually available to the property owner, who is generally restricted to placing classified ads in local newspapers or possibly *The Wall Street Journal.* When listing a property with a real estate broker, expect to execute one of the following contracts:

1. Exclusive agency (often has a multiple listing clause)
2. Exclusive right to sell (most desirable type from the broker's point of view—he gets paid no matter who procures the buyer)
3. Open listing, also known as nonexclusive or general listing
4. Option listing and net listing are two other forms of listings, both illegal in many states.[1]

For additional insights on marketing the manufactured home community—from a professional real estate broker's point of view and one who deals almost exclusively with manufactured home communities—see §§ **9.8** through **9.15.**

§ 9.5 Estimating the Value Range of the Property

Again, the property owner has an array of choices at this stage: consultant, appraiser, broker, or self-help. Just as a capable, experienced broker generally gives a property broadest exposure, the trained and

---

[1] Alvin Arnold, Real Estate Investor's Deskbook 1-3 (1994).

experienced real estate appraiser tends to prepare the most accurate and comprehensive (depending on level of appraisal report or opinion of letter value contracted) value appraisal of the property. A real estate broker, intimate with manufactured home communities will often have the best "market feel" value for this property type. In any event, seek to have the property valued from the three traditional perspectives:

1. Cost or replacement value approach
2. Market data or comparable sales approach
3. Income capitalization approach.

This should be all one needs to feel comfortable valuing a manufactured home community. One additional method, however, is the Valuation Calculation Worksheet or VCW. It is the first nontraditional valuation technique to be applied to manufactured home communities. The two main features of the system are the application of six key property characteristics and several adjustment factors to arrive at a valuation factor, which is then applied to the net operating income of the subject property. **Form 9–1** is an applied example of the blank form introduced in **Chapter 3**. See **Appendix T** for a detailed description of the VCW.

§ 9.6   Identifying the Target Markets and Planning Marketing Strategy

Who will purchase the manufactured home community? This is usually not a problem. Would-be buyers of manufactured home communities generally outnumber sellers by nine-to-one. Of course this is predicated on generally stable market conditions and properties of sufficient size and nature to produce an adequate and ongoing NOI. Who might be a buyer?

1. Small investors looking for their first income property—often young entrepreneurs or near retirees.
2. Partnerships looking to syndicate an acquisition to start or add to an existent portfolio of similar or dissimilar property types.
3. Larger investors—individuals and corporate—looking to expand portfolios or move into new geographic areas.

FORM 9–1

VALUATION CALCULATION WORKSHEET (VCW)
for owners and sellers of ground lease-type
MANUFACTURED HOME COMMUNITIES
operating at 85%+ economic occupancy✦

I. Name of the Property _____   Date: _____
    Physical Address: _____   Zip: _____
    Contact Person/Role: _____   Phone: (—) _____
    # Devoloped Acres: _100_   Average monthly site rent: $ _140-00_   Age of property: _20+_ yrs.(1974)
✦ # Sites occupied and paid: _475_ (+) # sites fully developed: _500_ (=) _95_ % economic occupancy✦

STEP A. KEY PROPERTY CHARACTERISTICS . . . viewed from owner/seller perspective of operation
  Assign points in 6 Key Characteristics, from low of 1/2 point to maximum of 2 points.

1. LOCATION. Remote and poor proximity = 1/2 pt.; Good desirability, accessibility and proximity = 1 pt.; excellent
    neighborhood, desirability, accessibility and proximity to employment, services, transportation = 2 pts. _1/2_ point(s)

2. NUMBER RENTAL HOMESITES. 5-49 = 1/2 pt.; 50-99 = 1 pt.; 100-199 = 1.5 pts.; 200+ = 2 pts.   _2_ point(s)

3. HOMESITE SIZES. All singlesection (4,999 sq. ft. and smaller) = 1/2 pt;
    approximately 50/50 mix = 1 pt.; All multisection (5,000 sq. ft. and larger) = 2 pts.   _1_ point(s)

4. UTILITIES. *1. Old, private and poor condition = 1/2 pt.; Private and OK condition = 1 pt.;
    Private and excellent condition or Public with fair rates and buried = 2 pts.   _2_ point(s)

5. AMENITIES. *1. None = 1/2 pt.; Minimal = 1 pt.; Top quality property with swimming pool and
    clubhouse - if desirable in local market = 2 pts.   _1 1/2_ point(s)

6. OVERALL CURB APPEAL. *1 Marginal to fair = 1/2 pt.; Good = 1 pt.; Excellent and better with
    landscaping, off-street parking, adequate setbacks, wide curvilinear (vs. grid pattern) streets,
    lap-sided and shingled homes = 2 pts.   _1 1/2_ point(s)

7. ADD POINTS from all 6 categories, deduct from 20, and put result here: _11 1/2 or 11.5_ point(s)

8. ACTUAL RENT COLLECTED (no new or resale home sales $, miscellaneous, or rental home
    income) during last 12 month period.*2. Is there a steady and growing income stream? Y/N _Y_ $ _798,000_ income

9. ACTUAL OPERATING EXPENSES (no debt service or depreciation $; consider including 5%
    for property management fee and 1% for capital reserves) for same 12 month period. $ _315,000_ expense

10. OPERATING EXPENSE RATIO (national OER = 37.8%; Model = 40%)
    Formula: total operating expense + total rent collected; line 9 + line 8 = OER benchmark   _39.5_ %OER

STEP B. VALUATION ADJUSTMENT FACTORS . . . viewed from owner/seller perspective of operation
  Decide whether each factor adds to or reduces property's value by maximum of ± $500/homesite

1. DENSITY OF HOMESITES.*1. 7+/acre = -$500; 6 or less/acre = +$500.   ± $ _+500_
    Density formula: # developed homesites + # developed acres.

2. ECONOMIC OCCUPANCY. Less than 84% = -$500; 85-94% = $-0-;
    95% and better = +$500. Formula: see ✦ at beginning of worksheet.   ± $ _+500_

3. PRESENT RENT LEVEL. *1. low for market = -$500; high for market = $-0-;
    mid-range for market = +$500.   ± $ _+500_

4. NUMBER OF RENTAL HOMES ON -SITE. *1. 3% + = -$500; 2% or less = +$500.   ± $ _-500_

FORM 9–1
(continued)

5. ADVERSE OR RESTRICTIVE LANDLORD-TENANT LEGISLATION AND/OR RENT CONTROL in effect locally? Yes = -$500; no = +$500.   ± $ *+500*

6. CONTIGUOUS RAW LAND AVAILABLE AND ZONED for like use? Yes = +$500; no = -0-.   ± $ *- 0 -*

7. OPTIONAL: e.g. licensed to operate, if appropriate. Yes = +$500 or No = -$500.   ± $ *+500*   optional

8. OPTIONAL: e.g. significant effect of miscellaneous income stream? *1 and *2.   ± $ *- 0 -*   optional

9. OPTIONAL: e.g. resident base and mix; pride in home ownership? Y/N   ± $ *- 0 -*   optional

10. OPTIONAL: e.g. effect of area occupancy level and rent structure.   ± $ *- 0 -*   optional

11. CUMULATIVE TOTAL OF VALUATION ADJUSTMENT FACTORS at ± $500/site, with cumulative total <u>not to exceed</u> ± $1,500/homesite on this line: ± $ *+2000* = *1500 max*

STEP C.   VALUATION CALCULATION . . . using data from STEPS A and B above . . .

1. RENT COLLECTED $ *798,000* *3 (-) OPERATING EXPENSES $ *315,000* = $ *483,000* NOI

2. a) NET OPERATING INCOME (from line above) divided by Key Point Total from Step A, expressed as a decimal (e.g. 9 points ÷ 100 = .09 divisor.
2. b) $ *483,000* NOI (÷) *.115* point divisor = preliminary value of $ *4,200,000*

3. Preliminary Value $ *4,200,000* (÷) *475* occupied and paid homesites = $ *8,842* per site

4. Value per site, $ *8,842* (±) *1500* adjustment per homesite from Step B = $ *10,342* adjusted site value

5. Adjusted Site Value of $ *10,342* (X) *475* # occupied and paid homesites = $ *4,912,450* value subtotal

6. Adjusted Site Value of $ *10,342* (X) *25* # vacant and unpaid homesites x .50 value <u>discount</u> = $ *129,275* value subtotal

7. ADD two subtotals (lines 5 and 6 above) together to obtain the TOTAL ESTIMATED VALUE of the MANUFACTURED HOME COMMUNITY . . . = $ *5,041,725* **Total Value**

FOOTNOTES:

*1. These characteristics (Step A) and factors (Step B) will be viewed and valued differently by owners estimating value and planning to hold vs. owners estimating value and planning to sell and wanting to attract serious prospective buyers now. The latter perspective will generally be similar to buyers of quality properties.

*2. Cable TV and phone commissions; MH brokerage; role of parts and service.

*3. A personal judgement call whether to include a 2% vacancy factor here or not.

DISCLAIMER. This VALUATION CALCULATION WORKSHEET FOR MANUFACTURED HOME COMMUNITIES is distributed as a handy, easy-to-use, self-help guide to estimating the possible value of a manufactured home community. The services of experienced, certified, licensed real estate value appraisers should always be retained for best results. Accuracy of results wholly dependent upon data selected and calculated by VCW user.

Designed by George Allen CPM, October 29, 1994

This form available for purchase in tablet format.
Property Management Form #118
Copyright Oct 1994
Revised January 1996

PMN Publishing
P.O. Box #47024
Indianapolis, IN 46247
(317) 888-7156

4.   Residents of the property who form a homeowners' association to purchase the property where they live. This is known as an R.O.C. or resident-owned community and may take the form of a cooperatively owned or condominiumized property.

5.   Local municipality wanting to purchase the property as a source of low-cost housing.

6.   Someone desiring to convert the property to another land use.

And the list goes on. The point is that there are generally more investors looking to acquire a manufactured home community than there are parties desiring to sell.

§ 9.7   Preparing and Executing the Marketing Plan

Not all sellers take the time to draft a formal Marketing Plan before putting their manufactured home community on the market, but they should. The exercise forces them to deal with specific and important issues and reckon with alternatives that may enhance the salability of the property, or lessen same if not dealt with properly. Because of the amount of money changing hands in this sort of transaction, it only makes sense to codify research, thoughts, plans, and anticipated actions.

A typical Marketing Plan, drafted for the purposes of selling a manufactured home community, usually has five parts:[2]

1.   **Introduction.** Simply a one- or two-paragraph overview of the seller's intent, general target market, and method of reaching same.

2.   **Target Market or Markets.** Identifies who might be interested in purchasing the property, including friends and associates who have expressed interest in the past.

3.   **Marketing Methods.** States how to reach the stated target, whether implemented by seller alone or with the assistance of one or more real estate brokers. Type of listing is important at this point. Advertising? If so, where placed, type and size ads, cost factors.

---

[2] George Allen, David Alley, & Edward Hicks, Development, Marketing and Operation of Manufactured Home Communities (John Wiley & Sons, Inc., 1994).

4. **Marketing Objective.** What type of deals are acceptable—all cash (and consequence of capital gains tax); a lease-option contract to postpone paying taxes; installment sale to save on taxes; even a 1031 tax exchange as a possibility?[3] The alternatives must be explored with flexibility.

5. **Marketing Budget.** Probably more owner/investor dollars are required when marketing oneself; less when using the services of a real estate broker.

There is no need for this to be a complicated or lengthy document. It is meant to simply be a tool. The Marketing Plan should suit one's purposes and be used to effectively market the manufactured home community. At this point, another perspective on the subject of marketing and selling a manufactured home community will be especially helpful.

ANOTHER PERSPECTIVE[4]
Michael Conley

§ 9.8   Introduction to Marketing Manufactured Home Communities

Marketing investment properties in the 1990s, specifically selling manufactured home communities, requires professionalism and specialization. To understand the requirements of successful investment property marketing, one must understand why people sell, the timing of the sale, and how to sell.

---

[3] As a 1031 tax exchange attorney states in his self-published book, *1031 Exchange Concepts,* "where there is a desire to continue to own real estate as an investment or for income-producing purposes, it makes more economic sense to use all of the equity in acquiring the new property rather than selling, paying the taxes from the proceeds, and then investing with the remaining proceeds." 180 Grand Ave., Suite 950, Oakland, CA 94612.

[4] Michael Conley of Marcus & Millichap's office in Chicago provides some unique insights and advice on the subject.

§ 9.9 Why People Sell

Based on an unscientific survey of 1,300 manufactured home communities over a five-year period, it has been observed that approximately 3 percent change ownership each year. Motivation to sell falls into two categories: (1) to solve a problem, and (2) to realize an opportunity. These two often overlap. Motivation is a mysterious consideration. In the realm of selling, it is generally considered important not to reveal true motivation. The reasons to sell are also related to who is doing the selling.

Certain types of owners display similar patterns of motivation. Single-community owners, as opposed to professional investors, are less likely to sell to take a profit or to get rid of a management problem. For the single-community owner, the decision to sell is likely to be more of a lifestyle decision than an investment decision. Both categories of sellers have their own complexities. It is helpful to consider some examples to better understand these dynamics. Then the next section considers investment analysis theory as it relates to choices owners may or may not make about selling their investment property.

Real Life Situations

One owner wants to sell to effect a great "deal" on another investment property that could be structured as a 1031 Exchange. Depreciation has run out on the manufactured home community for sale, and it has well water and lagoon systems that are causing an increasing array of problems with regulators. The seller is the original developer and would realize a substantial profit. This is a case of selling to solve a problem and realizing an opportunity.

Another owner is in litigation with the lender from whom the property has been purchased. Management is a mess, the property is being neglected, and everybody wants out. This is a clear case of a sale solving a problem.

Two partners have another dissimilar business that is growing fast and needs capital and time. Their 300-site manufactured home community is old. Their capital and time are clearly better spent on the business that has the greater growth potential. Here, a sale is motivated by another better opportunity.

A syndicator needs cash to stabilize some other investments that are not cash flowing, so selling his manufactured home community at a considerable profit seems to be a perfect solution. This is an example of solving a problem, even though the problem is not with the "for sale" property.

These examples are real life situations. Whether motivated by problems or prospects, all sellers have one common denominator—their decisions to sell are compelling. Smart investors just do not divest of an investment property without one or more very good reasons.

§ 9.10   —Investment Theory

The decision to sell generally cannot be limited to the property alone. It must also take into account external factors like the availability of alternative investments. Sometimes it is the opportunity toward which the seller is shifting time and money that drives the decision to sell as much as the property's specific considerations.

To summarize, the reasons why owners sell involve both internal and external factors. Internal property-specific factors generally include

- Realization of profit
- Loss of depreciation
- Avoidance of management problems
- Perceived declining yields
- Maxed-out rents
- Anticipated increases in operating costs, such as:
    Infrastructure maintenance and repair

    Homesite size obsolescence

    Excessive utility or property tax costs.

External non-property-specific factors may include

- The need for cash
- Other investment opportunities
- A period of high liquidity and strong demand in the local market.

The decision to sell is typically made when one or more of these factors are in place and present a compelling case to take action. The purpose of selling is to maximize gain and/or to minimize loss. Ultimately, the decision to sell is predicated upon the perceived opportunity to achieve basic and planned investment objectives. Generally, the objectives of the professional investor fall into the following basic categories:

- General preservation; safety
- Capital growth or the creation of wealth
- Income.

These are not mutually exclusive, and the interrelationship between them can be reflected in a risk-reward equation. Although each of the three objectives is important to the professional investor, the interrelationship among them, for each investor, is unique. It is this interrelationship that forms the foundation for the investor's strategy.

Investor strategy becomes even more personalized when the investor's objectives are established within the context of the investor's perception of asset and market characteristics. Although there is no typical investor, it is helpful to make some useful generalizations. For example, a model investor has a strong desire for creation of wealth and preservation of capital. In addition, the investor wants good regular income. Interestingly enough, it seems that manufactured home communities offer the investor excellent vehicles to maximize all three objectives. It is the realization of this that makes manufactured home communities so difficult to part with.

Such is the pervasive attitude in a marketplace that makes these investment opportunities hard to find, and it is the perceived lack of opportunities that, in turn, limits decisions to sell. The problem is this: most investors do not proactively consider selling. Instead, they tend to respond to outside stimuli. Therefore, realization of maximum long-term investment objectives is restricted by a market where sellers are scarce.

A Case for a Buy-Hold and Trade Investment Strategy

Let's say you have a property that was purchased for $2,500,000 five years ago with a down payment of $500,000. At the time of purchase, the NOI was $250,000. Of that, $193,000 (9 percent, 30 years) went to service debt and $57,000 was annual cash flow. Now, five years later, the NOI is $320,000 after roughly a 5 percent annual appreciation. Now instead of an 11 percent cash on cash return on the original investment, the return is $127,000 or 25 percent. That is a good return—or is it?

The market value of the property is now $3,370,000, assuming a 9.5 percent CAP disposition value (that is, capitalization rate). After netting out transaction costs and giving consideration to loan amortization, the net equity might be $1,270,000. The $127,000 cash flow now has a different perspective. It represents a 10 percent yield if considered as a return on unrealized pretax gain. A practical alternative here might be to trade out of this property into a larger one, a slightly more aggressive strategy with potentially greater long-term benefits.

Take the $1,270,000 proceeds and buy an income-producing property with a comparable capitalization rate as the original purchase, and presumably a similar appreciation potential, though it could be even better. This amount of cash could get you into a property of, let's say $5,000,000, with an NOI of $500,000 and D.S. debt service (at 9 percent, 30 years) of $360,000, leaving $140,000 as first year cash return, which is an 11 percent ROI. Now the investor owns a property twice the size, and theoretically, with an operating cost ratio that can even be more efficient. But the real benefit is what happens over the next five years. If annual appreciation is 2.5 percent on both properties, in year 10 the original property would have an NOI of approximately $362,000 and a cash flow of $169,000. After selling at a 9.5 percent CAP, the result is a net equity of $1,831,000. Not bad for just holding.

However, after trading into the larger property there would be an NOI of approximately $566,000. Utilizing the same parameters for selling would increase the net equity an additional $512,000. When considering the original $500,000 investment, the incremental increase to yield is generally enhanced. The example would be even more dramatic if appreciation had not slowed down in the last five years.

There are two assumptions to this example that warrant consideration. The first is a mortgage market with constant terms. Although this may be an oversimplification, it is important to hold this constant to make the point. In reality, it may be better or worse. If better, so is the example; and if worse, well, it has to be considered with all the other investment factors.

The other assumption that should be questioned is that of always buying at a 10 percent CAP (or capitalization rate) and selling at a 9.5 percent CAP. If investors had more confidence in their abilities to consistently buy low and sell high, there would certainly be more velocity in the market. If the right strategy is employed in the process of selling and buying, investors can generally realize a slight advantage, both in getting-in and getting-out of income-producing properties. It should be considered that this spread in capitalization rates is only .5 percent, but it makes a huge difference in performance over the long run. The selection of 9.5 percent and 10 percent for CAP rates is not intended to be a conclusion about market capitalization rates as much as it is intended to illustrate the relative significance of a small spread between in and out CAP rates on overall investment performance.

Additionally, at the risk of pointing out the obvious, compounding leverage and capital gains tax deferral are critical ingredients to the success of the buy-hold and trade investment strategy. However, this strategy may not always be available.

If more owners took the time to aggressively consider the possible benefits in a buy-hold and trade strategy, there would be more success stories and the market would be healthier. Some investors have used this approach successfully in the past. Others should consider using it in the future, not only to maximize quantitative financial objectives, but also to cull and prune portfolios on a qualitative level. Properties acquired years before may not reflect the current parameters of one's current organization. For reasons such as size, resident profile, utility configuration, or location, properties still in a portfolio may no longer be a good fit; consequently, these properties may be worth more to the next investor. It was Robert P. Vanderpoel who said, "The most successful businessman is the man who holds onto the old just as long as it is good and grabs the new just as soon as it is better."

In concluding this discussion of why to sell, the reader is reminded that the ultimate decision to sell can be at times quite simple, and at times quite complex. Serious consideration of whether or not to sell is too often lacking. The "do nothing" alternative does not always represent the optimum investment strategy.

§ 9.11 When to Sell: Timing

With respect to the question of when to sell, there are two basic answers. The first is when the reasons to sell outweigh the reasons not to sell. The second is to sell only when one does not have to! A fundamental dilemma arises when the reasons to sell are both compelling and time-sensitive. Obviously, an owner wants to avoid a forced sale at all costs. A forced sale is not part of any rational seller's investment strategy. It may, however, be a wonderful opportunity for a buyer.

In reality, there is no perfect time to sell. If there is an ideal time, however, it would be at that moment when all operating systems are stable—and have been for several years. Nothing significant appears to need fixing; rents are maxed-out, but somehow appear to have a long way to run; expenses are about to go through the roof, but have no appearance of doing so; and depreciation is gone.

§ 9.12   How to Sell Manufactured Home Communities

There are three fundamental questions that determine how to best market a manufactured home community:

1. What are the seller's investment and exit objectives?
2. What elements of strategy are necessary to ensure a high probability of maximizing these objectives?
3. What are the differences between selling the property without assistance, using open listings, or granting a real estate broker an exclusive listing?

§ 9.13   —Seller's Objectives

When it comes to maximizing the objectives of the seller, most often at the top of the list are sale price and terms. Most sellers prefer to sell all cash (assuming the ability to avoid or defer income taxes), at an astronomical price, and spend little or no time in negotiation (because for a seller, negotiation typically involves price erosion). Certainly a seller wants no part in spending time dealing with buyers' questions, probing audits, environmental studies, waiting for lenders, and resolving title issues. In short, the preferred sale is one where a foreign investor shows up one day in a helicopter with a suitcase filled with cash and asks, "How much? I must have this property; name your price and we'll close today." The better a seller's investment goals and objectives are defined, the better the probability of achieving,them.

§ 9.14 —Marketing Strategy

To maximize the probability of achieving the seller's objectives presupposes that those objectives are realistic. Without realistic objectives, the potential of being ignored by the market is substantial. To alienate the market is likely to result in neutralizing any exposure the marketing initiative will generate. The two pillars upon when any effective marketing strategy must be built are

1. Achieving maximum exposure to qualified buyers, and
2. Having realistic investment objectives.

Maximum Exposure

Achieving maximum exposure is important for two reasons. First, it increases the chances of finding the best buyer. The best buyer is typically a buyer that has an unusually favorable perception of the subject property, and ideally has some type of external motivation. External motivation is some set of circumstances propelling the buyer to buy that are independent from the buyer's interest in the subject property.

Second, it is the goal of exposure to find not only the best buyer, but the second best buyer, and the third, fourth, and so on. The purpose of this is to create competition, and it is the purpose of this competition to inspire the best buyer to prove it by making the best moves. As buyers, advantage is eroded by competition; conversely, as sellers, it is enhanced. To realize maximum exposure, one must first identify who buys.

Finding Buyers

Starting from scratch, the highest probability source of buyers is that group that has bought manufactured home communities recently. While recent acquisitions do qualify someone as a buyer, this does not necessarily provide a comprehensive buyer list. Considering this group alone, and adjusting out for multiple-properties buyers, assuming velocity of 3 percent and a market base of 10,000 investment-grade manufactured home communities nationwide, it is possible to estimate that there were 200 active buyers in the United States last year, assuming that some buyers made multiple purchases. Some are still active and some are not. The first step in establishing the market is to identify those proven buyers and determine their parameters, which tend to always be changing.

The next layer of potential buyers is less easily identified. These are the buyers that have not yet purchased any manufactured home communities, but are active investment real estate buyers. These "cross-over" buyers are often trading out of apartment investments and can be sold on the merits of manufactured home communities as superior investments when compared to their management-intensive cousins, the apartment complex.

After the cross-over buyers comes a broad category of "potential" real estate investors. This category is broad and deep, and isolating the performers from the pretenders is both difficult and time-consuming. This group represents active investors in areas other than real estate. Advertising is a good long-term strategy for isolating potential buyers in this category. However, in the short run, this is a very low-probability approach to finding highly motivated buyers for a given situation. When buyers from this category can be found, they often represent some of the best buyers around.

Another aspect of the market that is becoming more relevant today involves the public sector and nonprofit sponsorship. These groups, particularly in today's market, have access to relatively inexpensive bond financing and may buy on their own behalf, or on behalf of the residents. Understanding the needs and idiosyncrasies of this latter category is challenging because the sponsors do not always think like traditional investors. Working with these groups requires extraordinary patience because many of them are charting new waters in a highly politicized environment.

In summary, maximum exposure is not achieved without efficiently exploring each of the four categories of buyers just described. Again, these are

1. Proven active buyers of manufactured home communities
2. Proven investment property buyers or "cross-over" buyers

3. Potential real estate investors
4. Public/nonprofit sponsored buyers.

Pricing Objectives

As mentioned earlier, establishing realistic objectives as a seller influences the response from the marketplace. However, many sellers have a fear of being inundated by prospects who have read "How to Negotiate" paperbacks. Commentary on negotiation seems to revolve around one main theme, that is, how to buy for less. There never seems to be any instruction on how to sell for more. Consequently, sellers wanting a good price are encouraged to go to market at a price high enough to ensure a huge negotiating buffer. The problem with this strategy is that it is easily dealt with by experienced negotiators, so any benefits are greatly reduced because many buyers will not respond to a grossly overpriced property. Worse still, the most motivated buyers are often the least likely to respond because they are often under some real or perceived time pressure to close a deal. For them, the fear of wasting time with unrealistic sellers can be substantial. Fear of leaving money on the table is another common reason for putting properties on the market at prices that substantially exceed fair market value. Once again, the cost is high. Clearly, well-priced properties, given maximum exposure to motivated buyers, are most likely to be sold at levels that best accomplish the objectives of the seller.

Remember, one must have people to negotiate with. If the subject property is being shown, but not sold, it may be being used to make other properties on the market appear more attractive. A study by the National Association of Realtors illustrates this point: "When priced at fair market value, 60% of prospective purchasers will look at a property. At 5% over the market, the number drops down to 30% and at 10% over market, the number drops down to 2%."

The point is this: If there is competition for a property, it can be priced at or slightly above fair market value and held there. This strategy is that of a proactive seller who wants to enter into property marketing from a position of strength. To overprice real estate is clearly defeatist, especially if it is for purposes of winning a negotiation. Of course, the trick to all this is determining what the fair market value is for a given piece of property at a particular time.

Pricing

Pricing is clearly more of an art than a science, and credentials do not an expert make—that is, except for one, the consistent and successful track record in establishing and achieving demonstrably fair market value. According to Donald Henahan, "on the subject of wild mushrooms, it is easy to tell who is an expert and who is not. The expert is the one who is still alive." So it is with marketing investment property.

A critical and basic element to pricing a property is the pattern established by recent comparable consummated sales, and with comparable properties that have been on the market and not sold. There is little science to the process: simply research, document, and carefully compare.

Market facts on comparable properties must be aggressively sought out, checked, and cross-checked. But after the data is in, the fun begins. The art of pricing is in the interpretation of the data. What weight to place upon one set of facts versus another largely depends upon how one perceives the market's evaluation of the uniqueness of one property from the next. No two properties are ever the same. Generally, the market places either premiums or discounts on properties based upon specific characteristics, which have been described elsewhere in this text.

Another important consideration in comparing market information in pricing a property is making appropriate adjustments for terms. Seller financing, master leases, partial sale leasebacks, and earn-outs, to name a few, are all potential elements of deal structures that can significantly impact value. Ultimately, it is through a comprehensive analysis of market activity, viewed through the invaluable lens of experience, that patterns can be established. It is these patterns that provide a basis for pricing.

As Ray Krock, the founder of McDonald's once said, "It requires a certain kind of mind to see beauty in a hamburger bun." A certain kind of mind is most definitely required to effectively price manufactured home community investment properties in a complex and dynamic marketplace.

§ 9.15   —When and How to Use a Real Estate Broker

The next area of concern, whether of not to use a real estate broker, is easier to resolve. Sellers who are convinced that they have enough information to price their properties effectively, that they have access to large numbers of motivated buyers, and that they have enough time to get the necessary exposure to create competition, do not need to use brokers. However, for sellers not sure about these areas and who recognize the value of a "negotiating buffer" and having someone insulate them from a very time-consuming and management-intense process, then having a qualified and experienced real estate broker as a professional ally makes a whole lot of sense.

The choice whether or not to use a broker, in reality, is not a simple one to make. If a real estate broker can provide all the essential value-added elements of designing and implementing an effective marketing strategy, the seller will probably make more money by hiring one. The problem, however, is that like any profession, there is a huge variation in the quality of service provided between one broker and the next. If the broker is not successful, or if one is hired to do what the seller could do for himself (assuming, that one is willing to), then a mistake has been made.

But assume that finding a qualified professional is not a problem. Frankly, like in most things, a little research solves the problem. What then, are the seller's alternatives? There are really three:

1. Market the property without paying or using a real estate broker
2. Market the property on an "open listing basis" through the entire brokerage community
3. Market the property on an "exclusive listing basis" using a qualified and experienced broker.

Following are the advantages and disadvantages of these three choices.

Not Using a Broker

If the seller is going to market the property without paying or using a broker, the advantages are

- Saving a sales commission
- Maintaining control.

The disadvantages are

- Limited marketing and limited exposure to buyers
- Buyers discounting out the brokerage fee savings with lower offers

- A tremendous seller time investment fielding calls, presenting packages, facilitating showings, and so forth
- No intermediary or negotiation buffer
- Many buyers represented by brokers may not ever see the property.

Open Listings

If the seller is going to market the property on an open listing basis through the entire brokerage community, the advantages are

- Maintaining some control
- Getting more brokers scrambling to make a deal.

The disadvantages are

- No single-broker accountability
- Seller has the burden of qualifying buyers and brokers
- No seller representation; brokers are representing only buyers and themselves
- To some buyers and brokers, an open listing indicates the seller is not serious about selling the property; some exchange buyers avoid an open listing for this reason
- Seller may underprice or overprice property because of inexperience in the market
- No incentive for brokers to continue to work the deal after their immediate buyers reject the property
- A tendency of brokers to shop rather than promote the property.

Exclusive Listings

If the seller is going to market the property on an exclusive listing basis through a qualified broker, the advantages are

- Far greater potential market exposure
- Considerable time saving
- Having an intermediary and negotiating buffer

- Having commitment and accountability on the part of the exclusive broker
- Having someone to qualify buyers and brokers
- Prevents shopping by unqualified brokers.

The disadvantages are

- Perceived loss of control
- Potential for being "tied-up" by unqualified brokers or buyers.

Clearly, if the seller chooses not to market a property, an exclusive listing with an experienced and qualified real estate brokerage firm is the best alternative. However, the decision to put trust in someone for a job as important as selling an investment property can be difficult. This is because many owners got their start in this business by doing some degree of brokerage, or they find themselves today handling some or many of the aspects of a brokerage function.

But in these times, the investment real estate market is dynamic and unclear, and more than ever before the function of buying or selling investment property requires specialization. To specialize in the marketing of investment real estate involves much more than providing the fundamentals just discussed. Brokerage services have never needed to be more specialized and as value-added as they are today.

What to Expect from a Real Estate Broker

Sellers should expect the following essentials from a respectable and efficient real estate brokerage organization:

- A demonstrable ability to achieve the highest market price possible
- An established track record for closing escrows
- A proven ability as investment property specialists
- A known ability to arrange financing
- A network of highly trained investment property brokers
- A large established investor network
- Immediate access to prequalified exchange buyers

- A long-term advertising campaign that is constantly cultivating new buyers
- The ability to create competition
- An efficient system of other-office cooperation
- Proficiency in using tightly written contracts that are closing oriented— including short specific contingencies and large deposits
- Comprehensive marketing programs
- A seller-controlled broker co-op policy
- Established market credibility that endorses the integrity of an exclusive listing
- Clout with title companies, escrow companies, and lenders
- A large exclusive inventory that attracts a wide spectrum of buyers, some of whom are seeking exchange property opportunities
- Constant ongoing training of brokers
- Integrity of information
- Constant innovation.

For seller and buyers, there is clearly value in having representation. Only those brokerage firms that recognize this and strive to meet the complex needs of clients in the 1990s and beyond will survive. Recognizing that there is such a thing as value-added representation and demanding the highest quality of service is critical if one is to receive the greatest benefits from a brokerage company.

§ 9.16 Summary

When a manufactured home community is bought, managed, and sold "right," it can be truly said—as it is often joked about boat owners (but for different reasons)—the two happiest days in the life of a real estate investor are the day when he/she buys a manufactured home community, and the day it is sold! That in great measure has a lot to do with why this chapter and this book were written—to help would-be manufactured home community investors into and out of one of the best real estate investment opportunities available in the United States and Canada today.

CHAPTER 10

COMING FULL CYCLE

§ 10.1   Introduction

§ 10.2   Review of Major Themes

§ 10.1   Introduction

Together we've covered a lot of real estate investment territory in nine chapters. Everything from an introduction to manufactured housing and the manufactured home landlease community, to the basics of real estate investing, and through the consecutive but often overlapping stages of property search and evaluation, valuation, purchase, management, and disposition. But there is more to come. The appendixes alone contain enough valuable and related information to fill a separate volume. The purpose of this chapter, however, is to summarize what has been covered previously.

§ 10.2   Review of Major Themes

When all is said and done, there are really four major themes to this text. They are

1. How to <u>Find</u> a landlease manufactured home community to acquire
2. How to <u>Buy</u> it wisely and safely
3. How to <u>Manage</u> it profitably and professionally
4. How to <u>Sell</u> it when the time and circumstances are right.

Everything in this book, in one way or another, supports the accomplishment of these four stages of the investment real estate cycle.

As the first chapter of the text clearly stated, manufactured housing and manufactured home communities are enjoying nothing short of a renaissance. Not since the early 1970s have so many manufactured homes been produced. Today's manufactured homes are attractive and larger—mostly multisection in many parts of the United States—and equally destined for private building sites and manufactured home communities of all sorts: landlease and subdivision, retirement and all-ages, rural and suburban, large and small. Indeed, this first book written about the viability of a manufactured home community as a real estate investment makes its debut as the Decade (1995–2005) of Manufactured Housing and Manufactured Home Community dawns!

There really is not anything "new under the sun" where real estate investment basics are concerned. Would-be investors, and certainly those interested in manufactured home communities, continue to research, evaluate, and compare alternative property vehicles in terms of (1) availability—the influence of supply and demand; (2) degree of personal and corporate risk involved; (3) present and future value; (4) degree of desired and available financial leverage; (5) investor liquidity; (6) management intensity and requirements; and (7) effect(s) of taxation. Yes, all this is a complicated and interrelated array of circumstances and estimations, but an exercise that positions the investor for minimum, maximum, even negative return on and of one's initial investment. So learn the basics well and apply them wisely.

It has been established that there are seven steps toward acquiring a manufactured home community as an investment:

1. Know the type business or property one wants to purchase
2. Identify, visit, and research prospective acquisitions
3. Determine the seller's disposition motives, if possible
4. Negotiate, negotiate, negotiate
5. Make a bona fide offer to purchase
6. Verify the seller's information and keep mortgage underwriting guidelines in mind throughout
7. Close the transaction.

The second and third chapters of this text go to considerable length to mate the basics of real estate investment with the characteristics and peculiarities of manufactured home community operation. The better that would-be investors, and even some long-time present owners of manufactured home communities, understand these intricacies and inter-relationships, the better the opportunity to maximize their return on investment. This is especially true as real estate investors become comfortable with the concepts of

* Looking for good unchangeables and bad changeables during the property search and evaluation stages
* Learning to apply a practical problem-solving procedure (that is, scientific method) and popular Ms of Management as tools to ferret out details and organize data in a workable fashion
* Keeping these typical lender's seven touchstones in mind throughout the process:
  1. Location and physical condition of the property
  2. Tenancy (that is, resident) characteristics and mix
  3. Lease(s) and terms thereof
  4. Past, present, and future operating performance indicators and plans
  5. Property management considerations
  6. Ownership position of borrower(s)
  7. Presence or threat of hazardous materials.

While there are certainly other rules of thumb and investment guidelines to consider, these will take most interested parties a long way towards realizing their acquisition goals.

Probably one of the most significant values of this text has been, and continues to be, its worth as a resource guide for locating manufactured home communities to acquire. Heretofore, only industry insiders have known where to go and how to obtain lists of manufactured home communities in many states, and where these lists do not exist, who to contact for partial and specialty lists of this property type. It is entirely possible for any would-be investor to set reasonable investment parameters (for example, property size, location, type utilities, and degree of stability) then go out and find such manufactured home communities. He or she may have to exercise some patience in the process (that is, search and negotiations) and be willing to go a little further afield at times, but the deals are certainly there to be made when the time and conditions are right. On this final point, it is important for the buyer to realize that sellers' motives and motivations can change overnight with changes in circumstances. It is important to develop good relationships along the way to enhance one's opportunity to be the right investor at the right time with the right offer.

Negotiate, negotiate, negotiate—and make a bona fide offer. For many, this is the most exciting stage in the entire investment cycle. For others, it is an intimidating, even unpleasant, step one has to take to acquire an investment property. In either event, the accurate valuation of a prospective real estate investment acquisition is paramount. Here, independent and unemotional third-party input by a qualified *and* experienced professional is vital. At this juncture, a calculated guess or outright error can spell disaster throughout the holding period of an investment. So one should learn the basics of real estate valuation— the three traditional appraisal methods—and hire a professional for confirmation, assurance, or a reality check; in any event, protect one's assets and sanity. Speaking of professionals, once an offer has been made and accepted by the seller, assemble a well-qualified and experienced team of experts to perform the due diligence series of inspections in a thorough fashion. The physical property inspection tasks are just as important (and can be more so if discrepancies are uncovered) as the evaluation of a property's income stream, quality, and durability. So do not skimp in this area either. Once closing has been effected, the property management stage commences.

Property management—a subject as broad in scope as it must be high in priority. Professional property management, particularly as it applies to the landlease manufactured home community environment, goes well beyond the collecting of site rent. For here, the on-site manager or management team functions as a mayor of a small town. He or she is responsible for keeping the property attractive and inviting enough to interest homeowners in relocating their manufactured homes there. Once a prospective renter becomes a resident, the professional property manager is responsible for enforcing rules and regulations (also known as Guidelines for Living), keeping the property clean and in good repair, and collecting the rent in a timely fashion. Maintaining high occupancy and good resident relations and efficiently controlling operating expenses, the on-site manager helps "grow the value" of the income property for the owner. Virtually every ongoing problem with a manufactured home community, except for functional and economic obsolescence, can be traced back to less-than-satisfactory property management. So it is difficult to imagine a higher priority during the holding period for an investment like this.

An industry trend rarely described in industry literature is the strong interest that owners of older manufactured home communities have in rejuvenating their properties. At least two circumstances motivate this self-interest. First, the owner and property manager of an older community recognize that the maximum return (sale price) for an income property will only be realized when income is maximized, expenses minimized, and overall appearance is top-notch. The other scenario relates to the turnaround challenge. With the larger showcase properties already picked-over by major portfolio owners, REO (real estate-owned) and other disadvantaged or mismanaged manufactured home communities are the only way to go in some popular markets. So again, there is the strong interest in how to rejuvenate that older, unattractive, languishing property. In **Chapter 8,** the industry's guru on the subject outlined key steps, complete with photographs. And the turnaround aficionado will find practical advice and time-proven guidelines as well.

Time to sell? As with the acquisition stage, it is helpful to summarize this important phase with a list of appropriate steps:

1. Achieve the <u>best curb appeal possible</u>; everything should look and be clean and freshly painted.

2. Have complete and accurate financial records for the property for the past several years.

3. Arrange for a formal valuation of the property by a capable and experienced real estate appraiser familiar with manufactured home communities.

4. Set a realistic sale price (that is, what one would be willing to actually sell it for) and a slightly higher asking price.

5. Decide whether to sell on one's own or with the assistance of a qualified and experienced manufactured home community real estate broker. If appropriate, negotiate listing terms with such a broker and sign an agreement for a limited period of time.

6. Show the property to interested parties, or leave this responsibility entirely with the real estate broker. Request prospective buyers not to disturb staff or residents.

7. Receive and consider offers to purchase and decide accordingly, whether to accept or counter offer.

8. Once an offer to purchase is accepted , assist the prospective buyer throughout the due diligence inspections period.

9. Once closing is effected, confirm that the transaction is recorded and reported to appropriate authorities.

As was stated at the beginning of this chapter, we have now come full cycle with the typical landlease manufactured home community investment.

All that remains to be said now is that a manufactured home landlease community is indeed a desirable and generally profitable real estate investment. If interested in acquiring a first or additional such property, prepare ahead of time—learn the business principles and methods; search widely and diligently; and buy right. Then see to it that the property is professionally managed and that residents are respected and appreciated for their tenancy. Through it all, market and operate to keep the property full, earn a good financial return, and enhance value appreciation. When the time and circumstances are right, sell wisely and walk away from the experience feeling satisfied and realizing a good return on your investment.

This could well be the best opportunity to be an integral part of one of the most exciting and prosperous periods in our nation's economic and business history, as a housing provider and entrepreneur during the Decade of Manufactured Housing and the Manufactured Home Community!

APPENDIXES

Appendix A   **Top HUD-Code Manufactured Home Producers**

Appendix B   **History of the Manufactured Housing RV/MH Foundation**

Appendix C   **Marking the Decade of Manufactured Housing**

Appendix D   **The 1996 Allen Report on the Largest Community Owners**

Appendix E   **Institute of Real Estate Management Certified Property Manager/Members Experienced in the Management of Manufactured Home Communities**

Appendix F   **Manufactured Housing Industry Periodicals**

Appendix G   **History in the Making**

Appendix H   **Directory of National, Regional, State, and Provincial Manufactured Housing Related Associations and Institutes**

Appendix I   **Readying Your Community for Environmental Audits**

Appendix J   **Loan Amortization Charts**

Appendix K   **A Description of the Old Woodall STAR Mobile Home Park Rating System**

Appendix L   **Real Estate Brokers Specializing in the Marketing of Manufactured Home Communities**

Appendix M   **National Source List of Manufactured Home Communities**

Appendix N   **The 21st Century National Manufactured Home Landlease Community Rating System**

Appendix O   **Due Diligence On-Site Inspection Report**

Appendix P   **Typical Manufactured Home Community Operating Statements**

Appendix Q   **Manufactured Home Community Finance Sources**

Appendix R   **Monthly Manufactured Home Community Integrity Inspection Checklist**

Appendix S   **Directory of Products and Services for Manufactured Home Communities**

Appendix T   **Setting a Value on Your MH Community**

281

TOP HUD-CODE MANUFACTURED HOME PRODUCERS

TOP HUD-CODE MANUFACTURED HOME PRODUCERS

(based on 1994 Gross Sales Volume per *Automated Builder* magazine)

COMPANY ADDRESS CITY, STATE, ZIP TELEPHONE	GROSS SALES VOLUME # FLOORS PRODUCED TOP BRANDS PRODUCED
1. Fleetwood Enterprises Box 7638 Riverside, CA 92513-7638 (909) 351-3500	$1,310,044,787 65,781 Reflection Limited, Greenhill, Springhill
2. Champion Enterprises, Inc. University Dr., Suite 320 Auburn Hills, MI 48326 (810) 340-9090	$768,367,000 39,658 Dutch Chandeleur, Champion, Crest Ridge, Moduline
3. Redman Industries, Inc. Walnut Hill Ln., Suite 200 Dallas, TX 75229 (214) 353-3600	$562,875,210 21,843 NA

4.   Oakwood Homes Corp.
    S. Holden Rd.
    Greensboro, NC 27407
    (910) 855-2400

$506,187,000
NA
Oakwood, Freedom, Golden West

5.   Skyline Corp.
    By-Pass Rd.
    Elkhart, IN 46514
    (219) 294-6521

$505,668,000
$29,266
NA

6.   Clayton Homes, Inc.
    Box 15168
    Knoxville, TN 37901-5168
    (615) 970-7200

$358,194,442
23,335
Clayton

7.   Schult Homes Corp.
    Box 151
    Middlebury, IN 46540
    (219) 825-5881

$275,587,000
7,214
Schult, Marlette, Crest

8.   Cavalier Homes, Inc.
    Box 5003
    Wichita Falls, TX 76307
    (817) 723-5523

$217,438,361
10,018
Cavalier, Pacesetter, Brigadier,
Knox, Buccaneer, Challenger,
Parkwood, Mansion, more

9.   Horton Homes, Inc.
    Box 4410
    Eatonton, GA 31024
    (706) 485-8506

$205,000,000
12,000
Summit, Echo

10. Southern Energy Homes, Inc.
    Box 269, Hwy. 41, N
    Addison, AL 35540
    (205) 747-1544

$180,000,000
11,549
Southern Energy, Southern
Life/Style, Southern Homes

11. Belmont Homes, Inc.
    Box 280
    Belmont, MS 38827
    (601) 454-9217

$107,423,089
7,090
Premier, Glenwood

12. Guerdon Homes, Inc.
    SW. Meadows, Suite 131
    Lake Oswego, OR 97035
    (503) 624-6400

    $103,000,000
    4,750
    Guerdon, Magnolia

13. Cavco Industries, Inc.
    N. Central Ave., Suite 800
    Phoenix, AZ 85004
    (602) 256-6263

    $95,126,319
    4,983
    America's Pride, West Park, Cedar
    Court, Sunburst, Malibu, Catalina

14. Destiny Industries, Inc.
    Box 1766
    Moultrie, GA 31776
    (912) 985-6100

    $94,478,300
    5,059
    Omni, Peachtree

15. Homes of Merit, Inc.
    Box 1606
    Bartow, FL 33831
    (941) 533-0593

    $92,516,906
    6,895
    Twin Manor, Country Manor,
    Southern Manor, Pine Manor, Lake
    Manor, Bay Manor

16. Wick Building Systems, Inc.
    Box 490
    Mazomanie, WI 53560
    (608) 795-4281

    $90,826,000
    2,385
    Artcraft, Marshfield, Rollohome

17. General Mfd. Housing, Inc.
    Box 1449
    Waycross, GA 31502
    (912) 285-5068

    $67,400,000
    5,751
    General, Jaguar

18. Chandeleur Homes, Inc.
    Box 557
    Boaz, AL 35957
    (205) 593-9225

    $65,630,000
    4,478
    Chandeleur

19. Mfd. Housing Enterprises, Inc.
    State Rt. 6
    Bryan, OH 43506
    (419) 636-4511

    $49,000,000
    2,133
    Mansions

20. Nasau Homes of Idaho, Inc. $45,000,000
    Federal Way 1,345
    Boise, ID 83707 Nashua, Nashua Villa,
    (208) 345-0222 Castlewood

21. Cappaert Mfd. Housing $35,462,000
    Hwy. 61 South 2,627
    Vicksburg, MS 39180 Cairo, Pinnacle, Phoenix, Colony
    (601) 636-5401

22. Jacobsen Homes $35,000,000
    Packard Court 2,073
    Safety Harbor, FL 34695 Chancellor, Classic
    (813) 726-113

23. R-Anell Custom Homes, Inc. $35,000,000
    Box 428 1,378
    Denver, NC 28037 NA
    (704) 483-5511

24. Peach State Homes $34,839,800
    Box 615 3,001
    Adel, GA 31620 Peach State, Signature
    (912) 896-7420

25. Pioneer Housing System $34,734,000
    Glen Bass Rd. 3,345
    Fizgerald, GA 31750 Pioneer
    (912) 896-7420

26. Crest Ridge Homes, Inc. $32,718,636
    Box 1618 2,053
    Breckenridge, TX 76424 Crest Ridge, Western Manor
    (817) 559-8211

27. Crimson Industries, Inc. $29,981,411
    Box 1086 1,537
    Haleyville, AL 35565 Crimson
    (205) 486-9222

28. Summit Crest Homes
    Box 10
    Berthoud, CO 80513
    (970) 532-2632

    $29,000,000
    700
    Summit Crest

29. Kit Manufacturing, Inc.
    Box 848
    Long Beach, CA 90801
    (310) 595-7451

    $26,900,000
    785
    Golden State, Royal Oaks,
    Briercrest, Sea Crest, Limited, XL

30. Giles Industries, Inc.
    Box 750
    New Tazewell, TN 37825
    (615) 626-7243

    $21,468,000
    1,905
    NA

31. Grand Manor, Inc.
    Box 2657
    Thomasville, GA 31799
    (912) 228-0023

    $17,500,000
    1,174
    Grand Manor

32. Astro Mfg. Co., Inc.
    Box 189
    Shippenville, PA 16254
    (814) 226-6822

    $16,582,488
    1,024
    River Ridge, Buyers

33. Fleming Homes
    Box 426
    Flemingsburg, KY 41041
    (606) 849-4119

    $15,947,000
    1,313
    Fleming

34. Oxford Homes, Inc.
    Route 26, Box 167
    Oxford, ME 04270
    (207) 539-4412

    $10,000,000
    241
    Legacy, Platinum, Yankee Leader,
    Heritage, more

35. Hi-Tech Housing, Inc.
    C.R. 8
    Bristol, IN 46507
    (800) 837-6449

    $8,350,000
    82
    NA

36. Rochester Homes, Inc.
    Box 587
    Rochester, IN 46975
    (800) 860-4554

    $7,300,000
    212
    Rochester, Elite, Heritage Mod

37. Mid-America Homes
    Box 490
    Benton, KY 42025
    (502) 527-5006

    $1,425,000
    95
    Commonwealth, Princeton

APPENDIX B

HISTORY OF THE MANUFACTURED HOUSING RV/MH FOUNDATION

HISTORY OF THE MANUFACTURED HOUSING RV/MH FOUNDATION

Carlton Edwards

The legal name for the RV/MH Foundation is the RV/MH HERITAGE FOUN-DATION, Inc. The foundation owns their office, museum, and library facility at 801 Benham Ave., Elkhart, IN 46516. The RV initials in the name represent "Recreational Vehicles" and the MH initials "Manufactured Housing." The "Heritage" portion of the name reflects the purposes of the organization as:

1. to honor individuals who have made outstanding contributions to the industry. This is accomplished by their induction into the foundation's well-known Hall of Fame.

2. to maintain a library and archive of photographs, books, publications, and memorabilia about the industry.

3. to maintain a museum of industry products over the years.

All of these purposes are in place and ongoing, including the Hall of Fame gallery of 150 inductees since 1972. The library is well established with contributions catalogued for reference by writers, journalists, and researchers. The museum is a special attraction with several examples of early trailers and related products.

The Foundation is supported entirely by contributions from interested persons, companies, and the city of Elkhart. The Foundation is controlled by a Board of Directors elected to represent all segments of the industry and geographic areas. A managing director and assistants manage the day-to-day operations, including having the museum and library open daily for visitors. Money-raising events are scheduled periodically to add funds to pay annual operating expenses. Donations are also solicited directly from industry leaders and their companies.

The Foundation traces its history from early in the 20th century, when it was closely related to the automobile industry. In the 1920s when automobiles became reliable enough for distance travel with families, folks wanted to be assured of affordable eating and sleeping accommodations. So many "tourist cabins"and "tourist homes" sprang up all across the country. A few mechanics even remodeled autos and trucks to provide for family eating and sleeping. Others built "trailers" that could be towed behind autos, providing those facilities. As more and more homemade trailers took to the road, entrepreneurs saw a market for building trailers for sale. Thus an industry was born. Factory production began in the late '20s and early '30s and gained some momentum before World War II. The housing shortages near war production factories and training camps stimulated the use of such trailers for temporary housing. These trailers were intended for vacation and recreation use and lacked space and bath facilities for continued living. The vast numbers used, by necessity, for continuous living required parking sites with a community bath and laundry, electricity, potable running water, streets, and drainage for the water used in the home. As a result, large site developments were built, but since trailer dwellings were considered temporary, the sites were called "trailer camps."

Factories were built in Michigan, Indiana, and California to serve this new and sudden market. Along with manufacturing came "dealers" selling the products and site developers constructing locations with necessary support accommodations.

Owners of trailers provided a ready market for magazines and papers carrying news of these products and the people using them. Trade publications and trade associations quickly developed to serve the builders and suppliers of components and financing for consumers.

Trailers increased in size following World War II to satisfy the demands of families where the wage earner engaged in a seasonal occupation or one in which the location of the workplace changed frequently. Families also realized these trailers were a very affordable housing alternative. Complete bath facilities, bigger room sizes, and multiple bedrooms made larger trailers less movable with the family automobile. Special transport vehicles called "toters" were made by shortening the truck chassis and requiring experienced drivers to transport these homes from one locale to another. The homes were now called "mobile homes" to distinguish them from the smaller trailers moved with the family automobile. The latter became known as "travel trailers." The travel trailers were joined by "motor homes" in the late 1950s, and came to be known as RVs. The mobile homes were continually increased in size to meet demands for more living space by adding tip-out bays, extra attachable units, and finally multiple sections—known in the industry as "double wides" since they appeared to be two mobile home sections. Mobile homes have lost much of their mobile features with increased size. They have features comparable to site-built homes, along with quality appliances and components. The name manufactured home is more representative of these homes today. On the other hand, today's RVs are comprised of travel trailers in various configurations, motor homes, and camper vans.

In addition to the manufacturing and sales segments of the RV/MH industries, there are site developers, formerly known as "park operators," a name derived from the early placement of living trailers and mobile homes in close quarters adjacent to service facilities supplementing those within the home. This "park" designation followed the earlier name of "trailer camp." The contemporary industry term for areas for the placement of manufactured homes is a manufactured home community. With this recognition of the real estate–based segment of the industry, there are now two separate industries, RV and MH.

The formation of the Hall of Fame Foundation occurred during a meeting of the Mobile Home Manufacturers Association in 1972 when a group of the industry trade publication magazine owners, and association directors, thought it a good idea to have a Hall of Fame with the added features of a library and museum, to preserve records and memorabilia of both industries.

The publishers organized the Hall of Fame and provided funds to support the beginning activities. The organizing group included: Richard P. Robb, publisher of *Trailer Topics* magazine; Clifford H. Wilmath, publisher of *Florida Trailer News;* J. Brown Hardison, publisher of *Mobile Home Dealer;*

Ruth Kaseman, publisher of *Arizona Mobile Citizen;* Curtis Fuller, publisher of *Woodall's Trailer Travel;* Arthur Rouse, publisher of *Trailer Life;* Roy Kneip, publisher of *Mobile Home Reporter;* Ward Patten, publisher of *Mobile Living;* Thomas Lindsay, representing Herbert Tieder, publisher of *Mobile and Recreational Housing Merchandiser;* and Rex Cox, Executive Director, Indiana Mobile Home Association. Mr. Cox was elected president with directions to draft a charter and bylaws, and register the corporation with the Indiana Secretary of State as the "RV/MH Hall of Fame Foundation, Inc." Changes have been made in the name to better represent the scope and purposes of the organization and to facilitate obtaining Federal Tax Exemption status as Internal Revenue Code 501(C)3. Since August 20, 1984, the name in effect has been, "RV/MH HERITAGE FOUNDATION, INC."

Cox arranged the first Hall of Fame Awards Banquet for August 21, 1972, at the RV/MH Midwest Show at South Bend, Indiana. Fourteen industry pioneers were inducted. Hall of Fame awards have been made each year since, except 1976 when the organization was inactive.

An early activity to fulfill a part of the purpose for the Foundation was to compile a written history of the industry. The Board encouraged Prof. C.M. Edwards, a retired professor of housing at Michigan State University, to author the book entitled, *Homes for Travel and Living—the History and Development of the Recreational Vehicle and Mobile Home Industries.* The book published in 1977 was widely sold and distributed in the industry.

The Chairmen of the Board and their terms have been: Richard P. Robb 1972–74; J. Brown Hardison 1975–76; Herbert E. Tieder 1977–85; Vernon Sailor 1985–90; Jack Tuff 1990–91; Warren Jones 1991–92; Pete Callendar 1993; Virgil Miller 1994–95; and Dean Replogel 1996.

Men who have been President, Executive VP, or other designation have done the day-to-day work for the Foundation, and their terms have been: Rex Cox 1972–75; John Martin, Exec. Director, Mobile Home Manufacturers Association 1976; C.M. Edwards, President 1977–80; Herbert Reeves, Jr., Exec. VP 1980–83; Kenneth Rhoton, Exec. VP 1983; Gene Keener, Exec. VP 1984. From 1984 to 1990 Vernon Sailor, the Chairman of the Board, assumed the regular operating duties; followed by Jack Tuff 1990–91. Mike Jones was hired as the Foundation Exec. Director 1990–93, followed by Carl Ehry since July 1994. Dates of service overlap because officers did not serve on a calendar basis.

In 1982 Ricky and Agatha Bucchino formed the OLD TIMERS organization in Florida, hosting annual gatherings each winter. The events were attended by one to two hundred RV/MH industry pioneers. The Bucchinos compiled a list of several hundred persons as potential "old-timer" members, those who had many years of tenure in the RV/MH industry. Ricky Bucchino acquired hundreds of pictures depicting past industry people and events and mounted them on large display panels. These memorabilia have been turned over to the Foundation for the library and museum. The activities of the OLD TIMERS have been assumed by a committee of the Foundation, and the name of the group was changed in 1994 to the OLD TIMERS CLUB of the RV/MH Heritage Foundation.

During 1984 Gene Keener, retired director of the Ohio Manufactured Housing Association, became Executive Director of the Foundation. He developed an extensive plan for fund-raising involving many industry leaders who in turn were assigned to contact others for financial support. Vern Sailor in 1985 was a driving force in fund-raising and building construction for the Foundation's new headquarters. His wide and varied connections as a prominent industry supplier gave him access to company executives in both the RV and Manufactured Housing businesses. His sales ability and persistence resulted in the commitment of funds and materials for the construction of the center building in Elkhart. Jack Tuff was successful in having the City of Elkhart donate land for the building. The IRS tax exemption status 501(C)3 was helpful in obtaining donations. The principal source of funds for construction came from the sale of commemorative Bricks and Tiles. Bricks, engraved as commemoratives, were sold for $100 each. Floor tiles were $1000 each. The brick wall and floor were erected in a separate section of the building called "Memory Lane." The building was completed and dedicated in August 1990. The building houses the executive offices, conference room, Hall of Fame gallery, library, and exhibit area. The 18,000 square feet of floor area is heated and air conditioned. As of 1993, the museum contained 18 trailers dating from the 1920s, the library houses 6000 holdings, and the Hall of Fame gallery features more than 150 commemorative plaques.

Hall of Fame awardees are selected from nationwide nominations by a committee of the Board. Nominations listing the individuals' qualifications are made by industry peers, companies, or trade associations. The nominations describe the contributions of the individuals to the RV/MH industries in terms of time, money, and energy over a period of time. Hall of Fame inductions are effected at industry events such as trade shows and state conventions. Awardees, to date, are from the following states, which are listed, along with the latest date of induction:

Arizona	2	1981
Arkansas	1	1989
California	21	1992
Connecticut	2	1982
District of Columbia	1	1986
Florida	13	1990
Georgia	4	1986
Illinois	12	1993
Indiana	32	1994
Iowa	1	1983
Kansas	2	1982
Maryland	1	1980
Massachusetts	1	1975
Michigan	22	1991
Mississippi	2	1992
Missouri	2	1980
Montana	1	1993
New Jersey	2	1980
New York	1	1978
North Carolina	4	1994
Ohio	6	1983
Pennsylvania	4	1987
South Carolina	1	1994
Tennessee	1	1992
Texas	1	1993
Virginia	1	1982
Washington	1	1980
Wisconsin	1	1972

The RV/MH industries share the same historic roots and sell products to many of the same customers. So it is only fitting that they continue to jointly honor this rich heritage through the Hall of Fame, museum, and library of the RV/MH Heritage Foundation in Elkhart, Indiana.

MARKING THE DECADE OF MANUFACTURED HOUSING

MARKING THE DECADE OF MANUFACTURED HOUSING

As the old '60s song lyric went, "The times, they are a-changing!" And at what a rapid rate besides!

Only a year ago, manufactured housing industry leaders were whispering that the next 10 years just might be "our decade." But only the manufactured home community segment of the industry was bold enough to speak out and publicly proclaim the years 1995–2005 as "the Decade of the Manufactured Home Community." Bumper stickers, pens and terminology pledge cards soon appeared. Long dormant, the industry bandwagon was finally on the move.

What a difference a year has made! The bold community leaders have commanded the attention of MHI, the industry's information and lobbying nerve center, with a petition for equal representation on the MHI board.

With industry recognition of the vital role of the manufactured home community has come a desire to expand the decade-long celebration to encompass the industry as a whole. Now home producers, retailers and suppliers across North America are clamoring to know how they too can participate in the recognition of manufactured housing as affordable housing in its purest form.

Because of this interest, industry people in general now agree to officially designate 1995–2005 as "the Decade of Manufactured Housing." But it's not enough simply to state an industry theme and leave it at that. There must be solid, meaningful reasons for such recognition in the first place. These factors do exist.

There must also be planning, and that's the difficult part. So far, no national or regional manufactured housing trade group has stepped forward to assume leadership in promoting "our decade" to the home buying public. So, individuals and state industry leaders need to take the initiative and start incorporating the decade theme into their corporate literature and marketing materials.

In the meantime, let's review some of the reasons why the next 10 years should be an unprecedented decade for our industry. These could be summarized as follows:

* The production and distribution of manufactured housing units continues to grow. Following two successive years of 20 percent growth, 1995 continues close to that prosperous pace. The 1994 production total of more than 300,000 homes was the highest since 1974.

* On the national average, close to half of all new manufactured homes are permanently placed on scattered building sites. The rest are sited in manufactured home subdivisions and in rental communities.

* Nearly half (47 percent) of the homes produced today are multi-section models. The remaining 53 percent are still single-section homes.

* More than 150 publicly and privately owned manufacturers turn out homes at some 300 plants across the U.S.

* Since 1992, four major manufactured home community owners have gone public as Real Estate Investment Trusts (REITs). For the past three years, Wall Street's interest in manufactured housing has been unprecedented and all but insatiable. At least a half dozen monographs and studies have been penned by Wall Street analysts and other industry observers, describing the companies involved and their economic performance to date.

* The manufactured housing industry's leadership is powerful and respected. While manufacturing entrepreneurs and CEOs have long influenced home sales on state and national levels, they are now being joined by real estate

investment executives, whose assets are as large as those of their manufacturing counterparts.

* With its restructuring, MHI should emerge as a broader-based and considerably more effective trade association, able to deliver a more persuasive affordability message to its prospective customers and community residents.

* The manufactured housing industry has been blazing new trails in senior housing. As a product, the manufactured home has become a very desirable commodity for the growing population of retired people, thanks to its inherent flexibility in design, speed of production, transportability and overall cost-effectiveness. The very nature of community living lends itself easily to various degrees of independent living coupled with communal caregiving—a significant benefit for the elderly.

Taken as a whole, therefore, manufactured housing is an ideal vehicle for sheltering what is certain to be the fastest growing segment of the population in the 21st century, senior citizens. Nothing else offers such opportunity for assisted living and continuing, communal care in a retirement community. This is just one more reason to join the manufactured housing bandwagon for the exciting decade ahead.

* The manufactured housing industry in general and community segment in particular have become popular topics for discussion in articles and books. In the past five years, at least six books have appeared describing one aspect or another of the industry, including *Development, Marketing and Operation of Manufactured Home Communities,* released by John Wiley & Sons early in 1994. At least two more texts dealing with manufactured housing are scheduled to appear in the next two years.

* Industry statistics and education are two other areas where manufactured housing has been making significant strides. For a long time, MHI has been publishing information on the manufacturing side of the industry through its *Quick Facts.* More recently, the community segment has joined in with annual surveys of the largest community owners, published annually in this magazine.

Other indications of the growing importance of education and credentials in the industry has been the increasing number of Certified Property Managers (CPMs) who are taking leadership roles as heads of corporate property management companies, and the designation of the title, Accredited

Community Manager (ACM) by the Manufactured Housing Educational Institute (MHEI). Professional property management has been a long time coming for this industry, and now it is here.

   * Standard industry terminology is being adopted increasingly by state governments and members of the media. Manufactured housing is now a comfortable term for just about everyone, and most states have embraced the term "manufactured home community," in lieu of the outdated "p" and "t" words.

By now, it should be perfectly clear why we are on the threshold of what promises to be the manufactured housing industry's most exciting 10 years. It is especially fitting that this decade, 1995–2005, spans two centuries, linking the old with the new.

This is precisely what manufactured housing is uniquely suited to do: offer the homebuying consumer affordable and desirable home to move into, away from the old high-priced housing alternative.

So welcome to the Decade of Manufactured Housing! The next 10 years should be the best ever.

Manufactured Home MERCHANDISER
September 1995
Reprinted by permission

THE 1996 ALLEN REPORT ON THE LARGEST COMMUNITY OWNERS

Community Corner_____

DMN Publishing
Box 47024
Indianapolis, IN 46247

THE 1996 ALLEN REPORT ON THE LARGEST COMMUNITY OWNERS

By George Allen, CPM

George Allen is president of GFA Management in Indianapolis. GFA specializes in residential and commercial real estate management. For more information, contact Allen at GFA Management, Box 47024, Indianapolis, Ind. 46247. 317/888-7156.

The seventh annual Allen Report ranks 155 of the 500 largest owners and fee-managers of manufactured home communities operating throughout the U.S. and Canada during 1995.

More than 200 firms and individual owner/investors, or 40 percent of the 500 major owners and fee-managers responded to this year's questionnaire. To qualify for a ranking, individual owners, partnerships and companies must own or fee-manage at least 500 rental home sites or five land-lease communities.

[Let's make it clear from the start that we're talking about manufactured *home* communities; there is no such thing as a "manufactured *housing* community." Manufactured housing is the product our industry markets to the public. Once sold, the structure becomes someone's *home*, regardless of whether it is sited on a privately owned lot, in a subdivision or in a land-lease community. To refer to it as anything less is an affront to the home buyer who opted for this living environment and an indication of naïveté about the manufactured housing industry.)

Overall, the ranked companies operate 2,310 manufactured home communities, encompassing 531,795 rental homesites. These make up 4.6 percent of an estimated 50,000 manufactured home communities that exist nationwide, and 9.6 percent of some 24,000 considered to be "investment grade," or larger than 60 homesites.

These firms own an average portfolio of 15 manufactured home communities and 3,430 rental homesites. The average community size among those ranked in the report is 230 homesites per property. ROC Communities is the largest owner/manager of manufactured home communities, with 110 properties and 27,910 rental homesites. Overall, the five manufactured home community real estate investment trusts (REITs) own and manage 298 properties and 96,591 rental homesites. (See the table below.)

The emergence of the REITs, which first became evident in 1993, is an indication of the growth of the manufactured home community industry in recent years. This, along with the publication of the book, *Development, Marketing and Operation of Manufactured Home Communities* by J. Wiley & Sons in 1994 and the recent acceptance by MHI of the manufactured home community industry as deserving division status, has set the stage for 1995-2005, which has been called "the Decade of the Manufactured Home Community."

The trend is likely to continue in 1996 with the scheduled publication of second text, *How to Find, Buy, Manage and Sell a Manufactured Home Community as an Investment,* also by J. Wiley & Sons.

The owners and fee-managers surveyed have headquarters or operate manufactured home communities in 37 states, one Canadian province and the District of Columbia. The largest concentration of home offices continues to be in California (30), followed by Michigan (20), Florida (11), Illinois and New York (10) Arizona (eight) and Indiana (seven).

ROC Communities also owns properties in the most states (28), followed by MHC (20), Carlsberg Management (18), Ellenburg Capital (15), Uniprop (12) and Lautrec (10).

Eighteen firms not ranked last year were added to the 1996 report, while 11 firms dropped out due to downsizing, mergers or other reasons.

In all, 29 firms or 19 percent of the 155 ranked companies, including three of the five REITs, employ Certified Property Managers (CPMs) on staff as mid- and upper-level executive property managers. Seventy-five CPMs are active in the manufactured home community industry nationwide.

(CPM is the prestigious professional property management designation monitored by the Institute of Real Estate Management. The increased presence of CPMs indicates recognition of the need for professional property management. The Manufactured Housing Educational Institute's Ac-

---

HOME SITE GROWTH OF THE LARGEST REAL ESTATE INVESTMENT TRUSTS (REITs)

Year	ROC	MHC	Chateau	Sun	United	Total	Annual Growth
1995	27,910	26,237	19,594	18,000	4,850	96,591	9.0%
1994	26,231	28,407	15,689	13,500	4,623	88,450	37.8%
1993	20,142	14,700	15,261	9,036	5,050	64,189	17.8%
1992	18,745	12,873	10,032	7,600	5,200	54,450	N/A
1991	9,030	13,079	9,759	N/R	N/R	N/A	N/A

N/R = No report   N/A = Not applicable

NOTE: The 96,591 total sites counted for the top five REITs in 1995 make up 18.2 percent of the sites surveyed in the 1996 Allen Report. These sites are located in 298 REIT communities, which make up only 0.6 percent of the approximately 50,000 existing manufactured housing communities nationwide, or 1.2 percent of the 24,000 communities that are regarded to be "investment-grade." The community counts for the five major REITs are: ROC (110), MHC (69), Chateau (44), Sun (54) and United (21). The proportion of communities owned by each of the REITs compared to the others is: ROC (29%), MHC (27%), Chateau (20%), Sun (19%) and United (5%).

credited Community Manager [ACM] designation is a similar property management credential for on-site managers.)

Slightly more than 15 percent of the 2,310 communities surveyed are fee-managed. This represents 11.5 percent of the 531,795 homesites covered by this report.

Overall, 33 companies engage in fee-management to some degree, and 15 of them are primarily fee-management firms specializing in manufactured home communities.

Ninety-one firms reported a physical occupancy average of 93.6 percent nationwide, up from a 92.3 percent the year before.

Based on reports from 69 ranked companies, the average operating expense ratio (OER) was 38.6 percent nationwide, compared to 38.2 percent last year.

Using this data as a guide, one can estimate that all 500 major owner/managers probably operate about 7,452 or 15 percent of the total property inventory and 31 percent of the investment grade properties.

The top 10 firms in the Allen Report operate 587 communities, just 1.2 percent of the total inventory), and 2.5 percent of the investment-grade subgroup.

The accuracy and completeness of the statistics contained in the Allen Report are entirely dependent on information provided voluntarily by the respondents. A reasonable effort was made to verify this data, by requesting confirming signatures on the questionnaire and doing followup telephone interviews as appropriate. The author accepts no responsibility for sorting out properties owned or managed by more than one firm or individual cited in this report.

If your manufactured home community portfolio qualifies for inclusion in this report but was not listed, please call or write me. □

1996 rank	firm name	state or province	#sites owned/ managed	#comms. owned/ managed	#states or provinces	1995 rank
1	ROC Communities[1,2]	Colo.	18,078/9,832	66/44	28	2
2	Manufactured Home Communities[1,2]	Ill.	25,407/830	65/4	20	1
3	Ellenburg Capital[2]	Ore.	25,780/0	66/0	15	3
4	Lautrec Ltd.[2]	Mich.	22,652/0	58/0	10	4
5	Chateau Properties	Mich.	19,594/0	44/0	4	6
6	Clayton Homes	Tenn.	18,500/0	65/0	13	9
7	Clayton, Williams and Sherwood[1,2]	Calif.	17,244/834	45/4	9	5
8	Sun Communities[1,2]	Mich.	18,000/0	54/0	10	8
9	Uniprop	Mich.	14,648/0	39/0	12	7
10	Bloch Realty	Mich.	12,832/0	33/0	9	10
11	Bessire and Casenhiser[1,2]	Calif.	990/9,637	9/52	3	13
12	Aspen Enterprises[2]	Mich.	10,506/0	25/0	5	11
13	Kingsley Management[2]	Utah	9,500/0	29/0	7	12
14	Wilder Corp.	Fla.	7,900/0	22/0	3	14
15	CRF Communities	Fla.	6,383/0	24/0	1	15
16	Windsor Group	Calif.	6,200/0	29/0	13	17
17	J&H Asset Property Management[1,2]	Calif.	87/6,047	2/49	2	19
18	Buchanan Management	Mich.	4,121/2,007	5/7	3	16
19	Colo. Real Estate and Investment[1,2]	Colo.	5,200/249	25/2	6	18
20	Carlsberg Management[1,2]	Calif.	3,505/1,808	11/8	18	23
21	Kentland Corp.	Mich.	5,078/0	19/0	2	22
22	Choice Group	Mich.	5,024/0	20/0	6	25
23	Evans Management Services[1,2,3]	Calif.	115/4,786	1/31	2	24
24	United Mobile Homes	N.J.	4,850/0	21/0	5	27

1996 rank	firm name	state or province	#sites owned/ managed	#comms. owned/ managed	#states or provinces	1995 rank
25	Storz Management[1,2]	Calif.	2.602/2.201	19/17	3	29
26	Oakwood Land Development[1]	N.C.	4,400/300	12/1	8	44
27	Garden Homes Management Corp.	Ct.	4,450/30	66/1	3	28
28	The Blair Group[1]	Fla.	2,267/2,076	4/3	1	21
29	Meadows Management[1]	Calif.	3,655/430	8/1	3	31
30	Zeman MH Communities[1]	Ill.	3,719/350	20/2	2	35
31	Brandenburg, Staedler and Moore	Calif.	4.000/0	15/0	1	33
32	LCM Management	Calif.	3,973/0	25/0	3	34
33	Heritage Group	Ind.	3,840/0	24/0	6	46
34	Capital Development	Ill.	3,763/0	11/0	4	32
35	Brandywine Group	Pa.	3.725/0	14/0	2	38
36	Horner and Associates[1]	Kan.	2,720/972	10/2	5	37
37	Weiss and Nodel	Mich.	3.598/0	22/0	12	56
38	Chesapeake Mobilehomes[1]	Md.	2,940/613	10/7	3	42
39	Ashford Management Group[2]	N.Y.	3.530/0	19/0	8	40
40	Franklin Group	Mich.	3,526/0	20/0	2	36
41	McDay Corp.	Calif.	3,515/0	8/0	4	41
42	Newport Pacific Capital[1,2]	Calif.	1,005/2,490	7/20	3	49
43	PM Realty Advisors[2]	Calif.	3,378/0	9/0	4	43
44	Rudgate MH Communities	Mich.	3,378/0	7/0	1	53
45	Steiner and Associates[1,2]	Fla.	3,202/170	16/1	1	45
46	Apollo Properties[1,2]	Ariz.	0/3,304	0/9	2	48
47	Kort and Scott	Calif.	3,290/0	23/0	3	64
48	Katahdin Corp.	Maine	3,200/0	13/0	5	47
49	Wenner Management[1]	Calif.	0/3,162	0/7	2	39
50	E.T. Consultants[3]	Calif.	3,152/0	9/0	4	52
51	First Financial Realty Advisor	Wis.	3,059/0	25/0	2	51
52	Tunnell Companies	Del.	3,052/0	3/0	1	50
53	Burnham Properties[2]	N.Y.	2,997/0	22/0	7	30
54	Martin Newby Management	Fla.	2,550/135	9/1	1	67
55	Park Management Specialists[1]	Ohio	2,060/475	11/2	3	54
56	Lighthouse Home Center	Ind.	2,490/0	12/0	3	58
57	Progressive Rentals	Neb.	2,400/0	6/0	1	59
58	Western MHP Management[1]	Calif.	0/2,400	0/15	3	57
59	The Boston Group[3]	Utah	2,367/0	16/0	5	60

1996 rank	firm name	state or province	#sites owned/ managed	#comms. owned/ managed	#states or provinces	1995 rank
60	RHP Properties	Mich.	2,300/0	7/0	6	84
61	Essex Partners[1]	N.Y.	1,545/627	9/3	6	88
62	5005 Properties	Minn.	2,171/0	13/0	6	26
63	Mason Properties	N.Y.	2,117/0	29/0	5	66
64	Silver King Companies[1]	Ariz.	1,011/1,065	8/10	3	61
65	A.L.S. Properties	Minn.	2,035/0	9/0	3	74
66	Jennings Realty	Ill.	2,007/0	6/0	4	69
67	Cook/Park Investments	Ohio	2,000/0	20/0	4	82
68	Park Advisors[1]	Minn.	1,563/428	10/5	7	NR
69	Pittsford Capital Management	N.Y.	1,937/0	30/0	1	NR
70	Keystone Management	Mich.	1,890/0	15/0	3	70
71	Ballerina Parkhome	Okla.	1,876/0	14/0	3	72
72	PIC[1]	Wash.	1,630/170	20/3	3	73
73	LHI (Larry's Homes)[2]	Del.	1,793/0	16/0	3	114
74	QCA Management	Calif.	1,754/0	9/0	6	73
75	Richards and Associates	Calif.	1,734/0	10/0	3	62
76	DRS Realty	Mich.	1,730/0	9/0	4	79
77	Cannon MH Group	Ga.	1,724/0	9/0	4	75
78	Countryside Asset Management[1,2]	Colo.	1,321/399	4/2	3	77
79	Pegasus Group	Calif.	1,700/0	6/0	5	71
80	RIMCO Properties	Pa.	1,700/0	8/0	1	89
81	AL Larson	Ill.	1,690/0	6/0	3	NR
82	Holiday Homes	Ohio	1,674/0	6/0	2	78
83	NKS Group	Ariz.	1,671/0	2/0	2	80
84	Park Management and Investments	Ariz.	1,645/0	6/0	3	108
85	Patterson Management Group[1,3]	Ga.	0/1,594	0/3	3	85
86	NOI Corp.[1]	Wash.	1,593/0	2/0	1	86
87	Parkside Holdings	Alberta	1,590/0	5/0	2	94
88	Goldstein Properties	Calif.	1,577/0	5/0	1	87
89	Maumee Valley Mobile Homes	Ohio	1,501/0	13/0	1	102
90	Metro MH Management[3]	D.C.	1,500/0	4/0	3	90
91	Asset Development Group	Wis.	1,457/0	17/0	2	91
92	Ajax Property Management[2]	Vt.	1,444/0	12/0	3	83
93	Dolphin Real Estate Group[1]	Calif.	0/1,434	0/17	3	81
94	Bryn Mawr Properties[2]	Wash.	1,427/0	10/0	3	92

1996 rank	firm name	state or province	#sites owned/ managed	#comms. owned/ managed	#states or provinces	1995 rank
95	U.S. Park Investments	Ariz.	1,424/0	22/0	2	65
96	TOPS Home Center	Ind.	1,400/0	10/0	2	131
97	Canadian Heritage Homes	Alberta	1,377/0	9/0	2	95
98	Bertakis Management[1]	Mich.	1,303/0	5/0	1	96
99	Harvey J. Miller Inc.	Calif.	1,303/0	5/0	3	97
100	Real Estate Investment Partners	Ill.	1,284/0	9/0	3	98
101	Leichty Mobile Homes[2]	N.D.	1,258/0	1/0	1	121
102	Hanover Group	Ind.	1,249/0	7/0	1	99
103	Follett and Florence Investment	Calif.	1,217/0	6/0	4	137
104	Ashwood Communities	Wis.	1,207/0	9/0	2	107
105	Goldman and Associates	Ill.	1,200/0	5/0	2	103
106	Richard Kellam Associates	Va.	1,200/0	4/0	3	95
107	Novinger and Co.	Texas	1,150/0	8/0	6	109
108	Nationwide Investments	Ill.	1,147/0	3/0	2	106
109	Homewood Manor Enterprise	Miss.	1,142/0	7/0	1	111
110	Starview Sales	Pa.	1,125/0	10/0	1	110
111	Columbia Park	Ohio	1,109/0	12/0	1	113
112	Northern Properties[2]	Mich.	1,100/0	5/0	1	118
113	Kaufco Inc.	N.H.	1,099/0	5/0	3	112
114	Property Service of Fla.[1]	Fla.	0/1,083	0/7	1	NR
115	Harshaw Asset Management[1 2]	Texas	940/120	5/1	1	105
116	American MH Communities	Ill.	1,050/0	8/0	1	115
117	Camelot Village	Ohio	1,038/0	3/0	1	116
118	Caster Management[1]	Calif.	581/457	5/5	3	127
119	Investors Realty	Del.	1,001/0	7/0	1	119
120	Kahn Development	S.C.	1,000/0	7/0	2	122
121	K&R Mobilehomes	Ohio	1,000/0	5/0	2	NR
122	ALP Associates/Summit[2]	Calif.	952/0	2/0	1	NR
123	Jay R. Gelb and Co.	N.Y.	905/0	5/0	2	117
124	Abart Investment Corp.	Ill.	900/0	4/0	2	NR
125	PCF Management Service[1]	Wash.	686/169	7/2	1	NR
126	Orangewood MH Communities	Fla.	852/0	4/0	1	125
127	L.D. Flickinger[1 3]	Calif.	0/851	0/10	1	126
128	Interstate Properties	Mont.	805/0	3/0	3	93
129	Hastings Co.	Mass.	800/0	4/0	1	NR

1996 rank	firm name	state or province	#sites owned/ managed	#comms. owned/ managed	#states or provinces	1995 rank
130	Kurtell Growth Investment	Fla.	800/0	6/0	3	NR
131	MH Parks of Jeff Ossen	Ct.	800/0	10/0	3	123
132	Lakewood West Joint Venture	Texas	718/0	2/0	1	NR
133	Missouri Modular	Mo.	700/0	2/0	1	132
134	AMICORP Inc.	Fla.	696/0	5/0	3	NR
135	Realsearch Corp.	Calif.	675/0	4/0	3	133
136	Germano Management Co.	Mich.	659/0	3/0	1	NR
137	Vintage Real Estate	Ind.	649/0	6/0	3	144
138	WAS Development	Wis.	640/0	4/0	1	130
139	Sky Harbor Corp.	N.Y.	638/0	3/0	1	138
140	Heron Cay	Fla.	600/0	1/0	1	136
141	Cubb Properties	Vt.	596/0	17/0	4	139
142	R Homes Corp.	N.Y.	563/0	3/0	1	NR
143	Universal Housing Assn.	Fla.	554/0	4/0	1	NR
144	Riley Manufactured Homes	Ill.	500/0	4/0	1	140
145	Goldcoaster Park	Fla.	547/0	1/0	1	124
146	Greenbelt Properties	Ala.	508/0	3/0	1	142
147	White Properties	Nev.	488/0	4/0	3	145
148	Kenneth Everett Rentals	Ala.	487/0	6/0	3	147
149	Thomas P. Kerr Inc.	Calif.	407/67	6/1	2	NR
150	Capital Housing Corp.	Minn.	454/0	2/0	1	146
151	Royce Communities	Ind.	453/0	5/0	2	141
152	Act III Investments	Ind.	372/0	6/0	1	148
153	Wolfe and Associates	Calif.	371/0	3/0	2	NR
154	Charter Associates	Pa.	359/0	3/0	3	149
155	Schmitt Properties	Nev.	250/0	5/0	1	NR

[1]Firms that fee-manage manufactured home communities for other owners or function as general or managing partners for other properties in the 1996 Allen Report.

[2]Firms with one or more certified property managers (CPMs) on staff.

[3]Unconfirmed data.

NR = Not Ranked previously

Manufactured Home MERCHANDISER
January 1996
Reprinted by permission

APPENDIX E

INSTITUTE OF REAL ESTATE MANAGEMENT CERTIFIED PROPERTY MANAGER/MEMBERS EXPERIENCED IN THE MANAGEMENT OF MANUFACTURED HOME COMMUNITIES

**INSTITUTE OF REAL ESTATE MANAGEMENT
CERTIFIED PROPERTY MANAGER/MEMBERS
EXPERIENCED IN THE MANAGEMENT OF
MANUFACTURED HOME COMMUNITIES**

Allen, George F., Jr., CPM   (317) 888-7156
GFA Management, Inc.
Box # 47024
Indianapolis, IN 46247

Altschwager, Douglas J., CPM   (616) 784-1636
Northern Properties, Ltd.
1569 Beavercreek
Belmont, MI 49306

Beidler, Alan, CPM   (509) 662-3663
Sage Real Estate Services
135 S. Worthen, Ste. 200
Box # 1781
Wenachee, WA 98807

Bessire, Richard C., CPM   (909) 594-0501
Bessire & Casenhiser, Inc.
725 Brea Canyon Rd., Ste. 6
Walnut, CA 91789

Bower, Ronald L., CPM   (714) 721-5019
PM Realty Advisors
800 Newport Center Dr., Ste. 300
Newport Beach, CA 92660

Brennan, Robert E., CPM   (216) 749-1141
Western Reserve PM
1703 Brookpark Rd.
Cleveland, OH 44109

Brown, Weldon L., CPM   (909) 682-5454
Weldon L. Brown Co., Inc.
5029 LaMart Dr., Ste. C
Riverside, CA 92507

Burger, Eugene, CPM   (415) 461-8660
Eugene Burger Management Corp.
481 Via Hidalgo
Greenbrae, CA 94904

Burger, Lori, CPM   (415) 461-8660
Eugene Burger Management Corp. (EBMC)
481 Via Hidalgo
Greenbrae, CA 94904

Carman, Christine, CPM   (541) 773-6400
Commercial Property Management
711 E. Main St., Ste. 24
Medford, OR 97504

Casenhiser, Keith, CPM (909) 594-0501
Bessire & Casenhiser, Inc.
725 Brea Canyon Rd., Ste. 6
Walnut, CA 91789

Cruse, Rebecca, CPM (317) 587-8888
DMSI Asset Management Services
10333 N. Meridian St., Ste. 360
Indianapolis, IN 46290

Davis, Bruce, CPM (916) 797-1155
Horizon Management
4120 Douglas Blvd., Ste. 306-12
Granite Bay, CA 95746

Durand, Sandra, CPM (612) 349-6989
NHD Companies/Chateau Properties
3010 Plaza VII Tower
45 S. Seventh St.
Minneapolis, MN 55402

Elias, Richard, CPM (909) 594-0501
Bessire & Casenhiser, Inc.
725 Brea Canyon Rd., Ste. 6
Walnut, CA 91789

Esposito, Vincent, CPM (714) 837-6865
Management Services Associates
26365 Palomita Circle
Mission Viejo, CA 92691

Fannon, Brian W., CPM (810) 932-3100
Sun Communities, Inc.
31700 Middlebelt Rd., Ste. 145
Farmington Hills, MI 48334

Fisher, Gerald, CPM (619) 239-9641
Mitchell Management Co.
615 Ash St., Ste. 201
San Diego, CA 92101

Fudge, Bradley, CPM   (503) 244-2300
Commonwealth Real Estate Services
10725 S.W. Barber Blvd., Ste. 100
Portland, OR 97219

Funk, Donald, CPM   (714) 673-6030
Lido Peninsula Co.
710 Lido Park Dr.
Newport Beach, CA 92663

Geary, William W., Jr., CPM   (310) 450-9696
Carlsberg Management Co.
2800 28th St.
Santa Monica, CA 90405

Gruenke, Michael, CPM   (909) 985-9764
Premco Services
99 'C' St., Ste. 106
Upland, CA 91786

Hanks, William "Bill", CPM   (714) 974-0397
J & H Asset Management, Inc.
22875 Savi Ranch Pkwy., Ste. C
Yorba Linda, CA 92687

Hansen, Edward D., CPM   (206) 562-9292
The Allied Group, Inc.
14405 SE 36th St., Ste. 208
Bellevue, WA 98006

Harer, Steve, CPM   (206) 772-3000
Bryn Mawr Properties, Inc.
11326 Rainier Ave. South
Seattle, WA 98178

Harshaw, Curtis L., CPM   (972) 602-8500
Harshaw Asset Management Corp.
1517 N. Carrier Parkway, #124
Grand Prarie, TX 75050

Holland, Barbara, CPM   (702) 385-5611
H & L Realty & Management
720 S. Fourth St., Ste. 201
Las Vegas, NV 89125

Hoty, Zack, CPM   (216) 835-1199
Management, Inc.
837 Crocker Rd.
West Lake, OH 44145

Johnson, Norma, CPM   (714) 594-0501
Bessire & Casenhiser, Inc.
725 Brea Canyon Rd., Ste. 6
Walnut, CA 91789

Jones, Boyce, CPM   (714) 640-4200
Clayton, Williams & Sherwood
800 Newport Center Dr., Ste. 400
Newport Beach, CA 92660

Keenan, Thomas H., CPM   (813) 797-7674
Manufactured Home Communities, Inc.
28050 US 19 North, Ste. 406
Clearwater, FL 34621

Levine, Stuart M., CPM   (810) 637-9800
Property Management Group, Inc.
2100 E. Maple Rd., Ste. 500
Birmingham, MI 48009

Love, Robert, CPM   (404) 457-4395
Love Properties, Inc.
2951 Flowers Rd., South, Ste. 220
Atlanta, GA 30341

Montgomery, Guy, CPM   (502) 447-4030
Montgomery Realtors
4738 Dixie Hwy.
Louisville, KY 40216

Nachazel, Mary H., CPM   (303) 741-3707
ROC Communities, Inc.
6430 S. Quebec
Englewood, CO 80111

Neil, Michael, CPM   (714) 721-5018
PM Realty Advisors
800 Newport Center Dr., Ste. 300
Newport Beach, CA 92660

Nutt, Richard, CPM   (712) 252-0917
Valley Ventures
2951 Park Ave.
Sioux City, IA 51104

Pappas, Stephen G., CPM   (602) 898-1939
Apollo Properties, Inc.
307 W. Second St.
Mesa, AZ 85201

Petralia, Russell J., CPM   (315) 724-4900
Ashford Management
501 Main Street
Utica, NY 13501

Petrosky, Elaine, CPM   (403) 497-3900
Government Services
2nd Floor, 1000-9700 Jasper Ave.
Edmonton, Alberta, Canada T5J4E2

Placido, Richard, CPM   (216) 331-2575
Northern Lake Properties, Inc.
20220 Center Ridge Rd., #120
Rocky River, OH 44116

Ragin, Andrew "Pat", CPM   (404) 565-3304
Patterson Management Group, Inc.
Box # 70727
Marietta, GA 30007

Robideaux, Robert W., CPM   (509) 838-7970
R.W. Robideaux & Co.
421 Riverside, Ste. 620
Spokane, WA 99201

Rollar, Darlene, CPM   (813) 530-3431
Rollar Homes, Inc.
16100 49th St., North
Clearwater, FL 34622

Sharp, Stuart L., CPM   (913) 492-9700
Shyrock Realty Co.
10460 Mastin, Ste. 130
Overland Park, KS 66212

Stanciv, David, CPM   (703) 356-6400
Stanciv Management, Inc.
1320 Old Chain Bridge Rd., Ste. 435
McLean, VA 22101

Steinbaugh, Douglas, CPM   (612) 431-7504
12146 Gantry Lane
Apple Valley, MN 55120

St. Clair, Vernon G., CPM   (310) 791-1196
St. Clair Investment, Inc.
25550 Hawthorne Blvd., Ste. 106
Torrance, CA 90505

Stout, Deborah, CPM   (702) 227-0444
Stout Management Co.
2320 Paseo Del Prado Rd., Ste. B-101
Las Vegas, NV 89102

Sullivan, Michael, Jr., CPM   (714) 852-5575
Newport Pacific Capital Co., Inc.
17300 Red Hill Ave., Ste. 280
Irvine, CA 92714

Toothaker, Robert, CPM   (219) 234-9923
Real Estate Management Corp.
120 W. LaSalle St., Ste. 601
South Bend, IN 46601

Vaughn, Ron, CPM   (415) 461-8660
Eugene Burger Management Corp.
481 Via Hidalgo
Greenbrae, CA 94904

Winger, Paul F., CPM   (303) 758-5727
Winger Real Estate Co.
1160 Sherman St., Ste. 102
Denver, CO 80213

Rogosich, John, CPM   (810) 362-4150
Choice Properties
755 W Big Beaver, #1275
Troy, MI 48084

MANUFACTURED HOUSING INDUSTRY PERIODICALS

MANUFACTURED HOUSING INDUSTRY PERIODICALS

Allen Letter (The), PMN Publishing, P.O. Box 47024, Indianapolis, IN 46247. Monthly paid subscription newsletter for owners and managers of manufactured home communities in the United States and Canada.

ARR Newsletter, Association for Regulatory Reform, 1331 Pennsylvania Avenue, N.W., Suite 508, Washington, DC 20004. Membership newsletter.

Automated Builder, Box 120, Carpinteria, CA 93014. Free manufacturer-oriented monthly magazine targeting factory-built housing of all types.

FMO News, Florida Mobilehome Owners Association, Box 5350, Largo, FL 34649. Monthly manufactured housing homeowner magazine.

Journal of Manufactured Housing, Box 288, Manchester, GA 31816. Southeast regional tabloid publication for manufactured housing interest groups. Publishes several columns written by manufactured housing industry specialists.

Journal of Property Management, Institute of Real Estate Management, 430 Michigan Avenue, Chicago, IL 60601. Monthly paid subscription magazine for Certified Property Managers.

MANUFACTS, California Manufactured Housing Institute, 10390 Commerce Center Drive, Suite 130, Rancho Cucamonga, CA 91730. Manufactured housing industry's cutting-edge publicist of product and community design.

Manufactured Home Merchandiser, 203 N. Wabash, Suite 800, Chicago, IL 60601. Manufacturer, supplier, and retailer-oriented monthly trade publication. Features Community Corner column for landlease community owners and managers.

Manufactured Homes Magazine, Box # 55998, Seattle, WA 98155. A monthly subscription consumer magazine.

Manufactured Housing Attorney Network Newsletter, 2500 Financial Center, Des Moines, IA 50309. An occasional periodical.

Institutional Investor Newsletter, 477 Madison Ave., New York, NY 10022, telephone (212) 224-3800.

Manufactured Housing Today, Box 836, Forest Grove, OR 97116. Regional consumer-sales oriented tabloid.

Manufactured Structures Newsletter, Box # 6300, Battlement Mesa, CO 81636. Monthly paid subscription newsletter for manufacturers.

MHI Newsletter and Manufacturing Report, Manufactured Housing Institute, 2101 Wilson Boulevard, Suite 610, Arlington, VA 22201. Member newsletter and manufactured home shipment report.

Mobile Home Digest, Suite 1600, 150 Second Avenue N., St. Petersburg, FL 33701. A quarterly newsletter.

Mobile Home Monthly, Box 457, Highland, MI 48357, telephone (810) 887-5020.

Manufactured Housing Report, Crittenden Publishing Co., Box 1150, Novato, CA 94948, telephone (800) 421-3483.

MM Homelife, American Mobilehome Association, Inc., 12929 W. 26th Avenue, Golden, CO 80401. Monthly paid subscription.

Mobilehome Parks Report, 3807 Pasadena Avenue, Suite 100, Sacramento, CA 95821. Paid subscription newsletter for western manufactured home community owners and managers.

Professional Builder, Box 5080, Des Plains, IL 60017. Monthly magazine targeting homebuilders.

Shelter, 88 Old Street, London, Great Britain EC1V9AX (magazine).

Western Mobile News, 4043 Irving Place, Culver City, CA 90230. Consumer-oriented publication.

WMA Reporter, Western Mobilehome Association, 1007 7th Street, Suite 300, Sacramento, CA 95814. Monthly magazine for West Coast owners and managers of manufactured home communities.

Shelterforce, 439 Main Street, Orange, NJ, 07050, telephone (201) 678-3110.

HISTORY IN THE MAKING

HISTORY IN THE MAKING

—the maturation of the manufactured home community industry—

Today's manufactured home community owners and managers live and work in exciting times! Not many years ago we could identify only 20 multiproperty owners in our industry. Now the annual *Allen Report* profiles at least 150 of the 500 individuals and firms who own or fee-manage more than five communities or 500 rental homesites apiece. In 1989 we learned for the first time that our national average OER (operating expense ratio) for manufactured home communities was 37.8 percent (comparing very favorably to garden style apartments at 51.5 percent at the time); 1995–96 data suggests a slight adjustment to 38.6 percent for our type property. And starting in 1992, manufactured home community owners from across the United States and Canada began meeting annually in roundtable fashion to network, learn together, and chart their collective future as an industry.

Now for the most exciting ongoing development of all! Manufactured home community owners attending the second annual international Networking Roundtable in St. Petersburg Beach, Florida, decided to gather on August 31, 1993, in Indianapolis, for a daylong strategic planning meeting. The announcement for the event laid out seven planning and discussion items for the brainstorming sessions that would take place that day. As an industry, how would and could we—

- Effectively promote the manufactured home community lifestyle to all segments of the housing market?

- Further reduce regulatory barriers and stimulate manufactured home community development and expansion?

- Enhance our industry image to homebuying consumers, finance sources, government leaders, and the media?

- Encourage frequent, positive press coverage of manufactured housing and the manufactured home community lifestyle?

- Improve regional and national representation and lobbying on behalf of manufactured home communities?

- Stimulate regular and worthwhile property owner networking, manager training, and information exchange on regional and national levels?

And what a day it turned out to be! Breaking into cluster groups, the executives spent all day applying creative thinking, practical logic, and wise planning to the future of the manufactured home community industry. The result? An industry White Paper that was circulated to other property owners nationwide and to manufactured housing and real estate trade associations that might be interested in associating with or absorbing a group that could eventually number 55,000 manufactured home communities. The White Paper set forth 10 broad activity planning measures, along with eight specific educational and organizational measures. Two follow-up meetings were scheduled: one with Manufactured Housing Institute staff on September 23 in Las Vegas, the other a reconvening of the Industry Steering Committee (the first time this name was used) on October 26 in Dallas, Texas.

As exciting as the Indianapolis meeting had been for its novelty and precedent-setting nature, the Dallas venue convinced everyone of the serious nature of the project undertaken: to organize manufactured home community owners as an industry. At this gathering a Mission Statement was drafted:

> The manufactured home community industry is continually striving toward excellence, through education, communication and professionalism, with the goal of providing affordable housing and a quality lifestyle.

Furthermore, Seven Strategic Objectives were set forth as needs to:

- Share useful and accurate information within and outside the industry

- Improve industry image and encourage professionalism among peers

- Provide affordable landlease homesites

- Promote the manufactured home community lifestyle

- Encourage manufactured home community development and expansion

- Enhance communication at all levels throughout the industry

- Upgrade representation and lobbying efforts on state and national levels.

Seventeen "issues of note" were identified and rounded out the day's activities. The Industry Steering Committee (ISC) planned to meet again on April 4, 1994, at the National Manufactured Housing Congress in Las Vegas. Manufactured home community owners from Florida, California, Michigan, and New Jersey committed to prepare educational and regionally sensitive presentations on rent control, manufactured housing commissions, and property rights for that meeting.

In the meantime, the Mission Statement, Strategic Objectives, and Issues of Note were distributed nationwide to manufactured home community owners for their information and comment. More than 7 percent of recipients took time to respond to the information survey, indicating their overwhelming approval of what the ISC had accomplished to date. What an upbeat way to begin 1994!

The Las Vegas meeting was pivotal. Not only had the ISC's leadership doubled in size in just nine months, but landmark informal meetings were held between ISC and MHI leaders, agreeing to meet formally in July in Chicago. But before this, two preparatory meetings had to take place. An ISC-appointed core group met on May 24 at the offices of MHC Communities, Inc., to refine earlier objectives and issues into four categories of multistate-owner industry issues: state regulations, federal regulations, consumer/resident matters.

These, and their subcategory parts, were communicated to MHI staff for review prior to MHI chairman Jeff Wick's meeting with the ISC core group on July 13 in Chicago. There was no disagreement as to the issues raised by the ISC, simply concern that MHI's work in these areas, via staff and its Community Operations Committee, were not fully known and appreciated by manufactured home community owners seeking improved national and regional representation. A main point of concern, however, was if and how MHI might accommodate ISC within its existing organizational structure. So it wound up being a hopeful, but not wholly encouraging meeting.

Decision time had arrived. Should the Industry Steering Committee formalize and continue to search for an existent sister-industry trade group with whom to affiliate or continue to wait on MHI? August 3 in Detroit turned out to be a historic day for manufactured home community owners. Executives from nine of the largest multicommunity firms in the United States (MHC Communities, Inc.; ROC Communities, Inc.; Ellenburg Capital; Lautrec, Ltd.; Chateau Properties, Inc.; Choice Properties; Horner & Associates; Rudgate Company; and Ballerina Parkhomes) voted unanimously to formally organize under the temporary name of Industry Steering Committee. This would be an autonomous national group comprised of owners and fee-managers of manufactured home communities, and eventually their suppliers and state manufactured housing associations. The decision was also made to begin soliciting dues at 10 cents per rental homesite from firms that were active in the ISC at that point, and those who had expressed support as interested parties. ISC's agent, GFA Management, Inc., was directed to prepare a Business Plan for starting a new association or institute.

As a result of the earlier meeting with MHI chairman Jeff Wick, a summit meeting of sorts was held on August 31 in Chicago. Twenty-five MH industry leaders attended, representing ISC and MHI. The main result was that ISC was invited, through its newly elected chairman, Jeff Kellogg of Chateau Properties, Inc., to restate the group's issues of concern and prepare a formal request to MHI requesting that a new, separate and fully funded division be created to address the needs and concerns of manufactured home community owners nationwide.

On September 30, 1994, the first national meeting of the Industry Steering Committee was held in Scottsdale, Arizona. Close to 80 owners and managers attending the third annual Networking Roundtable participated in the historic meeting. Jeff Kellogg, with the assistance of Gary McDaniel of ROC Communities, Inc., and Randy Rowe of MHC Communities, Inc., explained where ISC was in its relationship with MHI—and how, in but a few days, that group would decide whether to accept or pass on our request for a new and separate division.

At MHI's annual meeting, 6&7 October 1994, the decision was made to create not just one but two new divisions, one for manufactured home communities and one for manufactured housing retailers. Soon thereafter task forces were named to facilitate this process. Dave Czeck of Tri-Park Investments and Tom Kimmell of Meadow Acres Manufactured Homes were named co-chairmen. The communities' subgroup consisted of Jeff Kellogg,

Randy Rowe, Gary McDaniel, Scott West of Ellenburg Capital, and George Allen.

The first task force meeting was held November 30 in Chicago. All appointees were present to work with MHI staff to develop an interim plan for creating and running the new manufactured home community division. This was accomplished and the task force agree to meet again at the Midwest Manufactured Housing Show in Louisville, Kentucky, on January 19, 1995, to finalize said interim plan for presentation to MHI's board for approval at their Winter Meeting in San Francisco, February 12–14, 1995.

So progress continues to be made. Manufactured home community owners in a year and a half have organized, and hopefully, will realize direct involvement and representation in a national trade group prepared to champion their dual interests as real estate investors and manufactured housing providers. The final chapter obviously has not been written. But the time has arrived for all manufactured home community owners to do their part to enhance our industry's image, promote our affordable lifestyle, and participate in the best business climate we have experienced in two decades. Is it any wonder that the next 10 years, 1995–2005, have already been declared "our decade," the Decade of the Manufactured Home Community?

This brief history would be incomplete without the names of the ISC leaders who have invested time and resources to bring our industry this far: Jeff Kellogg of Chateau Properties, Inc., Michigan; Randy Rowe, MHC Communities, Inc., Illinois; Gary McDaniel and Jim Grange, ROC Communities, Inc., Colorado; Jerry Ellenburg and Scott West, Ellenburg Capital, Oregon; Thomas Horner, Jr., of T. Horner & Associates; Martin Newby and Dick Leiter of MN Management, Florida; Ron Richardson, Ballerina Parkhomes, Oklahoma; Bill Williams, Shouhayib, Choice Properties, Michigan; Lynwood Wellhausen, Rudgate Companies, Michigan; Bill Geary, CPM, of Carsberg Management, California; Martin Lavin of AJAX Property Management, Vermont; Eugene Landy of United Mobile Homes, New Jersey; Brian Fannon, CPM, Sun Communities, Inc., Michigan; and Ed Zeman of Zeman Realty, Illinois.

The previous paragraphs appeared in the February 1995 issue of *The Journal*. Since that time MHI has formalized its recognition of manufactured home community owners and fee-managers by creating the Interim Communities Division (ICD); hired James Ayotte as executive vice president to head the new division; and named a board of directors that met for the first time in May of 1995 and again in October.

Charter members of the ICD board are

> Gary McDaniel, ROC Communities, Inc.—Chairman
>
> Wendell Verduin, Northwestern Mfd. Housing Community—Vice Chairman
>
> Fran Hirsch, Brandenberg, Staedler & Moore
>
> Thomas Bown, Charter Associates
>
> Jeff Kellogg, Chateau Properties, Inc.
>
> Craig White, ACM, of Craig White Associates
>
> Scott West, Ellenburg Capital
>
> George Allen, CPM, of GFA Management, Inc.
>
> Kristian Jensen, Jensen's Inc.
>
> Don Stockton, Lake Creek Ranch Mobile Estates
>
> Martin Newby of Martin Newby Management
>
> David Helfand, Manufactured Home Communities, Inc.
>
> Barry McCabe, Manufactured Housing Solutions
>
> Brian Fannon, CPM, of Sun Communities, Inc.
>
> Ted Weinhold, Terra Enterprises
>
> Dave Czech, Tri-Park Investments
>
> Steve Adler, Uniprop, Inc.
>
> William T. Poole, Williams Management Services, Inc.

At the fourth annual International Networking Roundtable held in Seaside, Oregon, in late October 1995, James Ayotte made the first formal public presentation of ICD goals and plans before manufactured home community owners and managers who had gathered from 23 states and Canada.

For further information about membership in and services of the Interim Communities Division, recently redesignated as the Manufactured Home Communities Council, contact Jim Ayotte at Manufactured Housing Institute, 2101 Wilson Blvd., Ste. 610, Arlington, VA 22201-3062, or call (703) 558-0400.

DIRECTORY OF NATIONAL, REGIONAL, STATE, AND PROVINCIAL MANUFACTURED HOUSING RELATED ASSOCIATIONS AND INSTITUTES

DIRECTORY OF NATIONAL, REGIONAL, STATE, AND PROVINCIAL MANUFACTURED HOUSING RELATED ASSOCIATIONS AND INSTITUTES*

—NATIONAL ASSOCIATIONS—

American Association of Housing Educators
College of Architecture
Texas A&M University
College Station, TX 77843

—no phone—

American Builders Consortium
227 Townhouse
Hershey, PA 17033

(717) 533-5935

---

* Researched and prepared by George Allen of GFA Management, Inc. and the staff of IMHA/RVIC, Indianapolis, Indiana.

American Consulting Engineers Council   (202) 347-7474
1015 15th Street, NW, Suite 802
Washington, DC 20005

American Mobile Home Association   (303) 232-6336
12929 West 26th Ave.
Golden, CO 80401

American Planning Association   (312) 955-9100
1313 60th Street
Chicago, IL 60637

Appraisal Institute   (312) 335-4100
875 North Michigan Avenue
Chicago, IL 60611

Association for Investment Management & Research   (804) 980-3647
Box 7947
Charlottesville, VA 22906

Association for Regulatory Reform   (202) 783-4087
1331 Pennsylvania Avenue, NW, Suite 524
Washington, DC 20004

Institute of Real Estate Management   (312) 329-6000
430 North Michigan Avenue
Chicago, IL 60610

Manufactured Housing Educational Trust   (714) 935-1900
500 North State College Blvd., Suite 1020
Orange, CA 92668

Manufactured Housing Institute   (703) 558-0400
2101 Wilson Blvd., Suite 610
Arlington, VA 22201

Mortgage Bankers Association of America   (202) 861-6554
1125 15th Street, NW
Washington, DC 20005

Multi-Family Housing Institute   (202) 857-1142
1200 19th Street
Washington, DC 20036

National Association of Home Builders   (202) 822-0200
15th & M Streets
Washington, DC 20005

National Association of Real Estate Investment Managers   (310) 479-2219
11755 Wilshire Blvd.
Los Angeles, CA 90025

National Association of Real Estate Investment Trusts   (202) 857-1142
1129 Twentieth St., NW, Suite 705
Washington, DC 20036

National Foundation of Manufactured Home Owners   (206) 885-4650
Box # 33
Redmond, WA 98073

Pension Real Estate Association   (203) 657-2612
95 Glastonbury Blvd.
Glastonbury, CT 06033

Property Management Network   (317) 888-7156
Box # 47024
Indianapolis, IN 46247

Urban Land Institute   (202) 624-7044
625 Indiana Avenue, NW
Washington, DC 20004

—CANADIAN ASSOCIATIONS—

Canadian Manufactured Housing Association   (613) 563-3520
150 Laurier Avenue West, Suite 200
Ottawa, Ont., CN K1P5J4

Manufactured Home Registry (government)
940 Blanchard Street
Victoria, BC, CN V8W3E6

Manufactured Housing Association of Alberta/   (403) 347-8925
Saskatchewan
Suite 201, 4921-49 Street
Red Deer, AB, CN T4N1V2

Manufactured Housing Association of British Columbia   (604) 850-1353
Suite 302, 32463 Simon Ave.
Abbotsford, BC, CN V2T5E3

Manufactured Housing Association of Nova Scotia   (902) 835-9125
67 Eaglewood Drive
Bedford, NS, CN V4A3B3

Manufactured Housing Association of Ontario   (519) 245-2000
Box 54
Sirathray, Ont., CN N7G3B1

Mobilehome Park Association of New Brunswick   (506) 458-8119
c/o Kelly's Cove
Fredrickton, NB, CN E3B6A5

Manufactured Home Park Owners Association of British Columbia
c/o Aldine Larsen
Crispen Bays
7790 King George Highway
Surrey, BC, CN V3W5Y4

—STATE and REGIONAL ASSOCIATIONS—

Alabama Manufactured Housing Institute   (334) 264-8755
60 Commerce Street, Suite 1212
Montgomery, AL 36104

Manufactured Housing Industry of Arizona   (602) 966-9221
1801 South Jen Tilly Lane, Suite B-2
Tempe, AZ 85281

Arizona Manufactured Housing Association   (602) 952-1102
4700 East Thomas Road Suite 103
Phoenix, AZ 85018

Greater Arizona Manufactured Housing Association (520) 887-0591
3833 North Fairview Ave., Suite 129
Tucson, AZ 85705

Arkansas Manufactured Housing Association (501) 771-0444
2500 McCain Place, Suite 203
North Little Rock, AR 72116

California Manufactured Housing Institute (909) 987-2599
10630 Town Center Drive, Suite 120
Rancho Cucamonga, CA 91730

California Manufactured Home Park Owners Alliance (916) 441-1882
7311 Greenhaven Drive, Suite 100
Sacramento, CA 95831

Western Mobilehome Association (916) 448-7002
1007 7th Street, 3rd floor
Sacramento, CA 95814

Colorado Manufactured Housing Association (303) 832-2022
1410 Grant St.
Denver, CO 80203

Colorado MH Parkowners Association (303) 757-2614
3592 South Hillcrest Dr.
Denver, CO 80237

Delaware Manufactured Housing Association (302) 678-2588
Treadway Towers, Suite 309
Dover, DE 19901

First State Manufactured Housing Institute (302) 674-5868
Box 1829
Dover, DE 19903

Florida Manufactured Housing Association (904) 222-4011
115 North Calhoun, Suite 5
Tallahassee, FL 32301

Georgia Manufactured Housing Association   (770) 955-4522
1000 Circle, 75 Parkway, Suite 060
Atlanta, GA 30339

Manufactured Housing Association of Hawaii
1051 7th Avenue
Honolulu, HI 96816

Idaho Manufactured Housing Association   (208) 343-1722
PO Box 8605
Boise, ID 83707

Illinois Manufactured Housing Association   (217) 528-3423
3888 Peoria Road
Springfield, IL 62702

Illinois Housing Institute   (708) 824-2224
140 North River Road
Des Plaines, IL 60016

Indiana Manufactured Housing Association   (317) 247-6258
3210 Rand Road
Indianapolis, IN 46241-5499

Iowa Manufactured Housing Association   (515) 265-1497
1400 Dean Avenue
Des Moines, IA 50316-3938

Kansas Manufactured Housing Association   (913) 357-5256
214 SW 6th Street, Suite 206
Topeka, KS 66603

Kentucky Manufactured Housing Institute   (502) 223-0490
2170 US 127 South
Frankfort, KY 40601

Louisiana Manufactured Housing Association   (504) 925-9041
4847 Revere Avenue
Baton Rouge, LA 70808

Manufactured Housing Association of Maine   (207) 622-4406
3 Wade Street, Lescomb Building
PO Box 1990
Augusta, ME 04330-6318

Manufactured Housing Institute of Maryland   (301) 797-5341
PO Box 1158
Hagerstown, MD 21740-1158

Michigan Manufactured Homes, Recreational Vehicles, &
Campground Association   (517) 349-8881
2123 University Park Drive, Suite 110
Okemos, MI 48864

Minnesota Manufactured Housing Association   (612) 222-6769
555 Park Street, Suite 400
Saint Paul, MN 55103

Mississippi Manufactured Housing Association   (601) 355-1879
PO Box 12227
Jackson, MS 39236-2227

Missouri Manufactured Housing Institute   (573) 636-8660
PO Box 1365
Jefferson City, MO 65102

Montana Manufactured Housing &
Recreational Vehicles Association   (406) 442-2164
PO Box 4396
Helena, MT 59604

Nebraska Manufactured Housing Association   (402) 475-3675
5300 West O Street
Lincoln, NE 68528

Nevada Manufactured Housing Association   (702) 737-7778
3160 East Desert Inn Road, Suite 3-165
Las Vegas, NV 89121

Nevada Mobilehome Park Owners Association   (702) 731-1900
4055 South Spencer Street, Suite 107
Las Vegas, NV 89119

New Jersey Manufactured Housing Association   (609) 588-9040
2382 Whitehorse-Mercerville Road
Trenton, NJ 08619

New Mexico Manufactured Housing Association   (505) 299-4070
Box 11607
Albuquerque, NM 87192-0607

New York Manufactured Housing Association, Inc.   (518) 464-5087
421 New Karner Road
Albany, NY 12205-3809

North Carolina Manufactured Housing Institute   (919) 872-2740
PO Box 58648
Raleigh, NC 27658-8648

North Dakota Manufactured Housing Association   (701) 667-2187
PO Box 2681
Bismarck, ND 58502

Ohio Manufactured Housing Association   (614) 258-6642
906 East Broad Street
Columbus, OH 43205

Manufactured Housing Association of Oklahoma   (405) 521-8470
PO Box 32309
Oklahoma City, OK 73123

Oregon Manufactured Housing Association   (503) 364-2470
2255 State Street
Salem, OR 97301

Manufactured Housing Communities of Oregon   (503) 391-4496
3857 Wolverine St., NE, Suite 22
Salem, OR 97305

Pennsylvania Manufactured Housing Association (717) 774-3440
PO Box 248
New Cumberland, PA 17070

Manufactured Homes Institute of South Carolina (803) 794-5570
PO Box 5885
West Columbia, SC 29171-5885

South Dakota Manufactured Housing Association (605) 224-2540
PO Box 7077 (605) 224-4022 (fax)
412 W. Missouri, Suite 8 (800) 657-4352
Pierre, SD 57501

Tennessee Manufactured Housing Association (615) 242-7395
240 Great Circle Road, Suite 322
Nashville, TN 37228

Texas Manufactured Housing Association (512) 459-1222
PO Box 14428
Austin, TX 78761

Utah Manufactured Housing Association (702) 737-7778
3160 East Desert Inn Road, Suite 3-165
Las Vegas, NV 89121

Virginia Manufactured Housing Association (804) 750-2500
8413 Patterson Avenue
Richmond, VA 23229

Manufactured Housing Communities of Washington (360) 753-8730
509 12th Avenue, SE, Suite 7
Olympia, WA 98501

Washington Manufactured Housing Association (360) 357-5650
PO Box 621
Olympia, WA 98507

Washington MH Dealer Association
PO Box 68397
Seattle, WA 98168

West Virginia Manufactured Housing Association   (304) 727-7431
205 First Avenue
Nitro, WV 25143

Wisconsin Manufactured Housing Association   (608) 255-3131
202 State Street, Suite 200
Madison, WI 53703

Central Wyoming Mobilehome Association
PO Box 40
Casper, WY 82602

READYING YOUR COMMUNITY FOR ENVIRONMENTAL AUDITS

READYING YOUR COMMUNITY FOR ENVIRONMENTAL AUDITS

By George Allen, CPM

Geroge Allen is president of GFA Management in Greenwood, Indiana. GFA specializes in residential and commercial real estate management. For more information, contact Allen at GFA Management, 1648B U.S. 31 South, Greenwood, Indiana 46143, 317/888-1703.

Times have changed. Gone are the days when all it took for a manufactured home rental community to change ownership was a motivated seller, a willing and capable buyer, and a finance source. Not any more. Today's transactions, more often than not, depend on the successful outcome of what is variously referred to as site study and testing, environmental audits, or the environmental real estate assessment.

Environmental liability, or even the threat thereof, is the driving force behind this recent addition to the traditional "due diligence" process occurring between acceptance of an offer to purchase and the actual real estate closing. Prospective buyers, lending institutions, and liability insurers are requiring these audits or assessments—tests to be performed well in advance of a deal's consumation. And it's even in the seller's best interest to see that this step is accomplished. Why? Because sellers, too, can be held liable, according to federal statute, to participate financially in the environmental cleanup of a property they once owned.

But I'm getting ahead of myself. Before worrying about liability and cleanup costs, you need to look at a definition and the three levels or phases of environmental auditing/assessment, a self-help checklist and resources to contact for assistance.

In a recent article about environmental liabilities, Dr. Albert Gray, PE, and vice president of JACA Corp. at Fort Washington, Pa., defined an *environmental audit* as "the systematic examination of a property by a certified environmental engineering company to *assess the presence, nature, and extent of contamination from past and present use.* It also can help pinpoint the causes of contamination."

What is the regulatory and impetus background that has given rise to environmental auditing? The primary federal statute is the Comprehensive Environmental Response, Compensation and Liability Act (CERCLA) also known as Superfund. This Act governs liability for hazardous waste cleanup and sets forth who can be identified as a "potentially responsible party" when hazardous waste contamination is documented. And because lending institutions can be left holding the bag when a mortgagor (borrower) defaults in the face of astronomic cleanup costs banks, savings and loans, etc. are requiring these audits. Also, several states (Illinois, New Jersey, Indiana) also have enacted legislation governing hazardous waste cleanup liability relative to real estate transactions in their areas.

Most environmental audit specialty firms describe a three-phase approach to environmental real estate assessments or testing. Some firms combine Phases II and III described in the following paragraphs.

Phase I
The Preliminary Audit or Investigation
This phase can include such activities as:
- Physical site visit and visual reconnaissance of all buildings, grounds, utilities, ponds, storage tanks, and waste disposal facilities.
- Aerial photograph analysis for environmental defects.
- Interviews with appropriate on-site staff.
- Review of on-site environmental-

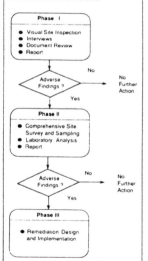

FIGURE I
Phased Approach to Environmental Audits

related documents, such as periodic water quality reports and wastewater treatment plant effluent reports.
- Review of public historical documents to ascertain past usage relative to environmental concerns.
- Evaluate all data collected pursuant to above-listed activities.
- Preparation of a comprehensive **Phase I** report.

On an encouraging note, most audits are concluded at the end of Phase I. Of 160 Phase I audits conducted by JACA, only 25 went on to Phase II, and only five of these were taken to Phase III.

Phase II
On-Site Survey
and Sample Analysis

This phase is only begun when possible or actual site contamination is suspected or identified. **Phase II** may include such activities as soil and water sampling, further site exploration (soil borings), effluent monitoring, and laboratory analysis.

This phase is generally more expensive than Phase I activities. Phase I costs generally average from $1,500 to $30,000. Phase II costs, however, will range from a low of $5,000 to $30,000 and more. And Phase III, the Remedial Design and Implementation phase, will run $20,000 and, possibly, much higher.

Phase III
Remedial Design
and Implementation

This phase is simply what it's entitled. The audit firm, at this point well familiar with the site in question, will prepare recommendations for hazardous material excavation; chemical, physical or biological treatment; and whatever other remedial steps are in order.

FIGURE I is taken from Galson's "A Guide to Environmental Audits" and is a good summary of the preceeding phases.

What should manufactured home community owners do in the meantime to prepare their property for eventual sale and the accompanying environmental assessment? Laventhol and Horvath, in their *L & H Perspective* newsletter (Nov. 1989), outline a self-help assessment analysis for owners of real estate assets in general.
1. Research general information on site history. What's happened at this site in the past and what's tak-

ing place today?
2. Implement management awareness and control programs. If a property has 10 or more employees, a formal, written hazardous or toxic substance familiarization program must be in place. Here, an ounce of prevention and preparation is certainly worth more than a pound of cure later.
3. Identify hazardous materials on-site.
4. Implement standard operating procedures (SOP) for handling, collecting, storage and disposal of hazardous materials.
5. Make sure recordkeeping is in compliance with appropriate regulations, licenses, permits, etc.
6. Become familiar with surrounding terrain and ecology. What's nearby that could have a detrimental effect on the subject property in the event of an environmental assessment?

Some states, such as Illinois and New Jersey, make environmental assessment checklists available to businesses. Check with your state to see if it does.

L & H also lists environmental *red flags* that real estate owners should be sensitive to in their area. They are:
- presence of hazardous materials, storage tanks, electrical equipment, pits, ponds or lagoons;
- stained soil or fouled surface water;
- proximity of flood plains, wetlands, coastal zones or surface water;
- evidence of excavation, filling or other earth-moving activities;
- proximity to known contaminated site;
- unfavorable press reports and

neighborhood complaints;
- regulatory actions against the owner and compliance status.

There are five major environmental risk areas manufactured home community owners/managers need to recognize:
1. stored hazardous materials.
2. buried wastes.
3. underground storage tanks.
4. asbestos in building materials.
5. PCBs in electrical transformers and capacitors.

Would you like to know more about environmental assessment and who to consider contacting for such services? The following is a list of firms that provide services and information.

Galson Technical Services of East Syracuse, N.Y. publishes "A Guide to Environmental Audits." For a free copy, call Cynthia Johnson at 315/432-0506, or contact my offices for a copy.

JACA Corp. of Fort Washington, Pa. has performed hundreds of audits and can be reached at 215/643-5466.

ATEC Environmental Consultants performs audits nationwide. Davies Batterton at 317/849-4990 can put you in touch with the appropriate regional office.

Laventhol and Horvath is also involved in this field. Check your telephone directory for a listing, usually under CPA services.

The *National Association of Environmental Risk Auditors* trains and certifies practioners as Certified Environmental Risk Auditors and Reviewers. Contact Tom Battle at 812/333-0077 for further information or write the association at 4211 E. Third St., Bloomington, Ind. 47401. ☐

GFA
MANAGEMENT
16488 U.S. 31 South
Greenwood, Indiana 46143
317-888-1703

Reprinted by Permission
Manufactured Home MERCHANDISER, January 1990

LOAN AMORTIZATION CHARTS

Allen Loan Amortization Chart for New and Resale Manufactured Home Sales

Factors per $1,000.00

YRS =	5	6	7	8	9	10	11	12	13	14	15	16	17	18	19	20
8	20.28	17.54	15.59	14.14	13.02	12.14	11.42	10.83	10.34	9.92	9.56	9.25	8.99	8.75	8.55	8.37
8 1/4	20.40	17.66	15.72	14.27	13.15	12.27	11.56	10.97	10.48	10.06	9.71	9.40	9.14	8.91	8.70	8.53
8 1/2	20.52	17.78	15.84	14.40	13.28	12.40	11.69	11.11	10.62	10.20	9.85	9.55	9.29	9.06	8.86	8.68
8 3/4	20.64	17.91	15.97	14.53	13.42	12.54	11.83	11.24	10.76	10.35	10.00	9.70	9.44	9.21	9.02	8.84
9	20.76	18.03	16.09	14.66	13.55	12.67	11.97	11.39	10.90	10.49	10.15	9.85	9.59	9.37	9.17	9.00
9 1/4	20.88	18.15	16.22	14.79	13.68	12.81	12.10	11.53	11.05	10.64	10.30	10.00	9.75	9.53	9.33	9.16
9 1/2	21.01	18.28	16.35	14.92	13.81	12.94	12.24	11.67	11.19	10.79	10.45	10.15	9.90	9.68	9.49	9.33
9 3/4	21.13	18.41	16.48	15.05	13.95	13.08	12.38	11.81	11.34	10.94	10.60	10.31	10.06	9.84	9.65	9.49
10	21.25	18.53	16.61	15.18	14.08	13.22	12.52	11.96	11.48	11.09	10.75	10.46	10.22	10.00	9.82	9.66
10 1/4	21.38	18.66	16.74	15.31	14.22	13.36	12.67	12.10	11.63	11.24	10.90	10.62	10.38	10.16	9.98	9.82
10 1/2	21.50	18.78	16.87	15.45	14.36	13.50	12.81	12.25	11.78	11.39	11.06	10.78	10.54	10.33	10.15	9.99
10 3/4	21.62	18.91	17.00	15.58	14.49	13.64	12.95	12.39	11.93	11.54	11.21	10.94	10.70	10.49	10.31	10.16
11	21.75	19.04	17.13	15.71	14.63	13.78	13.10	12.54	12.08	11.70	11.37	11.10	10.86	10.66	10.48	10.33
11 1/4	21.87	19.17	17.26	15.85	14.77	13.92	13.24	12.69	12.23	11.85	11.53	11.26	11.02	10.82	10.65	10.50
11 1/2	22.00	19.30	17.39	15.98	14.91	14.06	13.39	12.84	12.38	12.01	11.69	11.42	11.19	10.99	10.82	10.67
11 3/4	22.12	19.43	17.52	16.12	15.05	14.21	13.54	12.99	12.54	12.16	11.85	11.58	11.35	11.16	10.99	10.84
12	22.25	19.56	17.66	16.26	15.19	14.35	13.68	13.14	12.69	12.32	12.01	11.74	11.52	11.32	11.16	11.02
12 1/4	22.38	19.69	17.79	16.40	15.33	14.50	13.83	13.29	12.85	12.48	12.17	11.91	11.68	11.49	11.33	11.19
12 1/2	22.50	19.82	17.93	16.53	15.47	14.64	13.98	13.44	13.00	12.64	12.33	12.07	11.85	11.67	11.50	11.37
12 3/4	22.63	19.95	18.06	16.67	15.62	14.79	14.13	13.60	13.16	12.80	12.49	12.24	12.02	11.84	11.68	11.54
13	22.76	20.08	18.20	16.81	15.76	14.94	14.28	13.75	13.32	12.96	12.66	12.40	12.19	12.01	11.85	11.72
13 1/4	22.89	20.21	18.33	16.95	15.90	15.08	14.43	13.91	13.48	13.12	12.82	12.57	12.36	12.18	12.03	11.90
13 1/2	23.01	20.34	18.47	17.09	16.05	15.23	14.58	14.06	13.63	13.28	12.99	12.74	12.53	12.36	12.21	12.08
13 3/4	23.14	20.48	18.61	17.23	16.19	15.38	14.74	14.22	13.80	13.45	13.15	12.91	12.71	12.53	12.39	12.26
14	23.27	20.61	18.75	17.38	16.34	15.53	14.89	14.38	13.96	13.61	13.32	13.08	12.88	12.71	12.56	12.44
14 1/4	23.40	20.74	18.88	17.52	16.49	15.68	15.05	14.53	14.12	13.78	13.49	13.25	13.05	12.89	12.74	12.62
14 1/2	23.53	20.88	19.02	17.66	16.63	15.83	15.20	14.69	14.28	13.94	13.66	13.43	13.23	13.06	12.92	12.80
14 3/4	23.66	21.01	19.16	17.81	16.78	15.99	15.36	14.85	14.44	14.11	13.83	13.60	13.41	13.24	13.10	12.99
15	23.79	21.15	19.30	17.95	16.93	16.14	15.51	15.01	14.61	14.28	14.00	13.77	13.58	13.42	13.29	13.17
15 1/4	23.93	21.29	19.44	18.10	17.08	16.29	15.67	15.18	14.77	14.44	14.17	13.95	13.76	13.60	13.47	13.36
15 1/2	24.06	21.42	19.58	18.24	17.23	16.45	15.83	15.34	14.94	14.61	14.34	14.12	13.94	13.78	13.65	13.54
15 3/4	24.19	21.56	19.72	18.39	17.38	16.60	15.99	15.50	15.10	14.78	14.52	14.30	14.12	13.96	13.84	13.73
16	24.32	21.70	19.87	18.53	17.53	16.76	16.15	15.66	15.27	14.95	14.69	14.48	14.30	14.15	14.02	13.97

COMPUTED BY FINANCIAL PUBLISHING COMPANY, BOSTON, MASS. 02215

Property Management Form #113

DAN Publishing, Inc.
P.O. Box 47024
Indianapolis, IN 46247

Allen Loan Amortization Chart for Land and Manufactured Home Sales

Factors per $1,000.00

YRS =	10	11	12	13	14	15	16	17	18	19	20	21
5 *	10.61	9.87	9.25	8.74	8.29	7.91	7.58	7.29	7.04	6.81	6.60	6.42
5 1/4	10.73	9.99	9.38	8.86	8.42	8.04	7.71	7.43	7.17	6.95	6.74	6.56
5 1/2	10.86	10.12	9.51	8.99	8.55	8.18	7.85	7.56	7.31	7.08	6.88	6.70
5 3/4	10.98	10.25	9.63	9.12	8.68	8.31	7.98	7.70	7.45	7.22	7.03	6.85
6	11.11	10.37	9.76	9.25	8.82	8.44	8.12	7.84	7.59	7.37	7.17	6.99
6 1/4	11.23	10.50	9.89	9.38	8.95	8.58	8.26	7.98	7.73	7.51	7.31	7.14
6 1/2	11.36	10.63	10.02	9.52	9.09	8.72	8.40	8.12	7.87	7.65	7.46	7.29
6 3/4	11.49	10.76	10.16	9.65	9.22	8.85	8.54	8.26	8.01	7.80	7.61	7.44
7	11.62	10.89	10.29	9.79	9.36	8.99	8.68	8.40	8.16	7.95	7.76	7.59
7 1/4	11.75	11.02	10.42	9.92	9.50	9.13	8.82	8.55	8.31	8.10	7.91	7.74
7 1/2	11.88	11.15	10.56	10.06	9.64	9.28	8.96	8.69	8.45	8.25	8.06	7.90
7 3/4	12.01	11.29	10.69	10.20	9.78	9.42	9.11	8.84	8.60	8.40	8.21	8.05
8	12.14	11.42	10.83	10.34	9.92	9.56	9.25	8.99	8.75	8.55	8.37	8.21
8 1/4	12.27	11.56	10.97	10.48	10.06	9.71	9.40	9.14	8.91	8.70	8.53	8.37
8 1/2	12.40	11.69	11.11	10.62	10.20	9.85	9.55	9.29	9.06	8.86	8.68	8.53
8 3/4	12.54	11.83	11.24	10.76	10.35	10.00	9.70	9.44	9.21	9.02	8.84	8.69
9	12.67	11.97	11.39	10.90	10.49	10.15	9.85	9.59	9.37	9.17	9.00	8.85
9 1/4	12.81	12.10	11.53	11.05	10.64	10.30	10.00	9.75	9.53	9.33	9.16	9.01
9 1/2	12.94	12.24	11.67	11.19	10.79	10.45	10.15	9.90	9.68	9.49	9.33	9.18
9 3/4	13.08	12.38	11.81	11.34	10.94	10.60	10.31	10.06	9.84	9.65	9.49	9.35
10	13.22	12.52	11.96	11.48	11.09	10.75	10.46	10.22	10.00	9.82	9.66	9.51
10 1/4	13.36	12.67	12.10	11.63	11.24	10.90	10.62	10.38	10.16	9.98	9.82	9.68
10 1/2	13.50	12.81	12.25	11.78	11.39	11.06	10.78	10.54	10.33	10.15	9.99	9.85
10 3/4	13.64	12.95	12.39	11.93	11.54	11.21	10.94	10.70	10.49	10.31	10.16	10.02
11	13.78	13.10	12.54	12.08	11.70	11.37	11.10	10.86	10.66	10.48	10.33	10.19
11 1/4	13.92	13.24	12.69	12.23	11.85	11.53	11.26	11.02	10.82	10.65	10.50	10.37
11 1/2	14.06	13.39	12.84	12.38	12.01	11.69	11.42	11.19	10.99	10.82	10.67	10.54
11 3/4	14.21	13.54	12.99	12.54	12.16	11.85	11.58	11.35	11.16	10.99	10.84	10.72
12	14.35	13.68	13.14	12.69	12.32	12.01	11.74	11.52	11.32	11.16	11.02	10.89
12 1/4	14.50	13.83	13.29	12.85	12.48	12.17	11.91	11.68	11.49	11.33	11.19	11.07
12 1/2	14.64	13.98	13.44	13.00	12.64	12.33	12.07	11.85	11.67	11.50	11.37	11.25
12 3/4	14.79	14.13	13.60	13.16	12.80	12.49	12.24	12.02	11.84	11.68	11.54	11.43
13	14.94	14.28	13.75	13.32	12.96	12.66	12.40	12.19	12.01	11.85	11.72	11.61
13 1/4	15.08	14.43	13.91	13.48	13.12	12.82	12.57	12.36	12.18	12.03	11.90	11.79
13 1/2	15.23	14.58	14.06	13.63	13.28	12.99	12.74	12.53	12.36	12.21	12.08	11.97
13 3/4	15.38	14.74	14.22	13.80	13.45	13.15	12.91	12.71	12.53	12.39	12.26	12.15
14	15.53	14.89	14.38	13.96	13.61	13.32	13.08	12.88	12.71	12.56	12.44	12.33

COMPUTED BY FINANCIAL PUBLISHING COMPANY, BOSTON, MASS. 02215

Property Management Form #114

DMN Publishing, Inc.
P.O. Box 47024
Indianapolis, IN 46247

Allen Loan Amortization Chart for Land and Manufactured Home Sales   Factors per $1,000.00

YRS =	22	23	24	25	26	27	28	29	30	31	32	33
5	6.26	6.11	5.97	5.85	5.74	5.64	5.54	5.45	5.37	5.30	5.23	5.17
5 1/4 **	6.40	6.25	6.12	6.00	5.89	5.78	5.69	5.61	5.53	5.45	5.39	5.32
5 1/2	6.54	6.40	6.27	6.15	6.04	5.94	5.84	5.76	5.68	5.61	5.55	5.48
5 3/4	6.69	6.54	6.41	6.30	6.19	6.09	6.00	5.92	5.84	5.77	5.71	5.65
6	6.84	6.69	6.56	6.45	6.34	6.24	6.16	6.08	6.00	5.93	5.87	5.81
6 1/4	6.98	6.84	6.72	6.60	6.50	6.40	6.31	6.24	6.16	6.10	6.03	5.98
6 1/2	7.13	7.00	6.87	6.76	6.65	6.56	6.48	6.40	6.33	6.26	6.20	6.14
6 3/4	7.29	7.15	7.03	6.91	6.81	6.72	6.64	6.56	6.49	6.43	6.37	6.31
7	7.44	7.30	7.18	7.07	6.97	6.88	6.80	6.73	6.66	6.60	6.54	6.49
7 1/4	7.59	7.46	7.34	7.23	7.14	7.05	6.97	6.89	6.83	6.77	6.71	6.66
7 1/2	7.75	7.62	7.50	7.39	7.30	7.21	7.13	7.06	7.00	6.94	6.88	6.83
7 3/4	7.91	7.78	7.66	7.56	7.46	7.38	7.30	7.23	7.17	7.11	7.06	7.01
8	8.07	7.94	7.83	7.72	7.63	7.55	7.47	7.40	7.34	7.29	7.24	7.19
8 1/4	8.23	8.10	7.99	7.89	7.80	7.72	7.64	7.58	7.52	7.46	7.41	7.37
8 1/2	8.39	8.27	8.16	8.06	7.97	7.89	7.82	7.75	7.69	7.64	7.59	7.55
8 3/4	8.55	8.43	8.32	8.23	8.14	8.06	7.99	7.93	7.87	7.82	7.77	7.73
9	8.72	8.60	8.49	8.40	8.31	8.24	8.17	8.11	8.05	8.00	7.96	7.92
9 1/4	8.88	8.77	8.66	8.57	8.49	8.41	8.35	8.29	8.23	8.18	8.14	8.10
9 1/2	9.05	8.93	8.83	8.74	8.66	8.59	8.52	8.47	8.41	8.37	8.32	8.29
9 3/4	9.22	9.11	9.01	8.92	8.84	8.77	8.70	8.65	8.60	8.55	8.51	8.47
10	9.39	9.28	9.18	9.09	9.01	8.95	8.88	8.83	8.78	8.74	8.70	8.66
10 1/4	9.56	9.45	9.35	9.27	9.19	9.13	9.07	9.01	8.97	8.92	8.89	8.85
10 1/2	9.73	9.62	9.53	9.45	9.37	9.31	9.25	9.20	9.15	9.11	9.07	9.04
10 3/4	9.90	9.80	9.71	9.63	9.55	9.49	9.43	9.38	9.34	9.30	9.26	9.23
11	10.08	9.98	9.89	9.81	9.74	9.67	9.62	9.57	9.53	9.49	9.46	9.43
11 1/4	10.25	10.15	10.06	9.99	9.92	9.86	9.81	9.76	9.72	9.68	9.65	9.62
11 1/2	10.43	10.33	10.25	10.17	10.10	10.05	9.99	9.95	9.91	9.87	9.84	9.81
11 3/4	10.61	10.51	10.43	10.35	10.29	10.23	10.18	10.14	10.10	10.06	10.03	10.01
12	10.78	10.69	10.61	10.54	10.47	10.42	10.37	10.33	10.29	10.26	10.23	10.20
12 1/4	10.96	10.87	10.79	10.72	10.66	10.61	10.56	10.52	10.48	10.45	10.42	10.40
12 1/2	11.14	11.05	10.98	10.91	10.85	10.80	10.75	10.71	10.68	10.65	10.62	10.60
12 3/4	11.33	11.24	11.16	11.10	11.04	10.99	10.94	10.91	10.87	10.84	10.82	10.79
13	11.51	11.42	11.35	11.28	11.23	11.18	11.14	11.10	11.07	11.04	11.01	10.99
13 1/4	11.69	11.61	11.53	11.47	11.42	11.37	11.33	11.29	11.26	11.24	11.21	11.19
13 1/2	11.87	11.79	11.72	11.66	11.61	11.56	11.52	11.49	11.46	11.43	11.41	11.39
13 3/4	12.06	11.98	11.91	11.85	11.80	11.76	11.72	11.68	11.65	11.63	11.61	11.59
14	12.24	12.17	12.10	12.04	11.99	11.95	11.91	11.88	11.85	11.83	11.81	11.79

COMPUTED BY FINANCIAL PUBLISHING COMPANY, BOSTON, MASS. 02215

Property Management Form #115

DMN Publishing, Inc.
P.O. Box 47024
Indianapolis, IN 46247

Allen Loan Amortization Chart for Land and Manufactured Home Sales

Factors per $1,000.00

YRS = %	10	11	12	13	14	15	16	17	18	19	20	21
14	15.53	14.89	14.38	13.96	13.61	13.32	13.08	12.88	12.71	12.56	12.44	12.33
14 1/4	15.68	15.05	14.53	14.12	13.78	13.49	13.25	13.05	12.89	12.74	12.62	12.52
14 1/2	15.83	15.20	14.69	14.28	13.94	13.66	13.43	13.23	13.06	12.92	12.80	12.70
14 3/4	15.99	15.36	14.85	14.44	14.11	13.83	13.60	13.41	13.24	13.10	12.99	12.89
15	16.14	15.51	15.01	14.61	14.28	14.00	13.77	13.58	13.42	13.29	13.17	13.08
15 1/4	16.29	15.67	15.18	14.77	14.44	14.17	13.95	13.76	13.60	13.47	13.36	13.26
15 1/2	16.45	15.83	15.34	14.94	14.61	14.34	14.12	13.94	13.78	13.65	13.54	13.45
15 3/4	16.60	15.99	15.50	15.10	14.78	14.52	14.30	14.12	13.96	13.84	13.73	13.64
16	16.76	16.15	15.66	15.27	14.95	14.69	14.48	14.30	14.15	14.02	13.92	13.83
16 1/4	16.91	16.31	15.83	15.44	15.12	14.87	14.65	14.48	14.33	14.21	14.11	14.02
16 1/2	17.07	16.47	15.99	15.61	15.30	15.04	14.83	14.66	14.51	14.39	14.29	14.21
16 3/4	17.23	16.63	16.16	15.78	15.47	15.22	15.01	14.84	14.70	14.58	14.48	14.40
17	17.38	16.79	16.32	15.95	15.64	15.40	15.19	15.02	14.88	14.77	14.67	14.59
17 1/4	17.54	16.96	16.49	16.12	15.82	15.57	15.37	15.21	15.07	14.96	14.86	14.79
17 1/2	17.70	17.12	16.66	16.29	15.99	15.75	15.55	15.39	15.26	15.15	15.05	14.98
17 3/4	17.86	17.28	16.83	16.46	16.17	15.93	15.74	15.58	15.44	15.34	15.25	15.17
18	18.02	17.45	17.00	16.64	16.34	16.11	15.92	15.76	15.63	15.53	15.44	15.37
18 1/4	18.18	17.61	17.17	16.81	16.52	16.29	16.10	15.95	15.82	15.72	15.63	15.56
18 1/2	18.35	17.78	17.34	16.98	16.70	16.47	16.28	16.13	16.01	15.91	15.82	15.76
18 3/4	18.51	17.95	17.51	17.16	16.88	16.65	16.47	16.32	16.20	16.10	16.02	15.95
19	18.67	18.12	17.68	17.33	17.06	16.83	16.65	16.51	16.39	16.29	16.21	16.15
19 1/4	18.84	18.28	17.85	17.51	17.24	17.02	16.84	16.70	16.58	16.48	16.41	16.34
19 1/2	19.00	18.45	18.02	17.69	17.42	17.20	17.03	16.88	16.77	16.68	16.60	16.54
19 3/4	19.17	18.62	18.20	17.86	17.60	17.38	17.21	17.07	16.96	16.87	16.80	16.74
20	19.33	18.79	18.37	18.04	17.78	17.57	17.40	17.26	17.15	17.07	16.99	16.93

COMPUTED BY FINANCIAL PUBLISHING COMPANY, BOSTON, MASS. 02215

Property Management Form #116

DMN Publishing, Inc.
P.O. Box 47024
Indianapolis, IN 46247

Allen Loan Amortization Chart for Land and Manufactured Home Sales

Factors per $1,000.00

YRS =	22	23	24	25	26	27	28	29	30	31	32	33
14 %	12.24	12.17	12.10	12.04	11.99	11.95	11.91	11.88	11.85	11.83	11.81	11.79
14 1/4	12.43	12.35	12.29	12.23	12.19	12.14	12.11	12.08	12.05	12.03	12.01	11.99
14 1/2	12.62	12.54	12.48	12.43	12.38	12.34	12.31	12.28	12.25	12.23	12.21	12.19
14 3/4	12.81	12.73	12.67	12.62	12.57	12.54	12.50	12.47	12.45	12.43	12.41	12.39
15	12.99	12.92	12.86	12.81	12.77	12.73	12.70	12.67	12.65	12.63	12.61	12.60
15 1/4	13.18	13.12	13.06	13.01	12.97	12.93	12.90	12.87	12.85	12.83	12.81	12.80
15 1/2	13.37	13.31	13.25	13.20	13.16	13.13	13.10	13.07	13.05	13.03	13.02	13.00
15 3/4	13.56	13.50	13.44	13.40	13.36	13.32	13.30	13.27	13.25	13.23	13.22	13.21
16	13.75	13.69	13.64	13.59	13.56	13.52	13.50	13.47	13.45	13.44	13.42	13.41
16 1/4	13.95	13.89	13.83	13.79	13.75	13.72	13.70	13.67	13.65	13.64	13.62	13.61
16 1/2	14.14	14.08	14.03	13.99	13.95	13.92	13.90	13.87	13.86	13.84	13.83	13.82
16 3/4	14.33	14.27	14.22	14.18	14.15	14.12	14.10	14.08	14.06	14.04	14.03	14.02
17	14.53	14.47	14.42	14.38	14.35	14.32	14.30	14.28	14.26	14.25	14.24	14.23
17 1/4	14.72	14.67	14.62	14.58	14.55	14.52	14.50	14.48	14.46	14.45	14.44	14.43
17 1/2	14.91	14.86	14.82	14.78	14.75	14.72	14.70	14.68	14.67	14.66	14.64	14.64
17 3/4	15.11	15.06	15.02	14.98	14.95	14.92	14.90	14.89	14.87	14.86	14.85	14.84
18	15.31	15.26	15.21	15.18	15.15	15.13	15.11	15.09	15.08	15.06	15.05	15.05
18 1/4	15.50	15.45	15.41	15.38	15.35	15.33	15.31	15.29	15.28	15.27	15.26	15.25
18 1/2	15.70	15.65	15.61	15.58	15.55	15.53	15.51	15.50	15.48	15.47	15.47	15.46
18 3/4	15.90	15.85	15.81	15.78	15.75	15.73	15.72	15.70	15.69	15.68	15.67	15.66
19	16.09	16.05	16.01	15.98	15.96	15.94	15.92	15.91	15.89	15.88	15.88	15.87
19 1/4	16.29	16.25	16.21	16.18	16.16	16.14	16.12	16.11	16.10	16.09	16.08	16.08
19 1/2	16.49	16.45	16.41	16.39	16.36	16.34	16.33	16.31	16.30	16.30	16.29	16.28
19 3/4	16.69	16.65	16.61	16.59	16.56	16.55	16.53	16.52	16.51	16.50	16.49	16.49
20	16.89	16.85	16.82	16.79	16.77	16.75	16.74	16.72	16.72	16.71	16.70	16.70

COMPUTED BY FINANCIAL PUBLISHING COMPANY, BOSTON, MASS. 02215

Property Management Form #117

DMN Publishing, Inc.
P.O. Box 47024
Indianapolis, IN 46247

A DESCRIPTION OF THE OLD WOODALL STAR MOBILE HOME PARK RATING SYSTEM

A DESCRIPTION OF THE OLD WOODALL STAR MOBILE HOME PARK RATING SYSTEM

Motels, hotels, and restaurants regularly receive "quality and service" ratings from consumer-oriented magazines, automobile associations (who hasn't heard of or used the AAA-rating system?), and restaurant trade associations. Many years ago, mobile home parks used to be similarly rated, but not anymore.

For more than 23 years, the Woodall Publishing Company published an annual national directory of mobile home parks. In the early 1970s, when Woodall's *Mobile Home Park Directory* ceased publication, 13,000 of the 24,000 mobile home parks then in operation were deemed of high enough quality to be rated, from 1 through 5 STARS, and listed in the 950-page directory.

By that time, the Woodall STARS were highly desired by park owners and managers. Higher STAR ratings usually meant more business and were a source of pride for park residents as well.

Just what general requirements made up the Woodall STAR rating system? The following guidelines are quoted verbatim from the 1970 edition of Woodall's *Mobile Home Park Directory*.

Woodall One Star Park

The most important consideration for a one star park is overall appearance. If it is not a decent place to live, it will not be listed in Woodall's Directory. The following are general requirements:

1A.   Fair overall appearance.

1B.   Patios on most lots. May be concrete, asphalt, wood, or some suitable material.

1C.   Grass, rock or shell to cover ground.

1D.   Streets fair to good. May be dirt, asphalt or gravel in reasonable condition.

1E.   Restrooms clean, if any.

1F.   Adequate laundry or laundromat nearby.

1G.   If fences allowed, must be neat.

1H.   Mail Service

1I.   Homes may be old models but show evidence of care.

1J.   Manager available some hours of each day.

Woodall Two Star Park

In addition to the requirements for a one star park, a two star park will have the following:

2A.   Landscaping—some lawns and shrubs.

2B.   Streets in good condition. Must be dust free of crushed rock, gravel or shell minimum.

2C.   Neat storage.

2D.   Well equipped laundry or laundromat nearby.

2E.   220 volt connections available.

2F   If children accepted, park should have play area.

2G.   Park free of clutter, such as old cars and other abandoned equipment.

2H.   Well maintained and managed.

Woodall Three Star Park

What a three star park does, it does well but not as uniformly as higher rated parks. Many three star parks were once higher rated, but original construction does not allow for today's 10-foot, 12-foot, and double-wides or the 55-foot and 60-foot lengths. If children are allowed, there should be adequate play area. However, the disarray caused by children may at times be the determining factor that keeps a three star park at that level when it otherwise could be rated higher.

In addition to the requirements for a one and two star park, a three star park must have the following:

3A.   Attractive entrance.

3B.   All mobile homes must be in good condition.

3C.   Awnings and cabana rooms on some homes in southern area.

3D.   Some spaces for large mobile homes.

3E.   Paved or hand surfaced streets.

Woodall Four Star Park

(There are two categories. See item 4K)

Four star parks are luxury parks. In addition to the requirement for a one, two and three star park; a four star park must have the following:

4A.   Good landscaping.

4B.   Most homes skirted with metal skirts, concrete block, ornamental wood or stone.

4C.   Paved streets, edged or curbed.

4D.   Uncrowded lots.

4E.   Underground utilities if permitted by local conditions and authorities.

4F.   Most tanks, if present, concealed.

4G.   Any hedges or fences must be attractive and uniform.

4H.   Awnings, cabanas, or porches on most homes in southern areas. (Excepting double-wide units)

4I.   Most lots to accommodate large mobile homes.

4J.   Where row parking of homes exists, all must be lined up uniformly.

4K.   Community hall and/or swimming pool and/or recreation program. If a park is four star in all but this requirement, the fourth star will be printed as an open star indicating a four star park without park-centered recreation.

4L.   Excellent management.

Woodall Five Star Park

Five star parks are the finest. They should be nearly impossible to improve. In addition to the requirement for a one, two, three and four star park, a five star park must have the following:

5A.   Well planned and laid out spacious appearance.

5B.   Good location in regard to accessibility and desirable neighborhood. In some locations park should be enclosed by high hedges or ornamental fence.

5C.   Wide paved streets in perfect condition. Curbs or lawns edged to street, sidewalks, street lights, street signs.

5D.   Homes set back from street.

5E.   Exceptionally attractive entrance and park sign.

5F.   Patios at least 8 X 30 ft. (Excepting double-wide units)

5G.   Paved off-street parking such as carports or planned parking.

5H.   All homes skirted.

5I.   All hitches concealed. Any existing tanks concealed.

5J.   Recreation, some or all of the following: swimming pool (excepting areas with long, cold winters), shuffleboards, horseshoe pitching, golf course, hobby shop, hobby classes, games, potlucks, dances or natural recreational facilities.

5K.   Beautifully equipped recreation hall with kitchen. Room for community gatherings, tiled restrooms, etc.

5L.   Uniform storage sheds or central storage facilities.

5M.   All late model homes in excellent condition.

5N.   At least 60% occupancy in order to judge quality of residents which indicates park's ability to maintain a five star rating between inspections.

5O.   All empty lots grassed, graveled or otherwise well maintained.

5P.   If pets or children allowed, there must be a place for them to run and play without cluttering the streets and yards. Most five star parks are for adults only.

5Q.   Superior management interested in comfort of residents and maintenance of park.

Here is a sample entry from the 1970 edition of Woodall's *Mobile Home Park Directory:*

> **Sunny Lake Park, 123 Fourth St., 5 mi.n.b.c. WW HS 100L, Ch, FS. NP. ONS 10R.

This would indicate that the Sunny Lake Park if five miles north of the business center at 123 Fourth Street. It deserves a two-star rating, has accommodations for a hundred homes, laundry, community hall, separate section for families, does not permit pets, ten spaces for travel trailers, and maintains restrooms. The WW notation was an additional rating of the overnight or vacation facilities, and ranged from one through four Ws.

How were these STAR ratings determined? In 1970, 21 teams of Woodall men visited every mobile home park in the country. The directory editor also used postcard pages in the directory proper, encouraging mail-in opinions from park owners and managers, as well.

Why did all this STAR-rating stop? I asked George Goldman, owner of Woodall Publishing in Chicago, Illinois. According to Mr. Goldman, mobile homes had become "obviously immobile" by the mid-1970s, so consumers no longer really needed a national directory of mobile home parks. At the same time, however, the RV/campground industry was growing, and Woodall's *RV/Campground Directory* outperformed the mobile home park directory. In fact, the *RV/Campground Directory* is now the oldest and largest of such directories in the United States, commanding 51 percent of the consumer market.

The Woodall *RV/Campground Directory* is not only published as one major publication, but has spun off 19 other, less-expensive subdirectories as well. These are localized into east and west editions, and bistate (for example, Arizona and New Mexico) directories. The *RV Buyer's Guide* and *Tenting Directory* are two additional Woodall-family publications.

The interesting observation was made by George Goldman, that the RV industry increasingly exhibits nontransient characteristics of contemporary mobile home parks. More and more RV'ers spend more and more time in the RV at local and resort RV parks and campgrounds than ever before. It has definitely become a preferred lifestyle for many recreation-oriented consumers.

So there you have it, one through five STARS, the way mobile home parks used to be classified. Actually, it is still a helpful set of guidelines for park managers and owners. Why not clip the ratings and keep them handy to rate your own community from time to time?

APPENDIX L

REAL ESTATE BROKERS SPECIALIZING IN THE MARKETING OF MANUFACTURED HOME COMMUNITIES

REAL ESTATE BROKERS SPECIALIZING IN THE MARKETING OF MANUFACTURED HOME COMMUNITIES

1. AMERICAN NATIONAL REALTY
   Rte. 6, Box # 6859
   Hayward, WI 54843
   (800) 775-5899
   Steve Bodenschatz

2. BARBER & ASSOCIATES
   25431 Cabot Road, Ste. 200
   Laguna Hills, CA 92653
   (714) 472-1120

3. BIRCH MORTGAGE & REALTY
   2328 Livernois, Ste. B
   Troy, MI 48083
   (800) 589-7833

4. BITNEY REALTY
    108 Factory Ave. N., Ste. 1
    Renton, WA 98055
    (206) 255-1080
    Bob Viall

5. BUSINESS REAL ESTATE BROKERAGE CO.
    4380 La Jolla Village Dr., #200
    San Diego, CA 92122
    (619) 546-5416
    John Grant, Broker
    Vince Reynolds

6. CALIFORNIA COMMERCIAL REAL ESTATE
    1222 Lincoln Avenue
    San Jose, CA 95125
    (408) 279-5404
    Jim Wagar

7. CAMPBELL & ROSEMURAY REAL ESTATE
    (aka Campbell PM)
    1233 East Hillsboro Blvd.
    Deerfield Beach, FL 33064
    (305) 427-8686 & 946-0431
    Bob McSweeney, Broker

8. CENTURY 21 HERMAN BOSWELL
    1708 S. Cooper
    Arlingon, TX 76013
    (817) 274-2521
    Lori Scott

9. CHAPPEL REAL ESTATE
    534 Highway #58
    Swansboro, NC 28584
    (919) 393-6141
    J. Wm. (Dewey) Chappel

10. CHARLES H. STEVENS CO.
    c/o Emerald Lake Companies
    2205 U.S. Hwy. #27N
    Davenport, FL 33837
    (813) 424-5454
    Chuck Stevens

11. COMMONWEALTH COMMERCIAL CAPITAL BROKERAGE CO.
    10725 SW Barber Blvd., #100
    Portland, OR 97219
    (503) 244-2300
    Don Kilpatrick
    Mike Holman
    Jack Ward

12. CRAIG WHITE & ASSOCIATES
    13390 Harrison St., Ste. 120
    Denver, CO 80241
    (303) 457-1160
    Craig White

13. CULLEN INVESTMENT
    Box # 786
    Pacific Palisades, CA 90272
    (310) 459-8842
    Richard Cullen

14. DAUM CO.
    2300 E. Katella, Ste. 100
    Anaheim, CA 92806
    no phone #
    Chuck Gardner

15. DITTMAR REALTY
    Box # 129
    Menomonee Falls, WI 53052
    (414) 251-5800
    Clarence Dittmar

16. DON KUHN COMPANY
    1930 Cach Lane SW
    Cedar Rapids, IA 52404
    (319) 365-9496
    Don Kuhn (owns MHCs)

17. DYNAMIC REALTY
    1111 Church St.
    Flint, MI 48502
    (810) 238-3900
    John & Thomas Strittmatter

18. EASTERN GENERAL REALTY
    140 N. Orlando Ave. #150-9
    Winter Park, FL 32789
    (407) 740-8773
    Lamont Garber

19. ERA SUNCOAST REALTY
    1206 US Hwy. #19
    Crystal River, FL 34429
    (904) 795-6811
    Catherine Rooks Cassidy

20. FASTNET
    229 Oakland Avenue
    Audubon, NJ 08106
    (609) 546-0876
    Robert Laslocky

21. FENSKE, KRASNO & PAGE
    11 N. 5th Ave., #200
    Maywood, IL 60153
    (708) 345-3892
    Paul Fenske
    Andrew Krasno
    Rich Page

22. FIRST COMMERCIAL REALTY, INC.
    8136 Mall Rd.
    Florence, KY 41042
    (606) 371-9000
    Jim Lohr

23. FLORIDA CHOICE REALTY, INC.
    2929 E. Commercial Blvd. Ste. 200
    Ft. Lauderdale, FL 33308
    (305) 772-0613
    Loraine Leithiser
    Dan Marino

24. FLORIDA GROWTH REALTY
    511 E. Rosery Rd., Ste. 4H
    Largo, FL 34640
    (813) 596-9397
    Robert Lurie
    Donna Canada

25. FOLLETT & FLORENCE INVESTMENTS
    11344 Coloma Road, #480
    Gold River, CA 95670
    (916) 852-0112
    Robin Follett
    Matt Follett

26. FORTUNE REAL ESTATE
    4702-C 26th St. W.
    Bradenton, FL 34207
    (813) 755-1339
    Don McLavshlin
    Bob Smith

27. GOLDMAN & ASSOCIATES
    800 E. Northwest Hwy. #833
    Palatine, IL 60067
    (708) 359-1711

28. INVESTMENT PROPERTY GROUP
     3701 Birch St., 2nd Floor
     Newport Beach, CA 92660
     (714) 756-3232
     Al Gavsewitz
     Brian Fitterer

29. JAMES FOSTER & CO., INC.
     1290 Palm Ave.
     Sarasota, FL 34236
     (941) 954-4044
     Jim Foster

30. JEFFERSON GROUP LTD.
     12155 Wedgeway Court
     Fairfax, VA 22033
     (703) 385-6060
     Mary Frances de la Pava

31. KOHL CO. ASSOC., INC.
     5100 Round Lake Rd.
     Apopka, FL 32712
     Walter Kohl

32. LIPSCOMB REALTY
     183 Sargent Court
     Monterey, CA 93940
     (408) 373-3013
     Mike Lipscomb

33. MARCUS & MILLICHAP
     8750 West Bryn Mawr Avenue
     #750
     Chicago, IL 60631
     (312) 693-0700
     Mike Conley

34. MARCUS & MILLICHAP
     2626 Hanover Street
     Palo Alto, CA 93404
     Bill Bean

35. <u>MARCUS & MILLICHAP</u>
    One World Trade Center
    #1900
    Long Beach, CA 90831-1900
    (310) 436-5800
    Doug Danny

36. <u>MARCUS & MILLICHAP</u>
    2626 Hanover Street
    Palo Alto, CA 94304
    (415) 494-8900
    Bill Bean

37. <u>MARCUS & MILLICHAP</u>
    650 S. Cherry Street, Ste. 115
    Denver, CO 80222
    (303) 320-1300
    Brian Macey

38. <u>MARCUS & MILLICHAP</u>
    4040 E. Camelback Road, Ste. 130
    Phoenix, AZ 85018
    (602) 952-9669
    John McDermott

39. <u>MARCUS & MILLICHAP</u>
    750 Battery Street
    Fifth Floor
    San Francisco, CA 94111
    (415) 391-9220
    Jeff Mishkin

40. <u>MARCUS & MILLICHAP</u>
    1055 W. 7th Street, Ste. 1700
    Los Angeles, CA 90017
    (213) 623-7800
    Greg Parks

41. <u>MARCUS & MILLICHAP</u>
    10900 NE 4th Street, Ste. 2150
    Bellevue, WA 98004
    (206) 453-8330
    Ross Cano

42. <u>MELDEN REALTY</u>
    6200 S. Syracuse Way #125
    Englewood, CO 80111
    (303) 773-7123
    Ralph Melden

43. <u>MOUNTAIN VALLEY REAL ESTATE</u>
    11684 Westminster Dr.
    Waynesboro, PA 17268
    (717) 762-9329
    Jerre Snider

44. <u>MULKEY-HICKS, INC.</u>
    7520 W. Waters Ave. #16
    Tampa, FL 33615
    (813) 888-9841
    Dan Mulkey
    Ed Hicks

45. <u>NATIONWIDE PARK INVESTMENTS</u>
    5350 S. Roslyn St. #360
    Englewood, CO 80111
    (303) 796-8440
    Robert Murdock

46. <u>O'HARA REALTY</u>
    218 S. Lincoln Way
    Galt, CA 95632
    (800) OHARA-4-U
    Doris Klinkenberg

47. <u>PACIFIC WEST PROPERTIES</u>
    990 Highland Dr., Ste. 312
    Solana Beach, CA 92075
    (619) 966-5470
    Ron Temko

48. PALMER CO.
    11500 Hardwick Court
    Raleigh, NC 27614
    (919) 848-9376
    Robert Palmer

49. PARK SALES
    2223 5th St., Box 10826
    St. Paul, MN 55110
    (612) 426-1610
    Henry Votel

50. PARKBRIDGE CAPITAL
    5550 SW Macadam, #220
    Portland, OR 97201
    (503) 222-6400
    Lee Meekums

51. PICOR COMMERCIAL REAL ESTATE
    335 N. Wilmot, Ste. 505
    Tucson, AZ 85711
    (520) 748-7100
    Mike Hammond

52. PONTIAC REALTY
    1044 Rte. 23, Ste. 309
    Wayne, NJ 07470
    (201) 633-9609
    Warren Mackes, Pres.

53. PORTSER REAL ESTATE
    56 Harvard St. Ext.
    Natick, MA 01760
    (508) 655-9140
    Philip Portser

54. POGODA GROUP, THE
    31550 Northwestern Hwy. #150
    Farmington Hills, MI 48334
    (810) 855-9676
    Al Von Steeg, MHC Broker
    Darrel Brady
    Morrie Greener

55. PPI, INC.
    8383 Craig St. #325
    Indianapolis, IN 46250
    (317) 577-0800
    Doug Pelton (owns MHCs)

56. PREFERRED MOBILEHOME PARK INVESTMENTS
    5353 E. 2nd Street, Ste. 205
    Long Beach, CA 90803
    (310) 438-9971
    Jack Hale

57. QUADRELLE GROUP, INC.
    1 West Avenue
    Larchmont, NY 10538
    (914) 834-2600
    Lisa Loscalzo

58. REALSEARCH CORP.
    Box # 3660
    Palos Verdes, CA 90274
    (310) 541-2112
    Franz Fischer (owns MHCs)

59. REGENCY GROUP, INC.
    11711 SE 8th St., #310
    Bellevue, WA 98005
    (206) 454-4000
    Bruce Bobman

60. ROBERTSON & ASSOCIATES
    4865 Haines Street
    San Diego, CA 92019
    (619) 581-9377
    Bill Robertson

61. SAM SPENCER & ASSOCIATES
    16300 MillCreek Blvd., Ste. 105
    Mill Creek, WA 98012
    (206) 787-6200
    Sam Spencer

62. SIERRA VALLEY COMMERCIAL REAL ESTATE
    722 Sutter Street, Ste. F
    Folsom, CA 95630
    (916) 985-4944
    Gary Brown & Jim Cooper

63. SILVER KING COMPANIES
    11485 N. 103rd Place
    Scottsdale, AZ 85260
    (602) 949-0648
    Keith Vanderhout (owns MHCs)

64. SIMPSON'S MOBILEHOME PARK BROKERS
    10101 Slater Ave., #236
    Fountain Valley, CA 92708
    (714) 962-6336
    Donald Mehle

65. SPATARO REALTY & AUCTIONS
    209 McGregor Drive
    Canonsburg, PA 15317
    (412) 745-1886
    Anthony & Tom Spataro

66. STEVENS CO.—REAL ESTATE & DEVELOPMENT, THE
    6201 Hennessey Pkwy.
    Marion, IA 52302
    (319) 377-9955
    Joanne Stevens

67. STROUD, INC.
    217 US Hwy. 70 West
    Havelock, NC 28532
    (919) 447-8130
    Tom Stroud, CCIM

68. SUBURBAN MANAGEMENT & BROKERAGE
    2678 N. Main Street, #22
    Walnut Creek, CA 94596
    (510) 934-4550
    Scott Carter

69. <u>TOPPS REALTY</u>
    2512 Greenwood Road
    Northbrook, IL 60060
    (708) 564-3668 & (619) 327-1959
    Beatrice Shulkin (owns MHCs)

70. <u>UNITED NATIONAL REAL ESTATES</u>
    1600 N. Corrington
    Kansas City, MO 64120
    (800) 444-5044 Ask for Directory

71. <u>UNITED PROPERTIES</u>
    13612 Midway Rd. #250
    Dallas, TX 75244
    (214) 387-1503
    Tony Gange

72. <u>UNITED REALTY ADVISORS</u>
    12625 High Bluff Dr. #310
    San Diego, CA 92130
    (619) 755-1717
    Peter Andrews
    Bruce Kleege
    Rocky Maguire

73. <u>U.S. PARK INVESTMENTS</u>
    3515 N. 12th St., Suite 1
    Phoenix, AZ 85014
    (602) 230-0595
    Charles Irion (owns MHCs)

74. <u>WEST REAL ESTATE AGENCY</u>
    5528 William Flynn Hwy.
    Gibsonia, PA 15044
    (412) 443-1200
    Joe Mondello

75. <u>WRANGLER INVESTMENT CORP.</u>
    Box 280
    Cheyney, WA 99004
    (800) 733-1769
    Jim Parker

76. <u>ZEMAN REALTY</u>
    6547 N. Avondale
    Chicago, IL 60631-1597
    (312) 792-2515
    Bud Zeman (owns MHCs)

NATIONAL SOURCE LIST OF MANUFACTURED HOME COMMUNITIES

NATIONAL SOURCE LIST OF MANUFACTURED HOME COMMUNITIES

Chrissy Jackson, ACM

STATE	COMPLETE LIST	PARTIAL LIST	OTHER SOURCES
Alabama	None	None	**
Arizona	Space Finders Bill/Marian Stickler 2520 S. Rita Lane Tempe, AZ 85282 (602) 968-6307	Arizona Mfg Hsg 1840 West Van Buren Phoenix, AZ 85007 (800) 351-3350 ext. 7275	GAMHA 3833 N. Fairview #129 Tucson, AZ 85705 $2 ea/Tucson only
Arkansas	None	* 10 years old	**
California	Hoffman Books 1917 Milano Way Mountain View, CA 94040 (415) 968-4202 (415) 961-4909 Fax	Dept Hsg & Comm. Dev. P.O. Box 1407 Sacramento, CA 95812 Timothy Coyle, Dir. (916) 445-9471 $250 on disk Under $200 list only	**
Colorado	None	* $75 cost	

* See Appendix H, List of Manufactured Housing Associations.
** See Joseph J. Culligan, When in Doubt, Check Him Out (1993).

Connecticut	None	* Free to members Members only listed	**
Delaware	None	First State Mfg. Housing Institute Consumer Protection Unit P.O. Box 1829 Dover, DE 19901 (302) 577-3250	**
Florida	None	* Free to members Members only listed	HRS—HSES 1317 Winewood Bldg. Tallahassee, FL 32399-0700 (904) 488-4070 Free Lists all with wastewater plants
Georgia	None	* Free to members Members only listed	**
Idaho	None	None	**
Illinois	None	None	**
Indiana	Indiana Board of Health	* For Members Only $25 cost Members only listed	**
Iowa	None	* $26 cost	**
Kansas	None	* For Members Only Members only listed	** Not for solicitation
Kentucky	Cabinet for Human Resources 275 East Main St Frankfort, KY 40621 502/564-7181/3127	None	**
Louisiana	None	* Members only listed	**
Maine	State of Maine Mfg Housing Board, State House Sta. Augusta, ME 04333 David Preble, Exec Dir Cost about $50	* Free to Members Members only listed	**

Maryland	None	None	**
Massachusetts	None	* Free to members Members only listed	**
Michigan	Dept of Commerce Mobile Home Comm. P. O. Box 30222 Lansing, MI 48909 517/334-6203 Computer Report $40	* $20 to members $40 to non-members	**
Minnesota	None	* $45 cost	**
Mississippi	None	* $100 for total membership list	**
Missouri	None	* $150 cost	
Montana	Board of Health 1400 Broadway Helena, MT 59601 (406) 444-2544 (Must have notarized request stating purpose)	Ed McCue (406) 442-0080	**
Nebraska	None	None	**
Nevada	Nevada Div Mfg Hsng State Mailroom Las Vegas, NV 89158 (702) 486-4135 $75 cost	None	**
New Hampshire	None	* Free to members	**
New Jersey	None	None	**
New Mexico	None	* For members only 2-year-old list	**
New York	None	* For members only with board approval	**
North Carolina	None	* Free to members $10 to non-members	**

North Dakota	ND State Dept Health Consolidated Lab. P.O. Box 937 Bismarck, ND 58502-0937 (701) 328-6149 $12 approx. cost	* Members only	**
Ohio	None	* Free to Members $125 to non-members	**
Oklahoma	None	* For Members Only	**
Oregon	M/H Park Ombudsman 1600 State St. Salem, OR 97310 (503) 986-2016 No Cost	* No Cost	**
Pennsylvania	None	* Free Members only listed	**
Rhode Island	None	* Free to members	**
South Carolina	SC Dep't of Health & Environmental Control 2600 Bull Street Columbia, SC 29201 (803) 734-5000 $25 cost	None	**
South Dakota	None	* Free to members Members only listed	**
Tennessee	None	None	**
Texas	None	* Free to members Members only listed	**
Utah	None	None	**
Vermont	None	* Free to members Members only listed	**
Virginia	None	* Free to members Members only listed	**
Washington	None	None	**

West Virginia	None	* Free to members	**
		$50 to non-members	
Wisconsin	None	* $20 cost	**

Notes:

1. None of the Canadian Provinces have regulatory agencies at the province level nor are there any lists available of communities within each province.

2. In each of the states where "None" is entered under the center column, it is because the manufactured home communities in these states are regulated at the local level—either the municipality or the county where they are located.

3. American Business Lists, 5711 South 86th Circle, Omaha, NE 68127, (402) 331-7169, sells lists of manufactured home communities found in the yellow pages of telephone directories nationwide. The lists can be sorted by state, county, zip code, and so forth. In some areas of the United States, this would not be profitable, as the communities are all full and do not advertise. In other areas, such as in Montana, where the state association does not even represent communities, it may be helpful.

THE 21ST CENTURY NATIONAL MANUFACTURED HOME LANDLEASE COMMUNITY RATING SYSTEM

**THE 21ST CENTURY NATIONAL MANUFACTURED HOME
LANDLEASE COMMUNITY RATING SYSTEM**

Thomas Horner, Jr.

—a special preview of Tom Horner's soon-to-be-released text with that title—

Tom Horner's comprehensive new system offers A, B, C, D, and "unratable" designations for manufactured home communities. Each rating has a general definition (or overall appearance rating), location requirements, fifteen specific criteria, and five amenity considerations. By assigning appropriate alphabetical designations (or unratable) to the general appearance, location, fifteen specific criteria, and five amenities, one can tally the results and come to an accurate and informed conclusion as to the relative ranking of the property being rated. The individual explanations for each of these designations are presented on the following pages.

One important caution. It is imperative to compare manufactured home communities only with others in the same market area. Comparing an all-adult community in Southern California with a family community in Denver serves no purpose. Anyone undertaking a rating exercise must first identify a market area. It may be an entire state, county, large standard metropolitan statistical area, smaller city, or even a rural area.

The fifteen specific criteria and five amenities considerations are as follows:

SPECIFIC CRITERIA

1. General Layout and Design

2. Streets

3. Setbacks

4. Vehicle Parking

5. Entrance or Entries

6. Individual Homesite Improvements

7. Skirting

8. Towing Hitches

9. Outside On-Lot Storage

10. Individual Homes

11. Occupancy

12. Empty Homesites

13. Pets and Children

14. Rules and Regulations also known as Guidelines for Living

15. Management

AMENITIES

1. Swimming Pool or Pools

2. Clubhouse

3.   Clubhouse-Related Facilities

4.   Tennis Courts, Volleyball Courts, Basketball Courts, Shuffleboard Courts, Horseshoe Pits, Playgrounds

5.   Lake, Stream, Beach, or Other

The complete outline of the A, B, C, D, and Unratable considerations follow:

"A" RATING CLASSIFICATION REQUIREMENTS

GENERAL APPEARANCE AND DEFINITION

"A" rated manufactured home communities should be the finest in their geographic area. General appearance should not only be clean, neat, and attractive, but also inviting to any observer driving through the community. Positive "curb appeal" is a definite requirement of all "A" rated properties.

LOCATION

The location of a particular community is of critical importance to being rated an "A" community.

The location of an "A" rated manufactured home community must be the same as an above average to upper bracket single-family residential subdivision. That is, reasonable proximity to schools, churches, hospitals, shopping facilities, convenience stores, transportation facilities, employment centers, and recreational facilities. The property should front on or have easy access to freeways, highways, or major arterial streets.

Note: As an alternative, a specific manufactured home community may be somewhat removed from these traditional "location" criteria so long as it has within itself a specific "destination asset." Primary examples of a "destination asset" would be a golf course, lake, view of the ocean, view of the mountains, or a mountain valley with substantial facilities for residents on site so they won't need to go to and from the property as often as might otherwise be required.

Tenancy of the manufactured home community (for example, retired adults versus working individuals) will also dictate what is a good location. If the tenancy is all (or mostly) retired adults, then convenient proximity to employment centers is less important and this difference must be considered.

SPECIFIC CRITERIA

1.   <u>Layout or Design</u>: Well planned and laid out, spacious homesites. Homesite sizes must be able to accommodate large single- and multisection manufactured homes.

2.   <u>Streets</u>: Wide paved streets in well-maintained condition. Streets should be at least as wide (and of similar construction) as those in moderate and upper bracket single-family subdivisions in the same area. Streets must be curbed either with lazy-back, high-back, or combination sidewalk with curb, depending on what is customary in the geographic area for middle and upper (bracket) single-family subdivisions.

3.   <u>Setbacks</u>: Homes should be set back at least 7' off streets that are at least 40' in width; 25' setback on streets that may be as narrow as those required in area single-family subdivisions (normally 24' to 28') and which also have off-street parking.

4.   <u>Vehicle Parking</u>: At least 2 off-street parking spaces on each homesite, plus adequate cluster parking for guests in reasonable proximity to most homesites. Parallel, on-street guest parking should also be physically possible without restricting the normal flow of traffic throughout the community.

Note: Off-street parking spaces may be side by side, or one behind the other (and unprotected or under a carport), whichever is customary in the subject property's geographic area.

Home sizes vary from one geographic area to another. "A" rated communities should have no obsolescence, that is to say they must be able to accommodate the largest homes that are traditional or customary in the geographic and market area of which the community is a part.

5.   <u>Entrance or Entrances</u>: Entries in "A" rated manufactured home communities must convey the same image of quality the property itself offers. All entrances should feature attractive landscaping with trees, plants, and shrubs that are native or customary to the area. The sign (or signs) identifying the community must be attractive, neat, freshly painted, and well maintained.

6.   <u>Individual Homesite Improvements</u>: Improvements on individual homesites should feature large patios, paved off-street parking, sidewalks both

along the streets, and (if appropriate and depending on the design layout), from the street to the patio and entry to the home. These improvements should be of concrete construction, although asphalt is acceptable.

If homesite improvements are of asphalt, they must have a clean, fresh surface and be well maintained. The area under the home should have concrete runners or concrete "blocking support" piers or pads, depending on what is customary in the geographic area. The area under the home may be gravel or other suitable material as long as this is dry, clean, drains properly, and is of customary construction for the particular area.

7.   Skirting: The perimeter of the home must be skirted with an approved finished material. This material may vary from one geographic area to another, but the material must have a professional finish on it, and be properly installed.

8.   Towing Hitches: All hitches must be removed or attractively concealed.

9.   Outside Storage: Uniform storage sheds or central storage facilities must be provided or required. No individual outside on-site storage buildings are permitted.

10. Individual Homes: All homes must be in excellent condition, well maintained, and attractive in appearance.

11. Occupancy: Manufactured home community should have at least 50% occupancy in order to judge quality of residents and homes. Otherwise, occupancy should be compatible with the market area commensurate with the age of the property.

12. Empty Homesites: Vacant sites must be grassed, mowed, graveled, and otherwise well maintained in accordance with local practice and community rules.

13. Pets and Children: If pets and/or children are characteristic of the occupancy of a specific community, there must be facilities and adequate common "green areas" for them to run and play without cluttering or trespassing on yards and streets.

14. Rules and Regulations: An "A" class community must publish and enforce intelligent rules and regulations compatible with living habits that are

customary to the geographic area and the tenancy of the manufactured home community.

15. Management: The property must be competently managed with full-time on-site managers.

AMENITIES

Class "A" manufactured home communities must have most of the following, depending on what is customary for the better residential communities in the geographic area:

1.   Swimming pool or pools: Facilities may also include a wading or "baby" pool and related "hot tub" type facility and saunas.

2.   Clubhouse: It will have substantial meeting, dance, banquet, or meeting spaces and neat, clean, and adequate kitchen and restroom facilities to accommodate the activities (banquet, reception, birthday parties, etc.) that might be conducted in this space, or these spaces.

Size of the facility should depend on both the size of the community and the living habits (and demands) of the tenancy in a given geographic area. For example, "working" individuals don't place the same demands on community facilities as do "retirees." These differences in both specific properties and geographic areas must be recognized.

3.   Clubhouse must have other related facilities compatible with the geographic area and customary living habits of the tenancy, obviously, an adequate number of clean restrooms, outdoor decks, patios, or related areas, depending on the established (or anticipated) needs of the residents.

4.   Tennis courts, volleyball courts, basketball courts, shuffleboard courts, horseshoe courts, and well-equipped playgrounds: these are dictated by local custom and actual or anticipated tenancy.

5.   If a lake, stream, or beach is involved, then those facilities must also be of high quality, attractive, well maintained, functional, as safe as is reasonably possible, and denote quality and be an asset, rather than detrimental to the property. Same criteria applies to boats, boating facilities, docks, etc.

"C" RATING CLASSIFICATION REQUIREMENTS

DEFINITION

A "C" rated community is basically a neat, clean, functional residential manufactured home community in which to live, in an average location, with minimal obsolescence, in an average market, with average amenities for the market of which it is a part.

LOCATION

Since a "C" class property is "average" within the marketplace it is a part of, it should have an "average" location. Using the class "A" criteria, we can logically conclude that a "C" community would need to have some of the same location criteria as an "A," but obviously not all of them. The "A" requirement is as follows:

The location of an "A" manufactured home community must be the same as an above average or upper bracket single-family residential subdivision, that is, reasonable proximity to schools, churches, hospitals, shopping centers, and recreational facilities, and this difference must be recognized.

Accordingly, a class "C" manufactured home community should have a location similar to that which an "average" single-family subdivision might have. Similarly, it should obviously be in reasonable proximity to some (but not all) of the typical advantages we find in class "A." Class "C" communities could be in close proximity to employment centers, but some distance from some of the other "A" location requirements. Class "C" location might also be dictated by the neighborhood surrounding it as well as the price bracket of neighboring single-family homes.

SPECIFIC CRITERIA

1. Layout or Design and Homesite Size: Class "C" communities might have a well laid out and planned design but with some obsolescence in site size. It may be an older community where, with age, sites that were once large enough, today are too small for contemporary manufactured homes. "C" communities can have obsolescence on some of the sites, but obviously not all, or even a substantial number of them or else it rates as a class "D" property.

2.   Streets in a class "C" community should be about average in size and construction for what is typical of the marketplace. Likewise the condition (regardless of age) should be about average, within this same market.

3.   Setbacks: "C" communities may have a few setback problems that have evolved over the years. Assuming this is an "average" condition throughout the subject marketplace, then a specific property can still justify a "C" rating as long as the setback requirements can be dealt with within the jurisdiction of which the manufactured home community is a part and can still accommodate many of the large single- and multisection homes being produced.

Specifically, as long as 2/3 of the homesites in the subject community can accommodate large modern single- and multisection homes, the property (if meeting other appropriate criteria) can still qualify for an average or "C" rating. Over 1/3 obsolescence on homesite size would rate the property at below average or "D" rating.

4.   Vehicle Parking: An average or class "C" community must still provide adequate parking. This can either be provided as off-street parking (2 cars per site) or as parallel on-street parking with streets that are wide enough to provide for parallel on-street parking on both sides of the street and still accommodate an unrestricted flow of traffic.

5.   Entry: Class "C" properties must have an attractive entryway as what might be considered "average" for residential communities in the geographic area.

6.   Individual Homesite Improvements: The class "C" or "average" manufactured home community may have all, some, or most of the individual site improvements of an "A" or "B" community, but they may be smaller, older, or not quite as pristine as the "A" property. "C" or "average" properties may have smaller patios, blocking piers or pads (rather than all concrete runners or pads), and sidewalks that extend only from the street back to the site and not along streets and public walkways.

7.   Skirting: An "average" or class "C" manufactured home community requires skirting on all homes. It may be, however, that either due to the age of the community, the age of the homes in the community, or the economic circumstances of the residents, some of that material is less attractive. It may also be that in a class "C" property, enforcement of the skirting requirement may be more lax than in the higher rated properties that require and achieve timely compliance with this requirement.

8.   Towing Hitches: Towing hitches do not need to be removed in an average or class "C" property. If not concealed, they should be cleanly painted.

9.   Outside Storage: Uniform storage sheds or central storage is not a requirement of a class "C" or "average" community. Although no outside (on lot) storage will be permitted in a class "C" community, permitting residents some reasonable time period to comply and also allowing them to individually purchase a variety of individual storage facilities will mean that a class "C" community will probably always have some residents "in the process" of compliance, and therefore diminish the overall pristine appearance that would be required of an "A" community.

10.   Individual Homes: A significant number of the homes in a class "C" property would be of new or somewhat recent vintage. We acknowledge that a significant number of class "C" communities will be older communities with a mix of older and newer homes. The most important consideration regarding individual homes will not be their age so much as their general appearance and state of repair. A majority of homes in a class "C" community should be clean and well maintained. Having too high an incidence of both old and "unmaintained" homes would drop what might otherwise be a class "C" property down to a below average or "D" rating.

11.   Occupancy: Class "C" communities may feature a diverse mix of residents, typical of the city, county, and neighborhood of which it is a part. A class "C" property should be about "average" so far as occupancy is concerned. That is, if the property is in a market where other manufactured home communities and apartments are 95% occupied, then the subject property should have similar occupancy. If that is not the case, then those attempting to apply a rating should do enough market research to determine the occupancy trend of the subject property and, more importantly, the reasons for that trend. For example, a class "C" property could be one that has recently changed ownership or management, gone through refinancing, or had some deferred maintenance that is in the process of being corrected.

12.   Vacant Lots: Vacant lots in a class "C" property should be maintained on a regular basis but may not be as neat and well manicured as a class "A" property. Unmaintained lots in a class "C" community should be temporary situations, rather than a permanent condition, which would drop a rating down to a class "D" below average.

13. Pets and Children: Pets and children will probably abound in class "C" properties, much the same as they do in "average" single-family housing in the same geographic area. Although a class "C" manufactured home community will undoubtedly have some facilities for children, it will not have as many, and there will probably be incidences in some portions of the community where the children and pets, or lack of enforcement of rules regarding these matters, could drop what otherwise would be a class "C" property down to a below average or "D" community.

14. Rules and Regulations: A class "C" property may have a good set of rules and regulations. They may either be less restrictive than those of an "A" or "B" property, or the enforcement and compliance are not as strict.

15. Management: A class "C" manufactured home community may have both professional and competent on-site management as well as off-site support. Difference in this and an "A" or "B" community will be the quality of the results.

AMENITIES

In addition to having some of the amenities of a class "A" community, a class "C" manufactured home community must have what would be considered as "average" for both manufactured home and other single-family residential communities and apartment developments in the geographic area. Some of these requirements will obviously be dictated by both the climate and related living habits within the geographic area.

1. Swimming pool: A class "C" property should have a swimming pool, unless this is not typical to the area in other average housing communities (i.e., both single-family housing and apartments).

2. Clubhouse: A class "C" property should have a building on the property that serves as a clubhouse meeting or party room. In class "C" properties, the clubhouse facility will obviously be smaller than in a class "A" facility and some portion of it will probably also be used as the office.

3. Other amenities: A class "C" property may have one or two tennis courts, a playground, and perhaps one other facility, such as a basketball court, volleyball court, or whatever. Facilities should be compatible with the tenancy of the property and what would be considered "average" for all types of residential communities in the subject area.

Author's Note: Learning the "B" & "D" Portions of This System

This book is intended to be used as a reference by those wishing to rate manufactured home landlease communities. One should first read and become familiar with the "A" or best rating, then become familiar with the "C" or average rating classification. Having accomplished that, the logic of a "B" rating, which is above average (but not up to the "A" standards), and "D" rating, which is below the average or "C" rating, will become apparent.

The following pages present the DEFINITION, LOCATION, SPECIFIC CRITERIA, and AMENITIES requirements of the "B" and "D" ratings. In this section, the "A" and "C" details are restated so that anyone wishing to compare those other classifications may do so without having to turn back to other sections of the book for that information when reading or studying only the "B" or "D" classification explanations for those other contiguous rating classifications.

"B" RATING CLASSIFICATION REQUIREMENTS

GENERAL APPEARANCE AND DEFINITION

"B" rated communities should have an overall positive appeal and appearance. They must be above average for the market and geographic region of which they are a part. Being above average (that is higher that a "C" rating) but in a secondary location or lacking some of the specific criteria or amenities that would otherwise make the community an "A" property.

LOCATION

The location of a "B" rated community would undoubtedly be similar to the location of medium priced single-family housing in the same geographic area. It should have most of the same criteria as would be expected for a residential area (i.e., reasonable proximity to schools, churches, hospitals, shopping facilities, employment centers, and recreational facilities).

Note: A "B" rated community may not have "reasonable proximity" to all of these criteria. It may also be in proximity to good employment centers (and properly buffered), but may not then also be close to the other residential criteria. Obviously, if the property being rated had an "A" location and also complied with specific criteria and amenities requirements as an "A," then the property would be so rated.

A "B" property may be a compromise of any of the major qualifications (i.e., general appearance, location, specific criteria, and amenities). It may be very high in some of these but average in others.

Simply stated, a "B" community is not quite as good as an "A" community but must certainly be above the average (or a "C") community.

SPECIFIC CRITERIA

In order to properly define the various criteria for a "B" rated manufactured home community, it is necessary to recap what defines an "A" (or best) community, and also a "C" (or average) community. Obviously, the "B" rated community is either between these two in all respects or meets some of the requirements of an "A" community and some of those in a "C" community.

1.A   Layout or Design: Well planned and laid out, spacious homesites. Site sizes that will accommodate large single- and multisection manufactured homes.

1.B   Layout and Design, Site Sizes: Homesites may be smaller than an "A." The overall layout may not be as pleasing, density may be slightly higher, etc. To be a "B" rated community, however, the sites' layout and design must be above what is "average" for the geographic area, otherwise it would be a "C."

1.C   Layout or Design and Site Size: A class "C" community might have a well laid out and planned design but with some obsolescence in site size. It may be an older community where, with age, sites that were once large enough, today are too small for contemporary homes. The "C" community can have some obsolescence on some of the lots, but obviously not all or even a substantial number of them, or else it rates as a class "D" property.

2.A   Streets: Wide paved streets in well-maintained condition. Streets should be at least as wide (and of similar construction) as those in moderate and upper bracket single-family subdivisions in the same area. Streets must be curbed either with lazy-back, high-back, or combination sidewalk with curb, depending on what is customary in the geographic area for middle and upper bracket single-family subdivisions.

2.B   Streets in a "B" rated community may not be as wide or in as pristine a condition as streets in an "A" community. They should, however, be above average, otherwise the rating (at least so far as streets are concerned) would be "average" or a "C."

2.C   Streets in a class "C" community should be about average in size and construction for what is typical of the marketplace. Likewise, the condition (regardless of age) should be about average within this same market.

3.A   Setbacks: Homes should be set back at least 7' off streets that are at least 40' in width; 25' on streets that may be as narrow as those required in area single-family subdivisions (normally 24' to 28') and which also have off-street parking.

3.B   A "B" rated community should have setbacks similar to an "A" community, with minor variations. A "B" community should have adequate spacing and site sizes so that at least 80% of the lots can accommodate large single- and multisection homes commonly sold in the market and geographic area of which the property is a part.

3.C   Setbacks: "C" communities may have a few setback problems that have evolved over the years. Assuming this is an "average" condition throughout the subject marketplace, a specific property can still justify a "C" rating as long as the setback requirements can be dealt with within the jurisdiction of which the manufactured home community is a part and can still accommodate many of the large single- and multisection homes being produced.

Specifically, as long as 2/3 of the lots in the subject community can accommodate large modern single- and multisection homes, the property (if meeting other appropriate criteria) can still qualify for an average or "C" rating. Over 1/3 obsolescence on lot size would rate the property at a below average or "D" rating.

4.A   Vehicle Parking: At least 2 off-street parking spaces on each site, plus adequate cluster parking for guests in reasonable proximity to most sites. Parallel, on-street guest parking should also be physically possible without restricting the normal flow of traffic throughout the community.

Note: Off-street parking spaces may be side by side, or one behind the other (and unprotected or under a carport), whichever is customary in the subject property's geographic area.

Home sizes vary from one geographic area to another. "A" rated communities should have no obsolescence. That is to say, they must be able to accommodate the largest homes that are traditional or customary in the geographic and market area of which the community is a part.

4.B   A "B" rated community must obviously have adequate parking, but perhaps the configuration, incidence of, or location may be different from an "A" community. In most cases a "B" community will undoubtedly have the same parking as an "A" community but may be less desirable or functional in some other respects.

4.C   Vehicle Parking: An average or class "C" community must still provide adequate parking. This can either be provided as off-street parking (2 cars per site) or as parallel on-street parking with streets that are wide enough to provide for parallel on-street parking on both sides of the street and still accommodate an unrestricted flow of traffic.

5.A   Entrance or Entrances: Entries in "A" rated manufactured home communities must convey the same image of quality the community itself offers. All entrances should feature attractive landscaping with trees, plants, and shrubs that are native or customary to the area. The sign (or signs) identifying the community must be attractive, neat, fresh (rather than faded), and well maintained.

5.B   The entry of a "B" property will demand much of the same quality as an "A" community but may be less densely landscaped, may not have quite the quality on the signage, etc. Obviously, to be rated a "B" in this specific category it must be above average for the market and geographic area of which it is a part, otherwise it would be rated "average" dictating a "C" rating.

5.C   Entry: A class "C" property must have an attractive entryway as what might be considered "average" for residential communities in the geographic area of which it is a part.

6.A   Individual Homesite Improvements: Improvements on individual sites should have large patios, paved off-street parking, sidewalks both along the streets and (if appropriate depending on the design layout) from the street to the patio and entry to the home. These improvements should be of concrete construction, although asphalt is acceptable depending on what is customary in the area. If site improvements are of asphalt, they must have a clean, fresh surface and be well maintained. The area under the home should have concrete runners or "blocking support" piers or pads, depending on what is customary in the geographic area. The area under the home may be gravel or other suitable material as long as this is dry, clean, drains properly, and is customary construction for the particular area.

6.B   Site improvements in a "B" community may not be up to the standards required for an "A" rating, but they must be above average for the market and geographic area of which the community is a part.

For example: The incidence of sidewalks may be lower. The patios and other surface improvements may be smaller. The area under the home may be less substantial, etc. These improvements, however, must be above average or the property being rated would dictate a "C" rating so far as this requirement is concerned.

6.C   Individual Homesite Improvements: Class "C" or "average" manufactured home communities may have all, some, or most of the individual site improvements of an "A" or "B" community, but they may be smaller, older, or not quite as pristine as the "A" property. "C" or "average" properties may have smaller patios, blocking piers or pads (rather than all concrete runners or pads), and sidewalks may extend only from the street back to the site and not along streets and public walkways.

7.A   Skirting: The perimeter of the home must be skirted with an approved finished material. This material may vary from one geographic area to another, but the material must have a professional finish on it, and be properly installed.

7.B   "B" rated communities must have all the homes skirted and a vast majority of them must be neat, clean, and have a professional finished look to the installed material.

7.C   Skirting: An "average" or class "C" manufactured home community requires skirting on all homes. It may be, however, that either due to the age of the community, the age of the homes in the community, or the economic circumstances of the residents some of that material is less attractive. It may also be that in a class "C" property, enforcement of the skirting requirement may be more lax than in the higher rated properties that require and achieve timely compliance with this requirement.

8.A   Towing Hitches: All hitches must either be removed or properly concealed.

8.B   Towing hitches in a "B" rated community may not all be removed, but must otherwise be attractively concealed.

8.C   Towing Hitches: Towing hitches do not need to be removed in an average or class "C" property. If not removed they should be cleanly painted.

9.A   Outside Storage: Uniform storage sheds or central storage facilities must be provided or required. No individual outside (on-site) storage is permitted.

9.B   "B" rated communities may not have uniform or central storage facilities, but would most certainly require that residents provide some approved storage facilities on their individual lots. A "B" rated community may not be much different from an "average" or "C" community in this category except that a "B" community will obviously both require and achieve better compliance with this requirement.

9.C   Outside Storage: Uniform storage sheds or central storage is not a requirement of a class "C" or "average" community. Although no outside (on homesite) storage will be permitted in a class "C" community, permitting residents some reasonable time period to comply and also allowing them to individually purchase a variety of individual storage facilities will mean that a class "C" community will probably always have some residents "in the process" of compliance, and therefore diminish the overall pristine appearance that would be required of an "A" community.

10.A   Individual Homes: All homes in excellent condition, well maintained, and attractive in appearance.

10.B   Individual homes in a "B" rated community must have most homes in excellent condition, well maintained, and attractive in overall appearance.

10.C   Individual Homes: A significant number of homes in a class "C" property would be of new or somewhat recent vintage. We must acknowledge that a significant number of class "C" communities may be older communities with a mix of older and newer homes. The most important consideration regarding the individual homes will not be their ages so must as their general appearance and state of repair. A majority of homes in a class "C" community should be clean and well maintained. Having too high an incidence of both old and "unmaintained" homes would lower what might otherwise be a class "C" property, down to a below average or "D" rating.

11.A   Occupancy: Manufactured home communities should have at least 50% occupancy in order to judge quality of residents and homes. Otherwise, occupancy should be compatible with the market area commensurate with the age of the property.

11.B   "B" rated communities should have at least 50% occupancy (same as an "A" community in order to judge the quality of the residents and homes. Occupancy should similarly be compatible with the market area of which it is a part, commensurate with the age and mode of the community.

Tenancy (the makeup or mix of residents) may dictate a "B" versus an "A." "B" rated communities may not evidence the pristine condition and individual pride of ownership as an "A" rated community.

11.C   Occupancy: Class "C" communities may feature a diverse mix of residents typical of the city, county, and neighborhood of which it is a part. A class "C" property should be about "average" so far as occupancy is concerned. That is, if the property is in a market where other manufactured home communities and apartments are 95% occupied, then the subject property should also have similar occupancy. If that is not the case, then those attempting to apply a rating should do enough market research to determine the occupancy trend of the subject property and more importantly, reasons for that trend.

12.A   Vacant Lots: Vacant lots must be grassed, mowed, graveled, or otherwise well maintained in accordance with local practice and community rules.

12.B   Vacant Homesites: In a "B" community, these should be maintained in as clean, mowed, and inviting a condition as an "A" community. Difference in this aspect of rating may be minimal. Obviously, if vacant lots are unkept, unmowed, and of average appearance, the community (in this aspect of rating criteria) would dictate an "average" or "C" rating.

12.C <u>Vacant Lots</u>: Vacant lots in a class "C" property should be maintained on a regular basis but may not be as neat and well manicured as a class "A" property. Unmaintained lots in a class "C" community should be temporary situations, rather than a permanent condition, which would drop a rating to class "D" or below average.

13.A <u>Pets and Children</u>: If pets and/or children are characteristic of the occupancy of a specific community, there must be facilities and adequate common "green areas" for them to run and play without cluttering or trespassing on yards and in streets.

13.B Similar to class "A" properties, "B" rated communities must publish and enforce rules regarding pets and controlling children. The difference may be in the incidence or visibility of pets and children. It may also be that a "B" community has strict rules regarding pets, but a higher incidence of children in the tenancy of the community.

13.C <u>Pets and Children</u>: Pets and children will probably abound in class "C" properties, much the same as they do in "average" single-family housing in the same geographic area. Although a class "C" manufactured home community will undoubtedly have some facilities for children, it will not have as many and there will probably be incidences in some portions of the community where the children and pets, or lack of enforcement of rules regarding these matters, could drop what otherwise would be a class "C" property, down to a below average or "D" community.

14.A <u>Rules and Regulations</u>: An "A" class community must publish and enforce intelligent rules and regulations compatible with living habits that are customary to the geographic area and compatible with the tenancy of the manufactured home community.

14.B "B" rated communities must distribute and enforce intelligent rules and regulations compatible with the living habits of community residents. Difference between this and an "A" rated community may be in specific rules being slightly more lax or slightly more tolerant so far as enforcement is concerned.

14.C <u>Rules and Regulations</u>: A class "C" property may have a good set of rules and regulations. They may either be less restrictive than those of an "A" or "B" property, or the enforcement and compliance are not as apparent.

15.A Management: The property must be competently managed with full-time on-site managers.

15.B Management: For a property to be rated "B" it must have full-time on-site management. There may not be much difference (in this category) between an "A" and a "B" rated community since the opinion as to the quality of management may always be in a learning curve, in transition, and will also be different "in the eyes of the beholder."

15.C Management: A class "C" manufactured home community may have both professional and competent on-site management. The difference in this and an "A" or "B" community will be the quality of the results.

"B" RATING CLASSIFICATION AMENITIES

AMENITIES "B"

A "B" rated community must have most of the amenities of an "A" community that are considered customary for the climate and geographic region of which the community is a part. Obviously, to achieve a "B" rating those must also be in good condition, functional, and above average.

1.B Swimming Pool. "B" rated communities must have a swimming pool unless this is not considered as "normal" for better apartment, manufactured home, or site-built subdivisions in the geographic area. Size, related amenities, and condition may not be as attractive or functional as an "A" but must be above average for the area.

2.B Clubhouse in the "B" rated community should meet most of the requirements of an "A" community but may not be as impressive or have all of those accommodations. The facility must be above average, however, otherwise the property (so far as this specific item is concerned) would be rated a "C" or "average" community.

3.B Other Amenities. The "A" property classification has more requirements than the "C" and the "B" classification here being defined. "B" is obviously in the middle of these. "B" rated communities should have many amenities such as tennis courts, volleyball courts, playgrounds, etc., but not all of them. The facilities may also not be as extensive or in quite the condition as an "A" property in the same region.

"B" rated communities may have some of the items required to justify an "A" rating. It may also be that a "B" community might, for example, have an on-site lake but the lake is not as attractive, functional, or as well maintained as in an "A" rated community.

"D" RATING CLASSIFICATION

DEFINITION

A "D" rated community will be a hybrid of some good and some unacceptable conditions. It will, in many (or perhaps most) respects, be below average in overall appearance, site size, amenities, condition, etc. Many "D" rated communities will undoubtedly be older communities with considerable obsolescence.

A "D" rated community will fall below average in a majority of categories, which will dictate that it cannot be rated average for the marketplace or geographic region of which it is a part.

LOCATION

Typically a "D" rated community will have a secondary location. That is, it may be next to a junkyard, industrial type properties, or some other undesirable contiguous development and not properly buffered from such other area development. This does not mean all communities in such locations cannot be rated higher. We may find very attractive, clean, functional communities in such locations and which are properly fenced, buffered, or otherwise "stand on their own" so that a higher rating is not only possible, but justified.

Simply stated, a "D" rated community will be below average compared to a "C" rated community in the same market and geographic area. Viewing any significant number of manufactured home communities in an area will very quickly dictate what is below average. Obviously, a "D" rated community may not be below average in all respects, but will fail to meet many of the "average" criteria for the area, and accordingly fail to justify a "C" rating.

SPECIFIC CRITERIA

Inasmuch as this rating system is designed as a reference tool, it is important to refresh one's recollection as to what the "C" rating criteria are, in consideration of assessing a "D" rating. Following is a recap of the "C" or "average" criteria.

1.C   Layout or Design and Lot Size: A class "C" community might have a well laid out and planned design but with some obsolescence on lot size. It would probably be an older community where, with age, lots that were once large enough, today experience some obsolescence. A "C" community can have some obsolescence on some of the lots, but obviously not all, or even a substantial number of them, or else it drops to a class "D" property.

1.D   "D" rated manufactured home community Layout and Design will be below average for the area, that is, either nonexistent, insufficient, or having too much obsolescence. Many "D" properties will be significantly older properties that cannot attract (or where sites cannot physically accommodate) today's modern manufactured homes.

2.C   Streets in a class "C" community should be about average in size and construction for what is typical of the marketplace of which it is a part. Likewise, the condition regardless of age should be about average within this same market.

2.D   Streets in a "D" rated community will be below average for the market or geographic area of which they are a part, that is, either in width, type of construction, or physical condition. In all probability, typical "D" rated streets will be too small to accommodate parking and 2-way traffic, and they may also be in a poor state of repair.

Completely unpaved streets would drop what might be a "D" or below average rated community, to "unratable," that is, at least so far as this particular item is concerned.

3.C   Setbacks: A "C" community may have some setback problems that have evolved over the years. Assuming this condition is an "average" condition throughout the subject marketplace, then a specific property can still justify a "C" rating so long as the setback requirements can be appropriately dealt with within the jurisdiction of which the property is a part and the property can still accommodate many of the large single- and multisection homes currently being produced.

More specifically, so long as 2/3 of the homesites in the subject community can accommodate large modern single- and double-section homes, the property (if meeting other appropriate criteria) can still qualify for an "average" or "C" rating. Over 1/3 obsolescence on site size would drop the property to below average or "D" rating.

3.D   Setbacks: A "D" rated property will obviously have significant problems with homesite size and related setbacks. If more than 2/3 of the homesites could not accommodate current production models (i.e., large single- and multisection homes) and maintain required setbacks (within the jurisdiction that it is a part of), then these facts will dictate a below average or "D" rating.

4.C   Vehicle Parking: An average or class "C" community must still provide for adequate parking. This can either be provided as off-street parking (2 cars per site) or as parallel on-street parking with streets that are wide enough to provide for parallel on-street parking on both sides of the street and still accommodate 2-way traffic.

4.D   A "D" rated community will have inadequate parking both on individual lots and for guests.

5.C   Entry: A class "C" property must have an attractive entryway as what might be considered "average" for residential communities in the geographic area.

5.D   A class "D" community will, in all probability, not have adequate entry treatment, signage, or other appropriate identifying amenities. If it has, they would be below average for the area of which they are a part.

6.C   Individual Homesite Improvements: A class "C" or "average" community may have all, some, or most of the individual site improvements of an "A" or "B" community, but they may be smaller, older, or not quite as pristine as the "A" property. A "C" or "average" property may have smaller patios, blocking piers or pads (rather than all concrete runners or pads), and sidewalks may run only from the street back to the site and not along the streets or public walkways.

6.D   Individual Site Improvements: A class "D" property will, in all probability, not have significant individual site improvements. If it does, either the type, incidence of, or condition of these will be below average and accordingly dictate a "D" or below average rating. Most "D" rated communities will probably not have any concrete under the home parking site.

7.C   Skirting: An "average" or class "C" community will still require skirting on all homes. It may be, however, that either due to the age of the community, the age of the homes in the community, or the economic circumstances of the residents, that some of that material is less attractive. It may also be that in a class "C" property, enforcement of the skirting requirement may be more lax than in the higher rated properties which require and achieve timely compliance with this requirement.

7.D   Skirting in a "D" or below average community may (or may not) be required. It may be that skirting is required but either this requirement is not enforced or the type of material and workmanship is substandard or below average on a large enough number of the individual homes so that it diminishes the overall appearance and impression of the community.

8.C   Towing Hitches: Towing hitches do not need to be removed in an average or class "C" property.

8.D   Not much difference here between a "C" and a "D" property. Obviously, in a "D" or below average situation, few of the hitches would be removed. Very few or none would be concealed, and they may also be rusted, unsightly, and otherwise unattractive.

9.C   Outside Storage: Uniform storage sheds or central storage is not a requirement of a class "C" or "average" community. Although no outside (on-site) storage will be permitted in a class "C" community, permitting residents some reasonable time period to comply and also allowing them to individually purchase a variety of individual storage facilities will mean that a class "C" community will probably always have some residents "in the process" of compliance, and therefore diminish the overall pristine appearance that would be required of an "A" community.

9.D   Outside Storage: In "D" or below average circumstances, storage problems will be apparent, that is, with too much unsightly on-site storage, as a permanent condition, on too many of the individual sites.

10.C   Individual Homes: A significant number of the homes in a class "C" property would be of new or somewhat recent vintage, although we must acknowledge that a significant number of class "C" communities will be older communities with a mix of older and newer homes. Most important consideration regarding the individual homes will not be their age so much as their general appearance and state of repair. A majority of the homes in a class "C" community should be clean and well maintained. Having too high an incidence of both old and "unmaintained" homes would drop what might otherwise be a class "C" property down to a below average or "D" rating.

10.D   Individual Homes: Individual homes in a "D" rated community will be older, smaller homes. Too many of them will also, in all probability, be in a poor state of repair or unsightly to any casual observer, that is, unsightly to the point of being detrimental to the overall appearance of the property. It is significant to remember that in a typical manufactured home community 80% of the property is made up of individual homeowners' homes and the lots for which they (the residents) have responsibility. Accordingly, the size, appearance, and condition of the homes as well as how well the residents maintain those sites have a lot to do with the overall appearance of any community.

11.C   Occupancy: A class "C" community will undoubtedly achieve a diverse mix of residents, in all probability typical of the city, county, and neighborhood of which it is a part. A class "C" property should be about "average" so far as occupancy is concerned. That is, if the property is in a market where other manufactured housing communities (and apartments) are 95% occupied, then the subject property should (and undoubtedly will) also have similar occupancy. If that is not the case, then those attempting to apply a rating should do enough market research to determine the trend (filling up, or decreasing in occupancy) of the subject property and more importantly, reasons for that trend.

Note: A class "C" property could be one that has recently changed ownership or management or gone through refinancing and/or which has some physical neglect that is in the process of being corrected.

11.D <u>Occupancy</u>: Occupancy will probably not be a critical factor in determining a "D" rated community by and of itself. The lack of other qualifying criteria will undoubtedly dictate that many "D" rated properties have obsolescence and the related problems of maintaining occupancy with current production models (i.e., large single- and multisection manufactured homes).

12.C <u>Vacant Homesites</u>: Vacant sites in a class "C" property should be maintained on a regular basis but may not be as neat and well manicured as a class "A" property. Unmaintained sites in a class "C" community should be a temporary situation, rather than a permanent condition, which might drop a property down to a class "D" or below average rating.

12.D <u>Vacant Homesites</u> on a "D" rated property will undoubtedly be unmaintained or in a poor condition or poor state of repair. Here again, this condition will in all probability not be as significant as other criteria in distinguishing between an "average" or below average property.

13.C <u>Pets and Children</u>: Pets and children will probably abound in class "C" properties, much the same as they do in "average" single-family housing in the same geographic area. Although a class "C" community will undoubtedly have some facilities for children, it will not have as many and there will probably be some incidence in some portions of the community where the children and pets (or lack of enforcement of rules regarding these matters) could drop what otherwise would be a class "C" property down to a below average or "D" community.

13.D <u>Pets and Children</u>: Pets and children will probably abound in "D" rated communities. They will also be uncontrolled by appropriate rules and regulations and/or lack of enforcement. Lack of appropriate facilities in a "D" community will undoubtedly contribute to this situation.

14.C <u>Rules and Regulations</u>: A class "C" property may have a good set or rules and regulations. They may either be less restrictive than those of an "A" or "B" property or it may be that enforcement and compliance are not as strict.

14.D <u>Rules and Regulations</u>: Rules and regulations in a "D" rated property will either be nonexistent, inadequate, or not enforced. In turn, this will contribute to a below average appearance and circumstances so far as the living habits of the residents are concerned.

15.C   Management: A class "C" community may have both professional and competent on-site management as well as off-site support. The difference in this and an "A" or "B" property will be the quality of the results.

15.D   A "D" rated or below average community will, in all probability, not have competent on-site management and little apparent support from off-site owners.

"D" RATING CLASSIFICATION AMENITIES

The general explantation and criteria for "C" or "average" communities are here recapped before we consider "D" or below average amenities.

In addition to having some of the amenities of a class "A" community, a class "C" manufactured housing community must have what would be considered as "average" for both manufactured housing and other single-family residential communities in its geographic area. Some of these requirements will obviously be dictated by both the climate and related living habits within the geographic area.

1.   Swimming pool: A class "C" property should have a swimming pool, unless this is not typical to the area in other average housing communities (i.e., both single-family housing and apartments).

2.   Clubhouse: A class "C" property should have a building on the property that serves as a clubhouse meeting or party room. In class "C" properties, the clubhouse facility will obviously be smaller than in a class "A" facility and some portion of it will probably also be used as the office.

3.   Other amenities: A class "C" property may have one or two tennis courts, a playground, and perhaps one other facility, such as a basketball court, volleyball court, or whatever. Facilities should be compatible with the tenancy of the property and what would be considered "average" for residential communities in the subject area.

"D" RATED AMENITIES

A "D" rated community may either have none or only some amenities of a class "C" property. It may also be that although a specific "D" property has some of these amenities, those facilities are either below average, inadequate, or in a poor state of repair to the extent that a below average or "D" rating would be mandated.

UNRATABLE MANUFACTURED HOME COMMUNITIES

The rating system here presented offers certain requirements and criteria that, when consistently applied, will logically and fairly dictate which manufactured home landlease communities may be classified as A, B, C, or D.

There will obviously be attempts to rate other properties which do not conform to any of (or enough of) the criteria that would justify any of these 4 ratings. When that condition exists, the only logical conclusion a potential rater may arrive at will be to classify the property as "unratable."

The "unratable" conclusion should not have any implications other than a particular property does not meet the requirements (as here defined) to justify one of these ratings. It will also, obviously, be so determined "in the eyes of the beholder," which may be different from one individual to another, or from one period of time to another.

Many manufactured home landlease communities will also change for the better as they are improved or deteriorate over time if not properly maintained. Accordingly, the rating should also change to reflect these conditions. The manufactured housing industry today is at a crossroads. We are the fastest growing, most significant segment of the entire housing industry. We offer safe, functional, attractive, and affordable code-built housing at half the price of site-built housing.

Many landlease communities and manufactured home subdivisions are equal in appearance, amenities, and stature to many site-built single-family communities. We are the obvious answer to this nation's housing problem (as well as a solution to a portion of the restructuring) and megatrends changing society today. To continue to try to represent past, substandard, out-of-date, unsafe, unsanitary conditions or properties is no longer possible or beneficial to this industry. Those who choose (for whatever reason) not to bring their properties up to reasonable standards have chosen to fend for themselves and not move forward with this vital segment of the housing industry.

APPENDIX O

DUE DILIGENCE ON-SITE INSPECTION REPORT

DUE DILIGENCE ON-SITE INSPECTION REPORT

for buyers of groundlease-type

MANUFACTURED HOME COMMUNITIES

Name of Property _____

Date _____

Physical Address _____ Zip _____

Contact Person/Role _____ Phone ( )_____

Present Owner(s) _____ Phone ( )_____

Owner's Address _____ Zip _____

Inspection Report Preparer _____ Phone ( )_____

    Attorney _____ Phone ( )_____

    Surveyor _____ Phone ( )_____

    Environmental Auditor _____ Phone ( )_____

    Accountant or CPA _____ Phone ( )_____

    Engineer _____ Phone ( )_____

GENERAL PROPERTY CHARACTERISTICS

Developed acreage:_____; # undeveloped: _____ zoned? _____

Number of developed homesites: _____ Avg. size: _____sq. ft.

Smallest homesite size: _____sq. ft. Largest homesite: _____sq. ft.

Number of single-section sites _____ Number of multi-sec. sites: _____

Homesite services: Water _____, Sewer _____, Elec. _____, Gas _____, Ph. _____,

Cable TV _____ Number of partially developed &/or serviced homesites & why

_____

Property developed in what year(s): _____

Physical occupancy at time of inspection: _____% (# occup/total #)

Resident profile: family _____ or adult/retirement _____ or _____

Present street or call rent: $_____/mth. includes: _____

Rent range, if any: $_____ to $_____ Date last increase? _____

Legal description: _____ (attach copy)

Rental homes on-site? (Y/N) _____ Number: _____ # Occupied: _____

Additional Remarks:

_____

ADDITIONAL PHYSICAL CHARACTERISTICS

Number of entrances: _____ Security gate(s)? _____

Extent of landscaping: _____

Amount & type of fencing &/or walls: _____

Width & nature of street surface: _____

Presence of sidewalks _____, gutters _____, drains _____

Parking: _____ on street, _____ off street, other: _____

Extent of security lighting: _____

Mailboxes: _____# individual; _____ NDCBU (cluster)?

Set of architectural plans or "as built" drawings available? _____

Where? _____ (attach copy)

Any zoning restrictions? _____

Encroachments? (E.g., bldgs. too close, overhanging wires, ditches, walls

abutting, etc.) _____

Additional Remarks:

_____

UTILITIES (see utility subsections to follow)

All underground? Y/N _____ If not, what is above ground? _____

Water: private or public? _____ If private, number of wells _____,

pressure tank? _____ Quality of System: _____

If public, name & phone # of supplier: _____ ( )_____

Water &/or sewer submetered? _____ Who bills? _____

Sewer: private or public? _____ If private, nature & capacity of wastewater

treatment facility? _____ condition ? _____

If public, name & phone # of utility: _____ ( )_____

Electricity provided by: _____ metered? _____

Natural gas provided by: _____ metered? _____

Propane gas supplier: _____ Phone # (   )_____

Refuse removal by property owner: Y/N _____ or name of vendor: _____

Telephone service provided by _____

Cable TV service by property owner Y/N ____ or name of vendor: _____

Additional Remarks: _____

AMENITIES: (List the first three descriptions * following also on the
BUILDINGS FACILITIES list Bldg. #1–6 below)

<u>Insurance Value</u>

* Clubhouse(s) _____ size/type: _____ sq.ft. _____ $_____

    condition? _____ work needed? _____

* Office (in clubhouse) Y/N___ size/type: ___ sq.ft. _____ $_____

    condition? _____ work needed? _____

* Maintenance bldg.(s) ___ size/type: _____ sq.ft. _____ $_____

    condition? _____ work needed? _____

   Swimming pool(s) _____ size/type _____ cu.ft. _____ $_____

    condition? _____ work needed? _____

   Laundry facility _____ number of washers _____ number of dryers _____

    condition? _____ work needed? _____

Guest parking _____ #/location _____

    condition? _____ work needed? _____

Lakes & ponds _____ #/sizes _____ # acres _____

    condition? _____ work needed? _____

Playground(s) _____ #/equip. _____

    condition? _____ work needed? _____

Tennis court(s) _____ #/locations _____

    condition? _____ work needed? _____

Basketball court(s) _____ #/location _____

    condition? _____ work needed? _____

RV storage facility _____ secured? _____ sq.ft. _____

    condition? _____ work needed? _____

Shuffleboard court(s) _____ #/location _____

    condition? _____ work needed? _____

Golf course _____ #holes/type _____

    condition? _____ work needed? _____

Jacuzzi(s) _____ #/location: _____

    condition? _____ work needed? _____

Separate game & craft facilities _____ #/location: _____

    condition? _____ work needed? _____

                                    SUMMARY $_____

BUILDINGS FACILITIES

Insurance Value

Bldg. #1 _____, purpose(s) _____, size _____ sq.ft.____ $_____

Bldg. #2 _____, purpose(s) _____, size _____ sq.ft.____ $_____

Bldg. #3 _____, purpose(s) _____, size _____ sq.ft.____ $_____

Bldg. #4 _____, purpose(s) _____, size _____ sq.ft.____ $_____

Bldg. #5 _____, purpose(s) _____, size _____ sq.ft.____ $_____

Bldg. #6 _____, purpose(s) _____, size _____ sq.ft.____ $_____

SUMMARY $_____

General architectural design: _____

General condition of buildings: _____

   Exterior concerns (roof, walls) _____

   Interior concerns (floor, ceiling, walls) _____

All facilities in compliance with ADA regulations? _____

   Equipment concerns (kitchen, lighting, HVAC, etc.) _____

_____

Maintenance records available for: buildings ____; swimming pools _____;

wastewater treatment _____; water reporting _____; equipment

maintenance _____; operating manuals available for all above? _____

Additional Remarks: _____

EQUIPMENT, VEHICLES, INVENTORY, & FURNITURE (list here &/or as separate exhibit)

	Item	Condition	Cost
1.	vehicle: _____	_____	$_____
2.	vehicle: _____	_____	$_____
3.	vehicle: _____	_____	$_____
4.	sewer router _____	_____	$_____
5.	snowplow _____	_____	$_____
6.	mower: _____	_____	$_____
7.	mower: _____	_____	$_____
8.	mower: _____	_____	$_____
9.	other: _____	_____	$_____
10.	other: _____	_____	$_____
11.	manager's home, if any _____		$_____
12.	maint. mgr.'s home, if any _____		$_____

Description & amount of plumbing supplies: _____

_____ (attach list)

Description & amount of electrical supplies: _____

_____ (attach list)

Description of furniture & general condition of same: _____

_____ (attach list)

What improvements may be needed relative to: furniture _____,
carpeting _____, coverings _____

Attach copy of personal property inventory to this report.

Additional Remarks:

_____

INCOME SUMMARY

What is presently being collected:

Base site rent = $/mth _____ describe: _____

Utility charges: $/mth _____ describe: _____

Occupant upchg.: $/mth _____ describe: _____

Pet upcharge: $/mth _____ describe: _____

RV/heat storage: $/mth _____ describe: _____

Cable TV income: $/mth _____ describe: _____

Location premium: $/mth _____ describe: _____

Sale of product: $/mth _____ describe: _____

Sale of services: $/mth _____ describe: _____

Insurance sales: $/mth _____ describe: _____

Rental unit income: $/mth _____ describe: _____

New home sales: $/mth _____ describe: _____

Resale home sales: $/mth _____ describe: _____

Brokerage income: $/mth _____ describe: _____

Vending income: $/mth _____ describe: _____

Commercial rent: $/mth _____ describe: _____

Appraisal fees: $/mth _____ describe: _____

Notary fees: $/mth _____ describe: _____

other _____: $/mth _____ describe: _____

other _____: $/mth _____ describe: _____

other _____: $/mth _____ describe: _____

Attach copy of complete rent roll & Estoppel Certificates for <u>every</u> lessee and vacant site.

Specific location of resident files and rent records? _____

_____

Additional Remarks: _____

OPERATING EXPENSE SUMMARY

Utilities—related to new owner deposits and billing characteristics.

* Water. New deposit or assignable? _____ Amt. $_____

  How and when billed? _____

* Sewerage. New deposit or assignable? _____ Amt. $_____

  How and when billed? _____

* Electricity. New deposit or assignable? _____ Amt. $_____

  How and when billed? _____

*   Natural gas. New deposit or assignable? _____ Amt. $_____

    How and when billed? _____

*   Propane gas. New deposit or assignable? _____ Amt. $_____

    How and when billed? _____

*   Telephone service. New deposit or assignable? ___ Amt. $_____

    How and when billed? _____

*   Cable TV. New deposit or assignable? _____ Amt. $_____

    How and when billed? _____

*   Refuse removal. New deposit or assignable? _____ Amt. $_____

    How and when billed? _____

Any utility bonds in place? Y/N _____ Describe: _____

_____

Any hook-up charges billed to property &/or residents? _____

Additional Remarks: _____

EMPLOYEES PRESENTLY ON PAYROLL (or attach a payroll summary report)

Manager, name: _____

Address: _____ Phone (___) _____

Part or Full-Time? _____ Tenure: _____ mths./yrs.

Compensation: $_____/wk-mth-yr plus concessions? _____

   plus incentive? _____ plus utilities? _____

Assistant Manager, name: _____

Address: _____ Phone (___) _____

Part or Full-Time? _____ Tenure: _____ mths./yrs.

Compensation: $_____/wk-mth-yr plus concessions? _____

   plus incentive? _____ plus utilities? _____

Maintenance, name: _____

Address: _____ Phone ( ) _____

Part or Full-Time? _____ Tenure: _____ mths./yrs.

Compensation: $_____/wk-mth-yr plus concessions? _____

   plus incentive? _____ plus utilities? _____

Leasing Consultant, name: _____

Address: _____ Phone ( ) _____

Part or Full-Time? _____ Tenure: _____ mths./yrs.

Compensation: $_____/wk-mth-yr plus concessions? _____

   plus incentive? _____ plus utilities? _____

Security, name: _____

Address: _____ Phone (   )_____

Part or Full-Time? _____ Tenure: _____ mths./yrs.

Compensation: $_____/wk-mth-yr plus concessions? _____

   plus incentive? _____ plus utilities? _____

* Other _____, Name: _____

   Address: _____ Phone (   )_____

   Part or Full-Time? _____ Tenure: _____ mths./yrs.

   plus incentive? _____ plus utilities? _____

Attach copy of present organization chart—even if one has to be drafted—and copies of existent or new job descriptions for present staff.

Nature of present benefit package(s) re: health insurance, vacation policy, life insurance.

Additional Remarks: _____

KEY VENDOR CONTACTS

<u>ACCOUNT</u>
<u>NUMBER</u>

Trash Removal: _____ Phone (   )_____ _____

   (# times/wk. pickup): ___; curbside or dumpsters? ___

Snow Removal: _____ Phone ( )_____ _____

Swimming Pool Service: _____ Phone ( )_____ _____

Plumbing Service: _____ Phone ( )_____ _____

Electrical Service: _____ Phone ( )_____ _____

Sewer Router Service: _____ Phone ( )_____ _____

HVAC Service: _____ Phone ( )_____ _____

Underground Detector: _____ Phone ( )_____ _____

Laundry Service: _____ Phone ( )_____ _____

Fuel Oil Supplier: _____ Phone ( )_____ _____

Sign Painter: _____ Phone ( )_____ _____

Other: _____ : _____ Phone ( )_____ _____

Other: _____ : _____ Phone ( )_____ _____

Additional Remarks: _____ _____

LICENSES & PERMITS (attach copies of following items)

State &/or county permit/license to operate? Y/N _____

    contact: _____ Phone ( )_____

Business &/or retail permit or license? Y/N _____

    contact: _____ Phone ( )_____

Swimming pool permit or license? Y/N _____

    contact: _____ Phone ( )_____

Wastewater treatment EPA permit? Y/N _____

    contact: _____ Phone ( )_____

Retail Manufactured Home Sales license/permit? Y/N _____

    contact: _____ Phone ( )_____

Zoning letter? Y/N_____

    contact: _____ Phone ( )_____

Other: _____ Contact: _____

Additional Remarks: _____

WATER SUBCHECKLIST

* Who owns and maintains water distribution system? Utility or property?

    _____

* Water wells present; size of pump(s) and pressure tank(s) _____

    _____ Condition _____

* Type and size of water mains and lines: _____

* Adequate to service property now and in the future? _____

* Type of water risers: (galvanized, copper, PVC) _____

* Any ongoing or frequently recurring problems with present system?

    Y/N _____ Describe: _____

* Water softeners and/or conditioners required: Y/N _____

       In place new? Y/N _____ Describe: _____

* Water purification system needed/in place? Y/N _____

* Type hydrants; flushing only: Y/N _____ Number: _____

  other type (specify): _____ Number: _____

* Costs relative to system upgrade: _____

* Check health &/or environmental regulator files.

SEWER SUBCHECKLIST

* Who owns sewer/wastewater collection system? Utility or property?

  _____

* Septic tanks present and in use? Y/N _____ Number and size and

  location: _____

* Nature of percolation: _____ Location of leach fields: _____

* How often pumped? _____

* Sewer main material? _____

* Laterals clay or PVC? _____

* Any lift stations? Y/N _____ Number and location: _____

  _____ Condition: _____

* System adequate for present and anticipated needs? _____

* Present or future requirement to tie into a local municipal system?

  Y/N _____ When? _____

* Any ongoing or frequently recurring problems with present system?

  Y/N _____ Describe: _____

* Degree of infiltration: _____

Should lines be smoked to identify leaks? Y/N _____

* Costs relative to system upgrade: _____

* Additional remarks: _____

* Check health &/or environmental regulator files for past inspection reports.

ELECTRICITY SUBCHECKLIST

* Who owns distribution system? Utility or property? _____

* Copper or aluminum wiring underground? _____

* Amperage provided at each pedestal: _____ amps

Sufficient for present and anticipated needs? Y/N _____

* Any ongoing or frequently recurring problems with present system?

Y/N _____ Describe: _____

* Transformers owned by utility or property? _____

* Description of pedestals in place: _____

* Costs relative to system upgrade: _____

_____

* Additional Remarks: _____

NATURAL GAS SUBCHECKLIST

* Who owns the distribution system? Utility or property? _____

* Type gas lines: plastic _____, cast iron _____

* Any recent or recurring gas leaks on-site? Y/N _____

* Cathodic protection on gas lines? Y/N _____

    Type system: _____ Certification date: _____

* Gas leak survey performed? Y/N _____ When? _____

    How extensive? _____ (mains, laterals, under homes)

* System adequate for present and anticipated needs? Y/N _____

* Costs relative to system upgrade: _____

* Additional Remarks: _____

STORM SYSTEM SUBCHECKLIST

* Drainage over the surface or underground? _____

* Locations of storm runoff outlets: _____

    _____

* Flood hazard present? Y/N _____ Nature and extent? _____

    _____

* Street configuration: crown or reverse crown? _____

    Condition? _____

* Storm drains adequate and in good repair? _____

* General topography of the property: _____

    _____

* Catch basins? _____ Pumping stations? _____

* System adequate for present and anticipated needs? Y/N _____

* Costs relative to system upgrade: _____

_____

* Additional Remarks: _____

_____

RECOMMENDED INTERVIEWS

In addition to ones cited or implied earlier:

* Local Chamber of Commerce by area data, statistics, growth studies, demographics maps, etc.

* Local Realtors and/or appraisers for market comparables of other similar-sized, recently sold manufactured home communities

* Local tax assessor for county tax data, formulas, tables, and copy of subject property's tax record

* Local/state manufactured home trade association for industry data and contacts relative to competition in the area, retail sales centers, etc.

* Local aerial photographer for set of photographs taken from all four directions

* Local engineering firm to prepare comprehensive engineering report on the subject property

* Additional Remarks: _____

_____

ADDITIONAL ATTACHMENTS

In addition to ones cited or implied earlier:

* List of security deposits

* Phase I Environmental Audit Report

* Market Survey

* Copies of blank forms presently in use, e.g., application to lease, rental agreement and addendums, rules and regulations (a.k.a. Guidelines for Living)

* Copies of real and personal property tax bills

* Survey/plat map

* Agreement of employees (written)

* Proof of insurance

* Certificate of title for manufactured homes and vehicles

* Maintenance and service contracts

* Employee roster along with completed W-4s

* Past 3 years of operating statements

* Copies of existing notes, deeds, mortgages

* Copies of all promotional materials

* Additional Remarks: _____

_____

ADDITIONAL CONSIDERATIONS:

* Adjacent land use(s)

* Local school system

* Nearby shopping and retail facilities

* Accessibility to public transportation

* Zoning for other manufactured home communities

* Review of housing comparables in local market

* Number and list of manufactured homes "for sale" on-site and reasons why

APPENDIX P

TYPICAL MANUFACTURED HOME COMMUNITY OPERATING STATEMENTS

TYPICAL MANUFACTURED HOME COMMUNITY OPERATING STATEMENTS

Fred Goodman

CLIENT	8420
DEV.	X34
FYE	12

CLIENT NAME	
DEVELOPMENT NAME	
RUN DATE	7/25/95

REPORT NAME	OPERATING STATEMENT	
REPORT NO. C/F	CUSTOM	KEY 8420000X34
SQUARE FOOTAGE	44550	ACQUISITION DATE

DATE	7/31/94
PAGE	1
SEQ NO.	286

SAMPLE SINGLE PROPERTY INCOME STATEMENT

CURRENT MONTH		DESCRIPTION	PRIOR MONTHS		CURRENT YTD		REVISED BUDGETS	
JUL 1993	JUL 1994		MAY 1994	JUN 1994	YTD 1994	YTD VARIANCE	1994 ANNUAL	P.S.F.
		INCOME STATEMENT						
46,374.52	90,788.10	POTENTIAL RENT	44,363.67	45,394.05	363,598	45,750-	546,602	12.26
		LESS:						
9,953.27-	14,344.52-	VACANCIES	6,200.26-	7,172.26-	65,501-	16,023	88,038-	1.97-
36,421.25	76,443.58	NET RENTAL INCOME	38,163.41	38,221.79	298,097	29,727-	458,564	10.29
210.00	660.00	GARAGE RENT	371.94	355.00	3,029	309-	4,320	.09
43.00		OTHER INCOME	32.33	142.87	122-	321	800	.01
588.31	476.14	SERVICE CHARGE	50.99		1,974	1,680-	2,000	.04
554.14		INTEREST INCOME	476.14	476.14	3,333	309-	5,037	.11
37,816.70	77,579.72	TOTAL INCOME	39,094.81	39,195.80	306,312	31,705-	470,721	10.56
		TENANT REIMBURSEMENTS:						
62.61	45.60	MAINTENANCE CHARGES	142.25	172.50	739	445-	1,000	.02
2,646.97	5,915.40	UTILITIES	3,020.52	2,771.78	22,025	1,587-	34,073	.76
40,526.28	83,540.72	TOTAL INCOME & TENANT REIMBURS.	42,257.58	42,139.88	329,076	33,737-	505,794	11.35
78.53	84.19	NET INCOME AS % OF POTENTIAL	86.02	84.19	82	2-	84	
7,816.30	12,076.65	VACANCY TIMES NET INC AS % OF POT	5,333.46	6,038.32	53,697	11,923	73,855	

CLIENT 8420			
DEV. X34			
FYE 12			

CLIENT NAME	
DEVELOPMENT NAME	
RUN DATE	7/25/95

REPORT NAME	OPERATING STATEMENT		
REPORT NO.	CUSTOM	C/F	KEY 842000X34
SQUARE FOOTAGE	44550		ACQUISITION DATE

DATE	7/31/94
PAGE	2
SEQ NO.	226

CURRENT MONTH JUL 1993	CURRENT MONTH JUL 1994	DESCRIPTION	PRIOR MONTHS MAY 1994	JUN 1994	YTD 1994	CURRENT YTD YTD VARIANCE	REVISED BUDGETS 1994 ANNUAL	P.S.F.
		EXPENSES						
		COMMON AREA EXPENSES:						
		ADMINISTRATIVE						
350.00		LEGAL & AUDIT	350.00		1,550	50	1,550	.03
1,495.92	1,480.42	MANAGEMENT FEES	1,515.14	1,649.53	10,578	297-	18,560	.41
310.80	40.37	WAGES & SALARIES	198.29	228.19	840	735-	2,700	.06
72.18	60.25	OFFICE EXPENSE	67.37	59.77	745	150	1,120	.02
		MAINTENANCE						
355.38	2,895.29	WAGES & SALARIES	550.20	561.00	8,719	3,881-	13,500	.30
2.73	3.35	AUTO & EQUIPMENT	.92		35	21-	100	.00
602.28	180.25	ELEVATOR MAINTENANCE	180.25	180.25	1,261	34-	2,255	.05
239.68	254.66	LANDSCAPING	254.66	254.66	764	349-	3,038	.06
183.83	131.81	SUPPLIES	127.25	127.24	768	282-	1,800	.04
1,922.81	2,324.55	MAINTENANCE	718.12	4,355.88	9,151	26,167-	51,364	1.15
1,545.97	1,653.47	PAINTING & DECORATING	2,353.19		12,274	294-	20,900	.46
158.00	158.00	CLEANING	158.00	158.00	1,106	255	500	.01
		RUBBISH REMOVAL						
		SNOW REMOVAL			1,823	183-	2,050	.04
26,075.71	26,047.18	REAL ESTATE TAX	4,167.00	4,167.00	46,722	6,778-	50,000	1.12
20,303.71-	15,880.18-	*TAX RESERVE - NET CHANGE			17,553-	4,737		
237.00	225.00	INSURANCE	225.00	225.00	1,575		2,700	.06
		*INSURANCE RES - NET CHANGE						
		UTILITIES						
1,052.12	1,037.26	GAS	3,156.30	1,325.59	25,300	1,050-	31,000	.69
8,090.32	9,911.84	ELECTRIC	6,343.74	8,672.39	46,757	5,257-	75,250	1.68
5.00	62.43	TELEPHONE	63.41	64.15	498	29	800	.01
566.89	598.88	WATER	208.00	208.00	1,722	143-	2,500	.05
365.89-	390.88-	*WATER RESERVE - NET CHANGE						
22,597.02	24,794.05	TOTAL COMMON AREA EXPENSES	20,636.84	23,890.12	154,370	27,182-	283,382	6.36
		OTHER EXPENSES:						
49.28		ADVERTISING & PROMOTION	106.92	240.57	515	25-	850	.01
3.83		LEASE FEES & COMMISSIONS	4,610.85	9.50	5,052	11,048-	13,486	.30
		EVICTION & COLLECTION						
64.66		OTHER ADMINISTRATIVE	2.30	8.39	1,560	1,560-	3	.00
5.80		TENANT IMPROVEMENTS	2,072.24	1,026.38	5,091	15,909-	50	.25
2.29	307.21	TELEPHONE			1	1		
		OFFICE EXPENSE						
120.06	313.01	TOTAL OTHER EXPENSES	6,792.31	1,285.34	12,244	25,374-	25,909	.58
22,717.08	25,107.06	TOTAL EXPENSES	27,429.15	25,175.46	166,614	52,556-	309,291	6.94
17,808.20	58,439.66	NET INCOME BEFORE DEBT SERVICE	14,828.43	16,964.42	162,463	66,294-	196,503	4.41
		DEBT SERVICE:						
3,510.92	3,864.43	MORTGAGE PRINCIPAL	3,803.13	3,833.66	26,413		46,206	1.03

CLIENT 8420		CLIENT NAME		
DEV. X24		DEVELOPMENT NAME		
FYE 12		RUN DATE 7/25/95		

REPORT NAME			
REPORT NO. C/F	OPERATING STATEMENT	KEY 34200OX34	
CUSTOM		SQUARE FOOTAGE 44550	ACQUISITION DATE

| DATE 7/31/94 |
| PAGE 3 |
| SEG. NO. 288 |

| CURRENT MONTH | | DESCRIPTION | PRIOR MONTHS | | YTD 1994 | CURRENT YTD | REVISED BUDGETS | |
JUL 1993	JUL 1994		MAY 1994	JUN 1994		YTD VARIANCE	1994 ANNUAL	P.S.F.
10,996.33	10,642.62	MORTGAGE INTEREST	10,704.12	10,673.59	75,137		127,881	2.87
14,507.25	14,507.25	TOTAL DEBT SERVICE	14,507.25	14,507.25	101,551	1	174,087	3.90
3,301.95	43,926.41	NET INCOME AFTER DEBT SERVICE	321.18	2,457.17	80,912	86,289-	22,416	.50
		COMPUTATION OF TAXABLE INCOME ADD:						
3,510.92	3,864.43	MORTGAGE PRINCIPAL	3,803.13	3,833.66	26,413		46,206	1.03
		LEASE FEES ABOVE	4,610.85	9.50	5,052	11,048-	13,486	.30
64.66	307.21	TENANT WORK ABOVE	2,072.24	1,026.38	5,091	15,909-	11,523	.25
		LESS:						
5,954.00-	6,010.00-	DEPRECIATION	6,010.00-	6,010.00-	42,070-		72,125-	1.61-
575.00-	708.00-	AMORTIZATION	708.00-	708.00-	4,956-	4-	8,500-	19-
348.53	41,380.05	TAXABLE INCOME (OR LOSS)	4,089.40	608.71	50,443	59,241-	13,006	.29

CLIENT						DATE	7/31/94
8420			REPORT NAME	OPERATING STATEMENT		PAGE	4
DEV. X34			REPORT NO. CUSTOM C/F	KEY 8420000X34		SEG. NO.	288
FYE 12			SQUARE FOOTAGE 44850	ACQUISITION DATE			

CLIENT NAME							
DEVELOPMENT NAME							
RUN DATE 7/25/95							

CURRENT MONTH JUL 1993	CURRENT MONTH JUL 1994	DESCRIPTION	PRIOR MONTHS MAY 1994	PRIOR MONTHS JUN 1994	CURRENT YTD YTD 1994	CURRENT YTD YTD VARIANCE	REVISED BUDGETS 1994 ANNUAL	REVISED BUDGETS P.S.F.
		CASH RECONCILIATION						
3,141.77	18,463.00	BEGINNING CASH - OPERATING	34,018.51	21,674.29				
		CASH RECEIVED						
40,526.28	83,540.72	FROM TOTAL INCOME - PG 2	42,257.58	42,139.88				
7,044.20	13,677.45-	ADD:BEGINNING ACCTS. REC.	12,252.00-	14,861.48-				
7,991.13	7,137.63-	LESS ENDING ACCTS. REC.	14,861.48-	13,677.45-				
39,577.35	77,000.90	TOTAL CASH RECEIVED	44,836.98	40,955.85				
		CASH DISBURSED						
22,717.08-	25,101.06-	FOR EXPENSES - PG 2 /DISB.	21,428.15-	25,175.46-				
14,070.89-	13,992.87-	FOR OTHER ITEMS	20,992.68-	11,008.32				
36,787.97-	39,099.93-	TOTAL CASH DISBURSED	56,420.83-	14,167.14-				
		SECURITY DEPOSITS, INC/DEC	760.37-					
		MISC. NON-OPERATING INC/EXP						
5,931.15	56,363.97	TOTAL CASH AVAILABLE OR REQUIRED	21,674.29	48,463.00				
		OWNERS DISTRIBUTION/CONTRIBUTION		30,000.00				
5,931.15	56,363.97	RECONCILING ITEMS	21,674.29	18,463.00				
5,931.15	56,363.97	ENDING CASH - OPERATING ACCOUNT	21,674.29	18,463.00				
		ENDING CASH - RESERVE ACCOUNTS						
976.14-	808.14-	INSURANCE	1,258.14-	1,033.14-				
11,753.66-	24,710.46-	TAX	12,997.28-	8,830.28-				
80.75-	53.00	WATER	235.88-	443.88-				
12,810.55-	25,465.60-	TOTAL CASH FOR RESERVES	14,019.54-	9,419.54-				
6,879.40-	30,898.37	ENDING TOTAL CASH/ INC RESERVES	7,654.75	9,043.46-				
		MORTGAGE BALANCE	1,329,773.61	1,325,939.95				

CLIENT	8420
DEV.	16S
FYE	07

CLIENT NAME

DEVELOPMENT NAME

RUN DATE 7/25/95

REPORT NAME OPERATING STATEMENT

REPORT NO. C/F	KEY 8420000165
CUSTOM	
SQUARE FOOTAGE	77989	ACQUISITION DATE

DATE	7/31/94
PAGE	5
SEQ. NO.	288

CURRENT MONTH JUL 1993	JUL 1994	DESCRIPTION	PRIOR MONTHS MAY 1994	JUN 1994	YTD 1994	CURRENT YTD VARIANCE	REVISED BUDGETS 1994 ANNUAL	P.S.F.
		INCOME STATEMENT						
111,941.86	223,854.29	POTENTIAL RENT	111,712.38	111,636.82	1,452,659	112,049-	1,340,810	17.19
		LESS:						
14,357.87-	8,890.00-	VACANCIES	5,953.75-	4,445.00-	88,193-	52,470	49,421-	63-
5,130.00-	10,260.00-	ALLOWANCES			19,881-	9,130	13,101-	16-
92,453.99	204,704.29	NET RENTAL INCOME	105,758.63	107,191.82	1,344,785	50,449-	1,278,288	16.39
2,069.35	4,425.80	GARAGE RENT	2,250.00	2,250.00	26,992	2,592-	26,550	.34
756.87	1,665.68	STORAGE RENT	832.84	832.84	10,552	1,552-	10,000	.12
		REAL ESTATE TAX REFUND			17,138	17,138-		
		OTHER INCOME	289.65	13.25	2,042	42-	2,000	.02
		INTEREST INCOME			2,990	2,990-		
95,280.21	210,795.77	TOTAL INCOME	109,331.12	110,287.91	1,406,498	74,782-	1,317,138	16.88
		TENANT REIMBURSEMENTS:						
3,592.90	10,778.82	COMMON AREA MAINTENANCE	5,327.05	5,327.05	59,553	4,394	63,947	.81
115.45	168.10	MAINTENANCE CHARGES	310.11	315.15	2,677	677-	2,000	.02
8,313.14	17,594.20	UTILITIES	8,310.95	7,443.08	112,968	7,969-	106,038	1.35
107,301.70	239,336.89	TOTAL INCOME & TENANT REIMBURS.	123,079.23	123,373.19	1,581,696	79,014-	1,489,123	19.09
82.59	91.44	NET INCOME AS % OF POTENTIAL	94.67	96.01	93	4-	95	
11,858.16	8,129.01	VACANCY TIMES NET INC AS % OF POT	5,636.41	4,267.64	81,631	47,348-	47,113	

CLIENT	8420
DEV.	165
FYE	07

CLIENT NAME	
DEVELOPMENT NAME	
RUN DATE	7/25/95

REPORT NAME	OPERATING STATEMENT
REPORT NO.	KEY 8420000165
CUSTOM C/F	
SQUARE FOOTAGE 77089	ACQUISITION DATE

DATE	7/31/84
PAGE	6
SEQ NO.	218

CURRENT MONTH JUL 1993	JUL 1994	DESCRIPTION	PRIOR MONTHS MAY 1994	JUN 1994	CURRENT YTD YTD 1994	YTD VARIANCE	REVISED BUDGETS 1994 ANNUAL	P.S.F.
		EXPENSES						
		COMMON AREA EXPENSES:						
		ADMINISTRATIVE						
1,169.31	2,769.14	ADVERTISING & PROMOTION			4,261	1,261	3,000	.03
		LEGAL & AUDIT	500.00		2,050	550	1,718	.02
4,964.12	5,613.97	MANAGEMENT FEES	5,356.17	3,816.47	57,107	193-	56,500	.72
		WAGES & SALARIES			1	1	1	
	96.30	SECURITY			287	17	287	
41.24	42.93	OFFICE EXPENSE	40.36	37.40	891	291	834	.01
		MAINTENANCE						
1,930.23	5,465.24	WAGES & SALARIES	1,467.52	1,476.60	27,392	1,792	30,720	.39
2.40	1.45	AUTO & EQUIPMENT	1.18	.38	88	38	100	
230.00	236.90	ELEVATOR MAINTENANCE	238.90	433.40	3,413	433	3,020	.03
1,269.98	1,281.75	LANDSCAPING	1,281.75	1,452.49	13,133	133	12,754	.16
621.24	405.25	SUPPLIES	254.51	400.81	3,839	1,811-	5,550	.07
1,647.89	2,439.59	MAINTENANCE	1,649.94	3,598.51	32,066	2,368	30,457	.39
		PAINTING & DECORATING	773.58		3,368	2,352-	1,000	.01
3,644.90	4,099.98	CLEANING	3,970.33	4,081.25	51,498	4	52,350	.67
168.80	168.80	RUBBISH REMOVAL	168.80	168.80	2,054	2,417	2,050	.02
		SNOW REMOVAL			8,417	802-	8,097	.10
		OTHER TAXES			508	897		.00
77,930.78	73,051.69	REAL ESTATE TAX	12,500.00	12,500.00	146,103	4,523-	150,700	1.92
64,942.78-	60,551.69-	TAX RESERVE - NET CHANGE	12,500.00-	12,500.00-		386-		
571.00	500.00	INSURANCE	500.00	500.00	6,064	291	6,450	.08
		INSURANCE RES - NET CHANGE			291	291		
		UTILITIES						
512.92	461.90	GAS	2,302.91	693.52	18,852	5,648-	24,500	.31
17,971.43	17,138.42	ELECTRIC	11,629.86	14,253.52	151,519	6,981-	158,500	2.03
46.47	83.33	TELEPHONE	101.64	146.42	1,184	116-	1,300	.01
2,233.12	1,457.43	WATER	783.00	636.58	8,145	1,255-	9,400	.12
1,283.12-	674.43-	WATER RESERVE - NET CHANGE			2,086	2,086-		
48,729.93	54,087.95	**TOTAL COMMON AREA EXPENSES**	43,518.45	44,281.22	540,184	10,006-	559,384	7.17
		OTHER EXPENSES:						
110.35	15.00	ADVERTISING & PROMOTION	14.00	53.00	718	218	500	.00
27,928.70		LEASE FEES & COMMISSIONS		4,560.59	46,437	24,437	12,151	.15
5.50-	3.77	LEGAL & AUDIT			165	165		
		OTHER ADMINISTRATIVE	13.00	4.94	152	52	100	.00
50,435.04	747.45	TENANT IMPROVEMENTS	2,451.00-	65.50	80,526	41,526	32,839	.42
	1.53	TELEPHONE	1.17	.28	34	34		
		OFFICE EXPENSE			3	3		
78,468.59	767.75	**TOTAL OTHER EXPENSES**	2,422.83-	4,684.31	128,034	66,434	45,590	.58
127,198.52	54,855.70	**TOTAL EXPENSES**	41,095.62	48,965.53	668,218	56,428	604,974	7.75
19,896.82-	184,481.19	**NET INCOME BEFORE DEBT SERVICE**	81,983.61	74,407.66	913,478	22,586-	884,149	11.33

CLIENT 8420
DEV. 165
FYE 07

CLIENT NAME
DEVELOPMENT NAME
RUN DATE 7/25/95

REPORT NAME: OPERATING STATEMENT
REPORT NO. CUSTOM C/T — KEY 8420000185
SQUARE FOOTAGE 77989 — ACQUISITION DATE

DATE 7/31/94
PAGE 1
SEG NO. 288

DESCRIPTION	CURRENT MONTH JUL 1994	PRIOR MONTHS MAY 1994	JUN 1994	YTD 1994	CURRENT YTD VARIANCE	REVISED BUDGETS 1994 ANNUAL	P.S.F.
DEBT SERVICE:							
MORTGAGE PRINCIPAL	11,894.77	11,894.77	11,894.77	1,107,053	962,596	144,457	1.85
MORTGAGE INTEREST	30,154.08	27,438.51	30,243.07	337,315	32,245-	348,666	4.47
TOTAL DEBT SERVICE	42,048.85	39,333.28	42,137.84	1,444,368-	940,348-	493,123	6.32
NET INCOME AFTER DEBT SERVICE	142,432.34	42,650.33	32,269.82	530,880-	917,762	391,026	5.01
COMPUTATION OF TAXABLE INCOME							
ADD:							
MORTGAGE PRINCIPAL	11,894.77	11,894.77	11,894.77	1,107,053	962,596	144,457	1.85
LEASE FEES ABOVE	15.00	14.00	4,550.59	46,437	24,437	12,151	.15
TENANT WORK ABOVE	747.45	2,451.00-	65.50	60,526	41,526	32,639	.42
LESS:							
DEPRECIATION	35,067.00-	35,067.00-	35,067.00-	417,886-	2,931-	420,600-	5.39-
AMORTIZATION	3,859.00-	4,583.00-	4,583.00-	411,235-	3,277+	55,000-	
TAXABLE INCOME (OR LOSS)	115,439.56	12,458.10	9,140.68	234,030	117,501-	104,673	1.34

CLIENT 8420					
DEV 165					
FYE 07					

CLIENT NAME
DEVELOPMENT NAME
RUN DATE 7/25/95

REPORT NAME OPERATING STATEMENT
REPORT NO. C/F | KEY
CUSTOM | 8420000165
SQUARE FOOTAGE 77989 | ACQUISITION DATE

DATE 7/31/94
PAGE 8
SEQ NO. 288

| CURRENT MONTH | | DESCRIPTION | PRIOR MONTHS | | CURRENT YTD | | REVISED BUDGETS | |
JUL 1993	JUL 1994		MAY 1994	JUN 1994	YTD 1994	YTD VARIANCE	1994 ANNUAL	P.S.F.
		CASH RECONCILIATION						
64,768.02	133,778.12	BEGINNING CASH - OPERATING	182,234.07	119,707.12				
		CASH RECEIVED						
107,301.70	239,336.89	FROM TOTAL INCOME - PG 2	123,079.23	123,373.19				
12,593.81-	25,883.29-	ADD BEGINNING ACCTS. REC.	20,310.34-	342.18-				
9,510.93-	62,138.22	LESS ENDING ACCTS. REC.	342.18	25,883.29-				
104,218.82	151,315.38	TOTAL CASH RECEIVED	102,426.71	149,598.66				
		CASH DISBURSED						
127,198.52-	54,855.70-	FOR EXPENSES - PG 2 DISB.	41,095.62-	48,965.53-				
		FOR CAPITAL EXPENDITURES	12,424.29-	12,424.29-				
71,331.00-	92,077.36-	FOR OTHER ITEMS	126,307.71-	74,137.84-				
198,529.52-	146,933.06-	TOTAL CASH DISBURSED	167,405.39-	135,527.66-				
1,951.25		SECURITY DEPOSITS, INC/DEC	2,240.67					
		MISC. NON-OPERATING INC/EXP						
27,631.43-	138,160.44	TOTAL CASH AVAILABLE OR REQUIRED	119,707.12	133,778.12				
		RECONCILING ITEMS						
27,631.43-	138,160.44	ENDING CASH - OPERATING ACCOUNT	119,707.12	133,778.12				
27,631.43-	138,160.44	ENDING CASH - RESERVE ACCOUNTS	119,707.12	133,778.12				
2,273.68-	5,191.50-	INSURANCE	6,191.50-	5,891.50-				
64,051.92-	1,395.30-	TAX	32,656.39	45,156.39				
2,670.33	6,233.59	WATER	6,271.44	6,908.02				
64,546.27-	14,353.21-	TOTAL CASH FOR RESERVES	32,736.33	46,372.91				
92,177.70-	123,807.23	ENDING TOTAL CASH/ INC RESERVES	152,443.45	180,151.03				
		MORTGAGE BALANCE	4,892,947.11	4,881,052.34				

CLIENT NAME | DEVELOPMENT NAME | RUN DATE 8/8/95
CLIENT 9025 | DEV. | FYE

REPORT NAME DEVELOPMENT DETAIL COMPARISON STATEMENT
REPORT NO. KEY 8025000070 | COLINDEX C/F | SQUARE FOOTAGE | ACQUISITION DATE
DATE 4/30/95 | PAGE | SEQ NO 1 | 990

SAMPLE MULTI - PROPERTY INCOME STATEMENT

DESCRIPTION	BRIARWOOD	PINEGATE	HIDDEN PINE	HAZELWOOD	DRIFTWOOD	REDWOOD	HAPPY ACRES	OAK PARK
OPERATING INCOME								
OPTIMUM POTENTIAL RENT	68,535	201,185	99,880	264,760	142,065	20,200	12,960	18,440
POTENTIAL RENT	66,660	192,530	97,280	255,475	131,230	19,680	12,720	17,925
LESS-SUITE VACANCIES	1,264-	4,637-	4,119-	3,261-	2,393-	2,895-	860-	521-
GARAGE VACANCIES	598-	301-	308-	455-	925-	925-	195-	195-
ALLOWANCES	160-	1,448-	1,050-	5,150-	2,668-	840-		70-
ADD-SHORT TERM PREMIUM	100	950	685	1,020	690	30	40	50
NET RENTAL INCOME	64,739	187,094	92,487	247,609	131,944	15,825	11,995	17,189
COIN OPERATED INCOME	925	76	2,757	4,143	6,348	257	152	243
OTHER INCOME	3,287	8,037	5,071	11,642	2,382	25	257	125
TOTAL INCOME	68,951	195,207	100,315	263,394	140,674	16,107	12,403	17,557
OPERATING EXPENSES								
LEASING EXPENSE	1,398	4,096	2,242	3,872	3,915	418	2,760	36
MANAGEMENT FEES	3,187	9,994	5,090	12,764	7,180	792	579	872
ADMINISTRATIVE	731	5,735	3,734	6,269	2,024	214	191	229
SECURITY	1,528	3,495	2,496	1,839	1,060		160	80
POOL & RECREATION	152	269	176	1,238	505		40	
LANDSCAPING		2,833	1,845	2,953	854		742	
MAINTENANCE	4,920	13,647	8,125	36,831	15,222	3,123	2,237	4,771
APPLIANCE REPLACEMENT	96	83	334	3,916	719	549	420	44
CARPET REPLACEMENT		1,514	300	1,673	2,504			
DECORATING EXPENSE	40	1,505	498	3,502	3,122	1,670	6	160
TAXES AND INSURANCE	6,904	22,192	9,175	24,109	8,968	1,548	1,467	2,243
UTILITIES	7,946	18,555	16,904	41,445	16,254	1,843	2,027	1,993
TOTAL OPERATING EXPENSES	26,902	83,920	51,519	140,210	61,725	10,156	10,628	10,428
NET OP. INC. BEFORE DEBT SERVICE	42,050	111,287	48,785	123,183	78,949	5,950	1,775	7,129
DEBT SERVICE								
PRINCIPAL		7,723	13,473	9,072	5,129			
INTEREST		51,367	2,269	54,707	33,002			
REPLACEMENT RESERVE		6,450		13,100				
TOTAL DEBT SERVICE		65,540	15,742	76,879	38,131		1,775	7,129
NET OPERATING INCOME	42,050	45,747	33,093	46,304	40,818	5,950	1,775	7,129

CLIENT	B025
DEV.	
FYE	

CLIENT NAME	
DEVELOPMENT NAME	
RUN DATE	8/9/95

REPORT NAME	DEVELOPMENT DETAIL COMPARISON STATEMENT
REPORT NO. KEY	CURDEV C/F B025000070
SQUARE FOOTAGE	ACQUISITION DATE

DATE	4/30/95
PAGE	2
SEQ NO.	99

DESCRIPTION	BRIARWOOD	PINEGATE	HIDDEN PINE	HAZELWOOD	DRIFTWOOD	REDWOOD	HAPPY ACRES	OAK PARK
OTHER INCOME								
LATE FEE INCOME	75	1,650	1,010	1,620	755	25	50-	125
CABLE TV	1,176	6,237	4,061	9,502	114		307	
OTHER	2,036	150		520	1,512	25	257	125
TOTAL OTHER INCOME	3,287	8,037	5,071	11,642	2,382	25	257	125
LEASING EXPENSE								
ADVERTISING	532	1,249	813	1,483	1,441	1,134	139	
COMMISSIONS-OUTSDE AGTS/RES.				50	50			
WAGES & SALARIES	728	735	479	2,409	1,362		190	
OFFICE EXPENSES	62	759	467	249	398	9	18	10
MODEL SUITE RENT	83	342	223	326	274	25-	22	
COLLECTION FEES & BAD DEBTS	7-	928	245	903-	545	750-	2,090	27
VACANT SUITE UTILITIES	83		18	38	58			
TOTAL LEASING EXPENSE	1,398	4,096	2,242	3,672	3,915	418	2,760	36
ADMINISTRATIVE								
LEGAL								
WAGES & SALARIES	552	4,869	3,171	3,639	273	168	144	180
OFFICE EXPENSES	28	278	181	1,525	1,152		7	
DATA PROCESSING	142	550	358	837	569	43	37	46
OTHER ADMINISTRATIVE	9	37	24	268	390	3	3	3
					141			
TOTAL ADMINISTRATIVE	731	5,705	3,704	6,269	2,024	214	191	229
SECURITY								
GUARD SERVICE	613	3,495	2,276	1,730	923		160	
FACILITY & EQUIPMENT COST	915		220	108	138			80
TOTAL SECURITY	1,528	3,495	2,496	1,839	1,060		160	80
POOL & RECREATION								
WAGES - POOL			22	813	24			
MAINTENANCE & SUPPLIES-POOL	81	34	128	277	320		21	
WAGES-RECREATION	71	197	25	148	159		19	
RECREATION PROGRAMS		39			2			
RECREATION FACIL. & EQUIPMENT								
TOTAL POOL & RECREATION	152	269	176	1,238	505		40	
MAINTENANCE								
APPLIANCE REPAIRS	49			372	133	16	7	16
AUTO & EQUIPMENT	16			66			4	30

CLIENT	CLIENT NAME		REPORT NAME	DATE
9025	DEVELOPMENT NAME		DEVELOPMENT DETAIL COMPARISON STATEMENT	4/30/95
DEV.	RUN DATE		REPORT NO. COLMDEV C/F KEY 9025000076	PAGE 3
FYE	8/9/95		SQUARE FOOTAGE ACQUISITION DATE	SEQ NO. 99

DESCRIPTION	BRIARWOOD	PINEGATE	HIDDEN PINE	HAZELWOOD	DRIFTWOOD	REDWOOD	HAPPY ACRES	OAK PARK
BUILDING EXTERIOR								
CABINETS, VANITIES & TOPS		1,247	735	37	2,400	194	1,312	2,381
COIN OPERATED EQUIPMENT					98			
ELECTRICAL	321			541	625		123	
ELEVATOR	18	647	446	797	519	392	350	
EXTERMINATOR	382		165	693	453			37
FLOOR COVERINGS	34	238		300	68	40	18	92
GARAGES	70	319	93	213	134	184	125	
GLASS, SCREENS	239	75		237	215		63	6
HOT WATER TANK							6	
HVAC		325			32			
INTERIOR DOORS	1	48	225	788	414	193		
PLUMBING	173	511	256	461	297	191	110	51
ROOF & GUTTERS		350	324	371		134		
RUBBISH REMOVAL		633			516			
SITE WORK		500	325	675	322	110	58	155
SNOW REMOVAL	103	1,964	1,279	1,951	424	106	29	123
SUPPLIES-MAINTENANCE	63	178	116	148	112	98	27	
SUPPLIES-CLEANING	190	584	380	701	383	110	16	160
WALLS	84			1,054	60		49	
WAGES & SALARIES	3,088	5,890	3,836	26,350	8,463	1,099	1	1,720
	88	55	98-	210	168	2	893	8
TENANT RECOVERY	115-	115-		687	53-	315	23	
							980-	
TOTAL MAINTENANCE	4,920	13,647	8,125	36,831	15,222	3,123	2,237	4,771
DECORATING EXPENSE								
SUITE INTERIOR		1,505	498	3,334	2,209	1,670	6	160
BUILDING INTERIOR	40			168	313			
TOTAL DECORATING	40	1,505	498	3,502	2,522	1,670	6	160
TAXES & INSURANCE								
TAX RESERVE - NET CHANGE	6,508	20,917	8,333	22,192	8,033	1,433	1,375	2,133
INSURANCE RESERVE - NET CHANGE	396	1,275	842	1,917	933	113	110	110
TOTAL TAXES & INSURANCE	6,904	22,192	9,175	24,109	8,966	1,546	1,467	2,243
UTILITIES								
GAS	3,209	52	8,937	16,849	8,494	432	846	670
ELECTRIC	2,212	670	800	4,179	1,877	474	285	543
WATER	75	17,833	7,167	20,417	6,063	938	896	781
WATER RESERVE - NET CHANGE	2,450							
TOTAL UTILITIES	7,046	18,555	16,904	41,445	16,264	1,843	2,027	1,993

FINANCIAL STATEMENT

INCOME AND CASH FLOW ANALYSIS	AUGUST	SEPTEMBER	OCTOBER	YEAR-TO-DATE	BUDGET	BUDGET %	CURRENT MONTH %	YTD %
INCOME:								
RENTAL REVENUE	228,584.80	225,323.91	222,868.63	1364,406.61	1360,008.00	100.00	100.00	100.00
OTHER INCOME	10,879.19	9,859.99	19,769.74	69,127.63	63,489.00	4.67	8.87	5.07
TOTAL INCOME	239,463.99	235,183.90	242,638.37	1433,534.24	1423,497.00	104.67	108.87	105.07
OPERATING EXPENSES:								
TAXES AND INSURANCE	43,688.60	25,288.00	16,198.09	169,954.79	171,425.00	12.60	7.27	12.46
PROFESSIONAL SERVICES	11,788.58	11,845.55	11,523.70	72,287.02	71,976.00	5.29	5.17	5.30
UTILITIES	10,905.18	10,022.00	13,508.38	73,112.23	77,454.00	5.70	6.06	5.36
REPAIRS AND MAINTENANCE	18,219.84	18,068.04	14,984.70	94,326.31	131,642.00	9.68	6.72	6.91
SALARIES AND LABOR OVERHEAD	20,051.66	16,302.10	18,525.11	106,787.06	115,152.0	8.47	8.31	7.83
ADMINISTRATIVE EXPENSES	5,501.89	5,505.06	3,698.28	24,537.62	29,450.00	2.17	1.66	1.80
TOTAL OPERATING EXPENSES	110,155.75	87,030.75	78,438.26	541,005.03	597,099.00	43.90	35.19	39.65
NET OPERATING INCOME:	129,308.24	148,153.15	164,200.11	892,529.21	826,398.00	60.76	73.68	65.42
DEBT SERVICE-PRINCIPAL	2,485.15	2,507.00	2,529.05	14,847.41	14,851.00	1.09	1.13	1.09
DEBT SERVICE-INTEREST	129,471.12	129,449.27	129,427.22	787,197.56	787,180.00	57.88	58.07	57.70
CASH FLOW AFTER DEBT SERVICE:	2,648.03	16,196.88	32,243.88	90,484.24	24,387.00	1.79	14.47	6.63
INITIAL REPAIRS & MAINTENANCE	.00	1,604.40	.00	5,217.73	111,000.00	8.16	.00	.38
EXTRAORDINARY EXPENSES	.00	.00	.00	.00	.00	.00	.00	.00
CAPITAL IMPROVEMENTS	.00	.00	.00	.00	.00	.00	.00	.00
DEPRECIATION & AMORTIZATION EXP.								
NET CASH FLOW (LOSS)	2,648.03-	14,592.48	32,243.84	85,266.51	86,613.00-	6.37-	14.47	6.25

FINANCIAL STATEMENT

STATEMENT OF OPERATIONS-DETAILED	AUGUST	SEPTEMBER	OCTOBER	YEAR-TO-DATE	BUDGET	BUDGET %	CURRENT MONTH %	YTD %
INCOME:								
RENTAL NOTICE								
5010 RENTAL REVENUE-GROSS	235,337.00	237,646.00	239,996.00	1413,437.85	1431,504.00	105.26	107.67	103.59
5030 LESS VACANCIES	6,752.20-	12,322.09-	17,097.37-	49,031.24-	71,496.00-	5.26-	7.67-	3.59-
TOTAL RENTAL REVENUE	228,584.80	225,323.91	222,868.63	1364,406.61	1360,008.00	100.00	100.00	100.00
OTHER INCOME:								
5105 DEPOSITS FORFEITED	1,829.37	1,511.06	2,543.75	12,084.44	16,860.00	1.24	1.14	.89
5106 DAMAGE CHARGES	2,151.53	1,398.75	1,635.25	8,482.69	16,860.00	1.24	.73	.62
5110 VENDING MACHINE INCOME	99.42	.00	112.75	520.65	800.00	.04	.05	.04
5115 LAUNDRY INCOME	2,411.50	2,411.50	2,411.50	14,469.00	14,469.00	1.06	1.08	1.06
5120 NSF/LATE CHARGES	1,480.00	1,708.00	1,516.00	8,302.00	4,500.00	.33	.68	.61
5145 PET RENTAL	528.00	514.80	487.20	3,272.40	3,600.00	.26	.22	.24
5150 TRANSFER FEES	200.00	300.00	400.00	1,600.00	1,800.00	.13	.18	.12
5160 APPLICATION FEES	720.00	900.00	620.00	5,460.00	4,800.00	.35	.28	.40
5165 INTEREST INCOME	1,447.37	1,107.88	734.82	5,575.98	.00	.00	.33	.41
5195 MISCELLANEOUS INCOME	12.00	8.00	9,308.47	9,360.47	.00	.00	4.18	.69
TOTAL OTHER INCOME	10,879.19	9,859.99	19,769.74	69,127.63	63,489.00	4.67	8.87	5.07
TOTAL INCOME	239,463.99	235,183.90	242,638.37	1433,534.24	1423,497.00	104.67	108.87	105.07
EXPENSES:								
TAXES AND INSURANCE								
6010 REAL PROPERTY TAXES	22,800.00	22,800.00	22,800.00	136,900.00	136,900.00	10.07	10.23	10.03
6020 PERSONAL PROPERTY TAXES	2,187.00	2,188.00	2,188.00	13,126.00	13,125.00	.97	.98	.96
6030 LICENSES & FEES	2,581.60	300.00	136.00	3,746.20	3,400.00	.25	.06	.27
6040 INSURANCE	16,120.00	.00	8,925.91-	16,182.59	18,000.00	1.32	4.01-	1.19
TOTAL TAXES AND INSURANCE	43,688.60	25,288.00	16,198.09	169,954.79	171,425.00	12.60	7.27	12.46
PROFESSIONAL SERVICES:								
6105 PROPERTY MANAGEMENT FEES	11,777.78	11,880.55	11,613.70	69,901.22	69,480.00	5.11	5.21	5.12
6110 LEGAL FEES	10.80	35.00-	90.00-	2,385.80	2,496.00	.18	.04	.17
TOTAL PROFESSIONAL SERVICES	11,788.58	11,845.55	11,523.70	72,287.02	71,976.00	5.29	5.17	5.30
UTILITIES:								
6205 WATER/SEWER	2,444.03	1,994.68	6,572.98	25,011.26	28,002.00	2.06	2.95	1.83

CONTINUED ON NEXT PAGE

FINANCIAL STATEMENT

OCT. ACTUAL	OCT. BUDGET	OCT. VARIANCE	INCOME & CASH FLOW ANALYSIS	YTD ACTUAL	YTD BUDGET	YTD VARIANCE
			INCOME:			
222,868.63	222,800.00	68.63	RENTAL REVENUE	1364,406.61	1360,008.00	11,368.44
19,769.74	19,750.00	19.74	OTHER INCOME	69,127.63	63,489.00	5,638.63
242,638.37	242,550.00	88.37	TOTAL INCOME	1433,534.24	1423,497.00	10,037.24
			OPERATING EXPENSES:			
16,198.09	16,225.00	26.91	TAXES AND INSURANCE	169,954.79	171,425.00	1,470.21
11,523.70	12,250.00	726.30	PROFESSIONAL SERVICES	72,287.02	71,976.00	311.02-
13,508.38	13,950.00	441.62	UTILITIES	73,112.23	77,454.00	4,341.77
14,984.70	15,500.00	515.30	REPAIRS AND MAINTENANCE	94,326.31	131,642.00	37,315.69
18,525.11	21,525.00	2,999.89	SALARIES AND LABOR OVERHEAD	106,787.06	115,152.00	8,364.94
3,698.28	5,925.00	2,226.72	ADMINISTRATIVE EXPENSES	24,537.62	29,450.00	4,912.38
78,438.26	85,476.00	7,037.74	TOTAL OPERATING EXPENSES	541,005.03	597,099.00	56,093.97
164,200.11	157,074.00	7,126.11	NET OPERATING INCOME:	892,529.21	826,398.00	66,131.21
2,529.05	2,500.00	29.05-	DEBT SERVICE-PRINCIPAL	14,847.41	14,851.00	3.59
129,427.22	129,300.00	127.22-	DEBT SERVICE-INTEREST	787,197.56	787,160.00	37.56-
32,243.88	25,274.00	6,969.83	CASH FLOW AFTER DEBT SERVICE:	90,484.24	24,387.00	66,097.24
				5,217.73	111,000.00	105,782.27
32,243.88	25,274.00	6,969.83	NET CASH FLOW (LOSS)	85,266.51	86,613.00-	171,879.51

FINANCIAL STATEMENTS

| | CURRENT | | | | YEAR-TO-DATE | | | | ANNUAL | |
	ACTUAL	BUDGET	VARIANCE	PCT	ACTUAL	BUDGET	VARIANCE	PCT	BUDGETED	REMAINING
INCOME:										
RENTAL REVENUE	222,868.63	222,800.00	68.63	100.00	1,364,406.61	1,360,008.00	4,398.61	100.00	2,780,000.00	1,419,992.00
OTHER INCOME	19,769.74	19,750.00	19.74	8.87	69,127.63	63,489.00	5638.63	5.07	270,000.00	206,511.00
TOTAL INCOME	242,638.37	242,550.00	88.37	108.87	1,433,534.24	1,423,497.00	10,037.24	105.07	3,050,000.00	1,626,503.00
OPERATING EXPENSES:										
TAXES AND INSURANCE	16,198.09	16,225.00	26.91	7.27	169,954.79	171,425.00	1,470.21	12.46	380,000.00	208,575.00
PROFESSIONAL SERVICES	11,523.70	12,250.00	726.30	5.17	72,287.02	71,976.00	311.02-	5.30	150,000.00	78,024.00
UTILITIES	13,508.38	13,950.00	441.62	6.06	73,112.23	77,454.00	4,341.77	5.36	167,000.00	89,546.00
REPAIRS AND MAINTENANCE	14,984.70	15,500.00	515.30	6.72	94,326.31	131,642.00	37,315.69	6.91	261,000.00	129,358.00
SALARIES AND LABOR OVERHEAD	18,525.11	21,525.00	2,999.89	8.31	106,787.06	115,152.00	8,364.94	7.83	235,000.00	119,848.00
ADMINISTRATIVE EXPENSES	3,698.28	5,925.00	2,226.72	1.66	24,537.62	29,450.00	4,912.38	1.80	59,500.00	30,050.00
TOTAL OPERATING EXPENSES	78,438.26	85,375.00	6,936.74	35.19	541,005.03	597,099.00	56,093.97	39.85	1,252,500.00	655,401.00
NET OPERATING INCOME:	164,200.11	157,175.00	7,025.11	73.68	892,529.21	826,398.00	66,131.21	65.42	1,797,500.00	971,102.00
DEBT SERVICE-PRINCIPAL	2,529.05	2,500.00	29.05-	1.13	14,847.41	14,851.00	3.59	1.09	28,900.00	15,049.00
DEBT SERVICE-INTEREST	129,427.22	129,300.00	127.22-	58.07	787,197.56	787,160.00	37.56-	57.70	1,587,000.00	799,840.00
CASH FLOW AFTER DEBT SERVICE:	32,243.84	25,375.00	6,868.84	14.47	90,484.24	24,387.00	66,097.24	6.63	180,800.00	156,213.00
INITIAL REPAIRS & MAINTENANCE										
EXTRAORDINARY EXPENSES					5,217.73	111,000.00	105,782.27	.38	125,000.00	14,000.00
CAPITAL IMPROVEMENTS										
DEPRECIATION & AMORTIZATION EXP										
NET CASH FLOW (LOSS)	32,243.84	25,375.00	6,868.84	14.47	85,266.51	86,613.00-	171,879.51	6.25	55,600.00	142,213.00

FINANCIAL STATEMENT

DESCRIPTION	C/M LAST YEAR	OCTOBER	NOVEMBER	DECEMBER	JANUARY	FEBRUARY	MARCH	APRIL	MAY	JUNE	JULY	AUGUST	SEPTEMBER
INCOME:													
RENTAL REVENUE	223,300	222,868	228,580	225,450	224,300	225,335	225,320	223,300	219,800	225,300	225,000	228,584	225,323
OTHER INCOME	7,800	19,769	10,860	9,850	9,820	9,850	9,850	9,750	9,950	9,850	9,000	10,879	9,859
TOTAL INCOME	231,100	242,637	239,440	235,300	234,120	235,185	235,170	233,050	229,750	235,150	234,000	239,463	235,182
OPERATING EXPENSES:													
TAXES AND INSURANCE	25,100	16,198	23,680	45,200	25,280	25,850	25,800	25,250	23,220	25,200	25,200	43,688	25,288
PROFESSIONAL SERVICES	11,550	11,523	11,780	11,855	11,900	11,145	11,840	11,845	11,850	11,845	11,800	11,788	11,845
UTILITIES	10,005	13,508	10,905	10,240	10,000	10,620	10,220	10,250	10,100	10,020	10,000	10,905	10,022
REPAIRS AND MAINTENANCE	18,050	14,984	18,210	18,165	18,200	18,000	18,060	18,110	18,150	18,060	18,000	18,219	18,088
SALARIES AND LABOR OVERHEAD	16,150	18,525	20,055	16,325	16,250	16,150	16,330	16,300	16,300	16,300	16,300	20,051	16,302
ADMINISTRATIVE EXPENSES	5,450	3,698	5,500	5,550	5,650	5,500	5,500	5,510	5,450	5,505	5,500	5,501	5,505
TOTAL OPERATING EXPENSES	86,305	78,436	90,130	107,335	87,280	87,265	87,770	87,265	85,070	86,930	86,800	110,152	87,030
NET OPERATING INCOME:	144,795	164,201	149,310	127,965	146,840	147,920	147,400	145,785	144,680	148,220	147,200	129,311	148,152
DEBT SERVICE-PRINCIPAL	2,480	2,529	2,570	2,567	2,557	2,547	2,537	2,527	2,517	2,520	2,500	2,485	2,507
DEBT SERVICE-INTEREST	129,000	129,427	130,000	129,950	129,900	129,850	129,800	129,750	129,600	129,550	129,500	129,471	129,449
CASH FLOW AFTER DEBT SERVICE:	13,315	32,245	16,740	4,552-	14,383	15,523	15,063	13,508	12,563	16,150	15,200	2,645-	16,196
INITIAL REPAIRS & MAINT													
EXTRAORDINARY EXPENSES													
CAPITAL IMPROVEMENTS								1,400					1,604
DEPRECIATION & AMORT EXP.													
NET CASH FLOW (LOSS)	13,315	32,245	16,740	4,552-	14,383	15,523	15,063	12,108	12,563	16,150	15,200	2,645-	14,592

MANUFACTURED HOME COMMUNITY FINANCE SOURCES

MANUFACTURED HOME COMMUNITY FINANCE SOURCES

Jane Kelly

ACTIVE LENDERS FOR MANUFACTURED HOME COMMUNITIES

The following lending source information was supplied by Crittenden Publishing, Inc. Text was taken from the January 1996 "Crittenden Directory of Real Estate Financing" and the 1995 volume of "The Manufactured Housing Report" newsletter. Directories are updated by Crittenden every six months. Newsletters are printed twice monthly. For more information about these publications: Crittenden Publishing, Inc., P.O. Box 1150, Novato, CA 94948. Phone: (415) 382-2400.

Source	Territory	Loan Size	LTV/ DSC	Type	Typical Fees
Allied Capital Commercial Corp. (REIT)					
1666 K Street, Ninth Floor Washington, DC 20006	Nationwide	$750T–$10M	80% / 1.2	P	1–6 pts
American Savings Bank (Savings Bank)					
7717 Friars Rd. San Diego, CA 92108	California	Up to $5M	75% / 1.35	P	1–1.5 pts
Bank of America Commercial Mortgage Services (Bank)					
50 California St., 12th Floor San Francisco, CA 94111	Nationwide	$750T–$7.5M	75% / 1.2	C/P	1–2 pts
First Security Bank of Oregon (Bank)					
580 State St., P.O. Box 868 Salem, OR 97308	Oregon Washington	$200T–$3M	75% / 1.25	C/P/A	
General Electric Capital Corp. (Credit Company)					
260 Long Ridge Rd. Stamford, CT 06902	Nationwide	$3M and up	Negotiable	P	1 pt
GMAC Commercial Mortgage Corp. (Mortgage banker)					
8360 Old York Road Elkins Park, PA 19027	Nationwide	$500T and up	75% / 1.2	P/C/A	1–2 pts
Greyrock Capital Corp./Nationsbank (Credit Company)					
1 Canterbury Green Stanford, CT 06901	Nationwide	$2M–$35M	85% / 1.15	P	1 pt
Home Savings of America (Savings and Loan)					
3701 Wilshire Blvd., Suite 300 Los Angeles, CA 90010	California	$200T–$100M	75% / 1.15	P	1.25 pts
Home Savings Bank, FSB. (Savings Bank)					
P.O. Box 2168 Hollywood, FL 33022	Florida	Up to $30M	70% / —	C/P	2 pts

Source	Territory	Loan Size	LTV/ DSC	Type	Typical Fees
Imperial Thrift & Loan (Thrift and Loan)					
611 Anton Blvd., Suite 110 Costa Mesa, CA 92626	Arizona California Idaho Nevada Oregon Washington	$200T–$3M	70% / 1.15	P	1–3 pts
John Hancock Mutual Life Insurance Co. (Life Company)					
P.O. Box 111 Boston, MA 02117	Nationwide	$3M–$15M	75% / 1.25	P	4 pts
Key Bank of Oregon (Bank)					
828 N.E. Multnomah, Suite 478 Portland, OR 97232	Oregon Washington	$500T–$15M	75% / 1.25	C/P/A	1.5–2 pts
Lincoln National Life Insurance Co. (Life Company)					
200 E. Berry St. Fort Wayne, IN 46801	Nationwide	$5M–$100M	75% / 1.2	P	None
Local Federal Bank (Savings Bank)					
P.O. Box 26480 Oklahoma City, OK 73126-0020	Nationwide	$750T–$15M	75% / 1.25	P	1 pt
Love Funding Corporation (Mortgage Banker, HUD Direct Lender)					
1220 19th St. NW, Suite 801 Washington, DC 20036	Nationwide	$1.5M and up	90% / 1.1	C/P	None
Manufactured Housing Community Bankers/Imperial Credit Industries (Credit Company)					
1401 Dove St., Ste. 670 Newport Beach, CA 92660 (714) 261-1772	Nationwide	$1M and up	75% / 1.25	P	1 pt
New South Federal (Savings Bank)					
524 Lorna Square Birmingham, AL 35216	Nationwide	$1M–$20M	75% / 1.25	P	1–2 pts
Pacific Mutual Life Insurance Co. (Life Company)					
700 Newport Center Dr. Newport Beach, CA 92660	Nationwide (except New York)	$2M–$30M	75% / 1.2	P	1 pt

Source	Territory	Loan Size	LTV/ DSC	Type	Typical Fees
PriMerit Bank, FSB (Savings Bank)					
3300 W. Sahara Ave. Las Vegas, NV 89102	Nevada	$500T–$12M	75% / 1.2	P/C/A	1.5 pts
Sun Life Insurance Co. of America (Life Company)					
1 Sun America Center Century City, CA 90067	Nationwide	$2M and up	75% / 1.2	P	1 pt
Universal Bank, FSB (Savings Bank)					
1249 E. Katella Ave. Orange, CA 92667	Southern California	$200T–$2.2M	75% / 1.1	P	1–2 pts
Washington Mutual (Savings Bank)					
1201 Third Ave., Suite 1400 Seattle, WA 98101	Idaho Oregon Utah Washington	$100T–$5M	75% / 1.15	P	1.5–2 pts

COMMERCIAL MORTGAGE CONDUITS

The following is a list of several mortgage conduit partnerships. These partnerships consist of a lender and one or more loan originators. Mortgage conduit partnerships fund and pool commercial mortgages for securitization. Mortgage conduits recently have become a popular source for commercial property refinancing primarily because of the availability of funds and relatively quick deal closings. Conduit partnerships will consider deals nationwide.

Although most conduit lenders fund deals through their originators, it should be noted that some mortgage lenders cater directly to potential borrowers. These include Merrill Lynch, Lehman Brothers, Liberty Mortgage, and Nomura Asset Capital.

Source	Originators	Loan Size	LTV/DSC
Donaldson, Lufkin, Jenrette			
140 Broadway, 43rd Floor New York, NY 10005	Column Financial (404) 239-5300	$1M–$25M	80% / 1.25
Heller Real Estate Financial Services			
500 W. Monroe Chicago, IL 60661	Belgravia Capital (714) 724-8700	$1M–$5M	75% / 1.25
Lehman Bros.			
3 World Financial Ctr., 20th Flr. New York, NY 10285	Lehman Bros. (212) 526-5838	$800T and up	80% / 1.2
Liberty Mortgage Acceptance Corp.			
400 Capitol Mall, Suite 2300 Sacramento, CA 95814	Liberty Mortgage (916) 568-0100	$2M–$50M	75% / 1.25
Merrill Lynch Capital Markets			
250 Vesey St., N. Tower, 10th Flr. New York, NY 10281	CB Commercial (415) 772-0423	$1M–$15M	75% / 1.25
J.P. Morgan			
60 Wall St. New York, NY 10260-0060	Banc One (713) 785-3737 Home Savings (818) 814-7955	$1M–$15M	75% / 1.2
Nomura Asset Capital			
Two World Financial Ctr., Bldg. B New York , NY 10281	Bloomfield Acceptance (810) 644-8838	$1M–$15M	80% / 1.2
Prudential Securities			
One New York Plaza New York, NY 10292	Midland Comm. (800) 746-4623	$750T–$7.5M	75% / 1.2

Legend:

A= Acquisition Financing
C= Construction
DSC= Debt Service Coverage
LTV= Loan to Value
P= Permanent Financing
REIT= Real Estate Investment Trust

MONTHLY MANUFACTURED HOME COMMUNITY INTEGRITY INSPECTION CHECKLIST

MONTHLY MANUFACTURED HOME COMMUNITY INTEGRITY INSPECTION CHECKLIST

Jim Gossweiler

Community: _____

Manager(s): _____

Assistant Manager: _____

Maintenance Staff: _____

Month/Year: _____

I respectfully submit this monthly inspection report as evidence of my commitment to the success of this community, and the safety and well-being of the residents and community personnel.

_____
Manager

SOURCE: Federated Environmental, Baltimore, MD

INSPECTION ITEM	PASS or N/A	FAIL	CONCERN	ACTION TAKEN
ROAD SURFACES				
Streets free of debris, trash, and yard waste				
Streets free of potholes, rough spots, other				
Streets and drains free of sediment buildup				
Drain covers in good condition and secured in place				
Storm water draining from road surfaces				
Residents using permitted number spaces only				
Parking pads cracked, broken, oil-stained				
Curbs cracked, broken, missing, or oil-stained				
Other area(s)				
EXTERIOR LIGHTING				
Management office, walkways, parking				
Clubhouse/community mailbox building				
Laundry building(s)				
Maintenance building(s)				
Playground and recreational area(s)				
Basketball/Tennis courts				
Swimming pool(s)				
Community light poles, perimeter lights, gate				
INTERIOR LIGHTING				
Management office, covered walkways				
Clubhouse/community mailbox building				
Laundry building(s)				

INSPECTION ITEM	PASS or N/A	FAIL	CONCERN	ACTION TAKEN
Maintenance building(s)				
Swimming pool(s), i.e., lights in the pools				
Community-owned carports				
Other interior lighting				
COMMUNITY IMPROVEMENTS • roofs and rain gutters • sidewalks • exterior/interior walls • doors and hardware • paint/texturing condition • window assemblies • heating/cooling systems Management office				
Clubhouse/community mailbox building				
Laundry building(s)				
Maintenance building(s)				
Recreational pavillions, gazebos, others				
Swimming pool buildings, restrooms				
All community signage				
Other community improvements, walls, ornaments				
Leased and all owned homes				
COMMUNITY FENCING Community perimeter fencing				
Resident storage lot				
Interior fencing, i.e., on-lot well, wastewater treatment				
Other fencing				

INSPECTION ITEM	PASS or N/A	FAIL	CONCERN	ACTION TAKEN
UTILITIES/WATER				
Main water shut-off valve accessible and operational				
Main water valve flow meter operational				
Homesite water shut-offs operational (handles present and accessible)				
Submeter flow meters accessible and operational, no valve leaks				
Check valves or flow-back valves installed				
Resident reports of community leaks				
Residents warned to shut off water heaters during line repairs				
New home hook-ups checked for leaks, residents shown shut-off valve				
Submeter water valve sump covers in place and free of damage				
Exposed lines protected from freezing				
Residents are billed for usage if waste is detected (submetered homesites)				
• on-site water well				
Adequate chlorination supported with testing				
Well pump operation o.k., good pressure				
Cistern/water tank and lines free of leaks				
Regular testing conducted as required by state				

INSPECTION ITEM	PASS or N/A	FAIL	CONCERN	ACTION TAKEN
Wellhead/water lines protected from freezing				
High-pressure chlorine gas cylinders chained upright				
Resident reports of foul or strange-tasting water				
Well and water system secured against tampering				
Other items				
UTILITY/NATURAL GAS				
Main gas shut-off valve accessible and operational				
Main gas valve flow meter operational				
Main gas valve lock-out is <u>not</u> locked on!				
Main gas lines entering community not damaged				
Homesite gas shut-offs operational (wrench)				
Homesite gas valve lock-outs are <u>not</u> locked on!				
Submeter flow meters accessible and operational, no valve leaks				
Resident reports of gas leaks, strange odors				
Residents warned when gas is shut off				
New home hook-ups checked for leaks, residents shown shut-off valve				
• LPG tanks LPG cylinders at individual homes are chained upright				

INSPECTION ITEM	PASS or N/A	FAIL	CONCERN	ACTION TAKEN
Community LPG tanks inspected for leaks				
Community LPG tanks protected from damage				
Community LPG tanks placarded No Smoking				
Other items				
• Heating oil tanks Homesite tanks adequately supported				
Homesite tanks inspected for leaks				
Underground tanks and lines tested annually				
Other items				
UTILITY/SEWER Resident reports of leaks, clogging, or odors				
Sewer hook-ups secure on new homes				
Lift station(s) running properly				
Deoderant additive needed at lift station(s)				
Lift stations protected against tampering				
Other items				
• On-lot septic systems Resident reports of overflowing, odors				
Septic settling tanks adequately pumped				
Septic tank lids in good condition and in place				
Residents advised not to pour chemicals down drains				

INSPECTION ITEM	PASS or N/A	FAIL	CONCERN	ACTION TAKEN
Other items				
• Community sewerage treatment				
System operated by licensed company or Class A operator				
Resident reports of odors				
Proper management of chemicals, additives				
Appropriate discharge testing (if to sewer or creek)				
Discharge ponds handling flow				
Discharge area secured against trespassing				
Treatment system secured against trespassing				
Other items				
RECREATIONAL AREAS				
• Swimming pools				
Proper management of pool chemicals				
Filter room locked against tampering				
Available and stocked first aid kit w/eyewash				
Available life rings and shepherd's crook				
Appropriate placards and posted safety rules				
Certified lifeguard with current CPR certificate				
Baby pool suction drain cover in place and secure				
Regular testing of chlorine concentration				

INSPECTION ITEM	PASS or N/A	FAIL	CONCERN	ACTION TAKEN
"Buddy system" swimming only				
Adequate fencing around pool area				
Pool filter leaks or backflushing needed				
Pool filter is grounded and has ground fault interrupter switch				
Pool restrooms/changing rooms clean and in good repair				
Other items				
• Playgrounds				
Playground equipment in good repair				
Playground policed for broken glass, bottle caps, and pull tabs				
Playground equipment paint in good condition				
Playground inspected for potential dangerous conditions				
Is adult supervision of children on playground required?				
Other items				
GENERAL ITEMS				
Community free of litter and debris				
Vacated homesites clean within 24 hours				
No yard waste disposed in storm water ditches				
Notifications made to untidy residents				
Emergency numbers posted on office				

INSPECTION ITEM	PASS or N/A	FAIL	CONCERN	ACTION TAKEN
Community has contract with extermination company, resident reports				
Abandoned vehicles or other in resident storage disposed				
Abandoned homes removed or managed				
Residents warned of dangerous wild animals				
Residents with dogs and cats provide vaccination certificates				
Residents advised to have smoke detectors				
No resident dogs roam unattended				
No automobile repairs occurring on-site				
Large/dead tree limbs over/near homes trimmed				
Other items				
• Maintenance equipment All mowers/grass-cutting equipment in good repair				
Maintenance staff provided complete safety equipment and supplies				
Community vehicles in good repair and properly registered				
Equipment fuels/chemicals properly labelled & stored				
All vehicle and equipment damage reported				

DIRECTORY OF PRODUCTS AND SERVICES FOR MANUFACTURED HOME COMMUNITIES

DIRECTORY OF PRODUCTS AND SERVICES FOR MANUFACTURED HOME COMMUNITIES

Patti Greco

APPRAISAL AND COST ESTIMATION SERVICES

Allen & Associates
2000 N. Woodward Avenue,
　Suite 310
Bloomfield Hills, MI 48304
(810) 433-9630
Laurence Allen, MAI

Boeckh Building-Cost Manual
Box 510291
New Berlin, WI 53131
(800) 809-0016

Charles M. Ritley & Associates
23875 Commerce Park Road
Beachwood, OH 44122
(216) 464-8686 Roger Ritley, MAI

Cushman & Wakefield,
　Appraisal Division
150 S. Wacker Drive, Suite 3100
Chicago, IL 60606
(312) 551-1770 Mike Schaeffer

Datacomp Appraisal Systems
5250 Northland Drive, N.E.
Grand Rapids, MI 49505
(616) 363-8454 Ted Boers

F. W. Dodge Division
McGraw-Hill Publishers
1221 Avenue of the Americas
New York, NY 10020
(212) 512-2000

Kelley Blue Book
5 Oldfield
Irvine, CA 92718
(800) 444-1743

Marshall and Swift's Valuation
Services
1617 Beverly Boulevard
Los Angeles, CA 90026
(800) 526-2756

Mobile/Manufactured Home
Blue Book
29 North Wacker
Chicago, IL 60606
(800) 621-9907

N.A.D.A. Appraisal Guide
Box 7800
Costa Mesa, CA 92628
(714) 556-8511 Vince Pulsipher

APPRAISERS—REAL ESTATE

Act III
55 N., 200 W.
Lebanon, IN 46052
(317) 482-3984 Sharon Niccum

Brown, Chudleigh & Schuler
744 Cardley Avenue
Medford, OR 97504
(541) 772-8566 Greg Schuler

Field Adjusting, Inc.
112 Norcross St., Suite H
Roswell, GA 30075
(800) 864-0523 D. Arnold

Palmer, Groth & Pietka
110 SW Yarnhill Street
Portland, OR 97204
(503) 226-0983 T. Wright

Pardue, Heid, Church, Smith,
  Waller
4915 W. Cypress Street
Tampa, FL 33607
(813) 287-1020

Sheets, Hendrickson & Associates
3333 Henderson Boulevard,
  Suite 230
Tampa, FL 33609
(813) 871-3216 Bob Behrle

AUCTIONS

Manufactured Homes &
  Manufactured Home
  Communities
The Miles Company
Box 2228
Salisbury, NC 28145
(704) 637-2828 Jim Cox

**COIN-OPERATED LAUNDRY
SERVICES**

Automatic Laundry Co.
Box 39365
Denver, CO 80239
(303) 371-9274

Macke Laundry Service
122 Messner Drive
Wheeling, IL 60090
(800) 622-2141

WEB Service Co.
3690 Freemar Boulevard
Redondo Beach, CA 90278
(800) 421-6897

COMPUTER SOFTWARE AND COOPERATIVE PROCESSING SERVICES

American Computer Software
802 W. Broadway, #204
Madison, WI 53713
(608) 221-9449

Rent Manager
London Computer Systems
3246 Woodlake Court
Cincinnati, OH 45140
(800) 669-0871 Dave Hegemann

MRI Property Management
  Systems (cooperative processing)
23945 Mercantile Road
Cleveland, OH 44122
(216) 464-3225 Fred Goodman

PC Manager, The
170 East 17th Street, Suite 212
Costa Mesa, CA 92627
(714) 548-0303 Jim Washington

PRISM Computerized Solutions
8515 Douglas, Suite 17
Des Moines, IA 50322
(515) 270-0388 Jim Smidt

CONVERSION CONSULTANTS AND RESOURCES

Blair Group
5600 US 98 N., #7
Lakeland, FL 33809
(800) 274-5564 Bill Gorman

Brandywine Mobile Home
Community Services
2637 McCormick Drive
Clearwater, FL 34619
(813) 726-8868 Tod Eckhouse

Community Association Institute
(CAI)
1630 Duke Street, #300
Alexandria, VA 22314
(703) 548-8600

Florida Institute*
2530 State Road, #580
Clearwater, FL 34621
(813) 576-9480 Fred Yonteck
*a.k.a. National Society of
Homeowner Associations, Inc.

Lee Jay Celling & Associates, PA
20 N. Orange, #700
Orlando, FL 32801
(800) 330-1234

National Association of Housing
  Cooperatives (NAHC)
1614 King Street
Alexandria, VA 22314
(703) 549-5201

National Cooperative Bank
1401 Eye Street, N.W., Suite 700
Washington, DC 20005
(202) 336-7700

PMC Financial Services
2365 Skyfarm Drive
Hillsborough, CA 94010
(415) 375-8043 Deane Sargent

Van Alfus Financial Services
83 Montgomery Street
Jersey City, NJ 07302
(201) 434-6629 Art Goldberg

CREATIVE MARKETING BROCHURES

Greco Writing
902B Ridgefield Circle
Clinton, MA 01510
(508) 368-1022 Patti Greco
(Marketing communications
consultant)

CREDIT INFORMATION

Credit Information Corp.
5550 McKelvey Road, Suite 210
St. Louis, MO 63044
(800) 899-6396

Credit Interfaces
15050 Avenue of Science, #230
San Diego, CA 92128
(800) 456-4008

DEMOGRAPHICS

Claritas
53 Brown Road
Ithaca, NY 14850
(800) 234-5973

Equifax
5375 Mira Sorrento Place, #400
San Diego, CA 92121
(800) 866-6510

Market Statistics
355 Park Avenue South
New York, NY 10010
(800) 266-4714

DIRECTORIES

Fleets Guide to Financing
3343 Duke Street
Alexandria, VA 22314
(800) 336-3246

Manufactured Home
  Merchandiser (suppliers)
203 N. Wabash, #800
Chicago, IL 60601
(312) 236-3528 Herb Tieder

Meetings + Plus
Box 1981
Palm Springs, CA 92263
(619) 323-5462 Gordon Howe

RV & MH Aftermarket Association
11 S. LaSalle Street, #1400
Chicago, IL 60603
(312) 553-0300

DUE DILIGENCE

Credit Quality & Financial
   Consulting, Inc.
4334 Magnolia Street
Palm Beach, FL 33418
(407) 622-5893 George Gall, CPA

ENERGY MANAGEMENT & WATER CONSERVATION

Enviro-Check, Inc.
7121 Grand National Drive, #101
Orlando, FL 32819
(407) 352-2266

ENGINEERING AND LAND PLANNING SPECIALISTS

Alley and Associates
Box 897
Palm Harbor, FL 34682
(813) 787-3388 Dave Alley

Donald Westphal
512 Madison Avenue
Rochester, MI 48307
(810) 651-5518

Flint Survey & Engineering
5370 Miller Road, Suite 13
Swartz Creek, MI 48473
(810) 230-1333 Curt Karlson

Franklin Engineering
151 W. Jefferson Street
Franklin, IN 46131
(317) 736-7168 Steve Williams

Gerald Kessler and Associates
3760 Vance, #301
Wheat Ridge, CO 80033
(393) 756-1536 Gerald Kessler

IRIC
11 June Terrace
Lake Forest, IL 60045
(708) 234-8020 Herbert Behrend

McDermott Engineering
303 N. Placentia Avenue, Suite E
Fullerton, CA 92631
(714) 572-0376

QCI Development Consultants*
6541 N. Glade Way
Parker, CO 80134
(303) 840-9192 Bruce Melms
*a.k.a. Custom Comark Homes

Urban Research and Development
28 Bethlehem Plaza
Bethlehem, PA 18018
(215) 865-0701 Martin Gilchrist

Vaughn Shahinian & Associates
11185 Mora Drive
Los Altos, CA 94024
(415) 941-8592 Vaughn Shahinian

ENVIRONMENTAL CONSULTANTS

ATEC
8665 Bush Road
Indianapolis, IN 46256
(317) 577-1761

ENVIROTEL
1000 Nutt Road
Phoenixville, PA 19460
(610) 935-9177 Robert McIntyre

Federated Environmental
   Associates, Inc.
1314 Bedford Avenue
Baltimore, MD 21208
(410) 653-8434
Jim Gossweiler, Sr. V.P.

EXPERT WITNESS REGISTRY

TASA
1166 DeKalb Pike
Blue Bell, PA 19422
(800) 523-2319

FEASIBILITY CONSULTANTS

Consultants Resource Group
7520 W. Waters Avenue
Tampa, FL 33615
(813) 888-6341 Ed Hicks

Danter Co., The
30 Spruce Street
Columbus, OH 43215
(614) 221-9096 Kenneth Danter

Palmer, Groth & Pietka
2143 Hurley Way, #150
Sacramento, CA 95825
(916) 641-2206 Tim Wright, MAI

FEE MANAGEMENT FIRMS

Apollo Properties
307 W. 2nd Street
Mesa, AZ 85201
(602) 898-1939
Steve Pappas, CPM

Ashford Management Group
501 Main Street
Utica, NY 13501
(315) 724-4900 Russ Petralia

Bessier & Casenhiser
725 Brea Canyon Road, #6
Walnut, CA 91789
(714) 594-0501
R. Bessier, CPM, and
K. Casenhiser, CPM

Evans Management Services
871 38th Avenue
Santa Cruz, CA 95602
(408) 475-0335 Greg Evans

Love Realty
2951 Flowers Road S., #220
Atlanta, GA 30341
(404) 457-4395 Bob Love, CPM

Martin Newby Co.
3801 Bee Ridge Road
Sarasota, FL 34233
(941) 923-1456 Martin Newby

MDL Group
516 S. 6th Street, Suite 100
Las Vegas, NV 89101
(702) 388-1800 Tim Behrendt

Star Mobilehome Park
  Management
22992 Millcreek Road, Suite A
Laguna Hills, CA 92653
(714) 951-9565 Mike Cirillo

Steiner and Associates
5012 W. Lemon Street
Tampa, FL 33609
(813) 289-0500 Nelson Steiner

Storz Management Co.
9152 Greenback Lane, #3
Orangevale, CA 95662
(916) 989-5333 Jerry Storz

FINANCING FOR REAL ESTATE

Acquisitions Mortgage Co.
3146 Bristol Road
Warrington, PA 18976
(215) 343-9180

Belgravia Capital Corp.
19900 MacArthur Boulevard,
  #1100
Irvine, CA 92715
(714) 724-8700 Erik Paulson

Bloomfield Acceptance Co.
260 E. Brown Street, #350
Birmingham, MI 48009
(810) 644-8838 Dan Bober

Crown Capital Group
620 Crown Oak Centre Drive
Longwood, FL 32750
(407) 767-9553 Dean Hauck

Gorham Financial Corp.
1415 Nohilae Drive, #290
Minneapolis, MN 55422
(612) 546-9121 Frank Commers

Heller RE Financial Services
500 West Monroe Street,
  15th Floor
Chicago, IL 60661
(312) 441-6761

Love Funding Corp.
1220 19th Street N.W., #801
Washington, DC 20036
(202) 887-8475

Manufactured Housing
  Community Bankers
20371 Irvine Avenue
Santa Ana Heights, CA 92707
(714) 438-2643 David Young

Manufactured Housing Resources
  Group
1675 Broadway, #1020
Denver, CO 80202
(303) 592-4363 Roderick Knoll

Monte Klein Co.
Box 7481
Menlo Park, CA 94026
(415) 854-6355

SJS Realty Services
51 Sherwood Terrace
Lake Bluff, IL 60044
(708) 615-2250 Mark Siegel

Suburban Mortgage
7316 Wisconsin Avenue, #208
Bethesda, MD 20814
(301) 654-8616 Kyle Poole

FORMS AND BOOKKEEPING
SYSTEMS

Business Forms of America
9321 Kirby Drive
Houston, TX 77054
(800) 231-0329

Deluxe Business Forms and
   Supplies
980 Elkton Drive
Colorado Springs, CO 80907
(800) 843-4294

Jenkins Business Forms
Box "B"
Mascoutah, IL 62258
(800) 851-4424

McBee Systems
299 Cherry Hill Road
Parsippany, NJ 07054

NEBS Business Forms and Supplies
500 Main Street
Groton, MA 01471
(800) 843-4294

Peachtree Business Forms
Box 13290
Atlanta, GA 30324
(800) 241-4623

PMN Publishing
Box 47024
Indianapolis, IN 46247
(317) 888-7156

Professional Publishing
122 Paul Drive
San Rafael, CA 94903
(800) 288-2006

Reynolds & Reynolds
3555 S. Kettering Boulevard
Dayton, OH 45439
(800) 531-9055

Safeguard Business Systems
Box 7501
Ft. Washington, PA 19034
(800) 523-6660

Thompson Business Forms
2200 Warner Street
San Antonio, TX 78201
(800) 842-0191

HERITAGE GROUP

RV/MH Heritage Foundation and
   Museum
801 Benham Avenue
Elkhart, IN 46516
(219) 293-2344 Carl Ehry

HUMAN RESOURCES
ASSESSMENT

Stoneham Associates
235 Pine, Suite 1300
San Francisco, CA 94104
(415) 383-4820 Donna Stoneham

INDUSTRY STATISTICS

Berlin Research
731 Pacific Street, #1
San Luis Obispo, CA 93401
(805) 541-0171 Bronson Berlin

Business Trend Analysis
2171 Jericho Turnpike
Commack, NY 11725
(516) 462-5454

Dr. Thomas Nutt-Powell
100 Crescent Boulevard
Needham, MA 02194
(617) 449-7752

Dr. Waldo Born
Eastern Illinois University
Charleston, IL 61920
(217) 581-6201

Foremost Insurance Co.
5800 Foremost Drive, Box 2450
Grand Rapids, MI 49501
(800) 527-3905
(616) 956-8188 Ann Calomeni

George Carter and Affiliates
767 Park Avenue
Oradell, NJ 07649
(201) 265-7766

John DeWolf
11424 Waterview Cluster
Reston, VA 22090
(703) 437-0711

Joint Center for Housing Studies
79 John F. Kennedy
Cambridge, MA 02138
(617) 495-7908 William Apgar

Kammrath & Associates
1202 E. Missouri Avenue, #15
Phoenix, AZ 85014
(602) 263-5340 Bob Kammrath

Manufactured Housing Institute
2101 Wilson Boulevard, Suite 610
Arlington, VA 22201
(703) 558-0400 Jerry Connors

National Conference of States on
  Building Codes and Standards
  (NCSBCS)
505 Huntmar Park Drive, #210
Herndon, VA 22070
(703) 437-0100

Packaged Facts (reports)
625 Avenue of the Americas
New York, NY 10011
(212) 627-3228 David Weiss

PMN Publishing,
  "The Allen Report"
Box 47024
Indianapolis, IN 46247
(317) 888-7156 Nora Freese

Robert Siegel and Associates
26 Trianon Drive
Kenner, LA 70065
(504) 586-2000

Statistical Surveys, Inc.
1693 Sutherland Drive, S.E.
Grand Rapids, MI 49805
(616) 281-9898 Tom Walworth

Timberline Associates
11027 Timberline Drive
Shelby Township, MI 48316
(810) 731-2964 Paul Thacher

Welford Sanders
2658 N. Sherman Boulevard
Milwaukee, WI 53210

INSTALLATION SPECIALISTS AND EQUIPMENT

Manufactured Housing Resources
Box 9
Nassau, DE 19969
(302) 645-5552 George Porter

Soiltest, Inc. (pocket penetrometer)
Box 8004
Lake Bluff, IL 60044
(800) 323-1242

INSURANCE INFORMATION

Barrett & Associates
7 W. Square Lake Road
Bloomfield Hills, MI 48302
(810) 452-9881 Mark Barrett

Hogg Robinson of Michigan
Box 5007
Southfield, MI 48086
(313) 948-5650 Mark Barrett

John Carriero & Son
Box 312
Mechanicville, NY 12118
(518) 664-9882

LaRue Insurance
3089 Fairview Road
Greenwood, IN 46142
(317) 889-1000 Gary Cleveland

INVESTMENT INFORMATION RESOURCES

John T. Reed
342 Bryan Drive
Danville, CA 94526
(800) 635-5425
(RE-related publications)

LAKE MANAGEMENT SUPPLIES

Aquatic Control
Box 100
Seymour, IN 47274
(812) 497-2410

LANDSCAPING INFORMATION

American Nurseryman
77 W. Washington, #2100
Chicago, IL 60602
(800) 621-5727

LOAN AMORTIZATION TABLES

Financial Publishing Co.
82 Brookline Avenue
Boston, MA 02251
(800) 247-3214

MAILBOXES

Salsbury Mailboxes
1010 E. 62nd Street
Los Angeles, CA 90001
(800) 323-3003

MANAGEMENT CONSULTANTS

GFA Management, Inc.
Box 47024
Indianapolis, IN 46247
(317) 791-8114 George
Allen, CPM

JLT & Associates
9 Elmwood
Irvine, CA 92714
(714) 297-2921 John Turzer

John Lehman
820 Sylvan Avenue
Mountainview, CA 94041
(415) 968-7626

Manufactured Housing Solutions
3325 Bonnie Hill Drive
Los Angeles, CA 90068
(213) 882-6563
Barry McCabe

Robert Sage
Box 7783
Winter Haven, FL 33883
(813) 299-9941

MANAGEMENT RESOURCES

Construction Bookstore
  (mail order)
Box 2959
Gainesville, FL 32602
(800) 253-0541

"Find People Fast"
INFOMAX, Inc.
4600 Chippewa, #244
St. Louis, MO 63116
(314) 481-3000

Institute of Real Estate
  Management
430 N. Michigan Avenue
Chicago, IL 60610
(312) 329-6000
(CPM & ARM Programs)

J. Wiley & Sons, Inc.
605 Third Avenue
New York, NY 10158
(212) 850-6000

Lincoln Graduate Center
Box 12528
San Antonio, TX 78212
(800) 531-5333 Dr. Gary Dean

Manufactured Housing
  Educational Institute
2101 Wilson Boulevard, Suite 610
Arlington, VA 22201
(703) 558-0400 Ann Parnham
(ACM Program)

National Apartment Association
1111 14th Street N.W., Suite 900
Washington, DC 20005
(202) 842-4050
(CAM Program)

National Association of
  Homebuilders
1201 15th Street N.W.
Washington, DC 20005
(800) 368-5242
(RAM Program)

National Association of Real
  Estate Investment Trusts
1129 Twentieth Street, N.W.,
Suite 705
Washington, DC 20036
(202) 785-8717

PMN Publishing,
  "The Allen Letter"
Box 47024
Indianapolis, IN 46247
(317) 888-1703 Nora Freese

Texas Real Estate Research Center
Texas A & M University
College Station, TX 77843

Urban Land Institute
625 Indiana Avenue N.W., #400
Washington, DC 20004
(202) 624-7000

NEWSLETTERS FOR RESIDENTS

Newsletter Express
3500 DePauw, LL 1900
Indianapolis, IN 46268
(317) 876-8916

OUTDOOR FURNITURE

Texacraft Outdoor Furnishings
Box 741558
Houston, TX 77274
(800) 231-9790

PARKING CONTROL SUPPLIES

Peachtree Business Products
1284 Logan Circle
Atlanta, GA 30318
(800) 241-4623

PERSONNEL RECRUITING

Techention-Spangler and
   Associates
Box 718
Camdenton, MO 65020
(314) 346-4165

Vernon, Sage and Associates
Box 24582
Fort Worth, TX 76124
(817) 451-8785 Tony Vernon

PIERS—STEEL

C & R Pier Manufacturing
275 S. Rancho Avenue
Colton, CA 92324
(909) 872-6444

PROPERTY TAX RESEARCH AND APPEAL

Cocon, Inc.
Box 159
Belleville, MI 48112
(313) 699-3430

Easley McCaleb and Stallings
3980 DeKalb Technical Parkway,
   #775
Atlanta, GA 30340
(800) 843-0139
(404) 454-9998

Ennes & Associates
3275 N. Arlington Heights Road,
   #410
Arlington Heights, IL 60004
(708) 577-6500 Carl P. Pharr

RENTAL UNIT SALES

Homes Direct, Inc.
216 Third Avenue South
Jacksonville Beach, FL 32250
(904) 246-6688 James Stock

RESIDENT RETENTION

Let's Party! c/o Williams Design
P.O. Box 277
Yuma, AZ 85366
(520) 329-1262 Mindy Williams
(Activities Guide)

RESIDENT SCREENING

Americhek, Inc.
7825 North Dixie Drive
Dayton, OH 45414
(513) 454-1700

RETAIL SALES AND MARKETING CONSULTING SERVICES

The Housing Marketplace
145 W. Christina Boulevard
Lakeland, FL 33813
(813) 648-1487 Joe Adams

JCA
Box 704
Bettendorf, IA 52722
(800) 336-0339 Bill and Judy Carr

Developing Attitudes
9648 Kingston Pike #2
Knoxville, TN 37922
(423) 539-1504 Less Grebe

Nancy J. Friedman
  "Telephone Doctor"
30 Hollenberg Court
Bridgeton, MO 63044
(800) 882-9911

Roger Huddleston
Box 739
Mahomet, IL 61853
(217) 586-4444

R.S. Associates
2507 Eastland Avenue
Nashville, TN 37206
(800) 356-7065 Robert Skillen

Salesmaker Associates
Americus Center, #705
6th and Hamilton Streets
Allentown, PA 18101
(215) 434-2643
Grayson E. Schwepfinger

SCALE MODEL HOMES

Scale Model Homes Co.
Box 47024
Indianapolis, IN 46247
(317) 888-7156

SECURITY CONSULTANT

Dietz & Associates
709 Rush Creek, Suite 100
Allen, TX 75002
(214) 727-1415
John Dietz, CPP, CFE

SIGNS

Como Signs & Supplies
Box 5337, 806 Jefferson Street
Lafayette, LA 70502
(800) 232-0448

Grimco, Inc.
3928 Delor Street
St. Louis, MO 63116
(314) 481-4404

Mobile Advertising Sign & Display
Box 8952
Mattoon, IL 61938
(217) 967-5436 Don Dominix

Tri-Safety Symbol Signs
Box 45134
Baton Rouge, LA 70895
(504) 927-1478 Anne Stentiford

Vulcan Signs
Box 850
Foley, AL 36536
(800) 633-6845

SURVEYOR

AES Group, Inc.
605 State Street
Newburgh, IN 47630
(800) 867-8783 Tina Williams

SWIMMING POOL
CONSULTANTS AND SUPPLIES

Bel-Aqua
750 Main Street
New Rochelle, NY 10805
(914) 235-2200

Form Management Services (tags)
150 Airport Drive, #9
Westminster, MD 21157
(800) 541-2361

Recreation Supply Co.
Box 2757
Bismarck, ND 58502
(800) 437-8072

Recreonics
Box 34575
Louisville, KY 40232

Spear Corporation
Box 3
Roachdale, IN 46172
(317) 522-1126

Water Environment Federation
601 Wythe Street
Alexandria, VA 22314
(800) 666-0206

WATER LEAK DETECTION

Hydro-Tech, Inc.
805 S.E. 15th Street
Deerfield Beach, FL 33441
(305) 425-0954 Earl King

WATER METER INSTALLATION
AND BILLING

Aquameter, Inc.
520 South 5th Street
Columbus, OH 43206
(800) 860-0008 Kathleen Lyde

B & B Water/Wastewater
4402 S. Division Street
Moline, MI 49335
(616) 877-4196

Digital Metering, Inc.
8551 154th Avenue, NE
Redmond, WA 98052
(206) 885-0900

Park Utilities, Inc.
Box 998
Carmichael, CA 95609
(916) 944-1824 Tom Grant

SLC Water Meter Co.
3059 Dixie Highway
Pontiac, MI 48055
(313) 673-8539

U.S. Energy
500 Sun Valley Drive, #H-2
Roswell, GA 30076
(404) 998-3996

WaterMaster of Columbus
1255 North High Street
Columbus, OH 43201
(800) 444-9283 Tracy Harvey

SETTING A VALUE ON YOUR MH COMMUNITY

COMMUNITY CORNER

PMN Publishing
Box 47024
Indianapolis, IN 46247

SETTING A VALUE ON YOUR MH COMMUNITY

By George Allen, CPM

George Allen is president of GFA Management in Indianapolis. GFA specializes in residential and commercial real estate management. For more information, contact Allen at GFA Management, Box 47024, Indianapolis, Ind. 46247, 317/888-7156.

"How much is my manufactured home community worth?" This is the second most frequent question I'm asked by community investors. (The most frequent question I hear is, "Where can I find a manufactured home community to buy?")

Without a doubt, manufactured home valuation continues to be a lively and important question among investment property owners and managers.

Real estate professionals recognize three traditional approaches to estimate the value of a multi-family, income-producing property.

Replacement value is simply what it would cost to duplicate the same manufactured home community today. The methodology is simple—undepreciated raw land cost at current market value, plus the appropriately depreciated cost to replace existing improvements, such as utilities and street infrastructure and buildings, if any.

Various "building cost manuals" are referenced to support these calculations. The most accurate data, of course, would come from a duplicate manufactured home community just completed across the street from the subject property. But that's highly unlikely to exist.

Income capitalization is the second traditional valuation method. This procedure places a current value on the income stream—specifically the net operating income (NOI)—produced by a manufactured home community or any other residential, income-producing property.

A capitalization rate, or "cap rate," is usually calculated by researching and examining the NOI (rent collected minus operating expenses, but not including debt service or mortgage payments) and sale prices of recently sold similar properties within the same market area.

At the time of the sale, when the NOI of a given comparable property is divided by the selling price, the result is a cap rate (expressed as a percentage) that serves as a divisor to the subject property's NOI.

For example, a $250,000 NOI divided by an 11 percent cap rate equals an estimated $2,272,727. Obviously, the more comparable sales one has to work with locally, the more accurate is the cap rate in estimating the value of the manufactured home community.

The third traditional method of estimating value is the market approach. This means determining what other communities have sold for recently in the immediate market area.

Professional real estate appraisers research and compute values using all three approaches, weighing the alternatives based on the accuracy, immediacy and applicability of available data.

This is why a capable and experienced real estate appraiser is always preferred when calculating the value of a manufactured home community for sale, purchase or refinancing. And make sure the appraiser you select understands the peculiarities of manufactured home communities.

Recently, I have created an easy-to-use value estimation alternative for the owner/manager of a manufactured home community—the valuation calculation worksheet (VCW). It is designed solely for communities operating at an economic occupancy above 84 percent.

Economic occupancy

What is economic occupancy? It's the total number of rental homesites occupied and paid, divided by the number of rental homesites developed and available for occupancy. For example, 475 occupied and paid sites divided by 500 total available sites equals 95 percent economic occupancy. Obviously, unpaid and concessioned rental homesites would lower economic occupancy.

There are three major steps to use the worksheet:

Step A involves assigning values, from a ½ point to 2 points, to six key property characteristics.

Step B identifies and rates adjustment factors that will influence "per site" values later in the calculation. The adjustment range is plus or minus $500 per homesite.

Step C is the valuation calculation procedure that interrelates rental income, operating expenses, homesite point values and adjustment factors to calculate a total estimated value of a specific community.

All three steps and the respective data are viewed strictly from the property owner/seller perspective. Would-be investors and buyers will generally view several of the key characteristics and adjustment factors differently.

Characteristics in Step A and factors in Step B marked by a single asterisk (*) will be viewed differently by owners estimating value and planning to hold versus owners estimating value and planning to sell and wanting to attract serious prospective buyers now.

Steps marked with a double asterisk (**) require making a judgment call on whether to include a 2 percent vacancy factor.

Step A

Assign points in the following six key categories from a low of ½ to 2 points per characteristic:

1. Location: Remote and poor proximity equals ½ point; good desirability, accessibility and proximity to employment, services, transportation equals 2 points.

2. Number of rental homesites: If there are between five and 49 homesites, assign ½ point; 50-99 homesite equals 1 point; 100-199 homesites equals 2 points.

3. Homesite sizes: If all homesites are for single-section homes (4,999 square feet and smaller), assign ½ point; if there is a 50/50 mix of single- and multisection homesites, write in 1 point; if all homesites are multi-section (5,000 square feet and larger), mark down 2 points.

4. Utilities:* If the utilities are old, privately owned and in poor condition, assign a value of ½ point; if private and in fair condition, 1 point; if private and in excellent condition or public with fair rates and buried lines, 2 points.

5. Amenities:* If there are no amenities, factor in ½ point; minimal amenities merits 1 point; a top quality property with a swimming pool and clubhouse (if those qualities are desirable in your local market) deserves 2 points.

6. Overall curb appeal:* Marginal to fair curb appeal receives ½ point; good curb appeal gets 1 point; excellent curb appeal—with landscaping, off-street parking, adequate setbacks, wide curvilinear streets (versus a grid pattern) and homes with lap-siding and shingle roofs—merits 2 points.

Now add the points from all six categories, deduct them from 20 and determine the result. Next, factor in the dollar figures as follows:

• *Actual rent collected during the past 12 months:* This does *not* include income from new and resale home sales, nor miscellaneous or rental home income. Is there a steady and growing income stream? What is the income? Write it down.

• *Actual operating expenses during the past 12 months:* Debt service and depreciation dollars don't count here. Consider including 5 percent for a property management fee and 1 percent for capital reserves.

• *Operating expense ratio (OER):* The national OER is 37.8 percent. In the model, the OER is 40 percent. The formula divides total operating expenses by the total rent collected.

Step B

Decide whether each of the following factors adds to or reduces a property's value by plus or minus $500 per rental homesite.

1. Homesite density: If there are seven or more homesites per acre, subtract $500; if there are six or fewer homesites per acre, add $500. The density formula is the number of developed homesites divided by the number of developed acres.

2. Economic occupancy: If economic occupancy is less than 84 percent, subtract $500. If economic occupancy is 85-94 percent, write down $0. If economic occupancy is 95 percent or better, add $500. (See line item 1 for the formula.)

3. Present rent level:* If the present rent level is low for the market, subtract $500; if high for the market, indicate $0; if in the midrange for the market, add $500.

4. Number of rental homes on-site:* Above 3 percent equals –$500; 2 percent or less equals +$500.

5. Is restrictive landlord-tenant legislation or rent control enforced locally?: Yes equals –$500; no equals +$500.

6. Contiguous raw land available and zoned for common use: Yes equals –$500; no equals $0.

The following four items are optional:

• *Licensed to operate, if appropriate:* Yes or no?

• *Significant effect of miscellaneous income stream*:* Determine a positive or negative percentage.

• *Resident base and mix and pride of ownership:* Yes or no.

• *Effect of area occupancy level and rent structure:* Determine a plus or minus dollar figure.

Now, calculate the cumulative total of valuation adjustment factors at plus or minus $500 per site. The cumulative total should not exceed plus or minus $1,500 per homesite.

Step C

The data collected in Steps A and B are formulated here.

1. Rent collected $_____ ** minus operating expenses $_____ equals the net operating income (NOI) $_____.

2. The NOI (determined in line 1) divided by the key point total from Step A (expressed as a decimal).

The NOI $_____ divided by the point divisor _____ equals the preliminary value $_____.

3. The preliminary value $_____ is divided by the number of occupied and paid homesites, which equals $_____ per site.

4. The value per site $_____ plus or minus the adjustment per site _____ from Step B equals the adjusted site value $_____.

5. The adjusted site value of $_____ is multiplied by the number of occupied and paid homesites _____ which equals the subtotal value $_____.

6. The adjusted site value $_____ is multiplied by the vacant and unpaid homesites _____ multiplied by 0.5 (value discount) which equals the value subtotal $_____.

7. Add the two subtotals (line items 5 and 6) to obtain the total estimated value of the manufactured home community $_____.

This is an interesting way to evaluate your community. If you would like a free copy of this worksheet, contact me by phone or mail. I'd also appreciate your input, pro or con, about this new format and methodology. □

GFA
MANAGEMENT

P.O. Box 47024
Indianapolis, Indiana 46247
(317) 888-7156

Manufactured Home MERCHANDISER
May 1995
Reprinted by permission

VALUATION CALCULATION WORKSHEET (VCW)
for owners and sellers of ground lease-type
MANUFACTURED HOME COMMUNITIES
operating at 85%+ economic occupancy✦

I. Name of the Property _____ Date: _____
    Physical Address: _____ Zip: _____
    Contact Person/Role: _____ Phone: (   ) _____
    # Devoloped Acres: _____ Average monthly site rent: $ _____ Age of property: _____ yrs.
    ✦ # Sites occupied and paid: _____ (+) # sites fully developed: _____ (=) _____ % economic occupancy✦

STEP A. KEY PROPERTY CHARACTERISTICS . . . viewed from owner/seller perspective of operation
Assign points in 6 Key Characteristics, from low of 1/2 point to maximum of 2 points.

1. LOCATION. Remote and poor proximity = 1/2 pt.; Good desirability, accessibility and proximity = 1 pt.; excellent
    neighborhood, desirability, accessibility and proximity to employment, services, transportation = 2 pts. ____ point(s)

2. NUMBER RENTAL HOMESITES. 5-49 = 1/2 pt.; 50-99 = 1 pt.; 100-199 = 1.5 pts.; 200+ = 2 pts. ____ point(s)

3. HOMESITE SIZES. All singlesection (4,999 sq. ft. and smaller) = 1/2 pt;
    approximately 50/50 mix = 1 pt.; All multisection (5,000 sq. ft. and larger) = 2 pts. ____ point(s)

4. UTILITIES. *1. Old, private and poor condition = 1/2 pt.; Private and OK condition = 1 pt.;
    Private and excellent condition or Public with fair rates and buried = 2 pts. ____ point(s)

5. AMENITIES. *1. None = 1/2 pt.; Minimal = 1 pt.; Top quality property with swimming pool and
    clubhouse - if desirable in local market = 2 pts. ____ point(s)

6. OVERALL CURB APPEAL. *1 Marginal to fair = 1/2 pt.; Good = 1 pt.; Excellent and better with
    landscaping, off-street parking, adequate setbacks, wide curvilinear (vs. grid pattern) streets,
    lap-sided and shingled homes = 2 pts. ____ point(s)

7. ADD POINTS from all 6 categories, deduct from 20, and put result here: _____ point(s)

8. ACTUAL RENT COLLECTED (no new or resale home sales $, miscellaneous, or rental home
    income) during last 12 month period.*2. Is there a steady and growing income stream? Y/N___$ _____ income

9. ACTUAL OPERATING EXPENSES (no debt service or depreciation $; consider including 5%
    for property management fee and 1% for capital reserves) for same 12 month period. $ _____ expense

10. OPERATING EXPENSE RATIO (national OER = 37.8%; Model = 40%)
    Formula: total operating expense + total rent collected; line 9 + line 8 = OER benchmark _____ %OER

STEP B. VALUATION ADJUSTMENT FACTORS . . . viewed from owner/seller perspective of operation
Decide whether each factor adds to or reduces property's value by maximum of ± $500/homesite.

1. DENSITY OF HOMESITES.*1. 7+/acre = -$500; 6 or less/acre = +$500. ± $_____
    Density formula: # developed homesites + # developed acres.

2. ECONOMIC OCCUPANCY. Less than 84% = -$500; 85-94% = $-0-;
    95% and better = +$500. Formula: see ✦ at beginning of worksheet. ± $_____

3. PRESENT RENT LEVEL. *1. low for market = -$500; high for market = $-0-;
    mid-range for market = +$500. ± $_____

4. NUMBER OF RENTAL HOMES ON -SITE. *1. 3% + = -$500; 2% or less = +$500. ± $_____

5. ADVERSE OR RESTRICTIVE LANDLORD-TENANT LEGISLATION AND/OR RENT CONTROL in effect locally? Yes = -$500; no = +$500.   ± $_____

6. CONTIGUOUS RAW LAND AVAILABLE AND ZONED for like use? Yes = +$500; no = -0-.   ± $_____

7. OPTIONAL: e.g. licensed to operate, if appropriate. Yes = +$500 or No = -$500.   ± $_____   optional

8. OPTIONAL: e.g. significant effect of miscellaneous income stream? *1 and *2.   ± $_____   optional

9. OPTIONAL: e.g. resident base and mix; pride in home ownership? Y/N   ± $_____   optional

10. OPTIONAL: e.g. effect of area occupancy level and rent structure.   ± $_____   optional

11. CUMULATIVE TOTAL OF VALUATION ADJUSTMENT FACTORS at ± $500/site, with cumulative total not to exceed ± $1,500/homesite on this line: ± $_____

STEP C. VALUATION CALCULATION . . . using data from STEPS A and B above . . .

1. RENT COLLECTED $_____ *3 (-) OPERATING EXPENSES $_____ = $_____ NOI

2. a) NET OPERATING INCOME (from line above) divided by Key Point Total from Step A, expressed as a decimal (e.g. 9 points + 100 = .09 divisor.
2. b) $_____ NOI (+) _____ point divisor = preliminary value of $_____

3. Preliminary Value $_____ (+) _____ occupied and paid homesites = $_____   per site adjusted

4. Value per site, $_____ (±)_____ adjustment per homesite from Step B = $_____   site value value

5. Adjusted Site Value of $_____ (X) _____ # occupied and paid homesites = $_____   subtotal

6. Adjusted Site Value of $_____ (X) _____ # vacant and unpaid homesites / x .50 value discount = $_____   value subtotal

7. ADD two subtotals (lines 5 and 6 above) together to obtain the   **Total**
TOTAL ESTIMATED VALUE of the MANUFACTURED HOME COMMUNITY . . . = $_____   **Value**

FOOTNOTES:
*1. These characteristics (Step A) and factors (Step B) will be viewed and valued differently by owners estimating value and planning to hold vs. owners estimating value and planning to sell and wanting to attract serious prospective buyers now. The latter perspective will generally be similar to buyers of quality properties.
*2. Cable TV and phone commissions; MH brokerage; rule of parts and service.
*3. A personal judgement call whether to include a 2% vacancy factor here or not.

DISCLAIMER. This VALUATION CALCULATION WORKSHEET FOR MANUFACTURED HOME COMMUNITIES is distributed as a handy, easy-to-use, self-help guide to estimating the possible value of a manufactured home community. The services of experienced, certified, licensed real estate value appraisers should always be retained for best results. Accuracy of results wholly dependent upon data selected and calculated by VCW user.

Designed by George Allen CPM, October 29, 1994

PMN Publishing
P.O. Box #47024
Indianapolis, IN 46247
(317) 888-7156

This form available for purchase in tablet format.
Property Management Form #118
Copyright Oct 1994
Revised January 1996

GLOSSARY

Absorption: The filling of space, such as the rental of units or sale of a tract. The time or rate must be estimated and considered as part of the owner's (usually the builder) costs.

ACM: Accredited Community Manager. MHEI's designation for professional on-site managers of manufactured home communities. See MHEI.

Acquisition costs: Costs of acquiring property other than purchase price.

Ad valorem: "According to value." Using the value of the item taxed to ascertain the amount of tax.

Agent: One authorized to represent or act in behalf of another (the principal), usually in business matters.

Amenity: A feature or benefit in addition to the basic homesite; for example, swimming pool, clubhouse.

Amortization: Gradual repayment of a debt (that is, principal of a loan) through a series of payments made over a period of time.

Ancillary income: Income received from on-site sources other than homesite rent.

ANSI: American National Standards Institute. The national coordinating institution for voluntary standardization in the United States.

Appraisal: An opinion of value based on a factual analysis of the personal or real property being valued.

Appreciation: Increase in value over a period of time, usually caused by inflation, economic factors, and improvements to property.

APR: Annual percentage rate. The true percentage of interest charged on an annualized basis.

Back money: Refers to profit that the retailer receives for other than the sale of a manufactured home or accessories, on which the retailer pays no sales commission. The two major items in back money are retailer reserve (participation) and insurance commissions.

Balloon mortgage: Long-term loan paid off in a lump sum at a specific term.

Berm: Earthen mound used to control drainage or as a screening buffer between properties.

BOCA: Building Officials and Code Administrators.

Boot: Anything of value given or received in lieu of cash, for example, a boat, automobile.

Break-even: Percentage of income necessary for an income property to pay all operating expenses and mortgages.

Broker: One licensed by a state to conduct business as a broker of real estate, insurance, securities, and so forth.

CABO: Council of American Building Officials.

Cap or **Capitalization rate:** A current rate of return calculated by dividing the net operating income of a property by its estimated value.

Capital: Money used to create income, either as an investment in a business or income property.

Capital gain: The measure of taxable profit pursuant to the sale of an asset.

Cash flow: Flow of cash through a company; also the money a property owner can pocket after paying all expenses and mortgage.

Catch basin: A receptacle located where a street gutter opens into a storm sewer, designed to convey storm water.

CC&Rs: Conditions, covenants, and restrictions relating to a piece of real property.

Chattel: Personal property, as contrasted with real property.

Collage: Graphic grouping of photos in a display for marketing or information purposes.

Collateral security: Valuable consideration in addition to the personal obligation of a borrower.

Comprehensive plan: Social, physical, and economic development of a community described in a compilation of goals, policies, and maps.

Condominium: Individual property ownership of a specific homesite or apartment with an individual interest in the land and other parts of the structure or common area with other owners.

Construction loan: A loan to finance the improvement of real estate.

Contingencies: Plans subject to the occurrence of specified but uncertainly timed events.

Contour map: A map that uses lines (most always curved) to outline the configuration and elevation of surface areas.

Cooperative or **Co-op:** Right to occupy a unit or site is based on purchase of stock in the corporation owning the property or building.

CPM: Certified Property Manager. IREM designation of professional real estate manager.

Cul-de-sac: A street open at only one end, usually with a large rounded end.

Curb appeal: How a rental property looks to the casual passerby; its overall appearance, good or bad.

Curb cut: Apron of a driveway where curb has been cut away.

Curtailment: Reduction in principal owed on floor-planned manufactured homes in a retailer's inventory. This is in accord with lender and manufacturer's repurchase agreement, stipulating that principal be reduced per wear and tear and aging of homes.

Curvilinear: Having boundaries of curved lines; architectural design.

DC or **DSC:**   Debt coverage or debt service coverage. The degree by which an income property's annual NOI exceeds the amount of the annual mortgage on the subject property. Written various ways, but 1=1/1.0 indicates NOI exceeds DS by 10%.

Debt service: Mortgage payment, interest, and principal paid each month to mortgagor.

Decedents: Ones who have died.

Demographics: Statistical information relative to planning new business or expansion of same.

Density: Number of dwelling units in a given area of land.

Depreciation: Decrease in value owing to deterioration and/or obsolescence.

DER: Department of Environmental Regulation.

Due diligence: The process of property inspection and evaluation of financial records between the time a bona fide offer to purchase is made and accepted, and actual consummation of the transaction.

Earthwork: The moving and reshaping of surface contours.

Easement: A right that one has in the land of another, created by grant, agreement, prescription, reservation, or necessary implication.

EEOC: Equal Employment Opportunity Commission. A regulatory body charged with enforcing equality within the employment cycle.

Effluent: Flow of treated sewage from a wastewater treatment facility.

Elevation: Exterior design of a structure as viewed from the front or side.

Encumbrance: Lien, charge, or claim against real property, but does not prevent transfer of title.

EPA: Environmental Protection Agency.

Equity: Amount of capital one has invested in a property over and above any mortgage indebtedness.

Escrow: An instrument in the hands of a third party that is held for delivery until certain acts are performed or conditions fulfilled.

Estoppel Certificate: A legal document that, when completed fully and accurately, describes exactly who lessees are and the terms of their present lease.

FDIC: Federal Deposit Insurance Corporation. Insures deposits at commercial and savings banks.

FED or **FRB:** Federal Reserve Board. Nation's central bank.

Fee simple: The most complete form of real property ownership.

FEMA: Federal Energy Management Administration.

FHA: Federal Housing Administration. Provides a variety of home and loan insurance programs to lending institutions through the U.S. Department of Housing and Urban Development.

FHBM: Flood hazard boundary map.

FHLMC: Federal Home Loan Mortgage Corporation; a.k.a. "Freddie Mac." Increases the availability of mortgage credit and provides greater liquidity for savings institutions.

FIA: Federal Insurance Administration (part of FEMA).

FIRM: Flood insurance rate map.

Fixed expenses: Expenses that do not vary with occupancy; for example, taxes and insurance.

Floodplain: The extent of the land adjoining a river, which, because of its level topography, would flood if the river overflowed its banks.

Floor plan: Layout of a structure, indicating sizes of the rooms and purposes for each.

Floor planning: Inventory financing of a retailer's manufactured housing stock. Usually simple interest rates, 1 or 2 points over prime rate.

FMHA: Farmers Home Administration. Makes loans for rural housing, community facilities, and so forth.

FNMA: Federal National Mortgage Association; a.k.a. "Fannie Mae." Establishes a market for the purchase and sale of first mortgages for housing.

Foundation fascia or skirting: Visual screening and weather barrier, of permanent or semipermanent material, covering the airspace between the bottom of a manufactured home and the ground.

Frost line: Depth to which soil freezes.

FTC: Federal Trade Commission. A federal enforcement agency that promulgates trade regulations and rules.

GNMA: Government National Mortgage Association; a.k.a. "Ginnie Mae." A source of mortgage money backed by and insured by the federal government.

GRM: Gross rent multiplier. An investment rule of thumb that relates "sale price and rent rates at time of sale" at neighboring like properties to the present rent level of a subject property in an effort to estimate value. See **Chapter 3** for formula.

Groundlease: The transfer of possessory and right-to-use real property rights to a tenant for a specific period, in return for rent compensation.

Groundwater: Water in the subsoil or of a spring or shallow well.

Hardpan: A compacted layer of soil, usually containing clay, through which it is difficult to drain or dig.

Highest and best use: Property condition or development bringing greatest profit to its owner.

Holdback: Part of a loan commitment held back until additional requirements are met.

Homeowners association: Usually associated with PUD, condominium, and co-op properties, but can include any group of homeowners working together.

Homesite: Parcel of improved land upon which a manufactured home is permanently or temporarily sited. Usually complete with infrastructure utilities, piers, driveway.

HUD: Department of Housing and Urban Development. Oversees most federally sponsored housing programs.

Hydrology: The science dealing with the occurrence, circulation, distribution, and properties of the waters of the earth and its atmosphere.

ICBO: International Conference of Building Officials.

Infiltration: The movement of water through the soil surface into the soil; also used to describe movement of water through the soil into sanitary sewer lines through pipe cracks or separated connections.

Infrastructure: All common improvements and community features, such as water and sewer lines, streets, schools, and government facilities.

Interest: The charge made by a lender for the use of its money.

IREM: Institute of Real Estate Management. Professional trade association for real estate (property) manager. See CPM.

Iterative: Involving repetition, as with verbal and/or written actions and plans.

Land and home package: Occurs when a manufactured home is purchased for placement upon homeowner's parcel of real estate.

Landlease: The transfer of possessory and right-to-use real property rights to a tenant for a specific period, in return for rent compensation.

Landscaping: Modification of the landscape through grading, trees, and so forth.

Laterals: The sewer lines branching off the main sewer line.

Lease: Agreement between lessor and lessee whereby the former gives up right of possession and use for a period of time in exchange for specified consideration or rent.

Leasehold: An estate in realty held under a lease. In some states considered to be personal property.

Lessee: A person to whom a lease is given in exchange for rent.

Lessor: Property owner or agent granting the lease for a consideration (rent).

Leverage: Effecting an investment with as little cash (that is, down payment) as possible and maximum debt.

Lien: A charge placed upon a property for payment of a debt.

Liquidity: The measure of ease with which one can free-up invested funds. Real estate investments are not generally known for their liquidity versus commercial bank personal savings accounts.

Listings: Working agreement between a property seller and real estate broker; may be exclusive right to sell, exclusive agency, or open listing.

Loess: Deposits of windblown organic silt.

Lotline: The boundary line of a lot in a subdivision.

Lotting plan: A plan showing the lot (or homesite) layout and street arrangement in a subdivision or landlease community.

LTV: Loan-to-Value. Percentage relationship of loan or mortgage size to value of mortgaged property, for example, 75% LTV=loan amount is 75% of mortgaged property's value.

MAI: Member, Appraisal Institute. Professional designation awarded to real estate appraisers after completing comprehensive education and experience requirements as well as peer review.

MHCSS: Manufactured Home Construction and Safety Standards.

MHEI: Manufactured Housing Educational Institute. Nonprofit arm of MHI charged with educating manufactured housing industry managers, retailers, and so forth.

MHI: Manufactured Housing Institute.

Mortgage: The legal instrument used to obligate property to secure a loan.

Mortgagee: Party borrowing the money and granting the mortgage to mortgagor.

Mortgagor: Party lending the money and receiving the mortgage from mortgagee.

MSO: Manufacturer's Statement of Origin. Manufacturer's initiated document that originates title to a manufactured home.

Multisection: Denotes manufactured housing delivered to the homesite in two or more sections that are then joined together into one home.

NDCBU: Neighborhood Delivery & Collection Box Unit. U.S. Postal Service's name for cluster-type lockable mailboxes.

Net operating income: Amount left after adjustments and deductions for vacancy, credit loss, and operating expenses, but before mortgage is paid.

NFIP: National Flood Insurance Program.

NFPA: National Fire Protection Association.

NIMBY: Acronym for "Not in my backyard" attitude on part of homeowners against what they see as an undesirable land use next door.

NOI: Net operating income. Gross collected rent (income) less operating expenses is net operating income. Does not include debt service.

Nonrecourse financing: The party arranging the loan assumes sole liability should the retail consumer default. In order to provide nonrecourse financing, the lending institution may secure its position by obtaining mortgage guarantee insurance.

Obsolescence: A property condition or defect that may be caused by external influences (that is, economic obsolescence) or internal conditions (functional obsolescence).

Occupancy: In real estate leasing jargon, the measure of "how full" a property is versus vacancy or "how empty" it is.

OER: Operating Expense Ratio. A measure of operating efficiency for income-producing properties. The ratio of operating expenses to gross collected rental income.

OPM: "Other People's Money." Real estate investor jargon describing the leverage resulting from buying an income property using a partner or lender's funds.

Option: Right to purchase property at a negotiated price within a specific time period in exchange for a consideration.

Ordinance: Simply a law or statute.

Percolation: The absorption of liquid into soil by seepage.

Personal property: As opposed to real property, includes depreciable items such as carpet, equipment, appliances, vehicles.

Pier: Integral part of the foundation system for many manufactured home installations. Usually concrete block material.

Piezometer tube: A tube placed in the ground to measure groundwater levels.

PITI: Principal, interest, taxes, insurance.

Plat or **plot plan:** General street map of a community.

PMI: Private mortgage insurance.

Points: An additional loan charge put on a loan to increase the yield to the lender. One (1) point equals 1% of face value of a loan amount.

PRD: Planned residential development.

Principal: Money still owed on a loan at any given time, not including interest.

Pro forma: That which is provided in advance as a model or guide, as in an operating budget.

Pro rata or **prorate:**   To divide into appropriate shares, such as taxes, insurance, rent, and other items.

PUD: Planned urban development. Characterized by intensive unified use of land and site design with combination of private and common area improvements.

Purchase money mortgage: A mortgage given by the buyer to the seller as part of the purchase consideration, as opposed to a hard money mortgage.

Real property: Land and anything permanently attached to it.

Realtor: A designation given to a real estate broker who is a member of a board associated with the National Association of Realtors.

Rectilinear: A community layout wherein straight streets run parallel and at right angles to each other.

REIT: Real Estate Investment Trust. Public company with major holdings in real estate. The manufactured home community industry presently counts five REITs among its largest portfolio owners.

Remonstrators: Citizens in attendance at planning commission and board meetings who generally are against approving a particular land use approval or change.

REO: Real estate owned. How lending institutions often refer to the real estate they have "taken back" in foreclosure or in lieu thereof.

Repurchase agreement: The Manufacturer's Repurchase Agreement is a written agreement between the manufacturer and bank whereby the manufacturer agrees to repurchase units in the retailer's inventory should the retailer default on his obligations or go out of business. A Retailer Repurchase Agreement is a written agreement between the dealer and lender whereby the dealer agrees to buy back manufactured homes from the bank in which the retail consumer has defaulted on loan payments.

Retailer: Individual or firm in the business of marketing and selling new and resale manufactured homes.

Retailer buy rate: The difference between the cost of the financing to the retailer and the cost of financing to the consumer by the lending institution is known as the "buy rate." A good quality retail operation will normally have a more preferential buy rate, which allows the retailer to make more on participation, while charging the same interest rate to the consumer as a competitor might charge. Typically, if a retailer's buy rate is 6 3/4%, cost to the consumer would by 7 1/2% to 8 1/2%, depending upon how much the retailer can charge and still make the sale.

Retailer reserve (participation): A fixed amount of the interest rate set aside by the lending institution on behalf of the retailer to protect the lender on future repossessions should the leader go out of business. If the retailer remains in business, the reserve generally belongs to him or her once the loans are paid off.

Return on investment: Annual earnings on original cash down payment.

Right-of-way: A strip of land used as a roadbed, either for a street or railway.

ROC: Resident-owned community, usually characterized by cooperative or condominium ownership.

ROI: Return on and/or of investment. Return "on" investment relates to the amount of profit a venture generates. Return "of" investment relates to the time frame it takes to get one's total funds back from an investment.

RV: Recreational vehicle. A sister industry to manufactured housing. RVs are sometimes temporarily parked and used as temporary dwellings on manufactured housing rental homesites and often stored adjacent to manufactured home communities in storage lots.

SBCCI: Southern Building Code Congress International.

SCS: Soil Conservation Service.

Security agreement: A security agreement, as specified by the Uniform Commercial Code (UCC), replaces the trust receipt. A security agreement between the lender and retailer eliminates the need of having an individual document (trust receipt) initiated for each home floor planned. While most states accept the Uniform Commercial Code, finance companies, banks, and savings and loan institutions have been slower to change from the traditional trust agreement, which gives them more legal protection.

Seed money: Money needed for preliminary plans, reorganizing, controlling the site, and completion of feasibility studies.

Setback: The distance a structure must be set back or distanced from a street, lotline, or property to conform to a zoning or building code.

Simple interest: Interest charged on an annual basis, payable monthly, on the unpaid balance remaining.

Single-section: Denotes manufactured housing delivered to the homesite as one self-contained unit.

Skirting: Same as foundation fascia.

SMSA: Standard Metropolitan Statistical Area. U.S. Bureau of Census designation for larger cities in various geographic areas.

Soft market: Market condition when supply exceeds demand.

Streetscape: A pictorial view of or from a street.

Subdivision: A division of a single parcel of land into smaller parcels by filing a map describing the division.

Subordination: Willingness of a lien holder to accept payment after another creditor.

Swale: A valleylike intersection of two slopes in a piece of land.

Tag-along/tag section: A third section to a manufactured home.

Tiedown: An anchoring device used to secure a manufactured home to the homesite anchoring system, whether it be earth anchors or hardware secured in concrete.

Tight or **hard market:**   Market condition when demand exceeds supply.

Topography: Land surface contour.

Transporter: Single-axle over-the-road tractor designed to transport manufactured homes.

Trust deed: An instrument that is evidence of the pledge of real property as security for a debt where the title to the real property is held by a third party in trust, while the debtor repays the debt to the lender.

Turnover ratio: Number of move-outs in a 12-month period as compared with total number of homesites.

UCC: Uniform Commercial Code.

USCG: United States Coast Guard.

USDA: United States Department of Agriculture.

USGS: United States Geological Survey.

VA: Department of Veterans Affairs. Guarantees loans made to veterans.

Vacancy: In real estate leasing jargon, the measure of "how full" a property is versus vacancy or "how empty" it is.

Variable expenses: Expenses that fluctuate in proportion to physical occupancy, seasons, and so forth.

Water table: The depth, measured from the surface, at which natural underground waters are found.

Wetlands: Lands that have a wet and spongy soil, as with a marsh, swamp, or bog.

Wraparound mortgage: A second or junior mortgage with a face value of both the amount it secures and the balance due under the first mortgage.

Zero lotline: The construction of a building on any of the boundary lines of a lot.

Zoning: Planned division of a community into areas designed for designated uses, for example, residential, commercial, industrial.

BIBLIOGRAPHY

Allen, George. *Daily Management of Manufactured Home Communities,* Monograph #3. Indianapolis: PMN Publishing, 1995.

―――. *Development, Sale and Purchasing of Manufactured Home Communities,* Monograph #2. Indianapolis: PMN Publishing, 1995.

―――. *Mobilehome Community Management.* 2d ed. Indianapolis: PMN Publishing, 1991.

―――. *Real Estate and Property Management,* Monograph #1. Indianapolis: PMN Publishing, 1995.

―――. *Upper Management Related Reports and Directories for Manufactured Home Communities,* Monograph #4. Indianapolis: PMN Publishing, 1995.

Allen, George, and David Blakley. *Appraisal Guide for Mobilehomes.* Scottsdale: NAREA, 1990.

Allen, George, David Alley, and Edward Hicks. *Development, Marketing and Operation of Manufactured Home Communities.* New York: John Wiley & Sons, Inc., 1994.

American Appraisal Association. *Mobile-Manufactured Housing Cost Guide.* Milwaukee: Boeckh, 1995.

American Society of Planning Officials. Regulation of Modular Housing, with Special Emphasis on Mobile Homes. AMSPO, 1971.

Branson, Gary. *The Complete Guide to Manufactured Housing.* Cincinnati: Betterway Books, 1992.

Colorado Manufactured Housing Association and IREM, *Mobilehome Community Maintenance.* Denver: Colorado Manufactured Housing Association and IREM, 1986.

Commerce Clearing House. *State Tax Handbook.* Chicago: CCH, 1995 (updated annually).

Complete Guide to H.U.D. Mobile Home Standards Program. 2d ed. Atlanta: Compliance Systems Publications Inc., 1977.

Cooke, P.W., R.D. Dikkers, H.R. Trechsel, H.K. Tejuja, and L.P. Zelenka. *Model Documents for the Evaluation, Approval, and Inspection of Manufactured Buildings,* NBS Building Science Series 87. Washington, D.C.: National Bureau of Standards, 1976.

Culligan, Joseph J. *When in Doubt, Check Him Out.* Hallmark Press, Inc., 1993.

Cushman, Robert, and Neal Rodin. *Property Management Handbook.* New York: John Wiley & Sons, Inc., 1985.

Cymrot, Allen. *Street Smart Real Estate Investing.* Mountain View, Calif.: CR Publishing Co., 1993.

de Heer, Robert. *Realty Bluebook.* 29th ed. San Rafael, Calif.: Professional Publishing Corporation, 1993.

Design and Construction Manual for Residential Buildings in Coastal High Hazard Areas. Washington D.C.: HUD, January 1981.

Dodge Construction Cost Information System. *Manual for Building Construction Pricing and Scheduling.* Annual ed. Princeton, N.J.: McGraw-Hill Information Systems Company, 1992.

Downs, J. *Principles of Real Estate Management.* Chicago: IREM, 1990.

Federal Emergency Management Agency. *Design Guidelines for Flood Damage Reduction,* FEMA 15. Washington, D.C.: Government Printing Office, December 1981.

———. *Flood Insurance Study: Guidelines and Specifications for Contractors.* Washington D.C.: Government Printing Office, September 1982.

Federal Insurance Administration, National Flood Insurance Programs. "Reducing Flood Damage Through Building Design: A Guide Manual." In *Elevated Residential Structures.* Washington D.C.: 1976.

Federal Trade Commission, Bureau of Consumer Protection. *Mobile Home Sales and Service.* Washington, D.C.: Government Printing Office, August 1980.

Gordon, Sally, Young Chai, and Keith Lee. *Securities Collateralized by Manufactured Housing Communities.* Boston: CS First Boston, 1995.

Hall, Craig. *The Real Estate Turnaround.* Englewood Cliffs, N.J.: Prentice-Hall, 1978.

Haller, Edward J. *Simplified Wastewater Treatment Plant Operations.* Lancaster, Pa.: Technanic Publishing Co., 1995.

Hicks, Edward. *How to Get an FHA 207(m) Mobile Home Lot Rental Community Loan Guarantee From HUD.* Clearwater, Fla.: Consultants Resource Group, 1991.

Hoffman, Richard M. *Mobilehome Earthquake Bracing Systems in California.* Mountain View, Calif.: Hoffman Books, 1993.

Homel, Eric, and Steve Sakwa. *Manufactured Housing REITs—Study Long Term Fundamentals Support an Overweight Position.* New York: Morgan Stanley, 1995.

Jordan, Sloan. *Property Management Tactics in Manufactured Housing Communities.* Carlsbad, Calif.: SJ Publishing, 1990.

King, Carol, Gary Langerden, and Lyn Hummell. *The Successful On-Site Manager.* Chicago: IREM, 1984.

Kovacs, William D., and Felix Y. Yokel. *Soil and Rock Anchors for Mobile Homes: A State-of-the-Art Report,* NBS Building Science Series 107. Washington, D.C.: National Bureau of Standards, 1979.

Krigger, John. *Your Mobilehome Energy and Repair Guide.* Helena, Mont.: Saturn Resource Management, 1994.

Manufactured Housing/Mobilehome Parks, Info Packet Series #324. Washington, D.C.: Urban Land Institute, 1995.

Marshall and Swift Company. *Residential Cost Handbook.* Los Angeles: M&S Publishing, 1995.

McKie, Clint. *Do's and Don'ts of Mobilehome Repairing.* 2 vols. Manistee, Mich.: CM Publishing, 1990.

National Concrete Masonry Association. *Manual of Facts on Concrete Masonry (A).* 1983.

National Forest Products Association. *National Design Specification for Wood Construction.* National Forest Products Association, 1982.

NCSBCS/ANSI A225.1, NFPA 501A, *Manufactured Home Installations,* Washington, D.C.: NCSBCS, 1994.

Oahs, Daniel R. *Mobile Home Park Investment Guide.* Los Angeles: Manisha Publishing, 1988.

Pappas, Stephen. *Managing Mobile Home Parks.* Chicago: Institute of Real Estate Management, 1991.

Real Estate Center. *Guidelines for Mobilehome Park Development and Operations.* College Station, Tex.: Texas A & M University Press, 1988.

Robinson, Leigh. *Landlording.* El Cerrito, Calif.: Express, 1988.

Sahling, Leonard. *The Manufactured Housing Community Industry: The American Dream Re-engineered.* New York: Merrill Lynch & Co., 1995.

Sanders, Welford. *Manufactured Housing Site Development Guide,* Planning Advisory Service Report #445. Chicago: American Planning Association, 1993.

Sheldon, Jonathan, and Andrea Simpson. *Manufactured Housing Parks— Shifting the Balance of Power: A Model Statute.* Washington, D.C.: AARP, 1991.

Suchman, Diane. *Manufactured Housing: An Affordable Alternative,* Working Series Paper #640. Washington, D.C.: Urban Land Institute, 1995.

U.S. Department of Defense. *Flood-Proofing Regulations.* Washington, D.C.: Government Printing Office, 1984.

U.S. Department of Defense. *Protecting Mobile Homes from High Winds (TR-75).* Washington, D.C.: Government Printing Office, February 1984.

U.S. Department of Housing and Urban Development. *Guidelines for Improving the Mobile Home Living Environment.* Washington, D.C.: Government Printing Office, 1977.

U.S. Department of Housing and Urban Development. *Manual for the Construction of Residential Basements in Non-Coastal Flood Environs (CR-997).* Washington, D.C.: NAHB Research Foundation, March 1977.

Vellozzi, Joseph W. *Review of Proposed 1980 ANSI A58.1 Standard on Wind Forces Relative to Federal Mobile Home Construction and Safety Standards.* Washington, D.C.: Manufactured Housing Institute, May 1980.

Waldrip, Travis G. *Mobile Home Anchoring Systems and Related Construction.* June 1976.

Wallis, Allan. *Wheel Estates: History of the Manufactured Housing Industry.* New York: Oxford University Press, 1991.

Yokel, Felix Y., Riley M. Chung, Frank A. Rankin, and Charles W.C. Yancey. *Load Displacement Characteristics of Shallow Soil Anchors,* NBS Building Science Series 142. Washington, D.C.: National Bureau of Standards, 1981.

Yokel, Felix Y., Riley M. Chung, and Charles W.C. Yancey. *NBS Studies of Mobile Home Foundations,* NBSIR 2238. Washington, D.C.: National Bureau of Standards, 1981.

Yokel, Felix Y., Charles W.C. Yancey, and Christopher L. Mulen. *A Study of Reaction Forces on Mobile Home Foundations Caused by Wind and Flood Loads,* NBS Building Science Series 132. Washington, D.C.: National Bureau of Standards, 1981.

INDEX

ACCREDITED COMMUNITY
  MANAGERS (ACMs)
  Manufactured housing and
    manufactured home community
    § 1.8
ACTION PLAN AND BUDGET
  Turnaround challenge and
    rejuvenating older manufactured
    home communities § 8.4
ADVERTISING
  Manufactured home community,
    selling § 9.7
  Manufactured housing and
    manufactured home community
    § 1.7
  Property management §§ 7.14,
    7.17, 7.20
AFFORDABILITY
  Manufactured housing and
    manufactured home community
    §§ 1.1, 1.2, 1.5, 1.11
AFFORDABLE HOUSING
  Manufactured housing and
    manufactured home community
    §§ 1.1, 1.2, 1.5, 1.11
ALLEN MODEL
  See OPERATING EXPENSE
    RATIOS (OERs), ALLEN
    MODEL
AMENITIES
  Manufactured home community,
    how to find and buy §§ 4.3, 4.6
  Real estate investment, basics of
    § 2.9
  Turnaround challenge and
    rejuvenating older manufactured
    home communities § 8.2

AMENITIES (Continued)
  Value, estimating § 5.4
AMERICANS WITH DISABILITIES
  ACT (ADA)
  Manufactured home community,
    how to find and buy § 4.5
  Manufactured housing and
    manufactured home community
    § 1.7
  Property management § 7.29
AMORTIZATION LOAN
  Manufactured home community,
    what to look for § 3.6
  Real estate investment, basics of
    § 2.7
AMORTIZATION RATE
  Due diligence period: preparing for
    closing § 6.12
  Real estate investment, basics of
    § 2.7
AMORTIZATION TERM
  Real estate investment, basics of
    § 2.7
ANNUAL REVIEW AND
  REASSESSMENT
  Turnaround challenge and
    rejuvenating older manufactured
    home communities § 8.7
APARTMENTS, COMMUNITY
  Manufactured home community,
    how to find and buy § 4.6
  Manufactured home community,
    what to look for § 3.1
  Real estate investment, basics of
    §§ 2.1, 2.3
APARTMENTS, GARDEN-STYLE
  Real estate investment, basics of § 2.3

APPRAISERS
Due diligence period: preparing for
closing §§ 6.12, 6.13
Manufactured home community,
selling §§ 9.3, 9.5
Real estate investment: coming full
cycle § 10.2
Value, estimating §§ 5.1, 5.3, 5.4,
5.7
APPRECIATION, VALUE
Real estate investment, basics of
§§ 2.2, 2.3
ASSESSMENT
Turnaround challenge and
rejuvenating older manufactured
home communities § 8.4
Value, estimating §§ 5.3, 5.4
ASSISTED LIVING
Manufactured housing and
manufactured home community
§ 1.11
Real estate investment, basics of
§ 2.3

BAND OF INVESTMENT
TECHNIQUE
Value, estimating § 5.8
BENCHMARK, PROPERTY-TYPE
Manufactured home community,
how to find and buy § 4.3
Manufactured home community,
selling § 9.3
Manufactured home community,
what to look for § 3.2
Turnaround challenge and
rejuvenating older manufactured
home communities § 8.2
Value, estimating § 5.3
BENEFITS, ANCILLARY
Real estate investment, basics of
§ 2.2
BROKER, REAL ESTATE
Due diligence period: preparing for
closing § 6.11
Manufactured home community,
how to find and buy §§ 4.3, 4.4

BROKER, REAL ESTATE
(Continued)
Manufactured home community,
selling §§ 9.3, 9.15
Real estate investment, basics of
§ 2.3
Real estate investment: coming full
cycle § 10.2
Value, estimating § 5.4
BUDGET
See ACTION PLAN AND
BUDGET

CABLE TELEVISION
Due diligence period: preparing for
closing § 6.9
Manufactured home community,
how to find and buy §§ 4.3, 4.6
Manufactured home community,
selling § 9.3
Manufactured home community,
what to look for §§ 3.4, 3.6
Property management § 7.17
CANADA
Manufactured home community,
how to find and buy § 4.3
Manufactured home community,
selling § 9.16
Property management § 7.24
CAPITALIZATION RATE
Manufactured home community,
selling § 9.10
Manufactured home community,
what to look for § 3.6
CARETAKERS
Manufactured home community,
how to find and buy § 4.3
Property management § 7.2
CASH FLOW
Manufactured home community,
what to look for §§ 3.1, 3.6
Real estate investment, basics of
§§ 2.1–2.3
CASH FLOW BEFORE TAXES
Due diligence period: preparing for
closing § 6.10

CASH FLOW BEFORE TAXES
(Continued)
Manufactured home community,
what to look for § 3.6
Real estate investment, basics of
§§ 2.3, 2.6
CASH FLOW, FUTURE
Real estate investment, basics of § 2.2
CASH FLOW, PRESENT
Real estate investment, basics of § 2.6
CASH-ON-CASH RETURN
Manufactured home community,
what to look for § 3.6
Real estate investment, basics of
§§ 2.3, 2.7
CERTIFIED PROPERTY
MANAGERS (CPMs)
Manufactured housing and
manufactured home community
§ 1.8
Real estate investment, basics of § 2.2
CHART OF ACCOUNTS,
STANDARD
Property management § 7.14
CHASSIS, PERMANENT
Property management § 7.4
CLOSING TABLE
Due diligence period: preparing for
closing § 6.12
CLUBHOUSES
Manufactured home community,
how to find and buy § 4.3
Manufactured housing and
manufactured home community
§ 1.1
Property management § 7.4
Real estate investment, basics of
§ 2.10
Turnaround challenge and
rejuvenating older manufactured
home communities § 8.2
Value, estimating § 5.8
COMMUNITY
See MANUFACTURED HOUSING
AND MANUFACTURED
HOME COMMUNITY

COMMUNITY MANAGER,
ADMINISTRATOR
Manufactured housing and
manufactured home community
§§ 1.10, 1.11
COMMUNITY TO PURCHASE,
DEFINING TYPE OF
Manufactured home community,
how to find and buy § 4.7
COMPUTERIZATION
Property management § 7.28
CONDOMINIUMIZED
Manufactured home community,
selling § 9.6
Manufactured housing and
manufactured home community
§ 1.7
Property management § 7.2
CONDOMINIUMS
Manufactured home community,
how to find and buy § 4.6
Manufactured housing and
manufactured home community
§ 1.7
Property management § 7.2
Real estate investment, basics of
§ 2.3
CONGREGATE CARE
Manufactured housing and
manufactured home community
§ 1.11
Real estate investment, basics of
§ 2.3
CONSULTANT, SALES
Manufactured home community,
selling §§ 9.4, 9.5
Turnaround challenge and
rejuvenating older manufactured
home communities § 8.6
CONTINGENCY CLAUSES
Manufactured home community,
how to find and buy § 4.5
CONTINUING CARE
Manufactured housing and
manufactured home community
§ 1.11

CONTINUING CARE *(Continued)*
Real estate investment, basics of § 2.3
COOPERATIVELY-OWNED
Manufactured home community,
selling § 9.6
Manufactured housing and
manufactured home community
§§ 1.7, 1.8, 1.10
Real estate investment, basics of
§ 2.3
COOPERATIVES (CO-OPs)
Manufactured home community,
selling § 9.6
Manufactured housing and
manufactured home community
§§ 1.7, 1.8, 1.10
Property management §§ 7.2, 7.27
Real estate investment, basics of § 2.3
CORPORATE CIRCUMSTANCES
Manufactured home community,
how to find and buy § 4.2
Real estate investment, basics of
§§ 2.2, 2.3
COST OR REPLACEMENT
APPROACH
Manufactured home community,
selling § 9.5
Value, estimating §§ 5.5, 5.6
COST PROJECTIONS
Due diligence period: preparing for
closing. See DUE DILIGENCE
PERIOD: PREPARING FOR
CLOSING
Turnaround challenge and
rejuvenating older manufactured
home communities § 8.5
CURB APPEAL
Manufactured home community,
how to find and buy § 4.3
Manufactured home community,
what to look for § 3.6
Property management § 7.25
Real estate investment, basics of
§ 2.5
Real estate investment: coming full
cycle § 10.2

CURB APPEAL *(Continued)*
Turnaround challenge and
rejuvenating older manufactured
home communities § 8.1

DEFERRED MAINTENANCE
Real estate investment, basics of
§ 2.5
DELINQUENT ACCOUNTS,
SUMMARY OF
Property management; Form 7–7
§ 7.10
DEMOGRAPHICS, TRENDS
Manufactured home community,
how to find and buy § 4.1
Manufactured housing and
manufactured home community
§ 1.3
DENSITY
Real estate investment, basics of
§ 2.5
DEPRECIATION, ASSET
Manufactured housing and
manufactured home community
§ 1.3
Real estate investment, basics of
§§ 2.2, 2.3
DEPRECIATION, PHYSICAL
Manufactured home community,
selling § 9.9
Value, estimating § 5.6
DESIGN, FLEXIBILITY OF
Manufactured housing and
manufactured home community
§ 1.5
DISPOSITION, VALUE
Real estate investment: coming full
cycle § 10.1
DIVESTITURE PROCESS
Manufactured home community,
selling § 9.2
Real estate investment, basics of
§ 2.3
DOWN PAYMENTS
Real estate investment, basics of
§§ 2.2, 2.6

DUE DILIGENCE PERIOD,
INVESTIGATION TEAM
Due diligence period: preparing for
closing § 6.3
Manufactured home community,
what to look for §§ 3.1, 3.6, 3.8
Real estate investment, basics of
§ 2.2
DUE DILIGENCE PERIOD:
PREPARING FOR CLOSING
Generally §§ 6.1, 6.13
Assemble team § 6.3
Closing, preparing for § 6.12
Manufactured home community,
permits and licenses, and cost
projections
–Generally § 6.7
–Feasibility projections § 6.10
–Physical examination agenda § 6.8
–Regulatory agencies and utility
companies § 6.9
Manufactured home community
records and inventory § 6.6
Meetings, setting up § 6.5
Physical due diligence, purpose of
§ 6.2
Real estate investment: coming full
cycle § 10.2
Seller, information requested from
§ 6.4
Transaction financing, arranging
§ 6.11

EARTH ANCHORS
Manufactured home community,
what to look for § 3.4
Manufactured housing and
manufactured home community
§ 1.10
Property management § 7.18
EASEMENTS
Due diligence period: preparing for
closing § 6.12
Manufactured home community,
what to look for § 3.6
Value, estimating § 5.4

ECONOMIC AND FINANCIAL
FEASIBILITY
Real estate investment, basics of § 2.6
Value, estimating § 5.4
ENERGY SAVING IDEAS
Property management; Form 7–12
§ 7.25
ENVIRONMENTAL AUDITS
Due diligence period: preparing for
closing § 6.7
Manufactured home community,
how to find and buy § 4.5
Manufactured home community,
what to look for § 3.6
ENVIRONMENTAL CONDITIONS
Manufactured home community,
how to find and buy § 4.7
Manufactured home community,
what to look for § 3.6
Manufactured housing and
manufactured home community
§ 1.8
ENVIRONMENTAL HAZARDS
Manufactured home community,
how to find and buy § 4.7
EQUITY BUILDUP, DOWN
PAYMENT
Real estate investment, basics of
§§ 2.2, 2.3
EQUITY POSITION
Real estate investment, basics of
§§ 2.2, 2.3
ESTOPPEL CERTIFICATE
Due diligence period: preparing for
closing § 6.12
Manufactured home community,
how to find and buy; Form 4–1
§ 4.5
EVALUATION
Property management § 7.30
EXCLUSIVE AGENCY
Manufactured home community,
selling § 9.4
EXCLUSIVE RIGHT TO SELL
Manufactured home community,
selling §§ 9.4, 9.15

EXPENSES, ANCILLARY
Manufactured home community, what to look for § 3.6
EXPENSES, OPERATING
Manufactured housing and manufactured home community § 1.11

FACTORY-BUILT HOME
Manufactured housing and manufactured home community § 1.1
FAIR HOUSING ADVERTISING
Manufactured housing and manufactured home community § 1.7
FAIR HOUSING AMENDMENTS ACT OF 1988
Manufactured housing and manufactured home community § 1.7
Property management § 7.29
FARMLAND
Real estate investment, basics of § 2.3
FEASIBILITY, FINANCIAL
Due diligence period: preparing for closing §§ 6.2, 6.10
FEE SIMPLE
Value, estimating § 5.3
FIELDWORK PROPERTY RESEARCH SOURCES
Manufactured home community, what to look for § 3.3
FINANCIAL FEASIBILITY
See ECONOMIC AND FINANCIAL FEASIBILITY
FINANCIAL MATTERS
Property management § 7.14
FINDINGS, DOCUMENTING AND ORGANIZING
Manufactured home community, what to look for § 3.4
FORMS
Energy Saving Ideas; Form 7–12 § 7.25

FORMS (Continued)
Estoppel Certificate; Form 4–1 § 4.5
Incident/Accident Report; Form 7–6 § 7.10
Income and Expense Cash Flow Analysis Worksheet; Form 3–5 § 3.6
Invoice Distribution Summary; Form 7–9 § 7.10
Manufactured Home Community Guidelines; Form 7–8 § 7.10
Manufactured Home Community Investment Checklist; Form 3–4 § 3.6
Market Survey, Rental Community; Form 3–2 § 3.3
Marketing and Operations Summary; Form 7–4 § 7.10
Past Due Rent Notice; Form 7–10 § 7.15
Preliminary Loan Application; Form 6–1 § 6.11
Property Information Sheet; Form 7–2 § 7.10
Property Management Report Card; Form 7–14 § 7.30
Property Management Takeover Checklist; Form 6–2 § 6.12
Purchasing Comparison Chart; Form 7–13 § 7.27
Rental Prospect Qualification Summary for Multi-Family Income-Producing Properties; Form 7–11 § 7.21
Sample evaluation tool titled "How Does Your Community Measure Up?" Form 3–3 § 3.4
Sample Summary Offering Page; Form 3–1 § 3.2
Standard Shopping Report; Form 7–1 § 7.4
Summary of Delinquent Accounts; Form 7–7 § 7.10
Valuation Calculation Worksheet (VCW); Form 3–6, Form 9–1 §§ 3.6, 9.5

FORMS *(Continued)*
Weekly Marketing and Operations
Report; Form 7–3 § 7.10
Weekly Prospect Inquiry Report;
Form 7–5 § 7.10
FORMS AND RELATED AIDS,
START-UP PACKAGE OF
Property management § 7.10
FORMULAS FOR FINANCIAL AND
MATHEMATICAL
OPERATIONAL ANALYSIS OF A
MANUFACTURED
HOME COMMUNITY
Manufactured home community,
what to look for § 3.6
FOUNDATION, PERMANENT
Manufactured home community,
what to look for § 3.4

GEOGRAPHIC MARKET OF
INTEREST, IDENTIFYING
Manufactured home community,
how to find and buy §§ 4.2, 4.6
Manufactured home community,
selling § 9.6
GOAL SETTING
Manufactured home community,
how to find and buy § 4.2
GROUNDLEASE
Manufactured housing and
manufactured home community
§ 1.7
GUIDELINES FOR LIVING
Manufactured home community,
what to look for §§ 3.4, 3.6
Manufactured housing and
manufactured home community
§ 1.10
Property management § 7.12
Real estate investment, basics of § 2.5
Real estate investment: coming full
cycle § 10.2

HAZARDOUS MATERIALS
Manufactured home community,
what to look for § 3.4

HAZARDOUS MATERIALS
(Continued)
Real estate investment, basics of
§ 2.5
Real estate investment: coming full
cycle § 10.2
HOLDING COMPANY
Due diligence period: preparing for
closing § 6.11
Real estate investment, basics of
§ 2.2
HOLDING PERIOD
Manufactured home community,
selling § 9.3
HOMEOWNER ASSOCIATIONS
Manufactured home community,
selling § 9.6
Real estate investment, basics of
§ 2.3
HOMEOWNER/RENTER
Manufactured home community,
selling § 9.6
Manufactured housing and
manufactured home community
§§ 1.7, 1.10
Real estate investment, basics of
§ 2.3
HOMESITES, RENTAL
Manufactured home community,
how to find and buy §§ 4.2, 4.3
Manufactured housing and
manufactured home community
§§ 1.9, 1.10
HOSPITALITY INDUSTRY
Real estate investment, basics of
§ 2.3
HOUSING
See MANUFACTURED HOUSING
AND MANUFACTURED
HOME COMMUNITY
HOUSING, LOW-COST
Manufactured home community,
selling § 9.6
HOUSING, SENIOR
Manufactured home community,
how to find and buy § 4.2

HOUSING, SENIOR *(Continued)*
Manufactured housing and
manufactured home community
§ 1.11
Real estate investment, basics of
§ 2.3
HUD CONSTRUCTION
STANDARDS
Manufactured housing and
manufactured home community
§§ 1.5, 1.10

IMPROVEMENTS, BRICK &
MORTAR
Turnaround challenge and
rejuvenating older manufactured
home communities § 8.5
IMPROVEMENTS, BUILDING
Due diligence period: preparing for
closing § 6.5
Turnaround challenge and
rejuvenating older manufactured
home communities §§ 8.5, 8.6
IMPROVEMENTS, ON-SITE
Due diligence period: preparing for
closing § 6.5
Turnaround challenge and
rejuvenating older manufactured
home communities §§ 8.5, 8.6
IMPROVEMENTS, SITE
Due diligence period: preparing for
closing § 6.5
Turnaround challenge and
rejuvenating older manufactured
home communities §§ 8.5, 8.6
INCIDENT/ACCIDENT REPORT
Property management; Form 7–6
§ 7.10
INCOME AND EXPENSE
CASH FLOW ANALYSIS
WORKSHEET
Manufactured home community,
what to look for; Form 3–5
§ 3.6
INCOME APPROACH
Value, estimating § 5.8

INCOME CAPITALIZATION
APPROACH TO VALUE (IRV
FORMULA)
Manufactured home community,
selling § 9.5
Manufactured home community,
what to look for § 3.6
Value, estimating § 5.5
INCOME STREAMS
Due diligence period: preparing for
closing § 6.10
Manufactured home community,
how to find and buy §§ 4.3,
4.7
Manufactured home community,
what to look for § 3.12
Real estate investment, basics of
§§ 2.1, 2.3
INDIANA STATE DEPARTMENT
OF HEALTH
Manufactured housing and
manufactured home community
§ 1.7
INDUSTRIAL REAL ESTATE
Real estate investment, basics of
§ 2.3
INDUSTRY TERMINOLOGY
Manufactured housing and
manufactured home community
§ 1.10
INFORMATION CENTER
Manufactured housing and
manufactured home community
§ 1.10
Property management § 7.21
INFRASTRUCTURE, UTILITY
Manufactured home community,
how to find and buy §§ 4.3,
4.5
Manufactured home community,
what to look for § 3.1
Manufactured housing and
manufactured home community
§ 1.9
Real estate investment, basics of
§ 2.5

INFRASTRUCTURE, UTILITY
(Continued)
Turnaround challenge and
   rejuvenating older manufactured
   home communities § 8.2
INSPECTIONS, ON-SITE
Due diligence period: preparing for
   closing §§ 6.1, 6.7
Manufactured home community,
   what to look for §§ 3.2, 3.6
Real estate investment, basics of
   §§ 2.2, 2.5
INSTALLATION SITE
Manufactured housing and
   manufactured home community
   §§ 1.3, 1.5, 1.10
Property management § 7.25
INTERNATIONAL NETWORKING
ROUNDTABLE
Manufactured home community,
   how to find and buy § 4.4
Manufactured housing and
   manufactured home community
   § 1.8
Property management § 7.23
INTERNET
Manufactured home community,
   how to find and buy § 4.4
INVESTMENT CAUTIONS
Manufactured home community,
   how to find and buy § 4.3
Manufactured housing and
   manufactured home community
   § 1.9
Real estate investment, basics of.
   See REAL ESTATE
   INVESTMENT, BASICS OF
INVESTMENT RISK
Real estate investment, basics of
   §§ 2.2, 2.3
INVESTMENT THEORY
Manufactured home community,
   selling § 9.10
INVESTORS
Manufactured home community,
   how to find and buy § 4.2

INVESTORS *(Continued)*
Manufactured home community,
   selling § 9.6
Manufactured housing and
   manufactured home community
   § 1.8
INVOICE DISTRIBUTION
SUMMARY
Property management; Form 7–9
   § 7.10

LAGOON SYSTEMS,
COMMUNITY-OWNED
Property management § 7.18
LAND, RAW
Manufactured home community,
   how to find and buy § 4.7
Manufactured home community,
   what to look for § 3.1
Real estate investment, basics of
   § 2.2
Value, estimating § 5.6
LANDLEASE COMMUNITIES
Due diligence period: preparing for
   closing § 6.2
Manufactured housing and
   manufactured home community
   §§ 1.6, 1.7, 1.10
Real estate investment: coming full
   cycle § 10.2
Real estate investment, basics of
   § 2.3
Value, estimating § 5.1
LANDLORD,
LANDLORD-TENANT LAW
Manufactured home community,
   how to find and buy § 4.3
Manufactured housing and
   manufactured home community
   § 1.9
LANDLORD, LEGISLATION
Manufactured home community,
   how to find and buy § 4.3
Manufactured housing and
   manufactured home community
   § 1.9

LANDSCAPE, IMPROVEMENTS
Due diligence period: preparing for
closing § 6.7
Manufactured home community,
what to look for § 3.6
Turnaround challenge and
rejuvenating older manufactured
home communities §§ 8.4, 8.5
LEASE-UP COSTS
Value, estimating § 5.6
LEASED FEE
Value, estimating § 5.3
LEASEHOLD
Value, estimating § 5.3
LEASES
Due diligence period: preparing for
closing §§ 6.6, 6.11
Manufactured home community,
how to find and buy § 4.5
Manufactured housing and
manufactured home community
§ 1.10
Property management § 7.21
Real estate investment, basics of
§§ 2.1, 2.3, 2.5, 2.9
Real estate investment: coming full
cycle § 10.2
LENDERS
Due diligence period: preparing for
closing § 6.11
Real estate investment, basics of
§ 2.2
Value, estimating § 5.8
LESSEES
Manufactured home community,
what to look for § 3.6
Real estate investment, basics of
§ 2.2
LEVERAGE, DEGREE OF
Real estate investment, basics of
§ 2.2
LICENSE FEES
Manufactured housing and
manufactured home community
§ 1.5

LIQUIDATION VALUE
Real estate investment, basics of
§ 2.9
Value, estimating § 5.3
LIQUIDITY, DEGREE OF
Manufactured home community,
how to find and buy § 4.2
Real estate investment, basics of
§ 2.2
Real estate investment: coming full
cycle § 10.2
LOAN-TO-VALUE (LTV) RATIO
Manufactured home community,
what to look for § 3.6
Real estate investment, basics of
§ 2.2
Value, estimating § 5.8
LOCATION CONSIDERATIONS
Manufactured home community,
how to find and buy § 4.3
Manufactured home community,
what to look for §§ 3.1, 3.6, 3.10
Real estate investment, basics of
§§ 2.3, 2.5, 2.9
Real estate investment: coming full
cycle § 10.2
Turnaround challenge and
rejuvenating older manufactured
home communities § 8.2
LOSS CONTROL MEASURES
Property management § 7.18
Real estate investment, basics of
§ 2.2

MAINTENANCE MATTERS
Property management § 7.25
**MANAGEMENT ACTION PLAN
(MAP)**
Property management § 7.5
Turnaround challenge and
rejuvenating older manufactured
home communities § 8.7
MANAGEMENT IMPACT
Manufactured home community,
what to look for §§ 3.9, 3.11

MANAGEMENT IMPACT
(Continued)
Real estate investment: coming full
cycle § 10.2
Turnaround challenge and
rejuvenating older manufactured
home communities § 8.2
MANAGING BY THE NUMBERS
Property management § 7.16
MANUFACTURED HOME
Manufactured housing and
manufactured home community
§§ 1.1–1.10
MANUFACTURED HOME
COMMUNITIES
Manufactured home community,
how to find and buy §§ 4.2, 4.8
Manufactured housing and
manufactured home community
§§ 1.1, 1.3, 1.5–1.9
Real estate investment, basics of
§§ 2.1, 2.3, 2.7, 2.10
Real estate investment: coming full
cycle § 10.2
MANUFACTURED HOME
COMMUNITIES, WHAT TO
LOOK FOR
Generally §§ 3.1, 3.12
Fieldwork property research sources
§ 3.3
Findings, documenting and
organizing § 3.4
Formulas for financial and
mathematical operational analysis
of manufactured home
community § 3.6
Management impact § 3.9
Manufactured home community
investment checklist § 3.5
Primary considerations § 3.8
Project size § 3.10
Project types § 3.10
Property research sources, typical
§ 3.2
Risk and reward § 3.7

MANUFACTURED HOME
COMMUNITY CONDITION,
ASSESSING PRESENT
Turnaround challenge and
rejuvenating older manufactured
home communities § 8.4
MANUFACTURED HOME
COMMUNITY GUIDELINES
Property management; Form 7–8
§ 7.10
MANUFACTURED HOME
COMMUNITY, HOW TO FIND
AND BUY
Generally §§ 4.1, 4.9
Cataloging surveyed manufactured
home communities § 4.8
Community to purchase, defining
type of § 4.7
Geographic market of interest,
identifying § 4.6
Goal setting § 4.2
Property parameters § 4.3
Sources of manufactured home
communities for sale or otherwise
§ 4.4
Time to go looking § 4.5
MANUFACTURED HOME
COMMUNITY INVESTMENT
CHECKLIST
Manufactured home community,
what to look for; Form 3–4 § 3.5
MANUFACTURED HOME
COMMUNITY, SELLING
Generally §§ 9.1, 9.16
Manufactured home communities,
how to sell
–Generally § 9.12
–Marketing strategy § 9.14
–Real estate broker, when and how
to use § 9.15
–Seller's objectives § 9.13
Manufactured home communities,
introduction to marketing § 9.8
Marketing plan, preparing and
executing § 9.7

MANUFACTURED HOME
  COMMUNITY, SELLING
  (Continued)
Marketing process, recruiting
  right assistance in § 9.4
Marketing strategy, identifying
  target markets and planning § 9.6
Sale, preparation of property for
  § 9.3
Sale, timing of § 9.11
Sell, deciding right time to § 9.2
Selling, reasons for
–Generally § 9.9
–Investment theory § 9.10
Value range of property, estimating
  § 9.5
MANUFACTURED HOME
  LANDLEASE COMMUNITIES
Manufactured housing and
  manufactured home community
  §§ 1.6, 1.7, 1.10
Property management § 7.29
Value, estimating §§ 5.1, 5.2
MANUFACTURED HOUSING
Manufactured home community,
  how to find and buy § 4.4
Manufactured housing and
  manufactured home community
  § 1.11
MANUFACTURED HOUSING AND
  MANUFACTURED HOME
  COMMUNITY
Generally §§ 1.1, 1.12
Affordability § 1.2
Investment cautions § 1.9
Manufactured home communities
  as big business § 1.4
Manufactured home communities,
  trends among § 1.8
Manufactured home community
  § 1.7
Manufactured home community
  secret § 1.3

MANUFACTURED HOUSING AND
  MANUFACTURED HOME
  COMMUNITY *(Continued)*
Manufactured housing § 1.5
Manufactured housing industry
  terminology § 1.10
Manufactured housing, trends in § 1.6
Manufactured housing trends,
  overall § 1.11
MANUFACTURED HOUSING
  CONSTRUCTION & SAFETY
  STANDARDS ACT OF 1974
Manufactured housing and
  manufactured home community
  § 1.5
MANUFACTURED HOUSING
  EDUCATIONAL INSTITUTE
  (MHEI)
Manufactured housing and
  manufactured home community
  § 1.11
MANUFACTURED HOUSING
  INSTITUTE
Manufactured home community,
  how to find and buy § 4.4
Manufactured housing and
  manufactured home community
  § 1.11
MARKET ANALYSIS AREA
Manufactured home community,
  what to look for § 3.6
MARKET ANALYSIS, LOCAL
Property management § 7.7
MARKET ANALYSIS VALUE
Manufactured home community,
  how to find and buy § 4.5
MARKET SURVEY, RENTAL
  COMMUNITY
Manufactured home community,
  what to look for; Form 3–2 § 3.3
MARKET VALUE
Manufactured home community,
  what to look for § 3.6

MARKETING AND OPERATIONS
  REPORT, WEEKLY
  Property management; Form 7–3
  § 7.10
MARKETING AND OPERATIONS
  SUMMARY
  Property management; Form 7–4
  § 7.10
MARKETING MATTERS
  Property management. See
  PROPERTY MANAGEMENT
MARKETING PLAN, PREPARING
  AND EXECUTING
  Manufactured home community,
  selling § 9.7
MARKETING PROCESS,
  RECRUITING THE RIGHT
  ASSISTANCE IN
  Manufactured home community,
  selling § 9.4
MARKETING STRATEGY,
  IDENTIFYING TARGET
  MARKETS AND PLANNING
  Manufactured home community,
  selling § 9.6
MASTERPLAN
  Value, estimating § 5.4
MEETINGS, SETTING UP
  Due diligence period: preparing for
  closing § 6.5
METHODOLOGIES, CURRENT
  Turnaround challenge and
  rejuvenating older
  manufactured home communities
  § 8.8
MOBILE HOMES
  Manufactured housing and
  manufactured home community
  § 1.5
MODULAR HOMES
  Manufactured housing and
  manufactured home community
  § 1.5

MORTGAGE, CHATTEL
  Manufactured housing and
  manufactured home community
  §§ 1.6, 1.7
  Property management § 7.21
MORTGAGE, LEVEL-PAY
  Manufactured housing and
  manufactured home community
  § 1.6
MORTGAGE, REAL ESTATE
  OBLIGATIONS
  Manufactured housing and
  manufactured home community
  §§ 1.5, 1.6
MORTGAGE, SELF-AMORTIZING
  Manufactured housing and
  manufactured home community
  § 1.6
MORTGAGOR
  Manufactured housing and
  manufactured home community
  § 1.5
Ms OF MANAGEMENT
  Manufactured home community,
  what to look for § 3.4
  Real estate investment, basics of § 2.5
  Real estate investment: coming full
  cycle § 10.2
  Turnaround challenge and
  rejuvenating older manufactured
  home communities § 8.2
MULTISECTION HOMES
  Manufactured home community,
  how to find and buy § 4.3
  Manufactured housing and
  manufactured home community
  §§ 1.1, 1.6, 1.10
  Real estate investment: coming full
  cycle § 10.2
MYSTERY SHOPPING
  Manufactured home community,
  selling §§ 9.3, 9.4
  Property management §§ 7.4, 7.8

NDCBUs (NEIGHBORHOOD
DELIVERY AND COLLECTION
BOX UNITS)
Turnaround challenge and
rejuvenating older manufactured
home communities § 8.5
NET OPERATING INCOME (NOI)
Manufactured home community,
selling §§ 9.3, 9.6
Manufactured home community,
what to look for §§ 3.2, 3.6
Property management § 7.16
Real estate investment, basics of
§§ 2.3, 2.6
Value, estimating §§ 5.7, 5.8
NIMBY REPORT
Manufactured housing and
manufactured home community
§§ 1.2, 1.8
NURSING HOME
Manufactured home community,
what to look for § 3.6
Real estate investment, basics of § 2.5

OBSOLESCENCE, EXTERNAL
Real estate investment: coming full
cycle § 10.2
Value, estimating § 5.6
OBSOLESCENCE, FUNCTIONAL
Manufactured home community,
what to look for § 3.6
Manufactured housing and
manufactured home community
§ 1.9
Real estate investment, basics of
§ 2.5
Real estate investment: coming full
cycle § 10.2
Value, estimating § 5.6
OCCUPANCY, ECONOMIC
Manufactured home community,
what to look for § 3.6
Property management § 7.16
OCCUPANCY, PHYSICAL
Due diligence period: preparing for
closing § 6.9

OCCUPANCY, PHYSICAL
(Continued)
Manufactured home community,
what to look for §§ 3.4, 3.6
Property management § 7.16
Real estate investment, basics of
§ 2.5
OFFSHORE ISLANDS
Property management § 7.18
ON-SITE OPERATION, SETTING
UP AND RUNNING
Property management § 7.11
OPEN LISTING
Manufactured home community,
selling §§ 9.4, 9.15
OPERATING EXPENSE RATIOS
(OERs), ALLEN MODEL
Manufactured home community,
what to look for §§ 3.2, 3.6
Manufactured housing and
manufactured home community
§ 1.7
Property management § 7.16
Real estate investment, basics of
§ 2.6
Value, estimating § 5.7
OPTION LISTING
Manufactured home community.
selling § 9.4
OTHER PEOPLES' MONEY
(OPM)
Real estate investment, basics of
§§ 2.2, 2.3

PANELIZED HOMES
Manufactured housing and
manufactured home community
§ 1.5
PARKING FACILITIES
Manufactured home community,
what to look for § 3.4
Real estate investment, basics of
§ 2.3
Turnaround challenge and
rejuvenating older manufactured
home communities § 8.5

PARTNERSHIPS
Manufactured home community,
how to find and buy § 4.2
Manufactured home community,
selling §§ 9.2, 9.6
Manufactured housing and
manufactured home community
§ 1.7
Real estate investment, basics of
§ 2.1
PAST DUE RENT NOTICE
Property management; Form 7–10
§ 7.15
PAYROLL TAXES
Manufactured housing and
manufactured home community
§ 1.5
PER CAPITA CHARGES
Property management § 7.14
PERMITS AND LICENSES
Due diligence period: preparing for
closing. See DUE DILIGENCE
PERIOD: PREPARING FOR
CLOSING
PERSONNEL AND HUMAN
RELATIONS MATTERS
Property management § 7.13
PHYSICAL EXAMINATION
AGENDA
Due diligence period: preparing for
closing § 6.8
POLICIES AND PROCEDURES
Property management § 7.26
PORTFOLIO
Manufactured home community,
how to find and buy §§ 4.2,
4.3
Manufactured home community,
selling § 9.6
Manufactured home community,
what to look for § 3.11
Manufactured housing and
manufactured home community
§§ 1.8, 1.11
Real estate investment, basics of
§§ 2.2, 2.3, 2.5

PRECUT HOMES
Manufactured housing and
manufactured home community
§ 1.5
PRELIMINARY LOAN
APPLICATION
Due diligence period: preparing for
closing; Form 6–1 § 6.11
PRINCIPLE, MORTGAGE
Value, estimating § 5.7
PRIVATE LABEL HOMES
Turnaround challenge and
rejuvenating older manufactured
home communities § 8.8
PRO FORMA
Due diligence period: preparing for
closing § 6.10
Manufactured home community,
what to look for §§ 3.1, 3.4
Manufactured housing and
manufactured home community
§ 1.4
Property management § 7.14
Turnaround challenge and
rejuvenating older manufactured
home communities § 8.2
Value, estimating § 5.8
PRODUCTION STANDARDS
Manufactured housing and
manufactured home community
§ 1.5
PROJECT SIZE
Manufactured home community,
what to look for § 3.11
PROJECT TYPES
Manufactured home community,
what to look for § 3.10
PROPERTY FILES,
ESTABLISHING
Property management § 7.12
PROPERTY,
INCOME-PRODUCING
(PERSONAL TAXES)
Manufactured housing and
manufactured home community
§ 1.5

PROPERTY INFORMATION SHEET
Property management; Form 7–2
§ 7.10
PROPERTY INSURANCE
Manufactured housing and
manufactured home community
§ 1.5
Property management § 7.17
PROPERTY MANAGEMENT
Generally §§ 7.1, 7.31
Computerization § 7.28
Evaluation § 7.30
Federal laws affecting manufactured
home landlease communities
§ 7.29
Financial matters § 7.14
Loss control measures § 7.18
Maintenance matters § 7.25
Management action plan (MAP) § 7.5
Managing by the numbers § 7.16
Marketing matters
–Generally § 7.19
–Advertising § 7.20
–Leasing and sales § 7.21
–Public relations § 7.22
–Resident relations § 7.23
–Resident services enhancing
resident relations § 7.24
Maximizing income and
minimizing expenses § 7.17
Personnel and human relations
matters § 7.13
Policies and procedures § 7.26
Property files, establishing § 7.12
Property management information,
sources of § 7.6
Property management of a
particular property § 7.7
Property management, three levels
of § 7.3
Property management, two
categories of § 7.2
Property management visits and
inspections § 7.4
Property standard operating
procedure (SOP) § 7.9

PROPERTY MANAGEMENT
(*Continued*)
Property takeover checklist § 7.8
Purchasing matters § 7.27
Rent collection matters § 7.15
Setting up and running on-site
operation § 7.11
Start-up package of forms and
related aids § 7.10
PROPERTY MANAGEMENT,
PROFESSIONAL
Manufactured housing and
manufactured home community
§ 1.7
Real estate investment, basics of
§§ 2.2, 2.3, 2.5
Turnaround challenge and
rejuvenating older manufactured
home communities § 8.2
PROPERTY MANAGEMENT
REPORT CARD
Property management; Form 7.14
§ 7.30
PROPERTY MANAGEMENT
TAKEOVER CHECKLIST
Due diligence period: preparing for
closing; Form 6–2 § 6.12
PROPERTY PARAMETERS
Manufactured home community,
how to find and buy § 4.3
PROPERTY RESEARCH SOURCES,
TYPICAL
Manufactured home community,
what to look for § 3.2
PROSPECT INQUIRY REPORT,
WEEKLY
Property management; Form 7–5
§ 7.10
PUBLIC RELATIONS
Property management § 7.21
PURCHASING COMPARISON
CHART
Property management; Form 7–13
§ 7.27
PURCHASING MATTERS
Property management § 7.27

REAL ESTATE, ADVANTAGES
AND DISADVANTAGES
Real estate investment, basics of
§ 2.9
REAL ESTATE INVESTMENT,
BASICS OF
Generally §§ 2.1, 2.10
Cash-on-cash return § 2.7
Economic and financial feasibility
§ 2.6
Investment risk § 2.2
Manufactured home community,
how to find and buy § 4.2
Real estate, advantages and
disadvantages § 2.9
Real estate investment, search for
§ 2.4
Real estate investments, unique
characteristics of § 2.8
Real estate, motivation to invest in
§ 2.3
Research for right real estate
investment § 2.5
REAL ESTATE INVESTMENT:
COMING FULL CYCLE
Generally § 10.1
Major themes, review of § 10.2
REAL ESTATE INVESTMENT,
SEARCH FOR
Real estate investment, basics of § 2.4
REAL ESTATE INVESTMENTS,
UNIQUE CHARACTERISTICS OF
Real estate investment, basics of § 2.8
REAL ESTATE, MOTIVATION TO
INVEST IN
Real estate investment, basics of § 2.3
REAL ESTATE TAXES
(MORTGAGE, TRANSACTION)
Manufactured housing and
manufactured home community
§ 1.5
REASSESSMENT
See ANNUAL REVIEW AND
REASSESSMENT
RECONCILIATION
Value, estimating § 5.9

RECREATION
Manufactured home community,
how to find and buy § 4.3
Turnaround challenge and
rejuvenating older manufactured
home communities § 8.5
REFUSE REMOVAL
Manufactured home community,
how to find and buy § 4.6
Manufactured home community,
what to look for §§ 3.3, 3.6
Manufactured housing and
manufactured home community
§ 1.10
REGULATORY AGENCIES
Due diligence period: preparing for
closing § 6.9
REGULATORY BARRIERS
Manufactured housing and
manufactured home community
§ 1.10
REJUVENATION, PROPERTY
Manufactured home community,
how to find and buy § 4.2
Real estate investment: coming full
cycle § 10.2
RENT COLLECTION MATTERS
Property management § 7.15
RENTAL RATES
Manufactured home community,
how to find and buy § 4.6
Manufactured home community,
what to look for §§ 3.1, 3.6
Manufactured housing and
manufactured home community
§§ 1.7, 1.9, 1.10
Real estate investment, basics of
§ 2.9
REO (REAL ESTATE-OWNED)
Manufactured home community,
how to find and buy § 4.2
Real estate investment: coming full
cycle § i0.2
Turnaround challenge and
rejuvenating older manufactured
home communities § 8.2

REPLACEMENT APPROACH
Value, estimating § 5.6
RESALE CENTER
Manufactured housing and
manufactured home community
§ 1.10
RESALE HOMES
Manufactured home community,
how to find and buy § 4.3
Manufactured housing and
manufactured home community
§ 1.10
Property management §§ 7.1, 7.21
Turnaround challenge and
rejuvenating older manufactured
home communities § 8.8
RESIDENT MANAGER
Manufactured housing and
manufactured home community
§ 1.10
RESIDENT-OWNED COMMUNITY
(ROC)
Manufactured home community,
selling § 9.6
Manufactured housing and
manufactured home community
§ 1.8
RESIDENT RELATIONS
Property management § 7.23
RESIDENT SERVICES
ENHANCING RESIDENT
RELATIONS
Property management § 7.24
RETAIL, SALESCENTER
Manufactured housing and
manufactured home community
§ 1.10
RETIREES
Due diligence period: preparing for
closing § 6.11
Manufactured home community,
how to find and buy § 4.2
Manufactured home community,
selling §§ 9.2, 9.6
Manufactured home community,
what to look for § 3.10

RETIREES (Continued)
Manufactured housing and
manufactured home community
§§ 1.5–1.7
Real estate investment: coming full
cycle § 10.2
RETURN-OF-INVESTMENT (ROI)
Manufactured home community,
selling § 9.2
RETURN-ON-INVESTMENT (ROI)
Due diligence period: preparing for
closing § 6.10
Manufactured home community,
how to find and buy § 4.2
Manufactured home community,
selling § 9.2
Manufactured home community,
what to look for §§ 3.1, 3.6
Real estate investment, basics of
§§ 2.2, 2.3
Real estate investment: coming full
cycle § 10.2
REVERSION OF SALES PROCEEDS
Real estate investment, basics of
§ 2.3
RISK AND REWARD
Manufactured home community,
selling § 9.10
Manufactured home community,
what to look for § 3.7
RISK, DEGREE OF
Manufactured home community,
how to find and buy § 4.3
Real estate investment, basics of
§§ 2.2, 2.3
RISK TOLERANCE
Real estate investment, basics of
§§ 2.2, 2.3
RULES AND REGULATIONS,
ENFORCEMENT
Manufactured housing and
manufactured home community
§ 1.10
RULES OF THUMB
Manufactured home community,
what to look for §§ 3.4, 3.6

RULES OF THUMB *(Continued)*
Real estate investment, basics of
§§ 2.4, 2.5
Turnaround challenge and
rejuvenating older manufactured
home communities § 8.2
Value, estimating § 5.3

SALES APPROACH
Manufactured home community,
selling § 9.5
SALES CENTER, RETAIL
Manufactured housing and
manufactured home community
§ 1.10
Property management § 7.23
SALES COMPARISON
APPROACH
Manufactured home community,
selling § 9.5
Value, estimating §§ 5.5, 5.7
SALES, LAND
Manufactured housing and
manufactured home community
§ 1.6
Property management § 7.21
Real estate investment, basics of
§ 2.2
SAMPLES
See FORMS
SEAL-COATED
Manufactured home community,
selling § 9.3
Turnaround challenge and
rejuvenating older manufactured
home communities § 8.5
SELLER'S OBJECTIVES
Manufactured home community,
selling § 9.13
SELLING, REASONS FOR
See MANUFACTURED HOME
COMMUNITY, SELLING
SHOPPER
Manufactured home community,
what to look for § 3.3
Property management § 7.4

SHOPPER *(Continued)*
Value, estimating § 5.4
SHOPPING CENTERS
Property management § 7.19
Real estate investment, basics of
§§ 2.3, 2.9
SHOPPING REPORT, STANDARD
Property management; Form 7–1
§ 7.4
SIGNAGE
Manufactured housing and
manufactured home community
§ 1.8
Property management §§ 7.18, 7.20
Turnaround challenge and
rejuvenating older manufactured
home communities § 8.5
SINGLE-FAMILY HOMES
Real estate investment, basics of
§ 2.3
SINGLE-SECTION HOMES
Manufactured home community,
how to find and buy § 4.3
Manufactured housing and
manufactured home community
§§ 1.1, 1.5, 1.6, 1.10
SITE, RENT
Manufactured housing and
manufactured home community
§§ 1.6, 1.7
SITE, VACANT
Manufactured housing and
manufactured home community
§ 1.7
Turnaround challenge and
rejuvenating older manufactured
home communities § 8.1
SITE-BUILT HOMES
Manufactured housing and
manufactured home community
§§ 1.1, 1.5, 1.6, 1.10
SKIRTING
Manufactured home community,
selling § 9.3
Manufactured home community,
what to look for §§ 3.4, 3.6

SKIRTING *(Continued)*
Manufactured housing and
manufactured home community
§ 1.10
Property management § 7.18
SLURRIED
Manufactured home community,
selling § 9.3
SOLE PROPRIETORS
Manufactured home community,
how to find and buy § 4.3
Manufactured home community,
selling § 9.2
Manufactured housing and
manufactured home community
§§ 1.4, 1.7
SOUTH
Manufactured housing and
manufactured home community
§§ 1.6, 1.11
SOUTHEAST
Manufactured housing and
manufactured home community
§§ 1.6, 1.7
SOUTHWEST
Manufactured housing and
manufactured home community
§§ 1.6, 1.11
SPEED BUMPS
Property management § 7.18
STANDARD OPERATING
PROCEDURE (SOP), PROPERTY
Property management § 7.9
STORAGE BUILDINGS
Due diligence period: preparing for
closing § 6.8
Manufactured home community,
what to look for § 3.6
Property management § 7.18
Turnaround challenge and
rejuvenating older manufactured
home communities § 8.5
SUBCONTRACTS
Manufactured housing and
manufactured home community
§ 1.7

SUBDIVISIONS
Manufactured housing and
manufactured home community
§§ 1.6, 1.7, 1.10
Real estate investment, basics of
§ 2.3
SUBMETERING, UTILITY
Manufactured home community,
how to find and buy § 4.3
Turnaround challenge and
rejuvenating older manufactured
home communities § 8.2
SUMMARY OFFERING PAGE
Manufactured home community,
what to look for; Form 3–1
§ 3.2
SUNBELT
Manufactured housing and
manufactured home community
§ 1.7
SURVEYED MANUFACTURED
HOME COMMUNITIES,
CATALOGING
Manufactured home community,
how to find and buy § 4.8
SURVEYS, OFF-PREMISES
Due diligence period: preparing for
closing § 6.1
Manufactured home community,
what to look for § 3.3
SYNDICATORS
Manufactured housing and
manufactured home community
§ 1.4

TAKEOVER PROCEDURES
Due diligence period: preparing for
closing § 6.1
Property management § 7.8
TARGET MARKETS
See MARKETING STRATEGY,
IDENTIFYING TARGET
MARKETS AND PLANNING
TAX BENEFITS
Real estate investment, basics of
§§ 2.2, 2.3

TAX CREDITS
Real estate investment, basics of §§ 2.2, 2.3
TAX SHELTERS
Real estate investment, basics of § 2.2
TAXES, PERSONAL PROPERTY
Manufactured home community, what to look for § 3.3
Real estate investment, basics of § 2.9
TAXES, REAL ESTATE
Manufactured home community, how to find and buy § 4.2
Manufactured housing and manufactured home community §§ 1.5, 1.7
Property management §§ 7.14, 7.17
1031 TAX DEFERRED EXCHANGE FORM
Manufactured home community, selling §§ 9.7, 9.9
Real estate investment, basics of § 2.9
TERMINOLOGY
See INDUSTRY TERMINOLOGY
TIEDOWNS
Manufactured housing and manufactured home community § 1.10
Property management § 7.18
TIME-SHARING
Real estate investment, basics of § 2.3
TIMING: WHEN TO SELL
Manufactured home community, selling § 9.11
TOPOGRAPHY
Value, estimating § 5.6
TRANSACTION FINANCING, ARRANGING
Due diligence period: preparing for closing § 6.11
TRENDS
Manufactured housing and manufactured home community §§ 1.6, 1.8, 1.11

TRENDS *(Continued)*
Real estate investment, basics of § 2.5
TURNAROUND CHALLENGE
Manufactured home community, what to look for § 3.10
Real estate investment, basics of §§ 2.2, 2.3
Real estate investment: coming full cycle § 10.2
TURNAROUND CHALLENGE AND REJUVENATING OLDER MANUFACTURED HOME COMMUNITIES
Generally §§ 8.1, 8.3, 8.9
Action plan and budget § 8.6
Annual review and reassessment § 8.7
Assessment of present manufactured home community condition § 8.4
Methodologies, current § 8.8
Turnaround strategies § 8.2
Upgrade alternatives § 8.5
TURNOVER, EXPENSE
Manufactured home community, what to look for § 3.6
Manufactured housing and manufactured home community §§ 1.3, 1.7
Value, estimating § 5.10

UNITED STATES
Manufactured home community, selling § 9.16
Manufactured housing and manufactured home community §§ 1.2, 1.4, 1.5, 1.8, 1.9
Real estate investment: coming full cycle § 10.2
UPGRADE WORK, ALTERNATIVES
Turnaround challenge and rejuvenating older manufactured home communities § 8.5
UPREIT
Manufactured home community, how to find and buy § 4.2

UTILITIES
Due diligence period: preparing for
    closing § 6.9
Manufactured home community,
    how to find and buy § 4.6
Manufactured home community,
    what to look for §§ 3.4, 3.6
Manufactured housing and
    manufactured home community
    §§ 1.3, 1.5, 1.7, 1.9
Real estate investment, basics of
    §§ 2.5, 2.10
Turnaround challenge and
    rejuvenating older manufactured
    home communities § 8.2

VALUATION CALCULATION
    WORKSHEET (VCW)
Manufactured home community,
    selling; Form 9–1 § 9.5
Manufactured home community,
    what to look for; Form 3–6 § 3.6
VALUE, ESTIMATING
Generally §§ 5.1, 5.11
Future outlook § 5.10
Manufactured home community
    valuation § 5.2
Valuation
–Generally § 5.5
–Cost or replacement approach § 5.6
–Income approach § 5.8
–Reconciliation § 5.9
–Sales comparison approach § 5.7
Valuation of manufactured home
    communities, factors in § 5.4
Valuation premises § 5.3
VALUE RANGE OF PROPERTY,
    ESTIMATING
Manufactured home community,
    selling § 9.5

VENDORS
Manufactured home
    community, how to find
    and buy § 4.3
Manufactured home community,
    selling § 9.3
Property management § 7.17
VISITS AND INSPECTIONS
Property management § 7.4

WASTEWATER TREATMENT
Due diligence period:
    preparing for closing §§ 6.5,
    6.6, 6.9
Manufactured home community,
    how to find and buy §§ 4.3, 4.6,
    4.7
Manufactured home community,
    what to look for § 3.6
Manufactured housing and
    manufactured home community
    § 1.10
Property management § 7.12
Real estate investment, basics of
    § 2.5
Value, estimating § 5.8
WETLANDS
Manufactured home community,
    what to look for § 3.6
Value, estimating § 5.4

ZONING MAP
Value, estimating § 5.4
ZONING REGULATIONS
Due diligence period: preparing for
    closing § 6.7
Manufactured home community,
    how to find and buy § 4.6
Manufactured home community,
    what to look for § 3.6